Entrepreneurship

2nd Edition

by Dr. Kathleen Allen

for dummies®
A Wiley Brand

Entrepreneurship For Dummies®, 2nd Edition

Published by

Wiley Publishing, Inc.

111 River St.

Hoboken, NJ 07030-5774

www.wiley.com

For general information on our other products and services, please contact our Customer Care Department within the U.S. at 877-762-2974, outside the U.S. at 317-572-3993, or fax 317-572-4002. For technical support, please visit https://hub.wiley.com/community/support/dummies.

Wiley publishes in a variety of print and electronic formats and by print-on-demand. Some material included with standard print versions of this book may not be included in e-books or in print-on-demand. If this book refers to media such as a CD or DVD that is not included in the version you purchased, you may download this material at http://booksupport.wiley.com. For more information about Wiley products, visit www.wiley.com.

Library of Congress Control Number: 2022949439

ISBN: 978-1-119-91263-7 (pbk); 978-1-119-91265-1 (ebk); 978-1-119-91264-4 (ebk)

SKY10038930_112922

Contents at a Glance

Table of Contents

Introduction

Entrepreneurs like to do things that excite the world, bend the rules a bit, and make us look at something in an entirely new way. They are opportunistic, finding opportunities where others don't see them.

Although stereotyped as risk takers, the truth is that most entrepreneurs take *calculated* risks — most are not the gamblers people make them out to be. In their businesses, they assess their options and choose their course based on a calculated probability of success. They're not afraid to fail because they tend to measure their real success by how many times they learned from their mistakes and went on to try again. Entrepreneurship involves challenge, persistence, planning, and more persistence.

Entrepreneurship Has Changed

For the past two decades or longer, entrepreneurship has been viewed simply as a process for starting new businesses. Only recently have those of us who study this phenomenon concluded that entrepreneurship is more importantly about an opportunistic mindset and spirit. That's a significant distinction, because it means that everyone has the potential to benefit from understanding how the mind of the entrepreneur works. Whether you work in a large corporation, own a small business, run a nonprofit organization, or are at home raising children, you can find opportunities to improve your situation by applying this way of thinking to your life and work.

My approach to entrepreneurship starts with a mindset and then guides you in discovering the strategies, skills, and tools you can use to turn ideas into opportunities and opportunities into successful business concepts. You learn that customers define what a business is, what products and services it produces, and how successful it becomes.

About This Book

Entrepreneurship For Dummies contains practical information that can be used by anyone who aspires to start a business, work as an entrepreneur inside a large corporation, or just become more opportunistic by acquiring an entrepreneurial mindset. It doesn't matter whether you have ever owned a business or even have any business experience. You can use this book to think about the world of the entrepreneur and decide if it's right for you.

This book is grounded in the real world. It is based on research I and others have conducted in the field of entrepreneurship, the work I have done with hundreds of entrepreneurs starting new ventures, and my own experiences as an entrepreneur, so there are no hypothetical situations here. I pulled together the best information, the best tips, and the best examples of how to make entrepreneurship work for you.

Foolish Assumptions

Before I began this book, I made some assumptions about you — the reader. (I know that's not always wise, but I'm not afraid to take a risk!). I assumed that you want to understand what entrepreneurs do to create those exciting businesses you read about and see on TV. And I also assumed that you are ready to make an investment of time and effort in your future. Finally, I assumed that you want to know how to use entrepreneurial skills and attitudes in whatever endeavor you ultimately decide to undertake.

Icons Used in This Book

Throughout this book, icons in the margins highlight certain types of valuable information that call out for your attention. Here are the icons you'll encounter and a brief description of each.

A good idea, trick, or shortcut that can save you time and money.

A piece of information you shouldn't forget.

WARNING

A tip that can help you avoid disasters.

CASE STUDY

An example from the real world to illustrate the current point.

How This Book Is Organized

To make the content more accessible, I divided it into five parts:

» Part 1, "Getting Started in Entrepreneurship," gives you an introduction to the entrepreneur's world and the new environment in which businesses are being started.

» Part 2, "Testing the Feasibility of Your Business Concept," gets you started in the nuts and bolts of feasibility analysis, which is a way to test your business opportunity in the real world, before you spend time and money starting a business to make it happen.

» Part 3, "Designing a Company," tells you everything you need to know about business plans and how to develop them. You'll discover the right legal form for your business and the right business model to make money in your particular business.

» Part 4, "Growing a Company," covers how to take your business beyond startup and successfully grow it to a new level. You discover how to plan for growth.

» Part 5, "The Part of Tens," includes some of my best tips for reasoning why you maybe shouldn't start a business, and motivating yourself to get started with a business idea if you should start a business.

Where to Go from Here

If you want the most from this book and the full picture, I suggest you start at the beginning and work your way to the end. This book contains a wealth of information for you to explore, and I don't want you to miss any of it.

But, if you already have some business experience and not much time (like so many of us), you can skip from topic to topic depending on what interests you. The table of contents is organized to help you find what you need easily and quickly. For tips and tricks, you can also check out this book's online cheat sheet by searching for **Entrepreneurship for Dummies Cheat Sheet** at dummies.com.

No matter how you approach this book, if you have any questions or comments, I'd like to hear from you. Please contact me at kallen@marshall.usc.edu.

1
Getting Started in Entrepreneurship

Understand the world of the entrepreneur.

Explore current trends and understand how entrepreneurship has changed in our digital, global, post-COVID environment.

Learn to develop new product ideas and deal with obstacles.

Implement feasibility analyses and turn your idea into a business concept.

Chapter 1

Understanding Entrepreneurship

The term *entrepreneur* has become so much a part of everyday usage that some of the key attributes that define an entrepreneur have been worn away. The faces of entrepreneurs have become familiar to us, as they host podcasts and show us how it's done on YouTube and TikTok.

It's not surprising then that entrepreneurs come in an amazing variety of types and styles. And they *are* a unique breed. The ventures they create disrupt the market. That's because entrepreneurs change the way you and I do things — usually for the better.

For example, Heather Ward, founder of Hyperion Global Energy in Ottawa, Canada, led the development of a modular system that captures CO_2 from the smokestack emissions of heavy industry and uses the carbon to make materials. She and other *cleantech* entrepreneurs are one example of those who are taking on big, difficult problems that most believe can't easily be solved.

Any problem, even the most complex, can be broken into chunks, each one a smaller problem that may be easier to tackle. What you choose to tackle will depend on your reason for wanting to become an entrepreneur. We talk about that a bit later in this chapter.

Anyone Can Become an Entrepreneur

Now that's a bold statement. Anyone can become an entrepreneur? Yes, it's true, if they have the right mindset and certain traits that are common to entrepreneurs. Who exactly are these people at the center of *entrepreneurship?* In simple terms, an entrepreneur is someone who creates a new opportunity in the world of business and assembles the resources necessary — money, people, technology, and materials — to successfully exploit that opportunity. This admittedly is a broad definition that encompasses the different kinds of entrepreneurial ventures and many perspectives on entrepreneurship.

The growth in the number of entrepreneurs is a sign of changing times. In 2016, 25 million Americans were starting or running their own businesses. By 2019, 28 percent of American workers were engaged in some form of self-employment. Moreover, 83 percent of business owners started their companies from scratch. The United States is home to 8 million minority-owned businesses and 11.9 million small businesses owned by women.

Interestingly enough, the United States is not growing the fastest in number of small businesses. The country with the fastest growth rate, the Dominican Republic, has ten adults start a new business for every adult who owns an existing business. This is a common pattern in smaller countries, where jobs are few and entrepreneurship is the most promising road out of poverty. We do know that about 70 percent of entrepreneurs went to college, but that means that about 30 percent did not — which is still a sizeable number. Those who did not go to college likely found a way to take some business courses, maybe online, to help them understand the critical thinking, finance, management, and marketing sides of the business so they would be better prepared to run their companies.

Recognizing an Entrepreneurial Venture

People sometimes think of entrepreneurs only as big risk takers and shake-up-the-market types. For example, they look at what Uber did for the personal transportation industry. Uber's initial offering was ride hailing, but based on their success with that service they went on to offer food delivery, package delivery, couriers, and freight transportation. Uber found its opportunity at the intersection of smartphones, app stores, and customers' desire for on-demand work as part of the growing gig economy, something we talk about later.

It is also true that entrepreneurs invest in making improvements on products and services we're familiar with, from quick-service food to in-the-home health services. Entrepreneurs recognize customers' pain, and they know these pain points are associated with a compelling problem that is solvable. They know that if they can solve that big problem and take away that pain, the customer will be willing to pay a premium to get the solution. By identifying the solution for a problem where a real need exists, entrepreneurs can differentiate their solution from competitors' solutions and prioritize the resources they need to launch their business. Then, if they can move fast and run the business right (running it right is key), they can gain a foothold in the market niche, well before they have to go head-to-head with much bigger competitors.

REMEMBER

The bottom line is entrepreneurs are ordinary people who do extraordinary things. They take everyday ideas and give them some magic. You don't need a lot of experience or resources to be an entrepreneur. You do need passion, persistence, and a creative mind. You have to believe you can solve a problem like no one else.

CASE STUDY

That was certainly the attitude of the founding CEO of Uber, Travis Kalanick. However, an effective leader of a new company must also display a bit of humility and realize that no matter who they are, they didn't get to where they are without the help and guidance of others. Every entrepreneurial venture has stakeholders — investors, partners, employees, board members, and customers — and those stakeholders need to be heard. It often happens that once a startup becomes a big company very fast, the founding CEO no longer has the skills required to effectively run that larger company and is asked to step aside in favor of professional management with more experience. In the case of Uber, we have a wildly successful startup whose founder almost destroyed the company to feed his ego. His lack of professional management skills nearly took the company down. Check out the excellent documentary film on Uber, *Super Pumped: The Battle for Uber,* which is on Netflix and is based on a book by the same name.

Entrepreneurs are as human as anyone else. If your goal is as ambitious as to build "the next Uber," make sure you ask yourself why. Your reasons will be a clue to whether you can actually go the distance and keep your eyes on building a sustainable company for the long term and for the employees you need to help you get there. Uber is a great example of disruptive entrepreneurship. It is also an example of how even the best new ventures can implode when the needs of the stakeholders are not addressed.

CHECK YOUR ENTREPRENEURIAL INSTINCTS

Take this little quiz to see if you have the right stuff to become an entrepreneur. But don't take the results too seriously. I assure you that your answers will not determine whether you can succeed as an entrepreneur, but they may help you decide if entrepreneurship is right for you. The choices provided are the most common answers given by entrepreneurs in general.

1. Are you:
- Married or in a committed relationship?
- Single?
- Widowed?
- Divorced?

2. Are you:
- Male?
- Female?

3. Why do you want to start a business?
- To make a lot of money
- To be independent
- To give yourself a job
- To gain power
- To become famous

4. How comfortable are you with uncertainty?
- Very comfortable
- Somewhat comfortable
- Not comfortable

5. To become successful as an entrepreneur, what will you need?
- Money
- Luck
- Hard work
- A good idea
- All of the above

6. Concerning your willingness to take risk, are you:

- A high risk taker

- A moderate risk taker

- One who avoids risk

Answers

1. The most common response is married. This doesn't mean that all entrepreneurs are married when they start their businesses or stay married for the duration. Most entrepreneurs are married or in a committed relationship by the time they start a venture, possibly because having a working spouse gives them a steady income while they're risking time and capital starting a new venture. However, these days, you notice growing numbers of single entrepreneurs starting dot-com ventures while still in their teens.

2. It still is true that more men start new ventures than women, but that dynamic is changing. Women are starting businesses at a much faster rate than men, typically while they're in their 20s before they get married and start families or after their children are grown.

3. The common reason entrepreneurs give for wanting to start a business is to be independent. For most entrepreneurs, money is a by-product of operating a venture they are passionate about. However, money does motivate a certain class of entrepreneurs. When the media touts the riches of successful entrepreneurs, people may get the impression that entrepreneurship is a means to quickly create wealth. But if there ever was the allure of quick riches, it is vanishing. Even among venture capitalists, the focus is shifting to non-Internet technology companies that create new value and make a profit in about three years.

4. Most entrepreneurs are comfortable with uncertainty, because they understand intuitively that uncertainty brings opportunity with it. In general, people who must have a high degree of predictability in their lives are uncomfortable in the world of the entrepreneur.

5. To be successful as an entrepreneur, you probably need a little of all these things — money, luck, hard work (you need lots of that), and a good idea. Entrepreneurs will tell you, however, that they make their own luck by taking calculated risks and building a network of contacts.

6. Entrepreneurs are neither high risk takers nor do they avoid risk. They are moderate or calculated risk takers. They manage risk and make decisions based on what they believe their chances of success to be. Entrepreneurship is inherently risky, but so is driving a car and most everything else we do in life that has any significance. Entrepreneurs are typically better at judging risk and finding ways to manage it.

Understanding the Entrepreneurial Ecosystem

Entrepreneurial ventures are complex creatures. They have numerous parts, and the parts interact in a variety of ways. Look at Figure 1-1 to see all the major components of the entrepreneurial environment. Take a closer look at each of the parts:

>> **The Entrepreneur:** Though just one component, the entrepreneur is the driving force and coordinator of all the activities, resources, and people that need to be brought together to start a new venture. The entrepreneur's passion and vision give life to the business. The entrepreneur brings to the business experience, education, skills, a value system, and a network of people to rely on for help in getting the business started.

>> **Legal, Government:** Entrepreneurs conduct their business in a regulatory environment as prescribed by federal, state, and municipal laws, including the legal form of the venture (see Chapter 15) to the intellectual property it develops (see Chapter 8), to the contracts it writes, and to the employees it hires. Government — federal, state, and local — adds regulations to the mix in the form of taxes, fees, tariffs, and penalties for non-compliance.

>> **Suppliers:** Suppliers provide, among many other things, inventory, raw materials, parts, and even labor. Suppliers also help finance the new business by supplying lines of credit and extending payment periods.

>> **Competitors:** Competitors help determine if the market is hostile or friendly to the new venture. They have a huge impact on pricing, marketing strategy, and distribution-channel strategy.

>> **Customers:** Customers are the lifeblood of the business — without them, no business can exist. Customers influence everything the business does, from creating demand for the development of new products and services, to influencing market strategies, to improving support services, and to optimizing the quality of customer service.

>> **Technology:** Only a few years ago, no one described technology as a facilitator and driving force of an entrepreneurial venture. But now, technology is a prime facilitator of business processes, creating efficiencies and capabilities that businesses never experienced before. Think about it: How many businesses 15 years ago expected to be conducting some or all of their business on the Internet today?

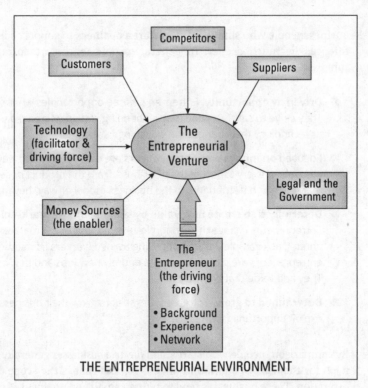

FIGURE 1-1:
The entrepreneurial venture.

(Diagram contents: Competitors, Customers, Suppliers, Technology (facilitator & driving force), The Entrepreneurial Venture, Legal and the Government, Money Sources (the enabler), The Entrepreneur (the driving force) • Background • Experience • Network)

THE ENTREPRENEURIAL ENVIRONMENT

>> **Money:** For most entrepreneurial ventures, money is the enabler. When all the other components of a successful business concept are in place — customer, value proposition, product/service, and distribution (you find out about these in Chapter 4) — then money comes into play as a resource that makes everything happen. Some entrepreneurial ventures, like those in biotechnology where product development times are long and costly, are naturally driven by money. Without sufficient capital, you can't survive the research and development phase long enough to bring the technology to market.

Distinguishing Entrepreneurial Ventures from Small Businesses and Why That Matters

As this chapter begins, I suggest that many small, startup ventures are likely to be called *entrepreneurial* even if they aren't. Let's face it, nearly every new business starts small, so physical size alone doesn't separate entrepreneurs from businesspeople who simply want to start a business to support a lifestyle. The differences lie much deeper. In general, people who start entrepreneurial ventures are

>> **Driven by opportunity.** Entrepreneurs see opportunities where others don't. They strive to satisfy a need that is not being served or create a new product or technology that changes the way things are done.

>> **Focused on innovation.** Entrepreneurs are creative and find ways to innovate in every aspect of their business, from the product or service to marketing and distribution, to the business model or way they make money.

>> **Determined to create new value by shaking up the marketplace.** Entrepreneurs change the economic environment of the marketplace they enter. One example: Instead of pulling trained workers from other businesses, entrepreneurs are inclined to create entirely new jobs and new opportunities. They add value that didn't exist.

>> **Determined to grow.** Entrepreneurs seek to grow their businesses and exploit opportunity to the fullest.

By comparison, people who start small *lifestyle businesses* generally do so to provide a job for themselves and family members, and that is the scope of their business aspiration. These businesses tend to remain small and are focused on serving a local community. The corner shoe repair shop, the pizza parlor, consultants in business for themselves, and the local manufacturer of rebuilt engines are examples of small, lifestyle businesses. Although such businesses represent most of all businesses in the United States, they are not the prime source of new jobs in the economy. Entrepreneurs generate the new jobs that we need for the economy to grow.

So, you need to decide what kind of business you want to start, because that decision will affect all the other decisions you'll need to make. If you plan to build a rapidly growing enterprise reaching a global market, you'll set different goals and make different decisions than if you want to confine your activity to your community. Both are worthy goals.

Considering the Many Ways to Be an Entrepreneur

If anyone tells you that all entrepreneurs take risks, that all entrepreneurs are optimists, that all entrepreneurs are egotistical, such opinions don't hold water. No one set of traits defines all entrepreneurs. You can find a variety of entrepreneurial types in the marketplace — they are as diverse a group of people as you'll ever see. But they do have a few things in common. For example, surveys find that virtually all entrepreneurs have cofounders. Starting a business is a lot of work, so it's best to share the load. I talk about teams and how to create them in Chapter 9.

In the following sections of this chapter, you find out about the many ways to become an entrepreneur.

The home-based entrepreneur

More than 15 million people are involved in home-based businesses. Why is starting a business from home so popular? Here are some reasons:

>> Because of technology, in particular the Internet, people can run their business from anywhere just by going online.

>> Because more resources are available to entrepreneurial businesses than ever before. Websites like Quora.com, AngelList.com, StartupCompanyLawyer. com, and AllBusiness.com are rich sources for answers to your questions such as how to find an angel investor, or get legal advice as a small business owner.

>> Because tax laws have grown friendlier to home-based businesses. On your personal tax return, you can deduct costs of running your home in proportion to the square footage devoted to the business (your home office), along with all of your other business expenses. Your home office must be dedicated to business and not have distractions like a big screen TV.

CASE STUDY

It's not always the biggest ideas that win the day. In fact, your home-based business could be started based on your success in something as unusual as a spelling bee competition. That's what happened to high school junior Cole Shafer-Ray, a three-time Scripps National Spelling Bee participant and 2015 runner-up. Shafer-Ray spotted an opportunity to turn his spelling superpower into a business of coaching other students how to outsmart the competition. Apparently, he discovered a real need because his clients are willing to pay him $100 an hour and they usually get coached twice a week via Skype. Not only that, he has a waiting list of more than 400 clients.

It sure beats the usual minimum-wage jobs that high school kids typically have.

Like any good entrepreneur, Shafer-Ray has a website, `spellingchamp.com`, where he sells lists of words used in major competitions with strategies for how to remember them. Some of his lists sell for $200 to $300 each. In this way, he can reach out to potential customers who aren't looking for one-on-one coaching.

His most prized product, which is not for sale, is his *Master List*, which contains 97.18 percent of the surprise words from the Scripps National Spelling Bee. In compiling the list, he calculated the statistical probability it would contain words from the national competition. He has been offered thousands of dollars for the list, but he refuses to sell because it would hurt the very competition that had been so good to him. Now that's an entrepreneur who operates from a set of values, not just the lure of financial reward.

The Internet entrepreneur

The Internet has given rise to a new kind of entrepreneur, the Internet entrepreneur. These businesses have no traditional, bricks-and-mortar locations for customers to visit. Like Amazon.com, some may have employees, offices, and warehouse space, but their only contact with customers occurs on the Internet. Some Internet entrepreneurs do everything online — work with strategic partners, employ experts, develop products, and deliver the goods to customers.

CASE STUDY

Carley Roney wouldn't go through her 1993 wedding again for anything — that is, unless she had the benefit of her own company, The Knot Inc. Planning her own nuptials, Roney quickly realized that the fairy-tale wedding preparations portrayed in bridal magazines don't paint an accurate picture of what most brides-to-be experience. Roney wanted to solve that problem. She came up with an Internet-based solution to the real problems people face when planning weddings. She calls her website TheKnot.com, and it has become the go-to source of information and ideas for anything related to tying the knot.

In 1996, Roney and her spouse presented their concept to America Online (AOL). The first round of seed money arrived shortly thereafter, and the business has provided an exciting ride ever since. TheKnot.com receives more than a million first-time visitors every month. They can search for everything from wedding gowns to cakes. The site also has its own gift registry. While the company is an Internet one, Roney & Partners are doing a few things to dip their toes into the real world. They introduced a magazine, negotiated a three-book deal with a publisher, and are in discussions on a series for PBS. In 2021, they celebrated 25 years of helping more than 25 million couples plan their weddings. You can learn more about this company by visiting its website at www.theknot.com.

The serial entrepreneur

Many entrepreneurs enjoy recognizing an opportunity and turning it into a business, but they don't enjoy running a business day-to-day. They prefer, instead, to leave that job to others who are more capable. Once the business is up and running, these entrepreneurs move on to the next opportunity.

Sir Richard Branson is a good example of a famous serial entrepreneur. Starting with a mail delivery record service, called Virgin, which grew into a recording studio and record store, he went on to develop concepts in the space industry, Virgin Galactic, as well as the travel, Virgin Atlantic, the beverage, and the broadcasting industries. Branson lets no moss grow under his feet. More than a serial entrepreneur, he is a *multipreneur* (I just made that term up). He starts and runs multiple businesses at the same time rather than leaving one to move on to the next. Branson does have a unique strategy that has generally served him well. He owns the brand "Virgin" but holds only a small stake in many of the companies that carry his brand. He also collects millions by licensing the valuable brand for others to use.

The downside to his approach is that his money is tied up in ventures around the world and can't be accessed like money in a bank. This became apparent during COVID-19. Because nearly all his businesses were severely impacted by the shutdowns (think aviation, cruise lines, hotels, and leisure), he couldn't easily move money from one company to another to save jobs, for example. Although he is reportedly worth more than $5 billion, he is asset rich and cash poor. And no one, it seems, felt sorry for him.

The gig economy entrepreneur

The easiest way to describe this type of entrepreneur is to think of them as a free agent or independent contractor who works for themself. You typically find these free agents participating in asset-sharing services like car sharing, parking space sharing, or equipment sharing; transportation-based services like ride-sharing, restaurant delivery, and goods delivery; professional services like coding, writing, and administrative work; and handmade goods and services. All of these free agents use digital platforms and apps to connect with potential customers and deliver their services. You are no doubt familiar with Uber and Lyft as well as Airbnb, DoorDash, and Etsy.

Those who make the most money have in-demand skills such as computer and information services, financial managers, software developers, analysts, and testers, and medical and health services administrators. Consultants also fall into this category.

Although gig work is a tiny percentage of the economy, it is growing rapidly and still offers many opportunities for new businesses. In fact, you may be surprised to learn that the highest-paying opportunities in the coming decade probably don't exist yet. If you need to upgrade your skills, now is the time to do it so you'll be prepared for whatever comes.

The traditional entrepreneur

Traditional entrepreneurs build brick-and-mortar businesses to a point where they can harvest the value they create. Before the Internet and e-commerce changed the face of things, this is how entrepreneurship worked. Actually, the traditional model is still the most common, but an increasing number of these mainstream business owners reinvent their enterprises by adding an Internet component, which expands their reach considerably.

CASE STUDY

You can start a traditional storefront business from scratch, or you can buy an existing business or franchise and build from there. For some types of businesses, starting with an existing base of customers is far superior to having to attract your first customer. That's exactly what Courtney Miller did. After she married, Courtney and her husband moved to the charming coastal community of Half Moon Bay, about 40 minutes south of San Francisco. There she discovered a small high-end children's boutique called P. Cottontail and took a part-time job to learn more about the business. She fell in love with children's clothing and soon began day-dreaming about what she would do if this were her store.

As luck would have it, the owner, who had started the business in 1985, became ill and decided it was time to sell the business. This was the opportunity Courtney had been waiting for. She bought the business and was pleased that so many of P. Cottontail's original customers were happy with her plans. Fortunately, she set up an e-commerce website, which served her well during the pandemic closures. Her sales continued to climb. Besides children's clothing, her other love was holidays. She was able to acquire empty space next to her boutique and, during the 2021 holiday season, she opened a Christmas store. She intends to change out what's offered by season so that she has year-round sales. She is a young woman who knows how to take advantage of an opportunity when she sees it. As the mother of two young children, it's not always easy to manage everything. But with the support of her husband and the kids as well as her mother, who spends about a week a month helping her with tasks such as inventory, packaging, and buying trips, she has made it work. Whether she grows the company beyond her current location is a decision for another day. Right now, she has the business she always wanted, and life is good.

The corporate entrepreneur

It may surprise you that entrepreneurs can be found inside large corporations. That, no doubt, sounds like an oxymoron; but it's true. The advantages of the entrepreneurial mindset and the lean startup approach are well known, so many large companies have looked for ways to use those approaches to gain a competitive advantage in the market. In general, corporate ventures differ from other types of projects that big companies take on in that they typically involve innovation and activities that are new to the company, so the risk of failure is quite high.

The corporate venture is typically handled by a project champion who, given the authority and appropriate resources, can test the idea and carry out an execution plan. Some companies, such as Google, encourage innovation at all levels in the company. Those ideas that meet the established criteria for selection can advance to a full-fledged company within a company.

In this book, we don't focus on the specific needs of corporate entrepreneurs, but startup activities such as recognizing opportunities, conducting feasibility analysis to test the concept, and developing a business plan for execution are the same skills and processes that take place inside large corporations.

Considering Your Personal Goals

This chapter gives you a taste of what entrepreneurship is all about. Are you still interested? Good! It's time to introduce some of the skills you need to succeed. Remember that the one thing I can't give you is the passion, that fire in the belly, that certain something that keeps you going when all the odds appear to be against you. Entrepreneurs have it, as do great people in every profession.

If the business you plan to launch doesn't complement your personal values and goals, it won't be a source of satisfaction, and chances are, you won't be as successful as you might be in a business you care deeply about. Before starting a new business, ask yourself the following questions. They can help you know yourself better and point you toward the right match.

Why do you want to start a business?

I know this is a deep question, but it's important and fundamental to your success as an entrepreneur. If, for example, you're thinking that starting a business provides financial security, you need to remember that most entrepreneurs take no money out of the business for the first couple of years, at least not until they can draw a salary and still leave the company with a positive cash flow (see Chapter 18 for more on cash flow). Likewise, remember that entrepreneurial wealth typically comes from appreciation in the value of the business, which also takes some time.

TIP

Do not be seduced by stories of personal wealth created by the proceeds of initial public offerings. For most businesses, building value and wealth for the founders takes hard work and time. I never recommend starting a business just to make money. Instead, start a business that you're excited about, (you'll have to spend a lot of time at the business, so you'd better at least like it), give it your best, and you'll increase your chances of creating wealth through that venture.

How will starting a business affect your personal life?

If you're young and have no special responsibilities other than to yourself, you can afford to take chances that an older person may not be able to take. You can afford to fail and lose money because you have more time to start over again. By contrast, if you're starting a business at an older age when you have commitments to a home and family, you may want to look for an opportunity that gives you some flexibility with your time and is well within your risk appetite.

You also want to consider the needs of your family and the responsibilities you have in addition to those you take on when you start a business. You definitely need the support of your family, and they need to understand what starting a business is going to mean to your family life. Some people believe you can have it all — the perfect family life and a very successful business. In practice, it's difficult to make that happen. Let's not mince words. Starting a business is not a walk in the park. It's hard work. Anyone who tells you differently has probably never started a business.

Are you in sufficient physical shape to start a business?

This may sound like a strange question, but it's not. A new venture demands long hours and focused effort. Are you up to it? Are you taking care of your health and getting the exercise you need to give you the stamina required to successfully launch this venture? I know too many entrepreneurs who work 14-hour days, 7 days a week just to get their new ventures to the survival stage. That kind of work is stressful and requires that you take care of your health — eat healthy foods, not fast foods, cut down on alcohol, exercise daily, and get a good night's sleep. Otherwise, you may not be able to enjoy the fruits of all that labor.

What aspects of business make you very uncomfortable?

We all have things that bother us or working situations that we don't particularly enjoy. It's important to recognize what your issues are so that you don't have to confront them daily in your business. If you don't like to carry any debt, for example, you probably don't want to start a business that requires debt to smooth out seasonality, like the clothing business. How do you feel about being a boss? If you don't like to deal with the issues related to managing employees, you probably want to consider starting a company that can outsource its personnel needs to other companies. If you don't work well under stress, you may want to stay away from advertising or social media marketing. Both can be stressful due to the need to meet constant strict deadlines and to generate interesting and original material quickly. Look carefully at how you like to work before you start a business. Then find opportunities that can be a potential match.

How will your feelings about your business affect its potential growth?

As an entrepreneur, you have the biggest impact on whether your business grows. You need to examine your attitudes about growth in general and all the ramifications of growing. For example, how do you feel about ownership issues such as how much of the company you want to retain as your own? If you have to bring on partners or investors to grow, that will mean giving up some of your ownership in the company. What about your ability to delegate control to other people? Can you trust others to share the work? Do you plan to build a company that will endure over many years, or do you want to get in and out quickly? Do you have a business education? You can find sources of entrepreneurship education online that will bring you up to speed on critical topics like finances, supply chains, and human resources.

TIP

Finding a mentor is an excellent way to get the support you need as you make important decisions. You learn how to create a mentor board in Chapter 9. Recognizing your attitudes about business helps you steer around potential hazards and make better decisions.

Clearing Up the Myths and Stereotypes about Entrepreneurs

Perhaps without realizing it, you may have developed some common stereotypes about entrepreneurs. It's not unusual and given that the media often engages in painting stereotypes as well, they seem to be everywhere. Let's take a moment to dispel some of the most egregious of these so you don't limit yourself.

You need a lot of money

This assumption is false. Thousands of businesses have started on little to no money; but to do it and succeed, you must have found a problem for which you have customers who need your solution. If you don't start with a ready stable of hungry customers, you will spend a lot of time and money to find them and convince them to buy from you. By contrast, if your customers really need what you're offering because it solves their problem, they will pay a premium to get it.

The types of businesses that can most easily be started with limited funds include service businesses, where you're essentially marketing your skills to people who need them; and consulting businesses, which are similar to service businesses in that you're selling a skill or knowledge that you have. For example, suppose you're very good at putting on events such as sporting events or conferences. If you do it right, you can sell advance tickets before you incur the major costs such as the venue.

A third type is a performance-based business, which typically involves musicians, speakers, and other performing artists. Again, you can often defer having to pay upfront costs if you can sell tickets in advance, pay the performers after the performance, and you've developed some good contacts in the industry who can help you.

The fourth type is very popular. In this version, the entrepreneur serves as a broker or intermediary who brings together people seeking information on a particular topic and the experts on that topic. You may have seen invitations in your inbox for online seminars on topics such as cryptocurrencies, eating healthy, preparing for disasters, and ways to deal with various health problems. You will need access to an e-commerce web platform that supports streaming and social media marketing strategies.

You need a great idea

It's not about having a great idea — it's about solving a real and compelling problem. Consider successful companies that have been in business several decades. It wasn't the idea that made them durable but starting with a great team that wanted to build an enduring company. Ideas come and go, but the ability to execute on a plan despite what happens in the market is their strength.

For example, VRBO (Vacation Rentals by Owner) started in 1995 with a stated goal of finding every family the space they need to relax, reconnect, and enjoy precious time away together. They brought together homeowners who wanted to rent their home temporarily and people who were looking to vacation in a home. This is the broker/intermediary model. VRBO put the business online to expand their reach, make it easier for customers to explore their offerings and to save money. They didn't have to depend on real estate brokers and, therefore, could scale quickly and inexpensively.

You must take big risks

In general, this has been an enduring mantra in entrepreneurship. "Go big or go home" as they say. If you take big risks, your rewards will be great. But that's not always the case. In fact, most of those "go big" ventures require investor capital. Investors are not fans of big risks because they need to protect their investment, especially when it involves other people's money, which is typical. You learn more about venture capitalists in Chapter 16. So, investors and entrepreneurs look to reduce the amount of risk the venture will face by testing the concept in the market before launch, validating a business model to ensure they can make money, and securing first customers. Instead of bragging that your big risk is going to produce a huge reward, you should be asking yourself if your business will make a big difference in the market.

You need to be young

Too many people believe that if you haven't started a business by the time you're 30, it's too late. Nothing could be further from the truth. In 2015, the Ewing Marion Kauffman Foundation reported that 24 percent of startups that year were founded by entrepreneurs aged 55-64 years old. That's up 71 percent from 1996. In 2018, the number of senior startups increased to 25.8 percent. Many seniors come to a startup with a wealth of business knowledge and experience that they want to continue to use. They become part of a startup's management team, start their own ventures, or become investors in new businesses. Today we see entrepreneurs across all age groups, which tells you that entrepreneurship can be a satisfying lifetime occupation.

Looking Ahead

Entrepreneurial opportunities rarely drop in out of the blue. You need to cultivate them. I talk about that in Chapter 3 (among other places) — things you can do to enhance your creative powers and coax opportunity out of hiding. I also talk about how to create a business concept and test it in the marketplace, and how to build a business that lets you execute the concept. This book is organized so that you can take a random walk through all the topics, dipping into chapters on a need-to-know basis, whether that means creating a concept, conducting a feasibility study, or plunging into the business planning process. So, welcome aboard! Feel free to go wherever you want — it's all up to you.

Chapter **2**

Entrepreneurship in the 21st Century

O ne thing we can say about the 21st Century so far is that every business needs to prepare for change. One could argue that the business environment is always changing — that's true. But in the 2020s, technology is driving enormous changes at an exponential pace, and those changes are likely to continue for some time. That is no exaggeration. Here are just a few of the technologies that didn't exist ten years ago and are now ubiquitous.

» Smart assistants (Siri, Amazon Echo)

» Smart watches

» Oculus Rift (virtual reality)

» Slack

» Tablet computers

We're so used to these applications, we've forgotten that their adoption happened very quickly, much faster than what you might normally see for new technology. We haven't seen this much rapid change since the Industrial Revolution and the introduction of the assembly line. Today, the ability to manage your business from a mobile device is no longer an option — it's essential. We certainly saw the importance of this during the COVID-19 pandemic when so many people had to work from home.

I'm not saying that technological change affects every business equally, but certainly every business is affected by the *perception* that information is readily available with a click. Today, most customers expect to connect with a business on many levels, through social networking platforms such as Facebook and Twitter and through video media such as YouTube and TikTok. In this chapter, you learn about some of the new fundamental truths about being in business today that are due to the impact of technology, augmented reality (AR) and artificial intelligence (AI) on businesses and on people's lives.

Dealing with the Boom and Bust Economy of the 2020s

The global events that began early in 2020 and continue to this day certainly left a mark on the startup community. But while the startup environment definitely changed and uncertainty became the name of the game, we still saw a lot of new ventures being started with high valuations, and venture capitalists (VCs) continued to invest in early-stage rounds. So, we witnessed good and bad news. Let's start on a positive note.

Finding the good news

A survey of 20,000 alumni at Stanford University produced information on almost 10,000 startups. That's remarkable. The research, led by graduate student Carrington Motley, examined the relationship between the conditions at the founding of a startup and the ultimate performance of the company over the long term. The research discovered that companies launched in times of economic uncertainty or instability, and that had agile teams that could handle multiple functions, outperformed businesses without these factors. It seems that starting a business under conditions of uncertainty may be an advantage. Maybe because uncertainty produces more opportunities, often more problems to solve. So, it's likely that running a business in times of uncertainty requires a different mindset and more resilience.

CASE STUDY

The largest startups by funding in 2020 included companies in real estate, consumer electronics, transportation, and financial services, according to Crunchbase News, a popular source for entrepreneurs. WeWork was the leader by far with funding of $22.5 billion. This company addressed the new workplace demand for dynamic workspaces to support hybrid working conditions and provide more flexibility. However, when it filed for a public offering in 2019, the filing revealed that its CEO Adam Neumann rented his own buildings to the company among many other behaviors that would not be viewed positively by the market. After the company canceled the initial public offering, it decided to change its name to The We Company and had to buy the rights from none other than its notorious CEO, Neumann. The company saw itself as a tech company, but it was really a real estate company, which was not nearly as sexy.

The We Company continued to grow rapidly, but it was also unprofitable and at one point faced laying off as many as 5,000 employees. Yet, one of its primary investors, SoftBank, encouraged Neumann to grow the company even bigger and faster. Ultimately, the CEO was ousted for a long list of misbehaviors. Financially, he made out quite well. The same can't be said of the shareholders and investors. Then in early 2019, the company announced that it was rebranding itself once again as WeWork with the intent to diversify into other types of co-living and working spaces. The company had to buy the naming rights from Neumann for several million dollars. Another less headline-grabbing company, DoorDash, won big during COVID-19 with its food delivery services. So, opportunities to solve big problems still existed during the pandemic, and those entrepreneurs who were paying attention found them.

You can complain about what's wrong or you can solve the problem and start a business to deliver your solution.

Funding with venture capital is strong at all levels

Although VCs saw their activity at about 70 percent of normal during COVID-19, this decline was not as much as they saw during the dot-com bust of 2001 or the financial crisis of 2008. Despite any challenges brought by the pandemic and its lockdowns, VCs remained very active with their portfolio companies. In general, they knew that economic volatility often results in increasing the value of companies in their portfolios. That's an opportunity they were not about to miss. That also probably explains why some VCs like SoftBank faltered on their due diligence as they fell prey to founder worship.

The good news is that investors are still seeking deals, and while the valuations of companies in some cases may be lower because of market conditions, that could turn out to be a blessing in disguise. Startups with lower valuations may find themselves in a stronger position for a follow-up round of funding when they need it.

Startups are still going strong

Against all odds, we now know from the National Bureau of Economic Research that the pandemic produced a huge surge — 4.3 million — in applications for new businesses. Did you catch the fact that the number of people quitting their jobs — 4.3 million — is the same number as applied for new business applications? An interesting coincidence to be sure. Non-employer businesses (those that don't have employees) increased the most, largely a result of the growth of the *gig economy* (discussed in Chapter 1). It is also likely that many of these non-employer businesses were started by people who had lost a job or who wanted to work from home. This was especially true in the retail trade and food services, which suffered huge declines during the pandemic. Tech, retailing, and construction businesses are now taking off.

The greatest number of entrepreneurs in the startup category were in the 45–54 age range, had not completed high school, and tended to be male immigrants of Hispanic origin. Some of the industries that captured much of the startup growth during the pandemic included utilities, wholesale trade, retail trade, transportation, warehousing, healthcare, social assistance, and food services.

Despite the problems associated with COVID-19, we saw several very successful startups come out of the pandemic, including Bird, the fastest company ever to reach *unicorn* status, which refers to a privately owned startup that grows to a valuation of more than a billion dollars. Bird is a dockless electric scooter rental service inspired by the success of Uber, which also became a unicorn. We talk more about *unicorns* in Chapter 3.

Dealing with the not-so-good news

We started with the good news, and it was satisfying to see a lot of it. Now we must recognize the challenges businesses face going forward. Some of them are tough, but entrepreneurs love to solve challenging problems. I hope you do too.

Competition for talent is tough

The U.S. Bureau of Labor Statistics tells a grim story about the *Great Resignation* during the pandemic, when more than 4.3 million people quit their jobs in December 2021, according to Forbes. In a futile effort to balance work and life during the pandemic, many chose life over work. So, what does this mean for an entrepreneur trying to find talent to fill key positions in their company? It's an extremely competitive environment, so it's important for you to know in advance what you need to offer to get someone to consider working at your company. Three things define what employees typically want today: higher compensation, flexibility in their work schedules, and personal and professional support. They want to do meaningful work in a place where they feel valued and safe, and that seems to be more important than compensation for a lot of people.

To compete for talent, you need to have a handle on the culture you're trying to build in your startup. Your company's culture is arguably the one competitive advantage that is difficult to replicate, so you need to take it seriously. Finding ways to make the workplace "sticky" is critical. You can do this by listening to the needs of the people you want to hire, then addressing their concerns, and finally creating a strong sense of community. If you succeed in these efforts, you will be able to tap the best people and keep them happy for the long term.

Digital platforms are more accessible to startups (and to everyone else)

The cloud and the digital platforms that run on the cloud have become a huge asset to businesses, large and small. For those who are not familiar with the term, the *cloud* is basically a global network of servers linked together so that they operate as a single ecosystem. Therefore, you can access anything anytime as long as you have permission. Using the cloud means your business doesn't have to own and maintain expensive hardware. Because you can access huge amounts of computer resources on demand, you can be assured that when you need storage capability or other computer resources, they will be available. The cloud has increased development speed and doesn't limit your ability to scale your business. In fact, it makes it easier and cheaper.

And now with the advent of the newest technologies, augmented reality and blockchain, the future is wide open for entrepreneurs to jump in and take advantage of this new environment to increase the value of their companies. It's the Wild Wild West, as entrepreneurs discover new ways to monetize cloud applications and deliver them to hungry customers.

What's really exciting is you have choices. You may start by investing in cloud-based operations such as IT infrastructure and accounting and financial tools. Alternatively, you can also choose to stay lean and outsource these capabilities to companies designed to deliver those services, such as Paychex or Gusto for payroll services (a very time-consuming activity for a young company) or online payment gateways such as PayPal or Google Pay to enable your customers to pay for goods and services. As your company grows, you can look at automating as many processes as possible. For example, you can connect employees and business partners so they can collaborate no matter where they're located. You can also connect with customers to develop lifelong relationships and reward programs.

No matter what you decide, it's important to think about how you can capture value from technology and the cloud. What's great is you can start small and gradually grow, adding applications and tools as you need them.

Some startups are too big to fail

Keep in mind that a startup's probability of failure is highest during the first two to five years of its life. This is due in large part to uncertainty — all the questions that haven't been answered or can't be answered. If yours is one of those startups with VC investments of $250,000 or more that are currently popular — namely advanced manufacturing and robotics, blockchain, agtech and big data — you are not as likely to fail outright even though about 75 percent of VC-funded startups fail. You are more likely to be acquired; hence you're too big to fail.

It's important to remember that when you take on investment capital, you need to think of it like debt because the investors are expecting a return of their capital plus a return on their investment. For example, if you took a seed round from VC or angel investors, they'll likely expect a return of 100X their investment because the risk of failure is great. This large return accounts for that failure and the dilution of their shares that will occur as the company goes through more funding rounds. If you waited until Series A (typically first round of VC capital), this is even early for many VCs, they may expect a return of 10 to 15 dollars for every dollar invested, based on the fact that the company is further along and has reduced some of the risk. But the amounts they are willing to invest are much higher than in the seed round. You learn more about investors at all stages in Chapter 14. Although we have seen high valuations with startup companies and the number of unicorns increased from 82 in 2015 to 390 or more in 2019, the fact is that your startup has a less than 1 percent chance of achieving unicorn status. And keep in mind, even unicorns can fail.

REMEMBER

As a startup, you may not survive, but the product you created and the talent you brought on board are valuable to a larger company with more resources. These acquisitions are called *aquihires*.

The Global Entrepreneurship Picture

Nearly every business today is a global business in some capacity. If you have an online presence, you have the capability of reaching customers and suppliers anywhere in the world. So, it's important to understand what's happening in entrepreneurship at the global level. The *Global Entrepreneurship Monitor* is the premier source of research on entrepreneurship ecosystems around the world. With a consortium of national country teams, GEM collects data directly from individual entrepreneurs. Here are some of the important findings from the 2021 report that can inform your thinking about a new company.

» More than half of survey participants claimed that the pandemic created new business opportunities for them in 2021. That was a significant increase over findings reported in 2020.

» Of the 47 national economies in the study, 22 reported that household income had decreased.

» The country found to have the most supportive environment for entrepreneurship was the United Arab Emirates. The UAE has a bold plan called Vision 2021 with six national priorities, including economic development and increasing entrepreneurship and intrapreneurship (corporate entrepreneurship). Instead of focusing on two huge industries, as the UAE has done in the past, they now want to place their attention on small- and medium-size businesses, while supporting innovation as a critical component of their culture.

» Total early-stage entrepreneurial activity (TEA) (which describes setting up a business and running it up to 3.5 years old) has fallen in most countries, with the notable exceptions of Saudi Arabia and the Netherlands, which both experienced increases in TEA.

» The biggest shifts in how entrepreneurs do business is seen by more businesses operating online or from home (again, likely online).

» In most economies, more men started businesses than women, and younger people more frequently than older people.

» The GEM study concluded that entrepreneurship will be the key to repairing national economies, creating more dynamic and vibrant communities, and solving some of the most challenging problems, such as clean water and power.

» The share of startups that consider the social implications of their businesses was more than half in all but two economies: Poland (44 percent) and Norway (41 percent).

» The share of businesses that consider environmental implications in their business decision-making was again more than half except for two economies: Poland (5 percent) and Kazakhstan (30 percent).

» Economies with higher levels of income have lower TEA rates. We can explain this best by the fact that there are generally more high-paying job opportunities in high-income economies.

» Higher-income economies tend to produce more startups in business and consumer services, while lower-income economies produce more startups in oil and gas, mining, and agriculture, largely due to their geography and natural resources.

>> Only five economies reported more than one in 100 adults starting a new business with new-to-the-world technologies or processes: Uruguay, the United Arab Emirates, Chile, the United States, and Luxembourg. If we consider the economies that are starting with technologies new to the area, but not necessarily new to the world, we find three stand-out economies: Chile, the Dominican Republic, and Canada.

When the GEM report looked at the motivations for starting a business, the number one motivation was to make a difference in the world, and that motivation was prevalent in seven out of ten Level C economies (economies that have the least supportive environment for entrepreneurship and have low GDP per capita numbers).

A different kind of entrepreneurship

Today everywhere you look, you can find an entrepreneur. It didn't used to be that way. When entrepreneurship became a "thing" in the early 1980s, it was the few, the brave, the big risk takers who achieved success and became known. Generally, they had work or professional experience, which meant they started their businesses in their late 30s and 40s. Female and minority businesses were few and far between. But that has all changed.

Entrepreneurs are getting younger, some electing to start businesses rather than go to college. Women-owned businesses have grown by 75 percent in the past ten years alone and now represent 40 percent of all U.S. businesses, according to the Women's Business Enterprise National Council (WBENC). Likewise, the number of minority business enterprises increased by over 79 percent between 2007 and 2017 to 9.3 million businesses, according to the SBA, U.S. Census Bureau. These increases can be attributed in part to the impact of technology, which has reduced startup capital requirements and enabled a small business to start and scale rapidly. Time for humane entrepreneurship, says the ICSB.

The International Council for Small Business (ICSB) supports small and medium-size entrepreneurial businesses. It believes that the entrepreneurs of the future can solve critical global problems by focusing on social, environmental, and economic dimensions. If you are looking to start a business that will have a potentially positive impact on the world, you may want to consider how the ICSB can help you achieve that goal.

In their words, humane entrepreneurship is a culture that focuses on doing good for employees, customers, the business, and the environment simultaneously. This culture fits well with how the workplace has changed over the past two years, a topic we consider in the next section. Employees are now looking for a more nurturing environment where they feel welcome and where they can grow their personal goals alongside the company's goals. In short, employee well-being is at the top of the agenda for savvy companies today.

The Internet and digital platforms can be an extension of your business or can be the entire basis of your business. Either way, you need them today to be successful tomorrow.

The need for speed

How do digital platforms and cloud-based technologies give your entrepreneurial venture a competitive advantage? In four big ways:

>> They provide easy, fast access to vital information.

>> They let you build sustainable size quickly.

>> They facilitate working with remote partners.

>> They enable your company to focus on what it does best, while you outsource other functions to companies that can do those things better and faster. Your customers will appreciate that.

Scaling quickly for competitive advantage

Businesses are getting smaller in terms of infrastructure and physical assets. Smaller? That may sound contrary to one of the basic tenets of entrepreneurial ventures — that they are growth oriented. The kind of *smaller* I mean isn't in conflict with that notion. Entrepreneurial businesses often form partnerships with other businesses to help them scale up functions that they aren't equipped to handle in-house.

So, for example, if you have invented a new product and you don't have manufacturing capability, you may seek that capability from a company that focuses on manufacturing. It's now possible to manage all those partnership relationships online, freeing up time, space, and resources for you to concentrate on what you do best. Besides, a dedicated manufacturer can probably produce your products for much less than you could do it, and you can pass along those savings to your customers.

The fundamental economics of startups have not changed. What has changed is the speed at which businesses are started, products are developed, and business is transacted. That speed has ramifications for everything from product development to service and delivery. That's why most businesses in any category have looked online for ways to connect with customers and give them the quick response they now expect. By doing that, they can keep their size in line to reduce costs.

If you want to move as fast as possible, keep your business as lean as you can and go online for as much as you can.

Harnessing technology for competitive advantage

Recently I've been studying the effects of technology on small businesses and comparing the results against similar businesses in the same industries that do not use technology as a competitive advantage. The differences are striking. Businesses that use technology to improve their competitive profile see opportunities and potential for their businesses that they were never able to see before.

CASE STUDY

One engineering design firm I worked with thought of itself as a small shop serving a very limited market in its seaside town in Southern California. The company believed that its biggest project capabilities were in a range of $5 million to $10 million. However, after installing and learning to use cloud technology and developing a website, the company found that it could optimize its inventory and design processes and could begin bidding on much bigger projects. Technology gave the company the speed and information it needed to compete against much larger companies and to do more complex projects.

CASE STUDY

Another company I know was offering office suites for lease to business tenants. The owner saw a need for space that provides services that companies need but maybe can't afford to own themselves. She spent some time investigating what technology was able to do for her business and its customers. As it turned out, technology totally transformed her already quite successful, but traditional, property management company into a state-of-the-art solution provider for businesses that need high-speed Internet access, a client/server network, cloud computing, video-conferencing, and so forth. Adding cloud technology to the product/service mix not only made this entrepreneur more efficient and effective, but it also created value for her customers and a huge competitive advantage in her marketplace.

What's the message in the stories in these case studies? Companies that attach technology to their processes achieve quantum leaps in productivity, leaps that are hard for competitors to match. That's why we're seeing huge differences in the performance levels of businesses that use technology to streamline their operations and processes and those that don't.

Turning information into intelligence

You probably know how to find information. What's more, you are probably being bombarded by more information than you care to receive, and it comes from every source imaginable. But are you leveraging that information to build intelligence — *knowledge*? Are you sharing information across every function of your business so that you can take advantage of the synergy of multiple sources of intelligence? Or are you leaving a lot of value on the table because it's not organized, filtered, or put into perspective in terms of the needs of your business? Think carefully about the downside to your business if you are not optimizing information.

If you want to build a company that uses its *knowledge* to create a competitive advantage, shift the spotlight away from information and focus it on intelligence. Technology is an enabler in the process of creating intelligence. Today, nearly every company can access sophisticated data analytics programs that enable them to deliver valuable insights to their customers and to everyone in the company. Data has become a product with its own operating and governance model. Teams associated with each data product can develop ways to use and monetize the data, improve on it, protect it, and ensure that it aligns with the company's values and ethics.

Chapter 3 has more to say about employing technology to exploit opportunity.

Managing the new work environment

The events of 2020-2022 caused some temporary changes in the work environment, but also accelerated the pace of more permanent changes. One example is the need to invest in digital and automation of basic day-to-day activities and decision-making. Doing this frees up your employees for more impactful work such as innovation and collaboration. Another is the need to be able to deploy remote processes to a greater extent than a company would have done in the past. No matter what type of business you have, it is important to learn from the experience of the past few years and be in a better position to deal with the next crisis that comes along. As the saying goes, "If Plan A fails, remember that you have 25 letters left."

Breaking the link between information and things

Selling products is not the same as selling information. The economics of the two are very different. When you sell a product, you no longer own it. But when you sell an idea, or a piece of music, or a blueprint, you still own it and can sell it again and again. The exciting thing about information is that it can be replicated at virtually zero cost and sold an unlimited number of times. This means that, unlike many other "things," information is not generally subject to the law of diminishing returns. Theoretically, you can continue to sell information over and over, forever.

What the Internet did for information was to separate it from the economics of things. We no longer need physically intensive media, like books, magazines, and newspapers, to deliver information. Breaking the link between information and things has freed information to go wherever it wants to go. So when the people in your company (or even outside the company) are electronically connected, information flows in every direction, for use by anyone who needs it.

REMEMBER

You can create value for your business by taking advantage of the freedom and mobility of information to create new products and services for your customers. Share company information to increase the intelligence of your business.

Consider this. Perhaps you are particularly good at something — maybe it's gardening or growing orchids. If you have picked up on important techniques and tricks over the years that would be of value to other people interested in orchids, you can share those ideas through an online newsletter, a website, a YouTube channel, branded products, consulting, and so forth. The possibilities are limited only by your imagination.

REMEMBER

Use the Internet to build a community of customers. Then listen to your customers and give them a stake in your success.

Cryptocurrency as an opportunity

You have no doubt heard about cryptocurrency. In simple terms, it is decentralized digital money designed as an alternative to money issued by governments. You can move crypto around and transfer value without the need for a bank. Why is it important for you to know about cryptocurrency? For one thing, it's becoming more common. Already several businesses are accepting crypto in payment for goods and services. Because crypto has the potential to address significant global problems, such as identity theft, economic inequality and freedom, and financial transfer fees, it's worth spending a bit of time learning more about it. Coinbase offers a website platform for accessing the crypto economy (www.coinbase.com). And yes, there is a *Cryptocurrencies For Dummies* book that should get you started. Take it slow. There's no rush to invest until you completely understand the risks and benefits.

Although you hear about crypto everywhere, you may not have come across NFTs (*non-fungible tokens*). They are called the digital answer to collectables — you know — your grandparent's baseball cards or coin collection. A fungible asset is something that can be exchanged for money. A non-fungible asset is unique, one of a kind, so it can't be interchanged with something else, and that's where tokens come in. Tokens are essentially digital certificates of ownership, proving that you own the original work of art or whatever the token represents, even though you don't have physical possession of it. Let's use art, because it's easy to understand.

You purchase a work of art from a local art dealer. The record of the purchase is recorded in a blockchain ledger (which is digital), much how crypto is recorded. You can now sell your token to someone else who wants to own the work of art, which still resides in the art gallery and will continue to reside there even after you sell your NFT. Jack Dorsey, Twitter founder, is promoting an NFT of his first tweet, and the bids are as much as $2.6 million. Seeing those numbers inspires many entrepreneurs to think about turning NFTs into a successful business. Beware that NFTs are highly speculative, so you will want to learn more and get lots of advice before you jump into the pool. No doubt entrepreneurs are looking at NFTs as an opportunity.

You don't have to do it alone. There is safety, power, and success in numbers, so create a network of people and businesses so everyone benefits.

Everyone's value chain is shorter

A value chain is a distribution channel. It's the highway for delivering your product or service to the end user. The traditional value chain looks something like Figure 2-1.

FIGURE 2-1:
The traditional value chain.

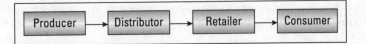

At each point along the channel, someone provides a service that increases the value of the product and allows that intermediary to mark up the price of the product or service. In the 1990s, we saw the shortening of the value chain by discounters like Price Club and Home Depot. They merged the retailer function into the warehousing operation (part of the distributor function), resulting in lower prices to the consumer.

But the Internet has now taken out the distributor as well, reducing a complex channel to a direct one where the consumer or end user deals directly with the producer. Thus, many value chains now look like Figure 2-2.

FIGURE 2-2:
Technology shortens the value chain.

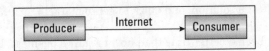

Now, industries such as travel, real estate, and financial services are seeing their traditional products and services being taken over by their customers who have the power to access the information they need via the Internet and control the transaction from start to finish with the click of a mouse.

Making yourself obsolete (before someone does it for you)

With the rapid pace of change in today's world, and recognizing that change is inevitable, every business needs to continually think about ways to put itself out of business, ways to make obsolete its current products and services before they become commodities. Here's a process that will help you do that:

>> Get your key decision-makers together in one group.

>> Identify the ways in which you are currently doing business.

>> Find all the holes in your current strategies that can be penetrated by technology in one form or another.

>> Develop ways to respond to these threats before they manifest.

>> Do rapid experimentation in small ways and get immediate responses from your customers.

>> Keep experimenting and modifying the product or service until you achieve what your customers want.

WARNING

If you don't find ways to make your current products or services obsolete, someone else will.

Facing technology disruption

I'm one of the many people who are rethinking the idea that technology is simply "an enabler." Considering the impact of technology on business and life in general, what appears to be true is that technology is also "a disrupter." Technology doesn't always just solve business or societal problems; sometimes, it creates them. But in the right hands, the new problem can become a new benefit.

To survive and prosper in a digital world, entrepreneurial companies are deconstructing — taking themselves apart and rebuilding — so that they can move faster and get new products to market more quickly. This dynamic environment is tailor-made for entrepreneurial businesses that are quick to see an opportunity, quick to test a solution, and quick to get to market.

There has never been a better time than now to start a business, but competition is coming quickly from high-growth emerging economies such as China, Hong Kong, Indonesia, Malaysia, Singapore, South Korea, and Thailand. These economies have all achieved or exceeded GDP growth of at least 3.5 percent over the past 50 years, according to McKinsey & Company. And they are just the first wave of competitors. As other countries adopt pro-growth policies, they will form a new wave. McKinsey reports that these outperformers generated an average total return to shareholders of 23 percent as compared to 15 percent for high performers in high-income economies. These are serious competitors.

What this means is that you need to think globally about competition and markets. In a highly connected world, Singapore is as close as San Francisco.

Being frugal in the beginning has another benefit. On the Internet, price matters. Customers, whether they're other businesses or consumers, can use the Internet to comparison shop. The Internet has made every product or service essentially a commodity, so price is pretty much all that matters to customers. Those companies that can keep their overhead down and operate lean and smart have a fighting chance. Those that can add value to a commodity in the minds of customers can win at this game. Entrepreneurs are good at creating value with limited resources, so the Internet is one startup environment that is perfect for them.

Wherever there's a customer need that hasn't been filled, there's an opportunity for an entrepreneur to satisfy that need.

Technology enables and disrupts constantly

I'm reminded of the often-quoted "Moore's Law," conceived by Gordon Moore, founder of Intel Corp., the semiconductor company. It essentially says that every 18 months, computer-processing power will double while costs will decline by half. In simple terms, this means that technology always moves toward smaller, cheaper, and faster. That's why the processing power of huge mainframe computers of years ago can now be found in palm-size video games.

The speed of technology innovation works for entrepreneurs whose ability to be flexible and fast gives them a distinct advantage in the market. So does that mean that in the next ten years, the problem of AR (augmented reality) optics will be solved? When you use an app to find your car in a crowded parking lot, you're using AR. But who wants to wear a large headset all the time? Eventually, we'll all be able to wear a pair of glasses instead of a headset that puts us in a virtual world. Recall that it took about ten years to move from WAP phones to iPhones. It was going to happen. The question was who was going to do it? Turns out it was Apple.

Everywhere, businesses are looking for ways to use technology to push back-office functions out the back door, so that they can focus on what they do best and remain quick on their feet. Today we have lots of options for doing that. Tomorrow there will be even more.

Understanding the Latest Big Trends

Trends come and go. Still, it's important to be aware of what the market is focused on at any point in time. At least knowing what customers want can put you a step ahead in preparing your business to be where it needs to be at any moment. I've put together some key trends that you should be aware of. Some will be more relevant to you than others, but it's important to at least recognize that these trends exist and are likely to be around for some time.

Easier access to entrepreneurship education

This trend has been a long time coming, but it's here. If you don't have access to a college or university entrepreneurship program, all is not lost. You can find a wealth of information online, including books like the one you're currently reading on how to become an entrepreneur. The advantage of a book like this is that all the information is in one place, and you can learn at your own pace. That's easier than having to search online for each topic.

Alternatively, some countries, such as India, have put course curricula online, as in the case of the Trainers' Training Programme on Entrepreneurship Development for PMYUVA Project of the Industrial Training Institute. (That's a mouthful) (see https://niesbud.nic.in).

Some U.S. universities offer online programs at reasonable costs. For example, Wharton offers an entrepreneurship acceleration program to help grow your business. It even culminates in a pitch to well-known venture capital firms like Sequoia Capital to get you the money you need to grow the business. Some countries like Turkey, for example, offer disadvantaged European students a program that covers their fees and travel. (See https://abroadship.org/training-course-powering-entrepreneurship-education-for-disadvantaged-youth-turkey/.)

The educational platform Coursera is another source of education in entrepreneurship and innovation as well as social enterprises. Many Coursera courses are free and offer flexible deadlines for completion. You can also focus on courses in specific areas that interest you. Most entrepreneurs will benefit from courses in accounting and finance. A legal course for business can't hurt either.

TIP

The U.S. Small Business Administration runs many programs in partnerships around the country to provide training and counseling to disadvantaged entrepreneurs. In addition to Small Business Development Centers (SBDCs), Women's Business Centers (WBCs), and Veterans Business Opportunity Centers (VBOCs), the SBA has service centers at Historically Black Colleges and Universities (HBCUs) across America.

Sustainable finance

The word *sustainable* has been thrown around a lot lately; we usually hear about it in terms of sustainable companies and environmental practices. But *sustainable finance* is something that's valued at about $30 billion, according to Bloomberg. What is it? It's the practice of investing in companies whose goal is to generate environmental and social returns for their shareholders. Is this something you need to think about as a new entrepreneur with a startup? The answer is yes. Some companies like Beyond Meat have built their entire concept around taking care of the planet by developing plant-based meat. That focus made them attractive to venture capitalists who see an advantage to investing sustainably.

Maybe your great business idea is not directly in the path of the sustainability crowd. That's okay, but you will enhance your chances of getting funding if you can show how your company is taking care of the environment and the well-being of its employees.

DIY coding

Over time, do-it-yourself versions of common skills emerge, capturing a new group of customers. Today it's *coding*, being able to write a script in a programming language that can be understood by a computer. Coding is how we end up with the apps on your phone, your Facebook page, and pretty much everything else you do online. New companies such as Zapier make it possible for your grandparent to build a digital product. And with the shortage of workers, you may need them, so that's a good thing. Webflow is a no-code platform that raised over $200 million in VC funding. And there's even a company that provides tutorials for building without code. It's called Makerpad.

Of course, these quick-and-easy ways to build are a boon to tech startups because they enable such companies to quickly develop minimum viable products and demonstrate the benefits of what they're offering to VCs and customers.

Sharing what you have

Whether you have a home, a car, or even a kitchen, you can make money by sharing it. And that's a business model that has seen huge successes such as Airbnb for vacation rentals, Uber for ride sharing, and most recently CloudKitchens, which provides kitchen spaces for delivery-only restaurants, a need that surged during the pandemic. In all three cases, entrepreneurs were able to launch their businesses without huge upfront costs. CloudKitchens, which was started by former Uber CEO Travis Kalanick after being forced out of Uber, has spurred the founding of dozens of new restaurants focused solely on delivery. That's quite a comeback.

Personalized and direct to customers

This is an example of technology as a driving force, not just an enabler. The availability of affordable AI (artificial intelligence) and 3D printing alone has inspired a new industry — personalized products designed by and shipped directly to the customer. It's known as DTC (direct to customer) and the annual increases in sales of DTCs have topped 20 percent per year in the past few years.

Let's look at FitMyFoot as an example. FitMyFoot is an online store that sells custom sandals and insoles made by their 3D printer according to a foot tracing that the customer does by hand when they place an order. FitMyFoot also has an app to take pictures of your foot for custom orthotics. They clearly solved a real problem for customers — foot pain and the high cost of custom-made orthotics. And they make it easy and quick to get their product. Their sales have doubled every year since they started. When you give customers what they need and want and make it easy to buy, you'll have delighted customers every time.

Using micro influencers for social media marketing

One of the biggest trends in marketing has been the rise of the micro influencer. Less expensive than celebrity influencers, the right candidate can have a significant impact on the acceptance of your product or service.

A *micro influencer* is someone, usually a blogger, YouTube, or Instagram personality who has gained a large and dedicated following. When they talk about and endorse your product, their followers are likely to purchase it or, at a minimum, talk about it and repost. Reposting is the name of the game, so you can extend your reach rapidly at no cost.

The trick for entrepreneurs is to figure out which influencer actually has influence! You might think it's about how many people follow the influencer, but that would only be partially correct. Recent research on the matter in the *Journal of Marketing Research* discovered that the most influential influencers did not follow other people, including their own followers, and that fact actually makes them more attractive to their followers. The reasoning is that the influencer is viewed as a primary source if they don't follow a lot of others. We're still early in understanding this phenomenon so, for entrepreneurs, choosing the right influencer could be hit and miss. It's important to consider what you're trying to sell and the type of platform your customers are most likely to use: Instagram, Twitter, Facebook, and so forth. It always makes sense to go online and view some influencers, read the comments from their followers, and decide if this environment is the right one for what you're offering.

It should come as no surprise that some entrepreneurs have taken advantage of this new marketing arena and have started companies such as #paid, which will help you find the right influencer for your brand and teach you how to set up a campaign.

Investing in climate tech is hot

Accounting giant PricewaterhouseCoopers reports that VC investment in climate technology is growing five times faster than other categories. As of 2019, VC climate tech investments stood at $16.3 billion. Some of the companies that have benefited include Pachama, which offers a monitoring technology for reforestation and conservation projects; Redwood Materials, which is recycling lithium-ion batteries and other e-waste; and Turntide Technologies, which produces motors that are 64 percent more efficient and don't use rare earth minerals. One startup, Climeworks, was able to raise $110 million in 2020 for its filtration system that removes carbon dioxide from the air and stores it underground.

If you're thinking about doing something in the climate arena, spend a lot of time thinking about the specific problem you're trying to solve. If you do develop a solution, make sure it is one you can protect. (I talk about intellectual property in Chapter 8.) You'll be going up against some big players, but if you've come up with something original and valuable, VCs are ready to put up the capital you'll need to make it happen. As mentioned, climate tech is hot right now and probably for some time to come, so it's a bit of a crowded space. The only thing that might change that calculus is if investors are unable to reap their desired returns in the timeframe they planned for.

Finally, it's always a good idea to keep up on business and market trends. Just because the current trends don't spark an idea doesn't mean a new trend won't emerge that you can take advantage of.

Chapter **3**

Preparing to Seek Opportunity

Would it surprise you to learn that ideas are a commodity, that everyone has them — dozens of times a day? When you say something like, "I think I'd like to go to a movie," that's an idea. We're generating ideas all the time. What makes entrepreneurial ideas different is that we can turn some of those ideas into opportunities that have commercial potential with a business. How does that happen?

In this chapter, I show you how to unleash your creative skills to recognize an opportunity, test it, and potentially come up with a business idea.

Understanding Ideas versus Opportunities, Creativity versus Innovation

To have a good discussion about opportunity, we need to understand some important terms. Let's start by looking at the difference between ideas and opportunities. Ideas are easy. Nearly everything you do involves an idea at the start. "I think I'd like to fix that broken door." The "I think" is a clue that you have an idea. And that's all it is, nothing more, nothing less. An opportunity, on the other hand, is more than an idea. It is something that has commercial potential or the potential to become a business.

Now let's look at creativity versus innovation. You'll see a similar relationship. Creativity is the ability to use your imagination to come up with original ideas. We'll test that ability in a minute. Innovation is creatively coming up with something — a product, service, or business — that has commercial value that people will pay for.

You can test your creative abilities by trying the following exercise. It's a classic:

> Choose a product that is part of your everyday life — for example, a glass jar. Then, list all the possible products you could make from the jar. Use your imagination and be as creative as possible with your ideas.

I have seen people come up with at least 30 different product ideas. You may not be able to match that number on the first try, but over time you'll find that you get increasingly better at looking at an object from a completely different point of view. Some typical products suggested for the jar are flower pot, fish bowl, and pencil holder. (Did you think to break the jar to do something with the pieces? That's real creative thinking.)

In doing this exercise, you used your creative skills to imagine a variety of uses. Once you have your list, consider whether any of them qualify as opportunities or potential solutions to problems that could lead to a business idea.

Every time you plan to do something, it involves an idea or a series of ideas. But, as you have probably figured out, not all ideas have the potential to become opportunities to make money.

REMEMBER

An opportunity (in a business sense) is an idea that has commercial potential. You can make money with it, develop a business around it, or in some other way, create value.

Starting with an Idea May Not Be the Best Idea

You need to get started somewhere, so why not right here? I want to get your creative juices going so that you are opportunity-focused for the rest of this chapter. Try these two exercises and see how creative you can be.

Changing an existing business

Choose a business in your community that is familiar to you. Then put yourself in the owner's shoes and see if you can identify a problem this business might have now or in the future. Make sure you understand the problem enough to think about a potential solution. For example, suppose you choose a restaurant that is operating in the traditional manner as a retail location where people enjoy a meal. Because many more restaurants are popping up in this part of town, this restaurant owner needs to think about how to grow their business and revenue. Through your analysis you discover there is unused capacity in the kitchen. You believe this is an opportunity to offer meals online for pickup and/ or delivery. Another possibility is leasing out your excess capacity to a non-competing business that needs kitchen facilities. In this exercise, you're applying creative thinking to an existing business to make it better. Now, to reinforce what you learned, use this example as a guide, choose a business in a different category and try the exercise again.

Solving a problem with creativity

Examine your home environment carefully to find a problem that needs to be solved. Ideally, it is something that requires a better process. This is an opportunity — an opportunity to solve a problem. *Now create an opportunity that will solve the problem.* For example, you have parents who are getting older and do not want to do their spring and fall cleaning. But the cleaning service companies are too expensive. Could students with the proper training meet the demand of a market niche that is being ignored? Could spring and fall cleaning become regular bi-weekly service calls? At this point you don't know because you haven't done any market research to find out how big this problem is. But it's a start.

Now it's your turn. Once you've completed the exercise, consider whether it was easy or difficult. If you struggled to come up with some ideas, you may be facing obstacles that you have inadvertently set up for yourself. We take care of those next.

Spotting Obstacles in Your Path

It may surprise you to discover that you are often your own worst enemy when it comes to improving your ability to be creative. Ask yourself a few questions:

» Do I let myself get so busy that I never have any time to think?

» Am I afraid of being criticized?

>> Am I having problems that seem to be constantly on my mind?

>> Am I under a lot of stress?

>> Do I believe that I'm not a creative person?

If you answered yes to any of these questions, you have identified an issue that could be stifling your creativity. The fourth one is the real killer of creativity, because it makes you less productive and less effective. If you are experiencing any of these five conditions, you probably won't do the things you need to do to become more creative. Therefore, the first step is to address the obstacles that are blocking your natural creativity.

Some obstacles — whether real or imaginary — that may keep you from being your creative best are addressed in the following sections.

You think you're not innovative (think again!)

Maybe in your family, your sibling was always referred to as "the inventor," because they could draw or build things. You, on the other hand, couldn't build things, even with an instruction manual. It's common for us to replay stories like these over and over in our minds. And the more we do this, the more we believe them. All is not lost. You simply need to change your story and look at things in a new way. Just doing the simple exercises in this chapter can start to retrain your brain. Time to do the jar exercise again, don't you think?

You dislike criticism (don't we all?)

Many times people don't try new things because they're afraid that people will criticize them or think they're crazy. Unfortunately, that attitude keeps these same people from realizing their full potential, because they're always being held back by their need to be accepted by others as rational human beings. Ideas that come out of left field may seem to have little in common with rationality, but the seemingly irrational idea often ends up leading you to the very solution you're seeking. Certainly, Gary Dahl wasn't thinking about what people would think of him when he came up with the idea of The Pet Rock. He just knew that he was tired of all the chores related to having a pet like a dog or cat, so he decided that people needed a pet that was no trouble at all. And what could be less trouble than a rock? He packaged the rocks with a "Pet Rock Training Manual" that he spent months writing and sold 1.5 million of them in 1975 for $3.95 a piece (over $21 in 2022 dollars). Now that's creative thinking.

And what about Harvard graduate Ken Hakuta, who started another fad when his mother sent him a rubber, octopus-shaped toy from Japan? What was unusual about this toy was that when you would throw it at a wall, it would stick; but then gravity would cause it to crawl down the wall. Hakuta licensed the North American rights to distribute the toy, called it the Wacky Wallwalker, and sold more than 250 million of the little beasts in the 1980s. He made more than $20 million.

CASE STUDY

Maybe you've noticed that some people are obsessed with taking and posting pictures of themselves on Instagram or Facebook. Maybe you're one of them. It seems as if they can't get enough of themselves. One clever entrepreneur decided to make fun of the selfie takers. He discovered he could mail a selfie to Vermont Novelty Toaster Corp., where they would make a metal impression of the selfie in the form of a small, metal plate. Then he could put the plate in his toaster and see his face burned onto his toast for breakfast. Imagine getting a Selfie Toaster for Christmas. Of course, building on the original idea, other innovative entrepreneurs came up with, for example, the Angry Toaster, with seven not-so-flattering phrases burned into toast. Not a very positive way to make someone's morning special. But you get the idea. You don't have to start from scratch. Sometimes you can build on someone else's idea as long as they don't hold a patent, which we talk about in Chapter 8.

You're a creature of habit (so is everyone)

Routines certainly have value. They let you complete regular and repetitive tasks more effectively. But if you rely too much on routines, you limit your thinking to those routines and you miss out on all the other ways of looking at things. In other words, you restrict the possible responses you might give in a particular situation. What that does is keep you from improving, finding new and better ways of doing things, and generally keeping up with change.

Instead of sticking to your daily routine, why not try taking a new route to work or school. Change your daily routine for a couple days and see if it helps you generate some new ideas. Here's some good advice. Turn off your phone for an hour a day and just play with ideas that come to your mind. Distractions are one of the biggest reasons people lose their innate creative abilities. Take some time to daydream. It's definitely worth it. And keep a notepad nearby to write down the ideas that come to mind. You'll be surprised.

You lack confidence (you can do it!)

Closely tied to a fear of being criticized is lack of confidence in expressing new and unusual ideas. If you are the kind of person who generally seeks approval from your social media pals for the things you do or the ideas you generate, you may be putting curbs on your ability to be creative. Many of the products we depend on today would never have existed if the people who invented them didn't have the courage to risk the "slings and arrows" of others who didn't have the inventor's vision.

CASE STUDY

Andrew Wilson, a Boston-based investment banker, was traveling through Memphis to visit the legendary home of Elvis Presley when he saw an amphibious military vehicle from the World War II era known as "the duck." It had been converted into a tour bus, but what Wilson saw was that it was perfectly suited to both land and water tours in Boston. Convincing city officials in Boston wasn't easy because at the time he didn't even own a duck boat that he could show them. But Wilson had confidence that he had found his dream opportunity. Finally, after much searching, he discovered Manuel Rogers, a collector of military vehicles, who owned a duck. Rogers loved the idea and helped Wilson raise the money to get started in 1994. By 1996, Boston Duck Tours was earning revenues of $3.4 million and looking for other cities to expand to. Today the company owns 28 Ducks and has 200 employees. It's one of the most popular tourist attractions in Boston.

You're overconfident (jumbo ego)

The opposite of a lack of confidence is having an ego so big that you think you already have all the answers, so you don't stop to consider new ways of thinking. It's fine to have strong beliefs and values that guide your thinking and decision-making, but you also need to suspend the limitations on your thinking once in a while so that you can be creative and grow.

CASE STUDY

Uber is a perfect example of great innovation by an entrepreneur who had a very large ego and didn't listen to his advisors or employees. Travis Kalanick set out to disrupt the taxi industry with a ride-hailing service via a mobile app in 2009. He succeeded in doing that beyond anything anyone thought possible, taking the company to a $17 billion valuation. However, his inability to take advice and his reckless behavior with the company caused the board to ask for his resignation as CEO, which he gave in 2017. As of December 2019, he had left the board and sold all his shares in Uber. He went on to found CloudKitchens, which rents out space to restaurants for delivery-only services. He says it will be bigger than Uber. Using the same aggressive culture that got him in trouble at Uber, he has already taken this company to *unicorn* status, proving that he does know how to recognize a hot opportunity. Kalanick is not alone in achieving huge success followed by crash and burn, proving it takes more than a great idea. Other companies that followed the same path include Theranos, a biolab, and WeWork, a provider of co-working spaces. In each case, we can point to a CEO who was overconfident and thought they could do anything, including taking extraordinary risks and skirting the law. So, it's probably best to check your ego at the door and learn from others' mistakes and successes. There's always a way to make an opportunity better. Be open to others' ideas and keep ethics front of mind. And remember, it takes more than a great idea to produce a successful company.

ASPIRING TO UNICORN STATUS: IS IT REALISTIC?

Unicorns are startups that reach $1 billion in valuation while they are still private companies. They used to be rare, about one a year as recently as 2013, but today one new unicorn is born every day. Unicorn companies are not valued based on their history, which is typically pretty short, but on their future potential, which comes from funding rounds or a potential buyout by a much larger company as well as the promise of an initial public offering (IPO). Privately held companies that become unicorns either have remarkable sales that justify a billion-dollar valuation, or they have such an innovative concept that investors are willing to roll the dice.

Among the top unicorn companies are Uber, SpaceX, Pinterest, Airbnb, and WeWork. Even unicorns fail or get into serious problems, as you learned with WeWork, Uber, and Theranos. SpaceX has had a remarkable run and as of 2022 was valued at $100 billion. Money can't always buy great strategy and effective management, however. All of the successful unicorns are based on innovative technology, and most are found in Silicon Valley. One peer-reviewed study of 135 unicorns found that the average company was overvalued by as much as 48 percent. That could explain why many unicorns don't experience successful IPOs. Uber went out at $45 per share and today trades at about $10 below its IPO price. It has yet to make a profit. One success story is Zoom, the darling of the pandemic. Its stock debuted in 2019 at $36 per share and for a short time exceeded $500 per share in late 2020.

Unicorn status brings with it fresh capital and a round of spending by founders. The risk of early startup is behind you. Investors typically keep a unicorn private as long as possible so they can achieve as high a valuation as possible before an IPO, which is their big payday. Employees don't often fair as well with unicorns because their stock options become very costly to exercise and an IPO is likely years away. Every new round of funding that the unicorn receives comes with a new 409A valuation of the fair market value of the options and the associated taxes that the employee has to pay as a result. Those taxes, which are usually based on short-term capital gains, must be paid upon the new valuation. That can be a huge burden and many employees have left their vested stock options on the table.

So, is it realistic to aspire to unicorn status? Probably not. Concentrate on coming up with a solution to a big problem that customers appreciate, and the money will take care of itself. Study the stories of several unicorns to learn from their mistakes as well as their successes.

Clearing Away the Obstacles

So what can you do to overcome all the obstacles you may have created for yourself that will keep you from being creative enough to become a successful entrepreneur? Help is on the way.

Going back to familiar territory

Most ideas come from environments and things with which you're familiar — your neighborhood, a comment from a friend, a suggestion of an employee, or a problem identified by a customer (probably the best kind). Too often we think we must look for opportunity outside what we know — it's the grass-is-always-greener syndrome. Actually, quite the opposite is true. Most ideas have very common roots in things we know and are comfortable with. Think Uber, Joe's Garage Coffee, and TaskUs. They were all born from things we know and understand. What turns these ideas into opportunities is the ability to look at the common from an uncommon point of view, to juxtapose things that normally are not associated with each other, or to tear things apart and put them back together in a new way. In doing so, you can come up with something customers want and will pay for. And that's called *innovation*.

Research supports the thought that most of our new ideas come from our prior experiences. Start taking an inventory of your experiences. Can you recall any problems you faced? Was it a problem that many people face? If so, you may have found an opportunity.

CASE STUDY

Anything can spark an idea for a business. Randall Thompson, who played for the Toronto Blue Jays for a short time as a free agent, remembered a trick his former coach used to get players to focus on their hands. He chopped off the top of a bat and had the players work with the rest of the bat. Thompson took it a step further and asked, why not create a mug from the fat end of the bat so you could serve a drink in it? He called his idea Dugout Mugs. With no plan for a company, he began selling the mugs and using the proceeds to finance the next batch of mugs. He did reach out for help to someone who knew how to scale businesses, Kris Dehnert, from the Dehnert Media Group. With Kris's guidance, the two have grown the company to $30 million in international sales. The future could hold an acquisition or an IPO. But for now, taking Kris's advice, they're simply operating a company that doesn't need to be acquired to succeed. Now that's good advice for any entrepreneur.

Tapping your personal network

Business associates are a popular source of new ideas for business ventures. Developing a personal network of people with a variety of skills and knowledge is a critical component in the opportunity recognition process. Your network will serve to open your mind to a variety of thoughts and ideas, one of which may become that great opportunity you were looking for. The key is to look at who's in your network. Have you surrounded yourself with people who are different from you? People who have different experiences and backgrounds? You want people who can provide critical feedback and take your ideas in directions you might not have thought of on your own. Building a network is a critical activity for any entrepreneur. Chapter 9 covers more about networks, where you'll learn that your network will be needed for every stage of your new business.

MEET DOUG HALL: NEW PRODUCT GURU EXTRAORDINAIRE

It has been said that Doug Hall, the unabashed guru of product innovation and creativity, can pull new-product ideas literally out of thin air like magic. In just three days he can get product companies like PepsiCo, Procter & Gamble, and Nike to come up with 30 viable products. That's a process that normally takes these companies three months. In fact, on average, you have about 18 products in your home that were first conceived at RSI, Hall's remarkable company based outside Cincinnati, Ohio.

Hall's base of operations is a grand old house he dubbed Eureka! Ranch to celebrate the Eureka! Stimulus Response, which is what you experience when you come up with what he calls a "wicked-good idea." The ranch is home to anything and everything that gets people to have fun and loosen up, from Nerf Ballzookas to Whoopee Cushions. Hall firmly believes that if you're laughing, you will come up with better ideas.

With tactics like the "Mind Dumpster," "Bulging," and "Smash Association," Hall can get his clients to suspend their old ways of thinking and embrace his wackiness. And while clients are focusing on ideas, Hall's "trained brains" (his team of creative people) wander through the room adding ideas, drawing packaging solutions, and sparking creativity wherever they feel it's lacking.

Food is a critical component of his creative strategy. According to Hall, "if corporations would double their food budgets, they'd get more than double their return on investment." So at Hall's invention fests, food and drink are plentiful, as is music, which he uses to stimulate ideas — Dixieland jazz to get acquainted, classic rock and roll to get things moving, and funky tunes like the theme from Gilligan's Island for his brain dump.

Hall's invention style has been studied to compare it with other methods in terms of effectiveness. Arthur VanGundy of the University of Oklahoma ran a comparison group

(continued)

(continued)

of Hall's people and his own and challenged them to come up with ideas for snack foods. VanGundy's groups averaged 6.5 marketable ideas in 45 minutes, while Hall's groups averaged 36.3 marketable ideas, or 558 percent more, in the same timeframe. From this experience, VanGundy learned that to successfully generate a greater volume of ideas, you must do three things:

- You have to believe that anything is possible.

- You have to create an environment that stimulates creativity.

- You have to use a variety of stimuli, both related and unrelated to the particular problem you're trying to solve.

According to Hall's website, Eureka! Ranch is a place where Eureka! Trailblazer Training leverages quantitative science and gritty street smarts to help managers think smarter, faster, and more imaginatively. Take a look at Hall's Eureka! Ranch website at www.eurekaranch.com. If you want a fun read, check out his book *Jump Start Your Brain*. It just may convince you that you can be creative.

Designing an Environment that Inspires Creativity and Innovation

If you want to use your creative abilities, you need to set yourself up for success. This section looks at some proven ways to spark your creativity and make the process a regular part of your life and talks about the best work environment to spark creativity.

Making time to be creative

If you do not think of yourself as a creative person, I'm guessing that one of the big reasons is that you've never allowed yourself time to be creative. Countless distractions occur on any given day, and if you let yourself be pulled away from what you're concentrating on by every little distraction that comes along, by email announcements to boring work and co-workers who take any opportunity to get away from their work and bother you, you will never find enough time to develop your creative skills.

Set aside some time for yourself to focus on building your latent creative tendencies. Here are some examples of things you can do during that precious time.

Find a favorite thinking space

Put on some thinking music (for me, anything by Mozart is good for this), sit in a comfortable chair or stretch out on a couch or on the lawn, close your eyes, and just free associate for a while. Let ideas and thoughts come in and out of your mind in any order. Be sure those thoughts are not about the work you were doing. The more you put yourself in this dream state, the more interesting and creative your thoughts will become. Alternatively, you can daydream while running, doing yoga, or floating in your swimming pool, but do be aware of your surroundings to keep yourself safe. Any activity that lets you be present and turn off distractions will work. Find the perfect spot and your mind will habitually become present when you go there.

Play with toys, games, and kids

Toys like Legos and K'NEX are great for stimulating creativity in a physical way. Various kinds of games, computer simulations, and video games also call for some creative thinking. They may kindle the more playful side of your creative thinking ability. Of course, playing with kids will let you see creativity and imagination in action. Kids can take the simplest tools — sticks, blocks, paper bags, and so forth — and turn them into props in an elaborate fantasy they build and act out. Suspend your adult intellect for a bit and try being a kid again. It will surprise you how easily you can look at your very familiar world in a new light.

Here's a list of some additional ways that you can enhance your creative ability:

>> **Keep an idea file or notebook.** You never know when an idea will strike, and even though you think it's the greatest idea you've ever had and you couldn't possibly forget it, write it down! In fact, keep a journal of all your ideas. You may not be able to make one happen right now; but who knows, sometime in the future may be perfect for turning that idea into an opportunity.

>> **Read, read, read.** Books, newspapers, magazines, and trade journals, and government websites are valuable sources of ideas and trends. Subscribe to websites where you can get validated content about trends and industry analysis and listen to podcasts. You may even learn about some new regulation that could mean an opportunity for you.

>> **Try thinking in opposites.** Pick something you're familiar with and then think about what it isn't. For example, a telephone is something you can't eat — or can you? AT&T brainstormed that opposite when their marketing people asked themselves what a telephone is NOT. As a result, they decided to create chocolate telephones to send to their best customers.

>> **Find new uses for old things.** 3M scientist Arthur Fry was working on developing bookshelf arranger tape when the idea for Post-it Notes, the sticky-backed bookmarkers, came to him.

Finding the right place for innovation

Too often entrepreneurs think that it takes a great idea — a great product — to build a great company. But that's not true at all. Thomas Edison's greatest invention wasn't the lightbulb; it was the modern research and development lab. Walt Disney's greatest creation wasn't Disneyland; it was Disney Imagineering, the source of all their great ideas. Successful companies create environments that stimulate creativity and produce a continuing flow of superb ideas. Why is your company's environment so important to creativity? Simply put, it's because environments have the ability to either stimulate your senses or dull them. Consider the following:

>> If you regularly work in an environment that is *rigid and hierarchical* (many layers of management), chances are your ability to think outside the box will be very limited because ways of doing things will tend to be standardized.

>> If your environment is hectic, *fast-paced, with many deadlines* — something you find in the world of advertising — you will probably have little opportunity to spend in contemplation, an activity that is generally necessary for creativity to happen.

Making your work environment friendly

The following are some actions you can take to handle your work environment and make it more conducive to creativity:

>> Find new and interesting ways to minimize the distractions in your life.

>> At the very least, you should devote some time each day to quiet contemplation to train your mind to be more attentive to creative opportunities.

>> Some people have found that a certain room or place allows them to relax and meditate. Dr. Yoshiro NakaMats, the prolific Japanese inventor (with over 2,300 patents for such things as the floppy disk, compact disk and player, and the digital watch), has developed an entire process to spark his creativity. He created some unique environments; for example, he starts his creativity process by sitting calmly in a room in his home — a sort of meditation room with only natural things in it — then he moves to a dynamic room, which is a dark room with the latest in audio/video equipment. Finally, he heads for the swimming pool where he swims underwater for long periods.

I'm not suggesting that you need to copy Dr. NakaMats to become creative. Find the process and location that works for you. The important thing to remember is that you will be more creative in some environments than others. Your task is to find the right environment for you.

REMEMBER

You are as creative as you want to be. Start looking at old problems in new ways and you're bound to spot a great opportunity.

Growing Ideas with Outside Help: Incubators and Accelerators

If you're fortunate enough to be attending a major research university with a good engineering school, you're in a hotbed of new inventions. Your university may even have a center focused on new technology ventures where you can get involved in commercializing a discovery or invention created at the university. Who knows? That invention you work on might turn into the company you start.

Today everyone is looking for new ideas, new solutions, and new products and processes; but for most businesses, doing R&D is an expensive proposition, one few can afford. Consequently, one of the biggest trends is joining an incubator or accelerator program where you can get support and access potential partners and investors. Many incubators have their own educational programs to help you acquire the skills you need to successfully launch your business. Dreamit Ventures is one of the most active incubators in the United States and it focuses on helping startups scale and secure needed capital. A global incubator, 500 Startups has supported thousands of companies with a four-month accelerator that provides hands-on learning, office space if needed, mentorship, and a $100,000 investment for 5 percent of the company. Amplify LA focuses on tech startups but their program is customized to the needs of each startup.

Before joining an incubator, ask yourself the following questions:

>> Have I done my research on the incubator? Do I know all the costs and requirements?

>> Have I contacted any of the alumni of the incubator?

>> Do I have a strong founding team? Incubators invest in teams first, ideas second.

>> Can I demonstrate that I have the ability to execute on my plan?

>> Do I know what I'm willing to give to get into this incubator?

WARNING

Do not use invention services that are advertised in TV infomercials or on websites with offers to help you patent and commercialize your invention. You don't need an invention service to patent your invention. You do need a good patent attorney.

And you need an entrepreneur, if you don't want to become one, to help you commercialize your product.

The best of the best accelerators — the elite — are tough to get into, probably because they produce some of the most iconic companies, such as Dropbox, Airbnb, and DigitalOcean. Here are some examples of what some of these accelerators are looking for.

>> **Techstars New York City:** Focus on a great application that leverages your network and any connections to the alumni of the accelerator.

>> **Y Combinator:** Build your minimal viable product. Have something to show.

>> **Dreamit Ventures:** Demonstrate that you've checked out their incubator and some of their alums.

WARNING

Be careful not to go after every accelerator in "spray and pray" fashion. They all know each other and want to feel like you chose them for a specific reason.

Spotting the Best Opportunities

This section covers some different ways to find opportunities from a more contrarian perspective.

Finding opportunity in failure (yours and others)

You have probably heard the oft-quoted phrases, "learn from your failures," and "you can't succeed without first failing." Trite but true.

The problem is that most people do not learn from their failures; instead, they head off in an entirely new direction only to fail again because they didn't apply the lessons learned from the previous experience. Don't make that mistake. Let's have fun with, and learn from, some of the more outrageous failures:

>> **Vessyl by Mark One.** I don't know what this entrepreneur was drinking when he picked this idea. It's a smart cup that knows what you're drinking and tells you by pinging your phone with an announcement of the ingredients. I don't know about you, but I usually know exactly what I'm drinking before I put it into a cup. In any case, their app didn't do a great job of getting the ingredients right. So when the first pass with customers didn't pass muster after all

the hype, they launched a second attempt, Pryme Vessyl, a smart water bottle which, after taking into account your height, age, weight, and sex, will tell you how many bottles of water you should drink to stay hydrated. Again, I don't know about you, but I never give my personal information to a water bottle, especially a smart one. Another flop. Part of the problem is they don't know how to spell. Pryme? Or is that Pry Me, which is even worse. And Vessyl? Eventually the company ran out of Kickstarter money and is now out of business. Lesson learned. Don't solve a problem that doesn't exist. Worse, don't create a problem that didn't exist in the first place.

» **:CueCat.** (yes, they put a colon before the C — maybe as eyes?) This hardware peripheral was a QR code reader that came out before the advent of cell phones with cameras. Maybe you see the problem already. But it gets worse. It could only scan barcodes in print magazines. Are you really going to scan a barcode from a magazine and then go online to register and go through all the hassle to buy something you saw in a print magazine? Probably not. Crazy as it sounds, the company was sending out the so-called "cats" free to get people to use them. Of course, no one was using them because they didn't solve a problem. The problem the company thought they were solving was being able to prove to advertisers that people actually saw their ads in magazines and acted on them. But that wasn't true. So eventually, magazines stopped including the bar codes in their advertising. And that was the end of a very bad business model. The interesting thing is that developers in the Linux community were able to reverse-engineer the "cat" and come up with some useful apps to take advantage of the scanner capability. But, :CueCat attempted to block them rather than recognizing the new opportunity for free product development so the cat could have a broader reach.

Lesson learned: Put a solid, validated business model in place but be prepared to modify it when conditions change.

Don't you think you're more creative than those two examples?

Finding opportunity for underrepresented communities

Digital and remote work adoption was accelerated during the pandemic of 2020-2022. The problem is that underrepresented communities such as indigenous people have had difficulty accessing these job opportunities. The Virtual Gurus seeks to solve that problem with its Talent-as-a-Service platform. The Calgary, Canada-based company provides virtual assistant jobs across a spectrum of tasks specifically to underrepresented groups and matches their virtual assistants to the needs of the customer. They curate those matches based on such things as availability, personality, and skill set.

Today, many impact investor funds are ready to provide funding to startups focusing on serving underrepresented communities, so it's definitely an opportunity worth considering.

CASE STUDY

Ritah Nakandi used to mentor Ugandan women in entrepreneurship in her native country. The problem she identified was the lack of a big market for these crafts-women to sell their unique items. In 2013, she founded the Afri-root Collective in Watertown, MA to connect these women to international markets. She has reinvested a portion of all sales into leadership training programs. The opportunity she created has had an enormous impact on the lives of these Ugandan women.

CASE STUDY

Brandale D. Randolph was tired of seeing the government throw money at the problem of poverty and never solve it because it didn't understand the problem. Randolph made it his mission to understand poverty and to rebuild underserved communities. He started in 2016 with his high-end bicycle assembly company, the 1854 Cycling Company, which gave jobs to formerly incarcerated people and then donated a portion of every bicycle sold to combat juvenile recidivism. He has even taken his message to a popular YouTube TEDx talk, "Stop Throwing Breakfast Sandwiches at the Poor," which is a call to solve the problem of poverty by offering skills training and counseling.

Finding opportunity in things that don't go together

In 1984, Virgin Atlantic Airways stunned the industry when it defied logic and took out its first-class seats and service. But Virgin was not acting precipitously without having done its homework. On the contrary, Virgin had figured out that they earned more profit on business class than first class. So they added value for their customers by putting in sleeper-recliner seats that their competitors didn't have, and providing free transportation to and from the airport. As Virgin's competitors began to copy its innovations, Virgin didn't rest on its laurels; it added state-of-the-art lounges where business passengers could do everything — take a shower, get their clothes pressed, and use the latest office equipment. Virgin saw itself as a solution provider rather than an airline, and that made all the difference.

Sometimes, doing what no one else is willing to do provides a huge opportunity and some space in which to exploit it before the skeptics discover that you were right all along.

IN THIS CHAPTER

» **Passing the entry exam**

» **Converting an idea into a business concept**

» **Running your concept past the critics**

» **Getting serious with a feasibility analysis**

Chapter **4**

Testing an Opportunity Before You Leap

S ometimes it seems that today's entrepreneurs come up with an idea over coffee one morning and by the next day or so, they're in business. At least, that's the way it appears from all the media stories, particularly those about Internet businesses. The reality is something quite different, however. Most businesses take a lot of time and preparation before they're ready to compete in the marketplace.

While it is true that companies like Amazon have made it theoretically possible for you to be doing business on the Internet in a matter of minutes, that doesn't mean that just because you have your website up, people will automatically flock to it. And even if they land on your site through a search engine or just by accident, it doesn't mean they'll stay, and it doesn't mean they'll purchase anything.

Every new business idea needs to be tested and proven in the marketplace, and that takes time and money. It's particularly difficult when your concept is very new and you don't have any benchmarks against which to judge how it will be received by customers.

In this chapter, you discover ways to take an idea that has been percolating in your mind and develop it into a form that you can test in the marketplace. That way, you can find out whether it's feasible before you spend hours of time and a lot of money trying to make a poorly developed business succeed.

Starting with Your First Risk: You!

That's right. The first risk you'll face in this process is yourself. But I've made it easier for you to look at how much of a risk you actually are. Start by responding to the questions listed in Table 4-1.

Questions 1–5 pertain to your personality and ability to adapt to new situations. Questions 6–10 address the stresses and challenges of being an entrepreneur. Questions 11–15 deal with skills and experience needed to successfully run a business. Just circle yes or no for each question. In general, the answer that first comes to mind is the most honest one. It's often called a gut response. These gut responses give you a lot of information about your ability to deal with an entrepreneurial environment.

TABLE 4-1   **Personal Inventory**

Question	Answers	
1. Do you enjoy making your own decisions?	Yes	No
2. Are you persistent in the face of challenges?	Yes	No
3. Do you regularly meet deadlines?	Yes	No
4. Do you like change?	Yes	No
5. Do you enjoy competing?	Yes	No
6. Are you willing to work 12–14 hours a day 7 days a week to get your business started?	Yes	No
7. Do you have excellent physical stamina?	Yes	No
8. Do you deal well with stress?	Yes	No
9. Are you willing to risk your savings?	Yes	No
10. Are you willing to change your lifestyle to make this business go?	Yes	No
11. Do you have the skills needed to run this venture?	Yes	No
12. Do you have the skills required to conduct the feasibility analysis?	Yes	No
13. Do you have a network of people you can tap for assistance and funding?	Yes	No
14. Do you have sufficient money to at least start the business?	Yes	No
15. Is this venture compatible with your life and career goals?	Yes	No

How did you do? You may want to revisit some of the questions that left you with more questions than answers, such as, do you have the skills to conduct a feasibility analysis. Read on a bit farther before you conclude anything definitively about that question since you might not yet understand the specific skills required for the analysis. By the end of this chapter, you will have a better understanding.

If you find that you circled a bunch of *yes* replies, the chances are good that you might have what it takes to start an entrepreneurial venture. If, on the other hand, you are answering *no* to several of the questions, it doesn't automatically mean that you'd better quit while you're ahead. What it does mean is that you may find some aspects of entrepreneurship uncomfortable or not compatible with the way you behave. Often you can resolve these issues by bringing partners on board who are good at doing what you are not.

REMEMBER

One point I want to make very clear. Your chances of becoming a successful entrepreneur are 100 percent if that's what you want for yourself and you're willing to do the work needed to make it happen. The person who most has to believe you can do it is YOU. You will encounter many naysayers during your journey, and it will only be your belief in yourself and your goals that will keep you from doubting yourself.

Turning Your Opportunity into a Business Concept

You already know what an *opportunity* is. But what exactly is a *business concept*? Put simply, a business concept is a way to define an opportunity so that it can be tested through a process known as a *feasibility analysis*. It's also a clear and concise way to tell someone about your business when they ask you to explain it.

A business concept, whether it's for an Internet business, a service business, or a manufacturing business, has four fundamental parts: the customer, the product or service, the value proposition, and the distribution channel. Assume for a minute that the business you want to start involves developing a portal site for manufacturers and retailers in the apparel industry who want to buy and sell from each other. Questions you can ask that lead you to completely defining the business concept include:

>> **What is the product or service you are offering?** In this case, you are providing a website that will link small apparel manufacturers with retail outlets.

>> **Who is your customer?** Your customer is the person or business that pays you, in other words, the source of your revenues. In this case, your customer is the small apparel manufacturer who pays a subscription fee to be listed on your site and display its products.

>> **What is the value proposition?** The value proposition is the benefit that you provide to the customer. In other words, why will the customers buy from you — what's in it for them? Here, the benefit is that small apparel manufacturers will be able to reach more outlets for their products.

>> **How will the benefit be delivered to the customer?** This is how you will reach the customer and deliver the benefit. In this case, your website is the distribution channel for this concept.

Benefits versus Features: What Do Customers Buy?

Entrepreneurs often confuse the terms *benefits* and *features*. Features are the particular characteristics of a product or service. In the case of the apparel manufacturer example, the features may be color, fabric texture, design, accessories, and so forth. Learning as much as possible about your customers will help you design the features they're looking for.

But here's the problem. Customers typically don't buy based on features. Oh, sure, they check to make certain all the features they need are present and accounted for. But the decision to buy is usually based on the *benefits* provided by the service or product. Here's an example to make this concept clearer. Suppose you own a clothing boutique. Some of the *features* of your business are:

>> Excellent location with lots of parking

>> Unique clothes not found in department stores

>> Great salespeople who learn what the customers' needs are

Those are important features that describe the business, but they tell us nothing about the benefits to the customer because they're not presented from the *customer's* point of view. They're presented from the *company's* point of view. Now think about how a customer *benefits* from these features.

>> Customers *save time* by being able to easily park right next to the boutique.

>> Customers will be able to *conveniently and quickly* find, *in one location,* the unique clothes they want.

> » Customers will *not have to waste time* trying to figure out what works on them and what piece of clothing goes with what. Customers will receive the personal attention they value.

An easy way to understand the benefits of the product or service you're offering is to put yourself in the customer's shoes and ask yourself, "What's in it for me?" In other words, "Why would I shop at this boutique?"

If you know what the customer values — for example, saving time by going to one location and getting expert help — you are better able to design your business concept to meet those needs. And that will result in more loyal customers.

Why isn't money part of the concept?

Recall that the four components of the business concept are the product or service, customer, value proposition, and distribution channel. Why doesn't the business concept include anything related to money? Isn't it important to know how much money the business will make, or how much it will need to get started? That's a good question, because money is certainly important to the startup of any business. However, remember that we're developing a concept and doing feasibility analysis because we don't yet know that we have a viable business. We don't yet know whether customers are interested in what we have to offer. If we don't know that, then we have no way of calculating revenues because we don't know what demand is.

Money is an *enabler*. It enables you to get a feasible business started. It doesn't, however, help you test for feasibility. Most entrepreneurs start businesses with very limited resources, mostly their own. So, most businesses start small and grow relatively slowly depending on the personal resources of the entrepreneur. Money is important, but you need to first find out whether you have a business that will attract customers.

Trying out your business concept skills

The best way to experience anything is to do it. Looking at the concepts of other entrepreneurs helps you see how they differentiated themselves, creating niches in the market where they could enter and survive long enough to build successful businesses.

Try these simple exercises, which will test your ability to identify the four components of a business concept so that you can understand completely what a business is about.

>> Go to the IndigoAg website at www.indigoag.com. Explore the website and then see if you can list what you believe to be its product/service, customer, value proposition, and distribution channel.

Now, let's see how you did. Indigo is seeking to increase the planet's capacity to produce more food in a sustainable and responsible manner by harnessing plants' natural microbiome or microbes, which have been disrupted by the use of chemicals and pesticides and adding them back to crops. Indigo provides technologies and tools to help farmers update their practices to be more sustainable, to increase their crop levels, and to make more money. So, farmers and farming operations are their customers who are seeking ways to overcome the productivity plateau that farmers have faced due to poor soil practices and climate-related issues. Dry bulk grain producers can access a transportation platform that connects shippers and carriers so they can find loads without a broker. So, farmers save time and money, and through the carbon credit program, can even make money.

>> Let's try one more — a service business this time. Go to gusto.com www.gusto.com and answer the same questions about product/service, customer, value proposition, and distribution channel without looking at the following paragraph.

This time, the company is offering payroll services to small businesses. The customers are entrepreneurs and small business owners who want an easier way to maneuver the complexities of handling payroll taxes and meeting all the government requirements. And there are many! The value proposition is saving time and providing the convenience of accessing accountants and human resource experts from one easy-to-use platform. The benefit is delivered directly via the Internet. Gusto expanded its initial payroll service to include hiring and on-boarding, human resource professionals, and managing employee benefits like healthcare and retirement. A simple concept statement for Gusto might look like this:

Gusto gives business owners the tools they need to hire, pay, and manage their team in one easy-to-use online platform.

TIP

A short, concise statement is valuable when you're trying to get a quick response from someone about your business idea. If you state your concept and the person being interviewed doesn't seem to understand what your business is, you need to go back and revise the concept to express more clearly what you're doing. It's rare to get the concept statement right the first time. Be open to suggestions and use the clarifying questions people ask you to figure out what aspect of the business is not clear.

Quick-Testing Your Concept: The Lean Method

Once you have your business concept refined and ready to go, you can do a preliminary test quickly at little to no cost We're going to use a methodology called *lean startup*. It is a popular way to quickly discover if what you're proposing to launch is viable, that is, able to make money. By constructing hypotheses about the business and testing them with real customers as well as iterating on the product, again with customer feedback, you can quickly learn what works and what doesn't. After that you'll be ready for a more in-depth feasibility study. Here are a couple of steps to take for a quick, gut test of your business concept:

>> **Talking with a few trusted friends to get their feedback is okay as an initial gut check.** Friends you know well enough to get an honest appraisal. Don't be surprised or discouraged if they tell you you're crazy. Here's a classic example. People thought Fred Smith was joking when he boasted about the ability to deliver a package anywhere in the United States overnight. They stopped laughing when he showed them how to do it in his new enterprise, Federal Express (more recently FedEx).

>> **Run a checklist on the forces in favor of your concept and the forces against it.** You may have done this kind of test when you were trying to make a major decision. You compared the advantages and disadvantages. You can do the same with your business concept. Ask yourself whether more forces are working for your concept than against it.

>> **Ask yourself some critical questions and be brutally honest with your answers:**

- **Am I really interested in this opportunity?** You had better be passionate about your concept because it's going to take a lot of time, energy, and money to make it happen. If you're not thinking about it day and night, maybe you don't want to do it badly enough. That's a red flag you need to check out.

- **Is anyone else interested in this opportunity?** You can't do a business alone — you need customers, employees, cofounders, investors, and others. If no one seems interested in what you're proposing, you need to reconsider or revamp your concept statement based on the feedback you get.

- **Will people pay for what I'm offering?** It's one thing for a person to tell you your concept is great, but is that person willing to use their credit card? And how much are people willing to pay for your product or service? Remember, your product or service must be perceived as sufficiently valuable so that you can charge enough to pay your costs and make a profit.

>> **Now ask yourself two final questions:**

- Why me?
- Why now?

These two questions are simple, but they get at the heart of what you're trying to do. Why should you be the one to execute this business concept? Why are you better than anyone else who comes up with the same concept?

>> **Why me?** This question addresses your level of confidence in yourself and your ability to make this business happen. It's one thing to come up with an idea and turn it into an opportunity. It's quite another to make it happen. Both talents are needed, and if they're not found in the same person, you need to find a partner who can fill the gap. If you're an idea person — an inventor type — you will probably want to team with someone who has business skills and knows how to successfully start and run a business.

>> **Why is this concept doable now?** Why hasn't anyone done it before? The why now question gets at the uniqueness and viability of the concept. If no one has ever done this before, is it because it's inherently not doable, or is it because you really have come up with something unique? You have to check out both possibilities.

Now that didn't take very long, did it? But look at how much more you know about this business that you want to start.

Getting Serious with Feasibility Analysis and the Lean Method

So you have some positive feedback on your initial concept and you're starting to see yourself as a successful entrepreneur. Maybe you're so excited you want to get going right away. Slow down just a bit. Before you get too excited and think that it's time to start finding space and hiring people, sit down for a minute and take stock of the fact that your homework has just begun.

For one thing, you've only done a quick test of your concept. You need a lot more information before you can feel confident enough to start dealing in the marketplace and talking to potential investors. What you need to do now is a feasibility analysis. Feasibility analysis is a process whereby you can test your hypotheses about various components of your business concept and arrive at some conditions under which you are willing to go forward with this business. No matter what type of business you intend to start — restaurant, manufacturer, retail outlet, Internet business — you will go through the same feasibility process. Of course, if you're looking to test a pure-play Internet concept without a physical footprint, you will probably go through this process much faster, but with the same amount of discipline.

At this point, you may be asking yourself why you wouldn't just create a business plan. It seems like that's what everyone says you need to be doing. Let's talk about this idea for a minute.

CASE STUDY

IT TAKES MORE THAN PASSION: IT TAKES PERSISTENCE

The story of the entrepreneur who falls blindly in love with a concept is not a new one — in fact, it's a common tale that often ends in failure and despair. If the ending is not failure, the journey is a bumpy one. It's not always a good idea to love your concept so much that you fail to see fatal flaws. But sometimes, passion will get you through the setbacks, failures, and rejections long enough to triumph. Such is the case with Tom Ashbrook, Rolly Rouse, and Shawn Becker and their business, eluxury.com. HomePortfolio is billed as the leading Internet destination for premium home design products. They feature top-of-the-line and hard-to-find products and direct you to your nearest retailers. It is also an online solution for technology and marketing, and a commerce site for makers and merchants of unique home-design products.

But, it wasn't always so. Going from idea to opportunity to a real business was a long and winding road. As Ashbrook reported in *Fortune Small Business*, back in 1995, Ashbrook, Becker, and Rouse had just discovered an idea that caught fire and took over every aspect of their lives. They lived and breathed Rouse's original idea and were determined that it would be their big hit. They definitely had passion going for them, but they also had several things working against them:

- No money
- No business degrees
- No technology background
- No acquaintances in the venture capital area
- No claim to young innocence — they were turning 40 at the time
- Tons of prior claims on their time and attention — spouses, kids, mortgages, and well-used credit cards

(continued)

(continued)

Most people with any sense and good jobs would probably back off after looking at this list of negatives, but they were in love and clueless about the challenges. They bought into the hype over the Internet and felt that they had to "digitize or die." They had the vision; they had the passion; after several months, they had the business plan; what they needed was the money. It always comes back to the money. Who pays you and why. Their business was a disintermediation play, which meant they were getting rid of the "middleman" or the person between the producer and the consumer. They planned to put the consumer in direct contact with manufacturers and retailers so they could buy direct. They also offered a feature whereby the customer could see the product in person by visiting the nearest retail outlet.

They began making the rounds of trade shows pitching their concept to the biggest names in the design world to positive feedback. Finally in 1996, they landed some seed money — $500,000 — from friends and family. Not as much as they really needed, but it validated their belief that the business would work. Or did it? By March of 1997, the seed money had run out and things really started to get tough. Credit cards (they had collected a lot of them) became their backup as they sought for money to pay bills that had soared to over a half million dollars. They had mortgaged their homes and had to borrow from relatives to survive.

Their full site finally went live in January 1998, to high praise from *The New York Times*. As manufacturers began to sign up, the venture money that had shunned them until then stepped up to the plate, with Scripps Ventures putting up a first round of $5 million. The site hosted a network of more than 1,800 top brands and 100,000 retailers. By 2000, they had secured five rounds of funding from 12 investors totaling about $68 million. In 2017, HomePortfolio.com was acquired by eLuxury (eluxury.com), a U.S. Veteran Owned company out of Evansville, Indiana.

As you can see from this story, as the company you launch based on your winning idea grows, it can change in ways you may not like. It is not uncommon to see entrepreneurs leave their companies for a time only to return to get the company back on track. *MIT Technology Review* turned this venture into a three-act drama. In Act 1, we find our heroes jumping up and down and running around like idiots so excited are they by their new venture idea and the big future they're going to have. In Act 2, we find Rolly suffering from heart problems due to stress over money and their financial condition is making his spouse sick. He decides to leave the business for a while. In Act 3, a venture capital firm commits $3 million to the venture, and Tom and Rolly (who returned to the business) are dancing again — all the stress forgotten. You can check out the website at eluxury.com.

Feasibility versus business plan: Double the work?

I've said that performing a feasibility study is a way to test your business concept to answer a lot of questions so you can reduce uncertainty and determine if the business has market potential. Doesn't a business plan do the same thing? Actually, no, it doesn't. A business plan describes not only a business concept but also the infrastructure, strategy, and operations that need to be in place to successfully execute the business concept. In other words, the business plan describes the company you are going to create. Table 4-2 shows a comparison of the components of the feasibility study with the additional components that you find in the business plan.

TABLE 4-2   **Feasibility Study versus Business Plan**

Feasibility Analysis	Business Plan (What's New?)
Executive Summary	Process Analysis or Operations Plan
The Business Concept	Organization Plan
	Marketing Plan
Industry/Market Analysis-Test of Customer	Financial Plan
Founding Team Analysis	
Product/Service Development Plan	Growth Plan
Financial Plan — Startup Capital Requirements	Contingency Plan
Feasibility Decision: Conditions Under Which to Go Forward	
Timeline to Launch	
Bibliography	
Appendix (A,B,C, and so forth)	

As you can see, the business plan assumes that you have a feasible business concept and can now add the operational pieces needed to create a company. I devote Chapter 13 to the business plan, but for now focus on the feasibility study. In this chapter, you get an overview of the parts of the analysis, but if you want more detail on each of the components, check out Chapters 5–12.

Introducing the feasibility analysis framework

Feasibility analysis consists of a series of tests that you conduct as you discover more and more about your opportunity. After each test, you ask yourself if you still want to go forward. Is there anything here that prevents you from going forward with this business? Feasibility is a process of discovery and during that process you will probably modify your original concept several times until you get it right. That's the real value of feasibility — the way that it helps you refine your concept — fine-tune it — so that you have the highest potential for success when you launch your business.

Today, you can often seek financing on the strength of a sound feasibility study alone. Certainly, in the case of Internet businesses, speed is of the essence, so many Internet companies get first-round financing on proof of concept alone and then complete their business plans before they go for bigger dollars in the form of venture capital. Let's look at the components of a thorough feasibility study.

Executive summary

The executive summary is probably the most important part of a feasibility analysis because, in about two pages, it presents the most important and persuasive points from every test you did during your analysis. An effective executive summary captures the reader's attention immediately with the excitement of the concept. It doesn't let the reader get away; it draws the reader deeper and deeper into the concept as it proves your claim that the concept is feasible and will be a market success.

The most important information to emphasize in the executive summary is your proof that customers want what you're offering. This proof comes from the customer discovery field work you do with customers to find out what they think of your concept and how much demand there is. The other key piece to emphasize is your description of the founding team. Even the greatest ideas can't happen without a great team, and investors put a lot of stock in a founding team's expertise and experience.

If you're creating an Internet business, you may want to prepare what's called a *proof of concept.* This is essentially a one-page statement of why your concept will work, emphasizing what you have done to prove that customers will engage with your site. That may be in the form of showing hits to your beta site or a list of customers signed up and ready to go when the site is finished. Similarly, if you're developing a new product, your proof of concept is your minimal viable product or market quality prototype.

Business concept

In this first part of the feasibility analysis, answer the following questions:

>> What is the business?

>> Who is the customer?

>> What is the value proposition?

>> How will the benefits be delivered?

It's important to be able to state your business concept in a couple of clear, concise, and direct sentences that include all four of the components of the concept. This is what is often called an "elevator pitch," because it's short enough to be given on an elevator ride. That means you have a few seconds to capture your listener's attention, so you better be able to get it all out quickly and confidently. If you're preparing a feasibility analysis for investors, you need to state your business concept right up front in the concept section. Then you can elaborate on each point as a follow-up. Here's an example based on the story you read about HomePortfolio:

> *HomePortfolio offers customers seeking home design products an easy online platform featuring more than 700,000 products from 100,000 retailers. With searchable style tags, customers will save time finding and saving products they like in their own portfolio that they can also share with others.*

As you find out more about your business concept, you'll also want to consider the various spin-off products and services you may be able to offer. It's always a good idea to identify more than one source of revenue for your company.

REMEMBER

One-product businesses have a more difficult time becoming successful than multi-product/service companies. You don't want to put all your eggs into one basket, and you want to give your customers choices so they'll keep coming back.

Industry analysis

Testing whether the industry in which you will be operating will support your concept is an important part of any feasibility analysis. An *industry* is a grouping of businesses that interact in the same environment as part of a value chain or distribution channel that delivers your product to customers. Here, you want to describe what the industry looks like, whether it's growing or not, where the opportunities are, who the opinion leaders are, and whether the industry readily adopts new technologies. You also want to see if there are other smaller, newer companies in the industry, so you have a chance to enter; and you want to understand where the industry is going in the future.

Don't forget that one way to identify a great opportunity is to study the industry first. For more details on how to do an industry analysis, check out Chapter 5.

Market/customer analysis

A business lives in an industry, but it competes in markets. For the market analysis, you perform customer discovery — you learn everything you can about who will buy your product or service. The goal is to find the "first customer," which is a person who has the major problem that your business is going to solve. If you correctly identified a compelling problem, you're halfway there. Now, if that problem is one that others have not addressed, you have found yourself a niche in the market, that is, a corner of the market that is not being served. That means you have a chance to make it yours and dominate that market.

In this part of the analysis, you will also look at what your potential customer wants by way of benefits and what the demand for your product/service might be. How many of those customers are there and how many will buy from you? You should also consider a variety of different distribution channels to deliver the benefit to the customer in the way they want it delivered. To find out more about market analysis, see Chapter 6.

Founding team analysis

Earlier you read that investors look very carefully at the founding team because even the best concept won't happen without a team that can execute. In this part of the analysis, you want to consider the qualifications, expertise, and experience of your founding team. If you are planning to do this as a solo entrepreneur, I urge you to reconsider. Most successful startups are done by teams, and the reason is that today's business environment is so complex and so fast-paced that no one person has all the skills, time, and resources to do everything themself.

Having said that, in Chapter 9, you can find lots of ways to make up for skills and people you lack. This is not to say that you can't start a business by yourself. You certainly can. But it probably should be a business that doesn't require professional investment capital, as investors typically don't favor solo startups.

Product/service development analysis

Whether you're planning to offer a product or a service or both (and that's often the case), it's going to take some planning. Consider which tasks must be accomplished to prepare the product or service for market, whether that is building a product from raw materials and perhaps going through the patent process, or developing a plan for implementing a service concept. Identify tasks and lay out a timeline for completion. Chapter 8 discusses several ways to perform an effective product/service analysis.

Financial analysis

Once you know you have a market and a team, it's finally time to consider money. (You probably thought we were never going to get to it!) In this part of the feasibility analysis, you want to figure out how much money you need to start the business and carry it to a positive cash flow, meaning you're bringing in more cash than you're spending. You also need to distinguish among the types of money — cash, investments, debt — which will be important in defining your financial strategy. You can find out how to do this analysis in Chapter 12.

Feasibility decision

Once you have gone through all the various tests that comprise the feasibility analysis, you are ready to decide about going forward. Of course, throughout the process of doing the tests, you may have decided to stop — because of something you found out from analysis of the industry, market, product/service, and so forth. But if you're still on the mission, now's the time to define the conditions you need to go forward.

Timeline to launch

It's important to end a feasibility analysis with an action plan so that you increase the odds that something will happen. Establishing a list of tasks to be completed and a timeframe for completing the tasks will increase the probability that your business will be launched in a timely fashion. It's also a good idea to associate capital needs with your milestones. The research you've done will pay off by helping you make wise estimates about the length of time it will take to complete everything and open the doors to your business.

Testing the Feasibility of Your Business Concept

Chapter **5**

Understanding Your Industry

T hink of an industry as the environment in which a business operates. The environment includes all the other businesses in the industry including those businesses that compete with your business in certain markets. The external environment includes such things as the state of the economy of the country where the business is based as well as taxes and fees that must be paid by the business. The industry is the focus of this chapter. If you position your company well inside a growing, healthy industry, you have a better chance of building a successful venture. By contrast, if your business niche is a weak position in a hostile, mature industry, your fledgling business may be doomed.

Before we go any further, I need to make a distinction between industries and markets:

>> An *industry* is a group of businesses that essentially operate within the same value chain, delivering similar products and services. For example, the telecom industry is an established industry with major companies such as AT&T and Verizon. They supply various products and services, some of which compete with each other in certain markets. Think of the industry as the environment in which your business operates and in which you will likely have suppliers and distributors. Your industry is defined by the products and services it produces.

>> *Markets*, on the other hand, are defined by customers who purchase the benefits of those products and services. You compete with companies in your industry when you are selling to the same customers. Identifying and validating your primary market is a critical step in the life of a new business. Chapter 6 addresses this topic in detail.

Industries have life cycles, just like people. They emerge, grow, go through difficult times, and reach maturity. Then they die or are reborn by some new technology or some other force that gives them new life. The stages of an industry's life cycle basically look like this:

>> **Birth.** A new industry emerges, usually based on some new technology that inspires multiple new products and services. Artificial Intelligence is one example.

>> **Emerging.** Blockchain is an example of an emerging industry with a disruptive technology. Entrepreneurs who enter an industry at this stage encounter nothing short of the Wild Wild West. They find few rules and plenty of opportunity. Companies with key disruptive technologies that are secured with patents enter at this stage with a plan to eventually become the industry standard.

>> **Differentiation, competition.** Over time, as the industry grows and matures, more companies are attracted to the industry and intense product differentiation results. Less uncertainty is evident because product standards have been established and proprietary rights have become less exclusive. The industry becomes highly competitive.

>> **Shakeout.** At the most intense point of competition, there is normally a shakeout, and companies that are unable to successfully compete leave. The most successful companies become the dominant players and at least one will set the standard for everyone else.

>> **Maturity.** The industry matures and a few firms dominate. The industry remains stable until an entrepreneur shakes it up with new technology, or it simply slowly disappears (think of computer manufacturing, coal products, and data recovery services made obsolete by the cloud).

The point at which you enter an industry with your startup determines your strategies and your ability to succeed. Let's look at how to discover the wealth of opportunity and possibilities in your industry.

Understanding Your Industry

We are in a time when new industries emerge on a regular basis. Examples of new industries include Artificial Intelligence (AI), renewable and alternative energy, and big data analytics. Since these are fundamental technologies, they can be deployed in many different markets to serve different types of customers. The Internet of Things (IoT), also called "wearables," is another hot industry that has seen its technology used in products that serve the fitness industry, the healthcare industry, and even agriculture. Are you surprised to learn that there are more devices connected to the Internet than there are people on the planet?

REMEMBER

An *industry* is defined by the goods and services it produces in a particular field.

All retail businesses have retail in common, and all manufacturers have manufacturing in common. Are retail and manufacturing industries as well? Yes, they are. Within retail, there are clothing retailers and book retailers, among many others. Is clothing an industry? Is publishing an industry? The answer to both these questions is yes.

Industries have layers, starting with the broadest terms and working down to more specific terms. As an example, consider an e-commerce business that everyone knows: Amazon.com. Figure 5-1 shows how Amazon.com is positioned.

FIGURE 5-1:
Amazon.com operates in the retail business sector of the e-commerce industry.

You can easily see that if we consider e-commerce to be an industry, a grouping of like businesses, then Amazon is part of that industry. In fact, it is the leading U.S. company in online retailing. Within online retailing, Amazon is also a retail business that happens to be using the Internet as its marketing/distribution channel. Within retail, it operates in the publishing, music, toys, and video industries, among many others, because it serves as a distribution channel for these industries. For the industry you chose for your feasibility study, start at the broadest definition of industry and work your way down to the segment that includes the product or service that you are providing. That is your primary industry.

Using a Framework of Industry Structure

One way to begin to look at the industry in which you're interested is to use a common framework. One framework that I particularly like is based on the work of W.H. Starbuck and Michael E. Porter, two well-known experts on organizational strategy. I adapt their ideas in Figure 5-2, where you see how entrepreneurs must be constantly on the lookout for forces that affect every area of their businesses.

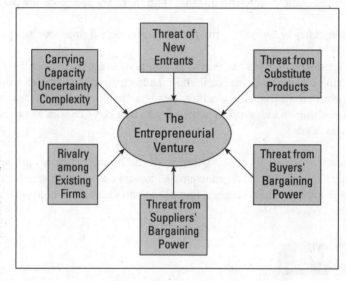

FIGURE 5-2: The success of your venture hinges on dealing with numerous incoming threats from your industry's environment.

If the entrepreneurial environment looks like a battlefield — well it often is! But for every threat there's a countermeasure. The first step is to understand these outside forces.

Carrying capacity, uncertainty, and complexity

This first environmental factor explains why so many industries today are changing, moving more rapidly, and making it more difficult for businesses to succeed. *Carrying capacity* refers to the extent to which an industry can accept more businesses. It may not have occurred to you that industries can become oversaturated with too many businesses. When that happens, the capacity of businesses to produce their products and services exceeds the demand for them. Then it becomes increasingly difficult for new businesses to enter the industry and survive.

Uncertainty refers to the predictability or unpredictability of the industry — stability or instability. Typically volatile and fast-changing technology industries produce more uncertainty. But these same industries often produce more opportunities for new ventures to take advantage of.

Complexity is about the number and diversity of inputs and outputs in the industry. Complex industries mean businesses have to deal with more suppliers, customers, and competitors than other industries. Biotechnology and telecommunications are examples of industries with high degrees of complexity in the form of competition and government regulation.

Threats to new entrants

Some industries have barriers to entry that are quite high. Entrepreneurs will need to study these barriers carefully before attempting to participate in the industry. Here are the main barriers you'll find:

» **Economies of scale:** These are product volumes that enable businesses to produce goods inexpensively. A new business can't compete with the low costs of the established firms. To combat economies of scale, new firms often form alliances that give them their own economy of scale.

» **Brand loyalty:** If you're a new business, you may face competitors that have achieved brand loyalty, which makes it much more difficult to entice customers to your products and services. That's why it's so important to find a market niche that you can control — a need in the market that is not being served. That will give you time to establish some brand loyalty of your own. Check out Chapter 6 to find out more about niches.

» **High capital requirements:** In some industries, there are high costs for the advertising, R&D, and plant and equipment you need to compete with established firms. Again, new companies often overcome this barrier by outsourcing expensive functions to other firms.

» **Buyer switching costs:** Buyers generally don't like to switch from one supplier to another unless there's a good reason to do so. To entice a customer to switch, entrepreneurs must demonstrate that their product meets a need that is not being met by the current product.

» **Access to distribution channels:** Every industry has established methods for getting products to customers. New companies must have access to those distribution channels if they are going to succeed. The one exception is where the new business finds a new method of delivering a product or service that the customer accepts. That was the case when the Internet became a distribution channel for online retail.

>> **Proprietary factors:** Established companies may own technology or a location that gives them a competitive advantage over new companies. However, new ventures have often entered industries with their own proprietary factors that enable them to enjoy a relatively competition-free environment for a brief time.

>> **Government regulations:** In some industries, a long and expensive governmental process, like FDA approval for foods and drugs, can be prohibitive for a new business. That's why many new ventures form strategic alliances with larger companies to help support the costs along the way.

>> **Industry hostility:** In some industries, rival companies make it difficult for a new business to enter. Because these rivals are typically mature companies with many resources, they can afford to do what it takes to push the new entrant out. Again, finding that niche in the market can help your company survive, even in a hostile industry.

Threats from substitute products/services

Remember that your competition comes not only from companies that deal in the same products and services that you do, but also from companies that have substitute products, products that may solve the same problem, but with a different method. For example, restaurants compete with other restaurants for customers based on food quality, variety of food items, and price. A competitor may offer all the same things, but in an entertainment setting. The Magic Castle is an example where the entertainment features magicians.

Threats from buyers' bargaining power

Buyers have the power to force down prices in the industry when they can buy in volume. For example, companies like Costco and Walmart have this kind of buying power. New entrants, by contrast, can't usually purchase at volume rates; therefore, they must charge customers more. Consequently, it's more difficult for them to compete if the only benefit to the customer is price.

Threats from suppliers' bargaining power

In some industries, suppliers have the power to raise prices or change the quality of products that they supply to manufacturers or distributors. This is particularly true where there are few suppliers relative to the size of the industry and they are the primary source of materials in the industry. Don't forget that labor is also a source of supply, and in some industries like software, highly skilled labor is in short supply; therefore, the price goes up.

Rivalry among existing firms

Highly competitive industries force prices down and profits as well. That's when you see price wars, the kind you find in the airline industry. One company lowers its prices and others quickly follow. This kind of strategy hurts everyone in the industry and makes it nearly impossible for a new entrant to compete on price. Instead, savvy entrepreneurs strive to find an unserved niche in the market where they don't have to compete on price. They compete on the benefits they offer.

Understanding the Value Chain

What is a value chain? In general, a value chain consists of all the companies that participate in the development and distribution of products and services coming out of that industry. For example, if your company is a supplier of a raw material like copper, it will be positioned at the top of the value chain, upstream from manufacturers who use the raw material. Companies that distribute and sell products and services are downstream from manufacturers because they deal in finished goods. Where your company lies in the value chain gives you an indication of the level of risk you face and specific skills you possess. The higher your company is in the value chain, generally the more risk it faces and the more specific technical skills are required.

The value chain also tells you who pays whom; see Figure 5-3.

FIGURE 5-3:
A simple
value chain.

As you can see in Figure 5-3, at each point along the value chain, the costs go up as each member of the chain marks up the product to cover its cost of sales and add a profit margin. It's a good idea to graph the value chain for your industry, which will enable you to do the following:

>> Calculate the time from manufacturing to the customer based on the lead time that each channel requires to do its part of the process.

>> Determine the ultimate retail price based on markups along the value chain.

>> Calculate the costs of marketing along the chain as each channel member needs to market to the next channel member

You probably noticed that the biggest price hike comes from the wholesaler to the retailer, which is normally passed along to the customer. The process of doubling the price from the wholesaler is called *keystoning* and is common in many industries. The reasons that costs go up along the value chain is that the costs of doing business go up the closer you get to the consumer. Keep in mind that every product or service has multiple channel options. That's why it's important that you consider all the viable options for your business and weigh the pros and cons before making a final decision.

Deciding on an Entry Strategy

The structure of your industry will largely determine how you enter the industry. Failing to consider the structure of your industry can mean that you spend a lot of time and money only to find that you have chosen the wrong entry strategy. By then, you may have lost your window of opportunity. For the most part, new ventures have three broad options as entry strategies: *differentiation*, *niche*, and *cost superiority*. This is a critical decision, so let's look at each of them in more detail.

Differentiation

With a differentiation strategy, you attempt to distinguish your company from others in the industry through product/process innovation, a unique marketing or distribution strategy, or through branding. If you can gain customer loyalty through your differentiation strategy, you will succeed in making your product or service less sensitive to price because customers will perceive the inherent value of dealing with your company.

CASE STUDY

What do you do when your company is stuck in one spot and not growing? If you're Jerry and Terri Kohl, you don't sit around waiting for something to happen. In the fashion accessory industry, where it's difficult to stand out in a crowd, the Kohls studied the industry and found a way to differentiate their company. They launched their company, Brighton, in 1991 with a line of leather belts, not an uncommon product. So how did the Kohls differentiate the company and their brand? They saw that the industry had a terrible reputation for sloppiness in operations, lost orders, poor manufacturing quality, and poor shipping. That's what had to change. The Kohls set out to create a new kind of belt company — lean, mean and customer oriented.

Their customers were not only consumers but retailers. Each had different needs. They quickly expanded their product offering to provide an extensive line of accessories from head to toe. They gave their designers the freedom to create something by hand and then follow the product to completion, which was not common in the industry. They wanted their products to be timely works of art, which is what their customers valued. For their retail customers, their salespeople can tap into industry reports on their laptops when they're in the field with customers. Those stats on how particular products are selling provide credibility when they're trying to convince a retailer that one color is selling better than another. The computer also helps the salesperson customize customers' inventories, so they are more efficient, ordering only what they need, when they need it. Salespeople can send in orders online and check the status of orders for their retail customers.

This effort was so successful at making information accessible that they went on to transform every other function in the business to make it more efficient and effective. Today, they own 180 Brighton Collectible stores and are also in more than 4,000 fine specialty boutiques and online. Differentiation worked for the Kohls in a very competitive industry (www.brighton.com).

Niche

The niche strategy is perhaps the most popular entrepreneurial strategy for new ventures because it enables an entrepreneur to enter a market with no direct competition for a time. It involves identifying and creating a place in the market where no one else is — serving a need that no one else is serving. This niche gives you space and time to compete without going head to head with the established players in the industry. It lets you own a piece of the market where you can establish the standards and build your brand loyalty before others invade your space.

CASE STUDY

Victor Echevarria thought he had found the perfect industry in healthcare data. His startup, Remedy Labs, was positioned to grow quickly. It addressed the huge financial burden of healthcare by helping its members uncover medical bill overcharges. Victor himself experienced the shock of medical debt for his 18-month-old son who was taken unresponsive to the emergency room in an ambulance. He thought his team had analyzed the industry sufficiently, attempting to identify the possible pitfalls and work out ways around them. Except that they didn't, and Victor now knows why. He had missed a fundamental problem with the industry. To be able to analyze health data, you need access to that data, which is protected under HIPAA medical privacy laws. He assumed wrongly that he and his patients would have electronic access to the data needed to benefit from his service. Unfortunately, that wrong assumption was the undoing of his business and in 2017, he closed the doors for good.

REMEMBER

When you're doing research to support your business decisions, look for all the factors that might kill your business first before you focus on the positive supporting factors. If you find any negatives, such as too small a market, or too much regulation, investigate them further. Negatives are perhaps the most important information you'll gather, so don't shy away from them.

Cost superiority

Being the low-cost leader is extremely difficult for a startup because the strategy relies heavily on volume sales and low-cost production, two things that a new venture cannot afford. Where a new venture can possibly take advantage of providing the lowest cost products and services is when it's part of an emerging industry where everyone shares the same disadvantage. In my experience, you want to avoid competing on price. With today's search engine capabilities, it's too easy for customers to go online to find the lowest price anywhere in the world. You want to compete on features and benefits, benefits being the most important. If your product or service does not solve a compelling problem for customers, you're going to have a hard time competing under any circumstances.

Researching Your Industry

Understanding your industry inside and out is critical to developing any business strategies you have. Yes, it's a lot of work, but it has the potential to pay off many times over.

Fortunately, today, it's much easier to research an industry with secondary sources of information; that is, information gathered by others, because that data is readily available from online sources. Using a reputable search engine is a good place to start. It will give you an idea of the general nature of the industry and current trends. Trade magazines, Gartner Inc. (a research and consulting firm famous for its hype cycle of emerging technologies), and your local college or university are also excellent sources of industry information. No matter the source you use, ask yourself questions about who authored the information, what their purpose was, and what their credentials are.

How do you check your sources? Here are some things you can do:

>> Ask yourself if the site or author is recognized for their authority or expertise in the field.

>> Ask people who are familiar with the industry you're researching if they've ever heard of that site or that person.

>> Compare what that site or person has said with what others are saying. If you find several sources that seem to agree, you're probably okay. If you find a lot of discrepancies, it's time to dig deeper. Of course, don't assume that just because many people agree on something, it's necessarily true; that's exactly how rumors get started.

Secondary data helps to paint a broad picture of the industry. However, be aware that secondary information may be dated. That's why it's important to conduct primary research on your industry. Primary research means getting into the field and talking with people who work in the industry. Some of these people include:

>> Industry analysts

>> Suppliers and distributors

>> Customers

>> Employees of key industry firms

>> Professionals from service organizations such as lawyers and accountants

>> Experts at trade shows

Answering key questions about your industry

As you begin to research your industry, you could find yourself overwhelmed with the quantity of data available. To manage the data, it's helpful to look at it from some key questions that you want to answer. Those questions include the following:

>> **Is the industry growing?** Growth can be measured in many ways: number of employees, revenues, units produced, and number of new companies entering the industry.

>> **Who are the major players?** You want to understand which companies dominate the industry, what their strategies are, and how your business is differentiated from them.

>> **Where are the opportunities in the industry?** In some industries, new products and services provide more opportunity; while in others, an innovative marketing and distribution strategy will win the game.

You want to look at your industry backward and forward in time to determine if what has happened in the past foreshadows what will happen in the future. It's helpful to consider what the industry prognosticators are saying about the future of the industry. But the best way to find out about the future of your industry is to get close to the new technology that is in the works and may not hit the market-place for five years. Here are some questions you might want to seek answers for:

>> **What is the status of new technology and research and development (R&D) spending?** You want to know if this industry innovates quickly and how much, in general, is spent on research and development.

>> **Does your industry adopt new technology quickly?** If your industry is an old established one, chances are it's slow to adopt new technology. On the other hand, a young industry is more likely to be quicker at technology adoption, so you need to be prepared for that.

>> **Is your industry technology-based or driven by new technology?** If you look at how much the major firms are spending on research and development of new technologies, you'll get a pretty good idea of how important technology is to your industry. You'll also find out how rapid the product development cycle is, which tells you how fast you have to be to compete.

>> **Are there young and successful companies in the industry?** If you see no new companies being formed in your industry, it's a pretty good bet that it's a mature industry with dominant players. That doesn't automatically preclude your entry into the industry, but it does make it much more expensive and difficult.

>> **Are there any threats to the industry?** Is there anything on the horizon that you or others can see that makes any part of your industry on the road to obsolescence? Certainly, if you were in the mechanical office equipment industry in the early 1980s, we hope you saw the handwriting on the wall with the introduction and mass acceptance of the personal computer.

>> **What are the typical gross profit margins in the industry?** The gross profit margin (or gross margin) tells you how much room you have to make mistakes. The gross margin is the gross profit (revenues minus cost of goods sold) as a percentage of sales. If your industry has margins of 2 percent like the grocery industry (sometimes even less), you have little room for error, because 98 percent of what you receive in revenues goes to pay your direct costs of production. You only have 2 percent left to pay overhead and make a profit. On the other hand, in some industries like software, gross margins run at 70 percent or more, so you end up with a lot more capital to cover overhead and profit.

Studying public companies

In most industries, public companies, those whose shares are traded on one of the stock exchanges, are the most established companies and often the dominant players in an industry, so it's a good idea to check them out. They can also serve as benchmarks for best practices in the industry. A host of online resources related to public companies is available. Here are a few of the best:

» **D&B Hoover's Online,** www.dnb.com/products/marketing-sales/dnb-hoovers.html: This is the home of Dun & Bradstreet, which provides the most comprehensive business data on more than 420 million global companies. It is an excellent source for finding high-value targets and key information on major players in your industry. You can try D&B Hoover's for free for a limited time.

» **U.S. Securities & Exchange Commission,** www.sec.gov: This site contains the SEC's Edgar database. It's not terribly user friendly but has great information on public companies.

» **Try Free Edgar,** www.freeedgar.com: This is a good place to research public companies and those that have filed to go public.

Searching for data at government websites

You will find an extensive network of government sites with mostly free information on economic news, export information, legislative trends, and so forth. Two sources link to most of these sites. They are

» USA.gov, www.usa.gov

» FedWorld, www.thecre.com/fedlaw/legal30/supcourt.htm

TIP

If you have trouble connecting to any of these sites, try using a different browser. I sometimes find that my Firefox browser is so good at detecting sites that track you, that sometimes I can't get to those sites at all, and I have to use a browser such as Edge.

You may also want to go directly to many other often-used sites like the following:

» **U.S. Department of Commerce,** www.doc.gov: Here you'll find everything you ever wanted to know about the U.S. economy.

» **U.S. Census Bureau,** www.census.gov: This is the home of the stats based on the census taken every ten years.

- » **Bureau of Labor Statistics,** www.bls.gov: This is another site full of information on the economy, with a focus on the labor market.

- » **Patent & Trademark Office,** www.pto.gov: This site is the home of everything you wanted to know about patents, trademarks, copyrights, and other forms of legal protection for your products and services.

- » **U.S. House of Representatives homepage,** www.house.gov: If you're tracking any kind of legislation that may affect your industry, this is the place to go.

Going offline for more research

The Internet is not the only place you can find important information. Some offline sources to consider include:

- » **Industry trade associations:** Virtually every industry has its own trade association with a corresponding journal or magazine. Trade associations usually track what's going on in their industries, so they are a wealth of information. If you are serious about starting a business in your industry, you may want to join a trade association, so you'll have access to inside information.

- » **Network, network, network:** Take every opportunity to talk with people in the industry. They are on the front lines on a daily basis and they will give you information that is probably more current than what you'll find in the media or on the Internet.

Benchmarking Against the "Perfect" Industry

Today, with industry boundaries breaking and changes occurring at a breathtaking pace, it isn't easy to find a perfect industry. In fact, the perfect industry doesn't exist. One city, Grand Junction, CO, was looking at the best industries to support and bring into the community to help their city grow. The public relations team identified four industry characteristics that led them to decide that growing their tourism was their best bet. The four characteristics of tourism that they found appealing were:

>> Brings in fresh money rather than recirculating existing dollars.

>> It's generally a clean industry that doesn't produce a lot of waste or require a lot of resources.

>> Helps recruit new companies to the community to support existing hotels and restaurants.

>> Grand Junction is already an attractive destination.

While these characteristics are specific to Grand Junction, they are not unique to Grand Junction, so other towns can potentially follow their example. Clues abound when it comes to the things you may want to consider when looking for an industry in which to start a business. Recognizing that there are no perfect industries, here are some benchmarks to get you started. Generally, you're seeking an industry that has more characteristics working for your business than against it — makes sense! So, look for an industry

>> With more than $50 billion in sales, because it is more likely to provide many niche opportunities that you can capture.

>> That is growing at a rate greater than the GNP (gross national product); in other words, one that's friendly to new entrants.

>> That will let your company make after-tax profits of more than 5 percent of sales within three to five years.

>> That is socially and environmentally responsible. You may get the added benefit of special grants and other types of funding given by the federal government to companies that produce products and services that are responsible.

Now that you have gathered a wealth of information about the environment in which your business will operate, it's time to make sense of all that data. I recommend that you start by using the Porter framework outlined in Figure 5-2 to come up with a description of the components of your industry. Then consider them against the following:

>> It's important to know how much power suppliers have. You can get an indication by looking at the income statements of the larger companies in your industry. You're looking to see what percentage of direct costs are spent on suppliers. Keep in mind that these are large companies that buy in volume so your supply costs will be even higher.

>> You also want to understand what power customers hold in your industry. If your industry supplies many downstream markets, customers do not have much power. But if your industry supplies only one or two types of customers, those customers will have more power and can strongly impact your company's strategy.

>> If you're in a fast-growing industry, suppliers have more power and charge higher prices. Not only that, but products tend to become commodities more quickly, which means that profit margins decline rapidly. For you this means that you must reach high volumes quickly and/or innovate on your product/service to be able to charge a premium and avoid becoming a commodity.

>> If you're in a popular, established industry that everyone is noticing, it will attract more competitors; you will find high barriers to entry in the form of brand loyalty and economies of scale, and few to no substitute products. This is great if your company is offering the product everyone is writing about or you have a viable, attractive substitute. Not so great otherwise.

You need to draw conclusions about your industry and what it means to your business strategy. What you probably want to avoid is an industry with low barriers to entry, which attracts a lot of competitors, strong supplier and buyer bargaining power, many substitute products, and strong competition. As a startup, you just won't have the resources and brand loyalty to survive that type of environment. The right industry will make all the difference in your journey to building a successful business. The bottom line — spend enough time understanding your industry.

Chapter 6

What Your Customers Can Tell You

You have no business without customers. Knowing this, it's remarkable that so many entrepreneurs fail to plan their businesses around the needs of their customers. Doesn't it make sense that if you design your business to fulfill a real customer need, you might have a ready market for your products and services?

Identifying a *target market* — the customers who are most likely to purchase from you — is perhaps the most important decision you'll make about your business. You do so by conducting a thorough feasibility analysis of your business concept. (See Chapter 4 for an overview of feasibility analysis.) Everything else about your business may appear viable, but if you can't demonstrate that sufficient customer demand exists, your business won't get off the ground.

In this chapter, you discover how to research and interact with potential customers so that you can gather enough data to make an informed decision about the future of your business, as well as your strategy to get there.

Conducting Customer Discovery

Recall from Chapter 5 that an industry is a grouping of businesses that operate within the same value chain. They transact with one another and compete with one another in various markets. *Markets* are groups of customers that an industry serves. Look at Figure 6-1 and you see that in conducting your feasibility analysis, you work your way down from the broader industry to the much narrower market niche.

Customer discovery is an approach to gaining information about customers that is empathic. It is also called a design thinking approach. What I mean is that your approach puts you in the shoes of customers so you can see what you're offering from their perspective. I cannot emphasize enough how important it is to assess your product/service from the customer's perspective. To do that, you need to deeply understand your customers and that takes some work — namely, customer discovery.

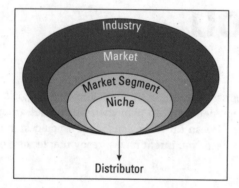

FIGURE 6-1:
Identifying
your niche.

You start the customer discovery process with a fairly loose definition of who you think your customers are. Keep in mind that as you learn more, you will refine this definition to be very precise.

To overcome being overwhelmed by the amount of data you find on markets you're interested in, you may want to keep these critical questions in mind:

>> What are the potential markets you could tap? Are they distinctly different? How big are they and are they growing?

>> Of all the markets you're considering, which customers are most in pain? In other words, who needs your solution most of all?

>> How do these customers buy and how frequently do they do so? How do they typically hear about the product or service?

>> How can you meet their needs? What are the specific benefits you're offering?

Just like the industry research you conducted, you want to first understand the broad market because it influences all the segments you'll eventually identify. Here is some of the information to collect to gain a fuller understanding of the total accessible market — all the possible customers:

>> How big is the market? The bigger it is, the more opportunities there are and the more niches you can capture, enabling your business to grow.

>> What are the demographics of the market? Demographics include age, income, race, occupation, and education. Demographics are often used to segment a market into target groups. Segmentation is covered in the next section. Note that demographics also apply to businesses as customers, for example, size, revenue levels, number of employees, market share, and so forth.

>> Which of these target groups is most likely to buy your product/service? Why?

>> Do you have a way to reach this target group? How do competitors currently reach the group? Is this group in a specific geographic region?

>> What marketing strategies have been successful with this group?

WARNING

At this point, all the information you're collecting comes from secondary sources, that is, other people's data. The research data you collect is only as good as your sources, so do compare data from more than one source to ensure you can rely on it for your calculations.

Segmenting your market

Within each broad market of customers are *segments*. For example, the broad market of people who buy books contains segments of customers who prefer, among other categories:

>> Travel books (or any other category of books)

>> Kids books

>> Books appealing to do-it-yourselfers

>> Audio books

Within each market segment, you can identify smaller *niches* — very specific needs that may not be served — such as:

>> Travel books geared toward people with disabilities

>> Kids books that target minorities

>> Books that teach DIYers how to deal with technology

>> Audio books that provide current journal articles to professionals

Market niches provide an opportunity for entrepreneurs to enter a market and dominate a niche before bigger companies take notice and begin to compete in the same niche. Having a small niche all to yourself gives you a *quiet period* during which you alone serve a customer need that otherwise is not being met. As a result, you get to set the standards for the niche and you get to refine your skills. In short, you're the market leader in that niche, at least for a while.

REMEMBER

As you zero in on your market, take care that the niche you ultimately choose is big enough to make money. The niche you select must have enough customers willing to buy your product so that you can pay your expenses and turn a profit. I talk about how to do that market research later in this chapter.

Defining your target market is about identifying the *primary or first customer* for your products or services — the customer most likely to purchase from you. You want to identify a first customer because creating customer awareness for a new product or service is time-consuming and costly, requiring lots of marketing dollars — dollars that few startups have at their disposal. So, instead of using a shotgun approach and trying to bag a broad market of very different customers, focusing on the specific customers who are most likely to purchase from you is far more effective. More important still, going to the customer who's easiest to sell to helps you gain a foothold quickly and start to build brand recognition, which makes selling to other potential customers easier.

REMEMBER

Not all customers are individuals; many are other businesses (B2B). In fact, the greatest dollar volume of transactions conducted on the Internet today is business-to-business. If a distributor, wholesaler, retail store, or manufacturer is paying you, your customer is a business, not an individual consumer. Businesses as customers can be described in pretty much the same way that you describe a person. Businesses come in a variety of sizes and revenue levels. Like consumers, they also have buying cycles, tastes, and preferences.

Don't forget that if your customer is another business, that business may not be the actual end user of your product or service. In that scenario, you also have an *end user* to deal with. The end user is the ultimate consumer, the person who uses the product or service. For example, look at Figure 6-2, which depicts a typical channel for distributing a product.

FIGURE 6-2:
Typical
distribution
channel.

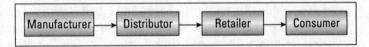

If the distribution channel in Figure 6-2 is filled with your products — refrigerators, for example — who is your customer? This depends on where your company lies in the value chain. If you are the manufacturer, your customer is the distributor who purchases the fridge from you to sell to retailers. The retailer, in turn, is the distributor's customer. The consumer, who uses the fridge, is the retailer's customer and your end user. (The easiest way to identify the customer is to find out who pays you — follow the money!)

Just because end users are not technically your customers doesn't mean that you can ignore them. On the contrary, you need to know as much about the end user as you do about the customer, because you must convince the distributor that a market for your product exists and that the end user will buy enough product so the distributor and retailer can make a profit. Thus, you must conduct the same kind of research on the end user that you do on the distributor. Sorry, that means double the work, but it will pay off.

Defining your niche

The main reason to define and analyze a target market is to find a way into the market so that you have a chance to compete. If you enter a market without a strategy, you're setting yourself up for failure. You are the new kid on the block. If customers can't distinguish your offering from the offering of your competitors, they're not likely to buy from you. People generally prefer to deal with someone they know, and if they've been happy with your competitors' products, they're not likely to incur the switching costs associated with buying your product.

Niche strategy is probably the premier strategy for entrepreneurs because it yields the greatest amount of control. As I've said, creating a niche that no one else is serving is the key to success. That way, you become the leader and can set the standards for those who follow. As the sole occupant of the niche, for a time, you can establish your business in a relatively safe environment (the *quiet period,* as I call it) before you develop any direct competitors. Fending off competitors takes a lot of marketing dollars, and when you're a startup company, you have better uses for your limited resources.

How do you find a niche that no one else has found? By talking to customers and looking for problems. The target market from which your business opportunity comes also holds the keys to your entry strategy. You will learn from your potential customers what's missing in your competitors' products and services. They also tell you what they need to be happy and satisfied with your product. Fulfilling that unmet need is your entry strategy. Don't forget that customers buy benefits, so listen for things like "saves time," "saves money," or "makes the customer younger, richer, thinner, or smarter." Behind every great solution is an entrepreneur who understands what customers value, and it's always something that benefits them directly.

CASE STUDY

SLEEP NICHE IS STILL HOT

Have you seen all the recent advertisements for mattresses? It used to be that this was an old, tired industry with customers who purchased a new mattress every 20 years. But guess what? The industry landscape has changed. With more of us focusing on the quality of our sleep and new technology emerging, it's not surprising that what you sleep on is a major contributor. Witness the rise of Purple, Casper, Tuft & Needle, Leesa, and Loom & Leaf. So hot is this market that some venture capital firms like Supermoon have focused on it.

The mattress industry was ripe for innovation. No one really enjoys spending time trying to find a mattress and having to deal with salespeople. The new mattress entrepreneurs recognized that busy young people were not going to shop around in physical stores to make what is a significant investment. So, they revamped the business model and made it a clickable purchase customized to the customer's needs and delivered direct to their residence in a convenient box smaller than the actual mattress and usually with a free trial period. An added bonus, the mattresses typically cost much less than retail store options, although not always. Even among this new group of products, there are luxury versions that cost much more.

Lesson learned: Studying traditional, old industries can sometimes yield new opportunities that lead to a sustainable business. The mattress industry is now an example of a hot industry.

Analyzing your competitors is critical, as customers will have expectations relative to materials, returns, and other key features. Leesa is an example of one company that chose to get certified as a B corporation, which means that it's focused beyond profits on a social mission. One way it meets that mission is with 100 percent American-made materials, and it donates one mattress for every ten sold to those in need. The company also invests locally with volunteer opportunities. Leesa is clearly going after Millennials who typically want to buy from companies with a social/environmental mission.

Discovering Your Customers

You have now segmented the broader market and maybe you have targeted the first customer, your target market. The research you do on your target market is probably the most important of all, because it helps you validate that this is in fact your primary or first customer. It also helps you begin to discover the level of demand for your product or service. Many new business concepts have failed because entrepreneurs misjudged their marketplace, envisioning more demand than actually existed. That's a costly error that you can avoid, maybe not totally, but substantially.

Good market research always begins with a plan. Your time is precious, so let's not waste it. The following sections cover basic components of a market research plan.

Finding the data you need

Before you take the time to collect data, decide how you're going to use that data and what you need to prove with the data. Here are some typical uses:

>> Demonstrate demand for your product or service

>> Describe the primary customer

>> Describe the buying patterns of your customers

Each of these points requires a different type of data. For example, demonstrating demand for your product or service may require you to find a similar product or service and use its adoption history to estimate demand figures for your enterprise. You might also set up a test site — a temporary, miniature version of the business — to gauge demand. To describe your customer, you need data on demographics like age, income level, and education. To discuss the buying patterns of your customers, you need psychographic data like buying behavior.

These are just a few of the things you may want to achieve through your market research. You want to determine your outcomes first so that you collect the right data. Nothing is more frustrating than doing your analysis and discovering you forgot to gather an all-important piece of information that you needed to present your case to a potential investor.

Looking at the total accessible market

The total accessible market (TAM) is the broad market of all potential customers you believe would buy from you eventually. You want to get a sense of how big that market is because it significantly influences how large your company can grow. If you're thinking you want to build a unicorn, a $1-billion valuation, you can't do that in a $100-million market because you'll never own the entire market, and even if you did, it's not big enough. Secondary research involves finding out what others have said about your target market. It's important to do this before you talk to people in the market yourself (called primary research). With the background information you gather from secondary sources, you will ask better, more accurate questions of the people you interview — you won't waste their time on the basics that you should already know from your research.

If your customers are consumers, a good place to start is the U.S. Federal Census Bureau, online at www.census.gov, where you can find all sorts of demographic information, such as age, education, income, and numbers of workers per household. You can define a geographic area and discover whether it is growing, declining, aging, or getting younger. To find some quick facts, just click on the dropdown menu of states and find the one that you're interested in. For example, if you select Colorado, you're directed to links to the Economic Census for the most recent year, income and poverty statistics, county business patterns for individual years, and many other useful facts. You can see whether the workforce is skilled or unskilled. These kinds of demographics help you determine whether your market has the disposable income you require for your products or services and the skilled workforce you might require for your company. You can also use census data to figure out how many customers are located within specific geographic boundaries and then segment out customers who meet your requirements.

In your community, you probably have an economic development department and a chamber of commerce that keep statistics on local population trends and economic issues. You may also find an office of the Small Business Development Corp., www.sba.gov/hotlist/sbdc.html. SBDC, a branch of the Small Business Administration, www.sba.gov, keeps tabs on new ventures and provides funding and loans.

Don't overlook trade associations as a rich resource. They provide information about your industry and track customers as well. Online, look at sites such as the following two associations and publications:

>> **American Demographics,** www.americandemographics.com: Contains a wealth of information about consumer markets

>> **American Association for Public Opinion Research,** www.aapor.org: Covers every topic imaginable in terms of public views on issues

Conducting customer discovery in the field

Customer discovery — called *primary research* — is the best way to get the most current and useful information about your target market. Nothing beats getting out in the marketplace and talking to customers and competitors.

REMEMBER

The biggest challenge of conducting a market analysis is proving that a market for your product or service exists and that it is large enough to make the business concept feasible. The most important data you collect will come from potential customers.

Don't make the mistake made by so many entrepreneurs of assuming they have a winning concept simply because friends and family are overwhelmingly positive about it. Maybe these admirers are right, but chances are they're flat out wrong and just want to support you. You need to determine with objective data that you have a winning concept.

To get good data from unbiased responses, you must choose a representative sample of your target market that is unknown to you — in other words, no friends and family. This is called a *random sample.* You want people who don't have a personal interest in seeing you succeed, because you want their honest responses. The form of your questions is another crucial concern. Just asking potential customers whether they would buy your product or service does not give you the kind of information you need — it's too easy for a respondent to simply say yes or no without giving you any useful information. You need answers to *why* questions, such as the following:

>> Why will you buy this product or service?

>> Why are you not interested in this product or service?

>> Why do you purchase in these locations?

>> Why do you buy the competitors' products? (This question confirms your competitors' advantage.)

>> What would it take for you to purchase this product or service? (This question gets at what is missing from your product, which is a feature or benefit.)

The answers to why questions give you information that helps you refine your business concept and ensure you're giving customers what they really want. They will also provide clues to who is your first customer, the one who needs your solution most.

Observing customers in their natural habitats

I call this the Jane Goodall approach to ethnographic research or customer discovery. Ms. Goodall is a highly regarded anthropologist who is known for her observations of gorillas in the wild in Tanzania, which gave us insights we never knew about these mammals that are more like us than we thought. Think of your customers as interacting in the wild. Your job is to observe them and draw meaningful conclusions about what you see. Here's a simple, yet very effective way to conduct this research:

1. Observe your customers, if possible, in their normal environment. If you're targeting hospital personnel, for example, you need to spend time observing the work patterns of these personnel in the hospital environment.

2. Interview your customers with open-ended questions so as not to bias their responses.

3. At the conclusion of the interview, explain to yourself what you observed or learned from the interview. (You can do this when you get back to your car or other private place.) Don't analyze, just note your first impressions.

4. Form a hypothesis about what you believe is true based on what you learned.

5. Test your hypothesis by going back into the field to see if you can validate it with a more focused group of customers.

6. Look at the preponderance of evidence you've gathered and draw a conclusion.

If you go through this process and are still not sure, repeat the process with different questions based on what you learned in the first round. Spending the time to do this properly early in the startup process will save you a lot of errors farther down the path when you can't afford them. I can't emphasize enough the importance of this primary research over anything else you do to validate your business concept. Without a customer, there is no business.

Survey by email and telephone

The first thing many people think of when they hear "primary research" is doing a survey, either by email or phone. Despite the advantages of ease and the ability to reach many people, email and phone surveys have significant disadvantages and are, therefore, not a very effective way to get the best data. Here are some of the reasons that I don't recommend them:

>> Questionnaires are not as easy to develop as you think. Some people spend whole careers studying the most effective ways to question people. If you do choose to use a questionnaire (perhaps as part of your interviews), here are a few tips to make it more effective:

- Keep it short.

- Don't ask leading or biased questions — a question that tends to direct the response.

- Ask the easy questions first.

- Ask the demographic questions last. (Don't forget to ask them because you'll need to segment your market by the responses to those questions to find out who your customer is.)

- Put answers to multiple-choice questions about age and income (which people resist anyway) into ranges so that respondents don't have to give an exact answer. It is well known that people responding to surveys typically lower their age one category and raise their income one category.

>> Response rates to email surveys usually are low, around 15 percent, and achieving even that level usually requires multiple follow-ups, which just annoys your prospective customers. Consider this: A 15 percent response means that about 85 of every 100 persons sampled did not respond. Think about what that non-response rate means: If 15 people responded and 10 of that number (a whopping two-thirds!) said they would buy your product, what do the other 85 think? You have no idea. The only way to resolve the non-response bias is to increase the response rate. That, however, takes money and time. Fortunately, other methods of collecting good data about your customers exist; I discuss those shortly.

>> You don't have the benefit of nonverbal communication, such as the visual clues to attitudes that you easily pick up in face-to-face interviews. This shortcoming of email and phone surveys is important, because it has been estimated that 85 percent of all communication is nonverbal.

>> With email surveys, you have no way of clarifying a response and no control over the accuracy of the information.

>> Phone surveys take much more time to conduct and are prone to interviewer bias. More importantly, think about how you feel when a survey marketer interrupts your dinner to catch you at your most likely time to be home. How much engagement do you believe you'll give?

Don't forget to collect demographic data such as age, sex, income, education, and so forth so you can segment the questionnaires when you're finished. This way you can better understand who exactly might purchase what you're offering.

SAMPLE QUESTIONNAIRE SUITABLE FOR EMAIL AND PHONE SURVEYS AND INTERVIEWS

This survey was created by two USC students, David Burlison and Joe Emerson, to obtain information about their potential customers for an Internet concept involving a prepaid purchasing account. It follows a proven method of construction to ensure unbiased responses. In general, the questionnaire should be short, with a lot of whitespace. It should contain no leading questions, but rather simple, easy-to-understand questions. This survey can also be used as the basis for in-person interviews.

1. Do you have an Internet account?

   Yes___ No___

   (This is a screening question so that you don't waste your time on people who don't have Internet access.)

2. How much time do you spend online each week?_____

   (This question is designed to ascertain how serious an Internet user the respondent is.)

3. What are your primary uses of the Internet?

   a. Email

   b. Research

   c. Shopping

   d. News

   e. Other _____

4. What primary method do you use for making purchases?

   a. Cash

   b. Check

   c. Credit Card

5. Do you have your own credit card? Yes___ No___

   (If no, answer Question 6. If yes, skip Question 6.)

6. Whose credit card do you use to make purchases online?_____

7. Have you ever purchased any goods or services online? Yes___ No___

8. What are your primary concerns with online purchasing?_____

_____

_____

_____

_____

9. If a system enabled you to make secure purchases over the Internet without the
need for a credit card, would you be interested in using it?

Yes___ No___Why?_____

_____

_____

Conduct interviews and focus groups

Personal interviews and focus groups may cost more time and money than email
and phone surveys, but you get what you pay for. These methods can be designed
to provide comparatively more valuable market information because:

>> You have more opportunity for clarification and discussion.

>> You gain the advantage of viewing nonverbal communication.

>> The response rate is high.

>> You can ask more open-ended questions.

>> You get the added benefit of being able to network and make new contacts.

A *focus group* is a group interview for which you bring together a representative
sample of potential customers to view a presentation of your product or service
and discuss its merits. The leader of the focus group (perhaps yourself, but more
likely someone trained in this interview technique, so that your own biases don't
creep in) introduces the product or service you offer, sometimes along with other
competing products and services, to solicit opinions from the group. For example,
suppose you're introducing a new kind of beverage. You may do a blind study,
offering several beverages (including your product) to the focus group and asking
group members to comment on taste, aftertaste, and so forth.

Focus groups and face-to-face interviews can prevent you from making a costly
error in product design or marketing strategy.

Building an early customer profile

A customer profile is what you construct from all the primary data you gather about your prospective buyer. It's a summary of your conclusions about the customer. The profile describes your typical customer in great detail, whether that customer is a person or another business, along with demographics, buying habits, and all other factors important to understanding who the buyer is and why and how they purchase. For example, your typical customer may be "a 35-year-old well-educated Hispanic female concerned about health issues, who earns $70,000 to $80,000 a year working principally in a management position and has a family with two children."

Knowing that much about your customer (and you certainly can add a lot more to this example) helps you tremendously when you design your marketing plan to reach this customer. The profile also helps you refine your business concept and your product/service design to ensure that you're meeting this customer's real needs.

CASE STUDY

GIVE CUSTOMERS WHAT THEY WANT

Knowing exactly what your customers want can mean not only more sales but also more initial interest in your venture from the people who provide the financing to get it off the ground. At least that's what happened to Gus Conrades and his partner Bryan Murphy. The two launched Wrenchead.com in 1999, which sold auto parts and car-care products through a B2C e-commerce channel.

The partners succeeded in raising a first round of $15 million on the strength of their business plan, which summed up their business concept in a simple sentence: "Wrenchead.com sells auto parts to consumers and professionals over the Internet." Investors had no trouble understanding the business. Of course, the partners were also able to demonstrate that the auto parts market was a hefty $32 billion a year at the time, promising potential for growth. Conrades and Murphy had both a clear vision of where the company was going and the data to support what they were saying. And they knew the auto parts business inside-out.

The partners also were wise enough to understand that warehousing and distribution is as important (if not more important) than the Internet itself. Their customer-oriented strategy worked: They are now the #1 provider of online e-business applications for the transportation industry. (For more details, go to www.whisolutions.com.)

Identifying more important people to interview

Beyond customers, there are other people who play important roles in your value chain, and you should get to know them. Here are five categories of such people:

>> **Gatekeepers:** These are the individuals who stand between you and the particular customers you're trying to reach. You will definitely encounter gatekeepers if your customers are major businesses or the U.S. government. For example, if you want to sell to the government, you need to qualify as a government contractor through the appropriate agency.

>> **Influencers:** I'm not talking about Instagram influencers here. I mean people whose approval is required for a purchase decision. For example, physicians often serve as influencers when you're trying to sell into hospitals or clinics. That is because the patient, who will benefit from access to the device you're selling, is generally not the one paying the bill. Whoever pays the bill is the customer and that could be an insurance company. Therefore, it's very important to understand how your industry works.

>> **Deciders:** These are the people who make the final purchasing decision for a company, and the decision is typically made based on their business strategy and their budget.

>> **Purchasers:** These are the people who have the authority to make the purchase.

>> **Users:** These are the beneficiaries of the purchase.

Graphing a customer segmentation matrix

Once you have a good understanding of your complete market and all the potential customers, it is helpful to graph a segmentation matrix so you can see more clearly where you should focus your selling efforts. Table 6-1 is an example of a segmentation matrix in the EdTech industry. Springboard is an EdTech company that teaches and certifies people in critical technology skills. You can make your matrix as large or as small as you need to cover all the areas you're investigating.

As you can see in the matrix in Table 6-1, I've identified three customers who have different needs. Additional columns you might add to support your decision-making are size of market, market growth rate, and barriers to entry. Once you have all this information, and assuming you have completed interviews with potential customers, you should be able to identify your first customer. Remember, this first customer should be the easiest to convince and reach.

TABLE 6-1   **Customer Matrix for Springboard (EdTech Industry)**

Customer	Pain or Need	Benefit	Distribution	Competition
Desiring UI/UX design skills	Need skills to get a job.	Learn current skills at own pace. Don't need to pay until secure a job.	Direct through Internet	Udacity
Seeking data analytics skills	Need certification in a tech area.	Online and flexible schedule	Direct through Internet	Thinkful
Seeking cybersecurity skills	Meet new SEC requirements for public companies. Better secure company's network.	Learn on your own schedule and get mentoring from an industry insider.	Direct through Internet	CBT Nuggets

Competitive Intelligence: Checking Out the Competition

One of the most difficult tasks you face is finding information about your competitors. I'm not talking about the obvious things that you can easily find by going to a competitor's physical location or website. I'm talking about the important stuff that can affect what you do with your business concept — things such as how much competitors spend on customer service, what their profit margins are, how many customers they have, what their growth strategies are, and so forth. If you're in competition with private companies (which is true most of the time), your task is even more difficult because private companies don't have to disclose the kinds of information that public companies do.

Here's some of the information you may want to collect about your competitors:

>> The management style of the company

>> Current market strategies and what they've done in the past, because history tends to repeat itself

>> The unique features and benefits of the products and services they offer

>> Their pricing strategy

>> Their customer mix

>> Their promotional mix

It's helpful to create a grid or matrix that lists all your competitors — direct, indirect, and emerging — so that you can immediately make comparisons with your company.

With a concerted effort and a plan in hand, you can find out a lot about your potential competitors. The following sections describe a step-by-step strategy for attacking the challenge of competitive intelligence.

Pounding the pavement

If your competition has physical sites, visit them and observe what goes on. What kinds of customers frequent their sites? What do they buy, and how much do they buy? What is the appearance of the site? How would you evaluate the location? Gather as much information as you can through observation and talking to customers and employees.

Buying your competitors' products

Buying your competitors' products helps you find out more about how your competition treats its customers and how good its products and services are. If you think that it sounds strange to buy your competitors' products, just remember, as soon as yours are in the marketplace, your competitors will buy them.

Revving up the search engines

From a search engine, type in the name of the specific companies or the general category of company you're interested in and see what comes up. True, this is not the most effective way to search; but it's a start, and you never know what you'll pull up that you otherwise may not have found. I can't tell you how many times a new entrepreneur has come to my office proclaiming that they have no competition. I immediately swivel my chair to pull up a search engine on my computer. I type in the generic category of product they're selling or the name of the company and voila! I always get at least a page or two of responses. Every business has competition.

Don't forget, many search engines are available. You don't get the same results from Google as you do from Duck Duck Go. Check them all out.

Forecasting Demand: Tough but Crucial

One of the more difficult aspects of market research is figuring out how much demand exists for your product or service. The problem is that no one best way to calculate it exists, so you must approach demand from several points of view. This process of using multiple approaches is called *triangulation*; I show you a trio of methods shortly.

You can certainly extrapolate demand figures from the work of others, but the best numbers come from your personal research in the market. Be forewarned, however, that five people telling you they will buy your product or service is not enough (as I caution you elsewhere in this chapter). You need to know, for example, that five out of six people questioned at random say they will purchase your product or service at a particular price. If you can come up with that kind of result each time you question a focus group, you have a pretty good sense of demand down the road.

WARNING

If you don't do a good job of forecasting now, you may create huge problems for yourself later, when your attention is occupied with meeting deadlines, looking for employees, and scrambling to find the customers you need to meet demand.

Here are a couple of suggestions to help you improve your forecasting:

>> **Quantify expectations.** You need to know how much you expect your business to grow on an annual basis in terms of sales, profits, and number of employees. For most businesses, growth is fairly predictable, but you can't always control demand. For instance, if you introduce a new technology or product that suddenly catches fire, you can experience what is known as *hockey stick growth* (think of the growth line on a sales chart). If you didn't anticipate that level of growth, you may not have the cash or the human capital available to keep up with customer demand.

>> **Ask the right questions and insist on real answers.** You must be able to support your numbers. If you're claiming that sales will grow from $1 million to $5 million by the second year, your investors will want to know what causes that growth. Are you spending more on marketing? Have you reduced costs? What is the basis for the increase? Let's hope it's demand. Just be sure that you can explain how you arrive at your figures.

Many factors affect a sales forecast. If any of the items in the following list are relevant to your business, think about them when you calculate sales growth.

>> **Seasons:** Nearly every business is affected by seasonal demand, that is, months, weeks, days, or even times of the day when customers buy more

than at other times. For example, more motorcycles are sold in the winter than in any other time of year. If you're selling motorcycles, that would be important to know. Customers get the best deals in the winter. The same is true for boats and a lot of other outdoor equipment.

>> **Holidays:** In the retail business, holidays are major sales times. That's why the majority of profit is made in the fourth quarter. By contrast, in manufacturing, holidays may represent a slow time of the year.

>> **Fashions or styles:** In the clothing industry, for example, you have to know how long a particular fashion is going to be in favor with consumers to be able to judge its economic life.

>> **Population changes:** Population shifts can cause certain regions, cities, or even neighborhoods to change such that a restaurant or boutique no longer enjoys a solid customer base.

>> **National and global developments:** Wars, elections, the stock market, pandemics, disrupted supply chains, and so forth affect consumers' buying habits.

>> **Competition:** If you have a lot of competition, for example, you probably have to bring your prices down, meaning you must sell more to make a profit.

>> **External labor events:** Labor shortages and strikes can depress productivity, and that can depress sales.

>> **Consumer earnings:** In good times, earnings are high and consumers buy. But in inflationary or recessionary economic times, consumers and businesses pull back.

>> **Weather:** Bad weather and catastrophes, like hurricanes, can be a boon to businesses like construction, but a bust to businesses located in affected regions.

>> **Product changes:** Changes in your products mean that customers have to become familiar with something new, so sales may decline for a period of time. In contrast, if the change is welcome, sales may rise exponentially.

>> **Credit policy changes:** Favorable credit policies may encourage more sales, while barriers to credit may discourage sales.

>> **Inventory shortages:** Shortages can discourage customers and send them elsewhere to shop, reducing your sales. By contrast, if a product that is in demand experiences a temporary shortage, sales may actually rise at a higher-than-normal pace once the product is available. We saw this happen during the supply chain disruptions in 2022.

>> **Price changes:** On goods and services that customers don't require to live or do business, a change in price can directly affect sales — positively if the price goes down and negatively if it goes up.

>> **Distribution channels:** On any product or service, customers have a preferred way to make their purchases. If you select the wrong distribution channel, you can lose sales.

Your challenge is to find the best and most reliable way to gauge demand for your product or service. As you do, don't fool yourself or take shortcuts — too much is at stake.

Triangulating to demand

Now, back to the business of triangulation. Triangulation involves approaching a demand number from three different sources. You simply get three or more different points of view concerning demand and decide on what appears to be the best information. In this section, I discuss three techniques or perspectives for developing demand data.

Use substitute products and services to gauge demand

If you're introducing a product or service that is an extension of something already in existence, you may be able to base your demand estimation on the level of demand established by the associated product or service. For example, demand for compact discs was derived from demand for cassette tapes. In other cases, you may be able to substitute another similar product that caters to the same customer base to help you judge demand.

Interview customers and intermediaries

The people who can give you the best estimates and insights about demand are those who work in the market daily: customers and intermediaries like distributors, wholesalers, and retailers. Spending some time talking with them about the market, the new product adoption patterns they're seeing, seasonality, and sales levels for products is time well spent. (To learn how to talk to industry people, see Chapter 5.)

Go into limited production with a test market

Sometimes the only way to gauge customer demand is to go into limited production so that you can see how customers respond to what you're offering. Customers who can hold and use your product or see how your service works are more likely to give you important feedback and they're also more likely to buy. You may want to do this after you've successfully tried the first two techniques I suggested. Putting a minimum viable product out in the market in a limited fashion elicits great feedback. That feedback can enable you to modify the product before you attempt to sell to a mass market, when modifications and returns are much more costly.

TIP

Putting up a temporary kiosk in a shopping center is a good way to gauge interest in a consumer product. Industry trade shows are excellent if you're selling B2B.

Software companies regularly ship prototype versions to the consumer and business markets in not-so-perfect fashion and count on their customers to report bugs to them. Then they create a *patch* to fix the bug and offer it free to download from their Internet site. Although not necessarily the best way to do things, it's typical in that industry, and customers haven't objected too strongly.

If you achieve a successful test market, you can expand to a more formal test market in a specific geographic market that is representative of your customers on a national level. Denver, Colorado, is often used as a test site because of its demographics, which are generally representative of the United States as a whole.

You now have a range of values for demand, and you can triangulate to a best estimate based on what you've learned about your customer. But keep in mind that total demand is not something you achieve on day one in the market. Products typically have adoption patterns, especially technology products. We address adoption patterns in detail in Chapter 16. However, the intermediaries in your channel should have a good handle on adoption patterns for your product, so be sure to discuss your thoughts with them.

Forecasting new product demand

Not accurately forecasting new product demand comes with a significant cost. A poor forecast can result in stockouts (running out of product), overstocking (increasing inventory costs), and damaged relationships with suppliers, not to mention customers. It's not just startups who miss the mark when estimating demand. Some very large companies have also missed and paid big time.

For example, Best Buy advertised great deals for the holiday shopping season in December 2011 and then had to notify customers that their orders would not be filled because they had miscalculated demand. Needless to say, these customers were angry at Best Buy's inability to correctly forecast demand at the most important buying season of the year. Some customers stopped buying from the company altogether. Others switched their business to Amazon. It's difficult and costly for a large company to recover quickly. It's nearly impossible for a small, startup company.

Triangulate demand with:

» Historical analogy of similar products or services

» Customer and intermediary feedback

» The entrepreneur's perspective based on experience or a test market

The lesson is this: Spend enough time understanding the buying patterns of customers in your market so that you're prepared to satisfy them with the appropriate number of resources.

Chapter **7**

Designing Solutions for a New Marketplace

Remember the scene in the movie *Superman* where Lois Lane is falling off a building, and Superman swoops in to catch her mid-air, saying, "I've got you," and she responds in a panic, "But who's got you?" Sometimes you just have to go for it.

That's pretty good advice for an entrepreneur on the trail of a new product or service in today's rapid-paced business environment — seize an opportunity in the moment and then make up the rules as you go. Practically everything that used to be considered gospel on the topic of designing new products and services is in the trash can today, thanks to advances in technology and a distribution channel called the Internet.

Yet, some things remain constant: It still costs a lot of money to design and build a working model (a *prototype*) of a new product. The new product's design and functionality have to meet or exceed the user's expectations. Reaching a customer still requires marketing, but traditional marketing has given way to newer concepts such as *mass customization and mass personalization*.

Mass customization is giving customers what they want, when they want it, and in the way they want it. One of my companies, for example, produces a combination air-compressor/generator that's usually painted cardinal and gold. But when one of our customers asked that we paint the machines they ordered in yellow and green to match other equipment they had, and to mount a different brand of compressor on the machine, of course we agreed. That's an example of modifying your product to meet the specific needs of your customers. We can do that with our machine because we designed the machine with interchangeable parts and mass customization in mind.

Mass personalization, on the other hand, is designing the product in a way that is personal to that customer. For example, when you revisit Amazon.com after registering the first time, the homepage greets you using your own name. Over time, Amazon.com tracks your purchases and suggests products for you to look at based on what you have bought previously. You're no doubt very familiar with this approach.

One more thing about the nature of product development today: The boundaries between products and services have faded. Product companies offer services; service companies develop products; and most companies offer a bundle of both. For example, UPS, the package delivery service, expanded its offerings to more effectively compete with the likes of FedEx. Today, UPS helps you personalize the treatment of your customers from your website to their doorstep. They offer business solutions for every stage of your company. However you define your company, think about developing both products and services to offer your customers.

In this chapter, I talk mostly about developing products, because it's a more complex process. But you can easily substitute the word *services*. Services need a development process, too, and it's virtually the same routine that you follow with products.

Zeroing-in on a Product Solution

Many entrepreneurs would like to deal in products, but they're not quite sure how to get started. Of course, you could import products from other countries or buy your products from domestic manufacturers. But if you like the idea of manufacturing and distributing a brand-new technology or other type of unique product, then you have three choices: invent something, team with an inventor, or license an invention. Let's look at these approaches in more detail.

Becoming an inventor

Most entrepreneurs are not inventors — not because they don't have the ability to invent, but because their focus is elsewhere. The mindsets of the entrepreneur and the inventor tend to be quite different, and it's unusual to find both in the same person. Not only are the mindsets different, but the skills required by each are very different. In general, pure inventor types aren't interested in the commercial side of things. They invent for the love of invention. Unless an entrepreneur comes along and points out an opportunity for their invention, it's likely that invention will not reach the marketplace.

I work with many types of inventors — engineers, scientists, and so forth — and most are more comfortable spending their time in the laboratory. You have to ask yourself which role feels right to you and do that. You can always find the other needed talents in someone else. In fact, most inventors never see their inventions in the marketplace because they don't understand the business process called the commercialization of new technology.

Teaming with an inventor

Entrepreneurs often team with inventors to commercialize a new product. That's what my husband and I did with our company (look at the sidebar "Genesis of a Product" to see how we recognized our opportunity). Often the opportunity to team with an inventor comes out of the industry in which you're working. You hear about someone who's working on a project; you investigate and discover an interesting invention. Don't hesitate to approach an inventor, but remember a couple of important things:

>> **Inventors are generally paranoid about their inventions.** They are sure that someone is out to steal their ideas.

>> **Inventors typically aren't business oriented and don't want to become businesspeople.** Their love is inventing, so don't expect them to be partners in a business sense.

REMEMBER

Structure an arrangement with your inventor that doesn't hamstring your efforts to commercialize the invention. You are each bringing something very important to the mix, so be sure you can work together well before you agree to anything in writing.

Licensing an invention

Companies, universities, the government, and independent inventors are all looking for entrepreneurs to commercialize their inventions. You gain access to these inventions through a vehicle known as *licensing*. Licensing grants you the right to use the invention in an agreed-upon way for an agreed-upon time. In return, you agree to pay a royalty to the inventor, usually based on a percentage of sales of the product that result from the invention. You can find out more about licensing in Chapter 8.

The government owns many core technologies developed for the military and the aerospace program, among others. You can license many of these core technologies and create a new application for use in a different industry. For example, if you go to the NASA technology site at `https://technology.nasa.gov/`, you can browse the Patent Portfolio for patents with commercial potential available through NASA's licensing program.

Alternatively, visit the technology licensing office at most major research universities and you'll find more opportunities. For example, the Stanford University Office of Technology Licensing evaluates, markets, and licenses technology owned by Stanford University. If you go to their site, `https://otl.stanford.edu/`, you will be guided through a process that could potentially lead to your licensing one of their technologies. You would start by familiarizing yourself with their licensing process; then look for a technology that interests you. Suppose you are interested in medical devices and want to see what kinds of technologies are available. If you go to their list of medical devices `https://techfinder.stanford.edu/technology_listing.php?search=recent&queryString=`, you will find a list of all the devices invented at Stanford University. Click on the docket number and you will be provided with a description and picture or schematic of the device and the name of the contact person.

Universities are a gold mine for new technologies that you can tap into. Of course, they require that you validate your ability to commercialize the technology. In other words, you need to demonstrate that you know your market and industry, and that you have access to resources to fund commercialization.

CASE STUDY

GENESIS OF A PRODUCT

In the early 1990s, my husband and I were doing commercial real estate development in the San Joaquin Valley in California. We had a group of subcontractors we regularly used on our projects, and one of them was a finish carpenter by the name of Bill Nelson. He had a passion for inventing things and was quite the character. One day he arrived at our home with a very curious-looking device in the back of his old pick-up truck. We quickly learned that it was an electric generator and an air compressor sitting on twin four-gallon air tanks and driven by a small gasoline engine. The concept was simple. When the user starts a power tool, whether air-powered or electric-powered, the machine senses which type of tool is being used and engages either the air compressor or the generator. No one had ever been able to do this before. Most contractors must carry around two separate units to accommodate their various tools.

We thought the concept intriguing; but at the time, we were busy divesting ourselves of some real estate deals because the market was in a downturn.

A year later, Nelson came back with an improved version of the machine. He confidently attached a hose to the machine with a power tool on the end, walked about 100 feet away, pulled the trigger of the power tool, the drive motor of the unit started up and the power tool started working. When he lay the tool down, the motor stopped. He also did the same with a small air-powered drill. The machine was designed to enable multiple users of air and electric-powered tools to operate them remotely and simultaneously from one power source, and it provided many other benefits over existing generators and compressors, saving time, money, and the environment.

Nelson had no business experience and no concept of what it would take to refine his invention to a marketable prototype, but we knew it would take a lot. He knew that we had the business experience he needed to commercialize the product and we saw the opportunity to take the product to a state-of-the-art level. We went into a licensing agreement with him and agreed to fund the development and patenting of the device. That was a risk because we had no way of knowing what development and patenting would cost. Let's just say that it was much more than we expected.

By the time product development was completed and the machine was introduced to the marketplace in 1998, it in no way resembled the original prototype in either design or function. It had now become an intelligent machine with three patents on it. We were able to take his very basic mechanical concept and transform it into a state-of-the-art electronic machine. The inventor continued to work with us until his untimely death, after which we sold the company and the patents.

Moving Rapidly to a Prototype: The Minimum Viable Product

Eric Ries's book *The Lean Startup* made popular the idea of a minimum viable product (MVP), which is an early version of a product that displays just enough of the functionality and value to attract early adopters, the first customers. Bill Nelson's mechanical prototype, discussed in the sidebar, was an MVP. If these early adopters like your product, that's great. But you need to understand specifically what they like and what they would like to see changed. Their feedback is critical to moving from an MVP to a complete product ready for the market. This is particularly true if your product involves incremental innovation; that is, it's built on existing technology that customers already understand. With incremental innovation, it's easier to determine if you are solving the customer's actual problem. However, the more incremental your product, the more important it is to introduce a fully functional MVP version, because your customers will automatically compare it to existing technologies in the market.

On the other hand, if your technology is new to the world — that is, disruptive — you have a different issue. You need customer feedback to refine the product, so you will likely introduce a series of MVPs, each one building on and improving on the feedback from the previous version. It's definitely a process, but one well worth the effort.

Bootstrapping Product Development

As an entrepreneur, typically you don't have enough money or enough people to do what you want to do relative to product development. I don't mean to discourage you right off the bat, but you need to be realistic. It's one thing to start from a concept and build a product that is market-ready when you have a staff of engineers, labor, and unlimited funds to make it happen quickly. It's quite another thing to try to do it when all you have are your own resources. Because you are working with limited resources, you will probably have to outsource some of the product development tasks. This means you will hire independent contractors to do things like aspects of manufacturing, designing, or prototyping.

For our product discussed in the sidebar, the intelligent power source, we outsourced everything but the final assembly. That meant we worked with 44 vendors, independent contractors, and suppliers. It was like being the ringmaster of a three-ring circus. But it meant that we got our welding and powder coating done without having to purchase very expensive equipment and learn new skills.

By now you may feel this will be a daunting task, but I want to encourage you to think of it as a challenge that you can meet. In fact, bootstrapping your way through product development can be a good thing. A lack of resources has propelled many an entrepreneur to seek innovative product and process solutions. In fact, research has found that new entrepreneurial companies are the most successful at introducing break-through innovations — products that change the way we do things. Big companies are better at building sustaining technologies; in other words, technology that is merely an improvement over something that already exists. So, take heart. It may not be easy, but chances are you can develop the next great product. Besides, many innovations today are software based, so they are much less costly and faster to produce.

Understanding the product life cycle

You learned about the industry life cycle in Chapter 5. A product has a life cycle as well, with equivalent periods of birth, growth, maturity, and decline or obsolescence. Some products have life cycles as short as 90 days (think fads). Others have cycles many decades long, such as appliances and automobiles. Even these life cycles can be extended through the introduction of new technology, such as the technology that gave us electric vehicles. Today life cycles are shrinking, and customers are demanding. Technological change has led to newer versions of products on a regular basis. That's why you don't want your company to be a one-trick pony. You need to plan for spinoff or derivative products from the beginning.

With that in mind, you want to design a new product and simultaneously design how it will be manufactured. They go hand in hand if you are ever going to be able to mass produce your product. Table 7-1 is a checklist of the product development process. It's quite a list, but doable if you stay organized.

TABLE 7-1   ## New Product Development Checklist

Task	Yes	No	More Investigation
Have we validated a first customer for the product?			
Do we have a niche market with no competition at entry?			
Do we have intellectual property rights?			
Have we identified a path to multiple customers?			
Are customer behavioral changes required?			
What is the primary benefit to the customer and is it validated?			
Have we identified any threats to the development of this product?			
Are there many opportunities to commercialize this technology?			
Are there serious threats to the development of the product?			
Can the product be manufactured easily?			
Is this a disruptive technology?			
Can we build an MVP rapidly and at minimal cost?			
Will we need to subcontract any of the manufacturing?			
Will the technology produce spinoff products or complementary products?			
Is the return on investment enough to justify the effort?			
Do we have the resources to do the product development?			
Do we have a validated business model for the product?			
Are the gross margins on the product high enough to be competitive?			

Once you've completed the product development checklist, do an honest assessment of where you stand. If you have several items that require more research to be able to answer the question, that research should be your next step. With a completed checklist in hand, you're positioned to determine if there are more forces working for this effort than there are against it. That will help you make the final decision.

It's rare when a new entrepreneur can answer "yes" to all the questions or even come close. That doesn't mean your dream has ended. It does mean that you need to consider your challenges and prepare to meet them.

Finding the money

I am fond of saying that for entrepreneurs, it's not just about the money. And, in general, that's certainly true. You're starting this business because you're passionate about your concept, you want to become independent, or you've always wanted to own your own business. But, if you're interested in starting a business that develops and markets new products, you're in a whole new ball game. Whether you're developing the next great toy, a medical device, or an Internet site, it takes a lot of capital up front. So, for these types of businesses, it really is about the money — not the money you make, but the money you spend. Product development is a sink hole for money, and you should know that before you begin.

The next thing you should know is that, for the most part, no one is out there excited to hand you money to turn your product concept (now only on paper) into the next great product. Most entrepreneurs must rely on their own resources to fund product development, at least until they get to a working prototype. That's because investors can't conceptualize the value of a product the way the entrepreneur/inventor can until they can see it, touch it, and use it. Then, and only then, might an investor understand the benefit.

The machine that my company developed (see the sidebar entitled "Genesis of a Product") took five years of effort and over $300,000 before it was ready to be marketed. My husband has a background in engineering, so he took the lead on running product development, while I did a lot of market research to discover the best customers and applications for the product. We each contributed financially to this process from other things we were doing. We took no outside capital. Remember, this was an industrial machine, not a sexy Internet startup. Five years to develop a product is a long time, but we moved it forward only as fast as the money came in. And we had to live and support our family at the same time. In addition to normal product development costs, we also had to pay for patents to protect what we had developed. It was not easy — there were times when we ran out of money and had to halt product development for a time — but we believed in the product and the benefit it would provide to the user. We resisted asking friends and relatives for help because we knew it would take a long time to build the company, and we didn't want to risk their hard-earned money.

REMEMBER

The exception to the rule of needing to use mostly your own resources is cutting-edge, new technology or technology platform — core technology that has the potential to spin off many applications in the form of new products that disrupt a market and has the potential to produce at least $25 million in sales within five years. In this case, you may qualify to apply for government grants or be able to obtain private or institutional venture capital. Let's look at some of these sources in more detail.

Seeking government grants

The government has come to the rescue of many an inventor or company that wanted to develop a new technology from scratch or access a technology that the government developed. I review here the major governmental agencies that provide seed and development capital to private companies.

>> **Small Business Investment Company (SBIC).** These entities are similar to private venture capital funds. Licensed by the Small Business Administration, the SBIC provides long-term loans and equity funding (capital in exchange for a stake in the business) to startup and growing businesses. Each SBIC is different; some focus on certain phases of funding, like early seed funding or growth funding, while others focus on certain types of businesses. You can find them through the SBA website at www.sba.gov.

If you receive funding from an SBIC, you also have access to mentoring and other support as you're developing your business. You can register your business at the SBA and find a wealth of information to support your efforts. A friend of mine who happens to be an inventor in medical devices used the support of the SBA to become a Woman-owned Small Business Federal Contractor, which means that she was able to sell her invention to the federal government. That's a big deal.

>> **Venture capital institutes and networks.** Many universities have begun to provide matching services to help local entrepreneurs find investors. The university takes no equity stake in the new venture, but merely acts as a go-between. Typically, the entrepreneur pays an admission fee and submits their business plan. The network tries to match the needs of the business with an investor. If an investor is interested in talking to an entrepreneur, contact is made. The success rate of these matching services is not high, but for entrepreneurs who don't have a large network of contacts with investor types, they're a good place to start. Investors sign up with these services voluntarily, so they're looking for good businesses to invest in.

>> **The Small Business Administration.** If you have previously owned or operated a business, you may qualify for an SBA-guaranteed loan for a new business. The SBA's focus is to provide funding to businesses that may not qualify under traditional banking criteria. If an SBA-backed loan recipient defaults, the SBA guarantees that it will repay the lending institution up to 90 percent of the loan. Although advertisements claim that qualifying criteria for SBA loans are less stringent than for traditional commercial loans, the reality is that most banks judge small, new businesses by the same standards they apply to established businesses. Thus, plan on doing a lot of paperwork if you get one of these loans. The SBA also has a micro loan program (amounts up to $25,000) for entrepreneurs with limited access to capital.

>> **Small Business Innovative Research (SBIR).** All federal agencies with research and development (R&D) budgets in excess of $100 million must earmark a portion of their budgets to funding grants for small businesses (under 500 employees) devoted to developing technologies in which the government is interested. You can find out what technologies interest the government by checking the solicitations published by the various agencies at www.sbir.gov/solicitations and the SBA Technology Transfer Program. Agencies like the Department of Energy www.energy.gov/science-innovation) describe the kinds of inventions the DOE is supporting.

Grants provided by government agencies go through three phases, the details of which are described at www.sbir.gov/funding and summarized here:

- **Phase I (the startup phase):** Provides awards of up to $100,000 for approximately six months to support and explore the merit or feasibility of an idea or technology.

- **Phase II:** Provides awards of up to $750,000, for as many as two years, to expand the Phase I results. During Phase II, research and development work is performed, and the developer evaluates commercialization potential. Only Phase I award winners are considered for Phase II.

- **Phase III:** Phase III innovation moves from the laboratory into the market-place. The small business must find funding in the private sector or other non-SBIR federal agency funding.

>> **State-Funded Venture Capital.** Several states — Massachusetts, New York, and Oregon, to name a few — provide venture funds to encourage startups to locate in their region of the country. For example, Texas has more than 44 state-based venture capital funds. States without venture funds may offer special loan or tax incentives to encourage startups. Check with the Secretary of State's office in the state you're interested in to see what's available.

>> **European Commission SME Funding for Product Development.** This is a program to help small and medium size enterprises pass through the "valley of death" or product development process and enter the global market. They offer between 50,000 EUR and 2.5 million EUR equity free, and they're looking for disruptive innovations that will change an industry or market. See `https://ec.europa.eu/info/funding-tenders/how-apply/eligibility-who-can-get-funding/funding-opportunities-small-businesses_endevelopment/`.

>> **Money for minority-owned small businesses.** Minority grants are no easier to obtain, but they are worth a try if you qualify. One example is the Merchant Maverick Opportunity Grants, which in 2022 is targeting Asian and Pacific Islanders who are U.S. citizens and who own a restaurant or other foodservice business. The Maverick website has a listing of other grant opportunities focusing on various underrepresented groups. See `www.merchantmaverick.com/business-grants-minorities/`.

>> **Be sure to check out Grants.gov, which is a searchable database of every grant program across 26 agencies of the U.S. government.** Although many of the grants go to cities and nonprofits, there are others geared toward minority business enterprises (MBEs).

Going after investor capital

Finding private investors who are willing to take the risk of investing in the very early stages of product development is rare. Unless you've just discovered the next AI equivalent, they probably won't even talk to you until you have a working prototype. However, once you have a prototype that's reasonably close to being market ready, some private investor groups — the ones that have carved out a niche in the gap between your personal resources and large-scale private and venture capital — may be willing to provide you with seed capital if you can provide proof of concept, market, and business model and show that there is an outsized market for what you're offering.

I've sat in on sessions between investors and inventors enough times to know that too often the inventor has no understanding of what it takes to develop a product from the drawing board, the laboratory, or the garage to production quality — something that can be mass produced and that people will buy. Investors, like customers, need to see proof of the utility of your product. Look at Chapter 14 to find out more about sources of money for starting and growing your business. Keep in mind that the toughest time to raise capital is during product development, also known as "the valley of death," because it carries so much risk. If you can find a way to bring down that risk, investors may listen to you.

Crowdfunding

Getting potential customers to invest in product development as stakeholders is one popular use of crowdfunding sites such as Kickstarter, Indiegogo, and GoFundMe. They are best for funding in the five to six figure range. One advantage is that crowdfunding is a good way to test the market's interest in what you want to build. Another is that these early adopters are eager to be involved in design and development; and if you use their feedback to improve the product, they will have your back when you go to market and encounter naysayers. You will have developed a group of micro-influencers who will promote your product for you. And that saves you a lot of money.

Crowdfunding is not free, however (nothing really is). At Kickstarter, for example, they will take a percentage of the money you raise and then there is usually a payment processing fee applied to each individual pledge. Together, these amount to about 8-10 percent of what you raise. The best-funded startups on Kickstarter have been in the technology space, namely wearables. Another big category has been games, mostly card games.

WARNING

The biggest Kickstarter in the history of Kickstarter was Pebble Technology with its smartwatch. It had a goal of raising $500,000 but came away with over $20 million from 78,000 backers. Two years later Pebble was purchased by Fitbit for $23 million. Fitbit then promptly shut it down and laid off 60 percent of the employees. Pebble had used Kickstarter three times as it faced a highly competitive smartwatch market by 2017. It appears that Fitbit did not want the competition. The first mover is not often the winner when there are huge companies like Google, Apple, and Samsung waiting in the wings for you to prove demand. Then they swoop in with unlimited resources and take out the first mover.

All that being said, crowdfunding is still an excellent way to secure product development funding if you have a product that is easily understood and creates some excitement.

REMEMBER

If you're thinking the least bit about developing a new product, start saving your money and thinking about potential resources now. You will probably need money in stages, so it's always wise to plan ahead so you know where to go when the time comes. Later in this chapter, you find out ways to save money on product development and to get help from others so that you can go through the process more quickly.

Developing New Products: The Process

Product development is a process comprised of many tasks. It used to be that you could depict the product development process in a linear fashion that looked similar to Figure 7-1. Each task was completed before the next was started in a logical, orderly process.

FIGURE 7-1:
The traditional product development process.

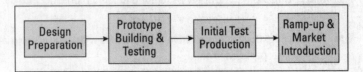

This process works fine in a marketplace that's stable and predictable, but it can't survive in today's dynamic and unpredictable markets. Today, companies focus on fast-cycle product development with a more integrated approach. What I mean by *integrated* is that all the company's functions are represented in the planning, design, and development processes. As a result, you derive input from engineering, manufacturing, marketing, finance, and the customer from the beginning and throughout the process. Dynamic product development looks more like Figure 7-2.

FIGURE 7-2:
Dynamic product development replaces the traditional, linear approach with total, simultaneous input from all company functions.

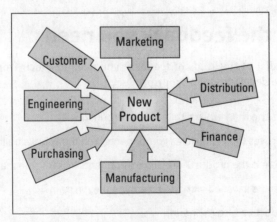

The advantage of getting everyone involved in the process from the beginning is that the ultimate product will reflect each participant's input individually and as a group and, therefore, be more complete. For example:

>> **Customer:** Provides valuable information about the product design and functionality so that the customers get what they need.

- >> **Engineering:** Uses comprehensive product information to design the product right the first time.

- >> **Finance:** Follows production costs and warns developers if they're choosing a component or part that will be too costly in the final product.

- >> **Manufacturing:** Makes sure that a viable process with the appropriate tooling for producing the product exists.

- >> **Marketing:** Adjusts strategy as needed to launch product into a receptive market.

- >> **Purchasing:** Establishes reliable relationships with vendors to make sure that they deliver parts on time.

Notice that I refer to these functions as if they're major departments in your company; they are not. You may outsource many of these functions or have only one person responsible for a particular function. Perhaps your area of expertise is engineering, and your partner's expertise lies in finance. You'll likely have to hire or partner with employees, companies, and other independent contractors to perform the remaining functions to complete your development project.

TIP

If you get everyone involved in the process, you can develop your product much faster — and that's important in a world where customers' preferences can change overnight. You need to be prepared to change as well.

Getting the feedback you need

Here's a checklist of the kinds of feedback you need to solicit from all the people involved in the development of your product:

- >> What does the marketplace think of the product?

- >> What improves the product, its components, and the way it's built?

- >> How reliable is the product? Are any components less reliable than others?

- >> Are customers satisfied with the prototype they've seen?

- >> Is the product easy to maintain?

- >> How will you service the product?

- >> How will you handle complaints?

- >> How will you get positive publicity for the product?

Answers to these questions are the basic information you need during the process of product development. You may think of more specific questions to ask about your product or service. The more, the better.

Overcoming scarce resources with a plan

Many solutions are available to help you overcome the limitations of a startup company's scarce resources. Here are a few of them:

» If you have several products in mind, prioritize and start with the one that will bring you the biggest return on investment the fastest. Alternatively, if one of the products is the easiest and least costly to develop and you can validate its market potential, you may want to start with that one, because it will use the fewest resources and quickly get an income stream going.

» Don't reinvent the wheel. Don't try to manufacture products that others already do very well. Focus your energies on what you do well and outsource everything else. Doing so is called focusing on your *core competencies.* Later, when your company is well established and you have more resources, you can think about bringing some outsourced tasks in-house to save money, control quality better, and speed up your processes.

Tasks that you may want to outsource include component design, materials specifications, machinery to produce, ergonomic design, packaging design, and assembly drawings.

» Wherever possible, purchase off-the-shelf parts and components. They are usually cheaper and more readily available.

» Look into *job shops,* which are small companies that make certain products for one customer at a time. They can do some of the work for you. Make sure that they will work as quickly as you need and that they're used to working with entrepreneurs and your type of product.

Developing in a digital world

Today you can collaborate online to create your product designs. Let's say you just designed a new part for your product. You can email that design to a rapid proto-typing shop, where the design enters a computerized CNC or 3D printer that spits out your part in metal or another medium you've chosen. This way you don't need to own the equipment that produces the parts, although because prices are falling on 3D printers, you'll soon want to have one in your place of business for the convenience.

If your outsourcing partners are online, coordinating work and receiving regular progress updates are a snap. If you want to really go all the way, you and your partners can install digital cameras so that you can view what they're doing for you.

Why consider the digital route to product development? Here are some of the many reasons:

» By outsourcing, you share the resources of other companies and spread the risk and expense of product development.

» When you link the core competencies of several companies, you get better product innovations because everyone is doing what they do best.

» By integrating the knowledge and skills of many companies, you can reduce your time to market.

» Your relationships with other companies give you access to new markets.

» It will be easier to sell solutions rather than products.

WARNING

Of course, I don't want to make it sound as if partnering in cyberspace has no disadvantages. The fact is that strategic alliances with other companies for product development are like any other partnerships: They can be fraught with problems if you don't choose your partners carefully. So, choose partners that believe in what you're doing and have similar company cultures and ways of doing business.

Moving Rapidly to the Prototype Stage

One critical component of success in product development today is the ability to advance quickly to the prototype stage. When you have a physical model, you can see product features that are sometimes difficult to see clearly in either a blueprint of a design or a computer-simulated model.

Ergonomics, the study of how equipment, furniture, and so on affect the human body in workplace situations, is a design feature that becomes more apparent in a physical prototype. When we first designed our PowerSource machine, the design engineer put the handles down low near the wheels. Not until the first prototype was built did we discover that this placement would never work, because even though the prototype handles provided greater leverage to lift the machine, you would hurt your back doing it. The design was not ergonomically correct, so we moved the handles to a better position. It was a problem not readily visible in the drawings. It had to be experienced.

REMEMBER

One thing you need to know about prototypes: They can cost up to ten times as much as the final product costs to produce, because you're not ordering parts in volume and you're paying your independent contractors a premium for building one or two units instead of 100 or more at a time.

TIP

While you're looking for parts for your prototype, ask manufacturers for samples. Usually, they will send a small sample for free, because often, in the case of a small part, it's more expensive for them to invoice you than it is just to send it. But if your supplier sees a huge market opportunity, you may be surprised at what they're willing to donate to your NPD effort.

Designing right the first time

The design of your new product represents an estimated 8 percent of your budget for product development, but it determines fully 80 percent of the final cost of the product and its subsequent price to the customer. That's an important figure! What it means to you is that if you can make your design right the first time, you'll save a lot of time and money. Redesign — which entails reengineering, new drawings, and a reworking of the prototype — ends up being more costly than the original design, not to mention the potential for a lost opportunity in the marketplace by not getting there quickly.

I can't go into all the technical elements of engineering design, but here are some key elements to ponder when you begin to design your product:

>> **Start with a clear product definition.** A good definition takes feedback from all the functions of your business (I discussed this in the section "Developing New Products: The Process," earlier in this chapter), especially from your customers. Changing the handlebars on our machine after the first prototype cost us a lot of time and money. Get as much feedback as possible as early as possible.

>> **Ask customers what they need, expect, and want.** What customers *need* are the features that they must have to be satisfied with the product. What customers *expect* are the standard features that would be basic to any product of this type. What they *want* are the special features that apply to their individual circumstances — their wish lists.

You definitely want to prioritize these items, because the cost of putting everything the customer wants into the product may be too high.

>> **Deploy quality function.** A lengthy discussion of Quality Function Deployment (QFD) aside, you may want to consider this method for letting the customer design the product by identifying critical customer preferences and requirements and incorporating them into the design. Software is available to walk you through the process, and some consultants specialize in facilitating QFD. Check this site for more information at www.productplan.com/glossary/quality-function-deployment/.

>> **Design for manufacturability.** Designing your product with the process of producing it in mind is wise. By doing so, you can significantly reduce manufacturing costs and increase productivity. If you plan to outsource the manufacture of your product, be sure to include that manufacturer in your design phase. Factors you're trying to achieve in designing for manufacturability include

- Minimizing the number of parts.

- Simplifying components and using common or standard off-the-shelf parts.

- Minimizing electrical wiring.

- Making parts independently replaceable so that it's less costly for customers to repair.

- Eliminating adjustments of manufacturing equipment.

- Eliminating fasteners to simplify assembly and reduce direct labor. It saves time.

- Eliminating jigs and fixtures (devices that hold parts of your product in place while it's being worked on so that each product produced is exactly the same) to reduce changeover costs.

>> **Design for quality.** If you wait to think about quality until you're manufacturing your product, you're too late. Inspecting for quality can raise production costs by as much as 50 percent. If you plan for a quality product and process during the design stage, you can engineer a reliable and stable manufacturing process, which will speed up the process and reduce the costs.

Sourcing your materials

One product development task that many entrepreneurs overlook in planning the timeframe for product development is the sourcing of materials and parts for their products. Materials and parts account for about 50 percent of total manufacturing cost, so you need to choose them carefully. Locating vendors to supply your material needs is not a difficult task — there are thousands of them — but finding the best vendors at the right price is the hard part. It took almost a year for my company to source all the components for our machine and arrive at 44 vendors that could give us high-quality parts and components at the best prices. If you don't factor that time and effort into your calculations for how quickly you can get your product to market, you could end up being way off in your timing.

Your first decision is whether to use more than one vendor to supply a single part. A big advantage to using a single vendor to supply as many of your needs as possible is that you'll probably get better service for buying parts in larger quantities and bigger discounts because you're buying more. The main disadvantage is that if something happens to that lone vendor — their warehouse burns down or they raise prices, for example — you won't have a backup that you can turn to quickly. Cover yourself by always having a backup. Perhaps you can purchase 80 percent of your parts from the main vendor and 20 percent from the backup.

Questions to ask yourself when looking for the best vendors include the following:

>> Can this vendor deliver what I need when I need it?

>> How much will freight cost using this vendor?

>> What services does this vendor provide?

>> Is the vendor familiar with the product lines I'm using?

>> What are the vendor's maintenance and return policies?

TIP

Go online to search for vendors. Several sites help you compare prices across many companies. And be sure to carefully compare prices. A simple bolt can range in price from a few pennies to more than a dollar!

Making your minimum viable product

You don't have to be a manufacturer to produce a product. In fact, setting up a manufacturing facility is a very expensive undertaking. More and more entrepreneurs are taking advantage of technology and strategic alliances to outsource manufacturing and save money. That way, they don't have to invest in a plant and equipment at a time when the product is unproven in the market and resources are limited.

Finding someone to manufacture your product is a task that you need to undertake at the same time you're beginning to design the product so that you can integrate product and process in the most effective way. Plenty of manufacturers can do what you need in the United States and throughout the world. When you did your industry analysis for feasibility, you probably discovered some of these manufacturers and learned whether products in your industry are typically manufactured domestically or in foreign countries. Knowing where competitors manufacture their products is important, because if they are manufacturing for a low cost in China and you choose to manufacture domestically at a higher cost, you must find a way to make up the difference so your price to the customer isn't out of line with the rest of the industry.

The one-minute product solution plan

A product plan doesn't have to be a long, drawn-out document with pages of information. However, it should answer the following questions:

>> What is my product?

>> Who will design the product?

>> Who will build the prototype?

>> Will the product require patents?

>> How will the product be produced?

>> Who will manufacture the product?

>> How much will it cost?

>> How long will product development take?

If you choose to outsource manufacturing overseas, keep in mind the following words of caution:

>> Never choose your outsourced partner based solely on price. The lowest price often comes with a lot of risk. When the first edition of this book was published in 2001, it was common to outsource to China to bring costs down and compete more effectively. Today, however, we have all seen the perils of a supply chain that's thousands of miles long.

>> It's important to keep your customers close to your product development, which is not easy to do when it's happening thousands of miles away in another country.

>> If you hold patents or other intellectual property that you must protect, it will be very difficult to do so in many countries where those rights are not respected and hard to enforce.

>> Your costs for managing a geographically dispersed team will go up. You also need to factor in shipping costs and supply chain problems.

Spending enough time on the frontend design of your product and determining how it will be produced will save you time and money — savings that can be passed along to your customers.

Chapter **8**

Protecting Your Products and Services

When entrepreneurs start businesses, they acquire or create assets, both tangible and intangible. They create new knowledge, which is an example of an intangible asset. Products and manufacturing equipment are examples of tangible assets. Whereas in the past, businesses owned more tangible assets than intangible, today the reverse is frequently the case.

Understanding Intellectual Property Rights

We generally identify three categories of knowledge as intangible assets. They are listed here from the weakest to the strongest:

» **Intellectual capital** is perhaps the most common form of knowledge as an asset because it arises from the regular daily activities in the business: employees chatting in the lunchroom or meeting informally to brainstorm an idea. The knowledge that arises from these activities is sometimes called *tacit knowledge,* which simply means that it is not codified or written down. It's the general knowhow one gets from working around other people, and it's extremely valuable.

» **Intellectual assets** consist of explicit knowledge that one documents in a physical manner such as in a manual or in computer files.

» **Intellectual property** is the most valuable form of asset, because it can be protected through legal means with recourse through the courts.

Intellectual property (IP) has become the ultimate asset for today's entrepreneurs. They protect those assets through patents, trademarks, copyrights, and trade secrets.

Intellectual property is a driving force for technology innovation, art, and culture. Many companies stockpile this IP in a way they've never done before. They know that patents and trademarks are like gold; they can be sold for huge amounts or licensed to other companies and individuals, providing new revenue streams. For example, movie production companies such as Disney earn billions of dollars licensing the rights to use their valuable trademarks such as Marvel, Mickey Mouse, Star Wars, and The Muppets, to name a few. Even very small companies are benefiting from this wave of enthusiasm for IP. In addition to creating revenue from licensing, a small company with an important patent can find itself being acquired for many times its earnings.

CASE STUDY

In June 2020, Google announced that it had acquired Looker, an analytics and business intelligence company, to become part of the Google Cloud. The price? An eye-popping $2.6 billion. But in 2018, the company had just received Series E funding to the tune of $103 million and was enjoying the benefits of growth as a SaaS (Software as a Service) company. When you deliver applications over the Internet instead of locally on machines, you reach a point where you focus on expanding the customer base rather than the products to increase your revenue. Looker's solid customer base was the gift that kept on giving. CEO Frank Bien believes that you can't have happy customers if you don't have happy employees, and he had happy employees. The acquisition by Google let Looker leverage the scale of the Google Cloud platform to reach new customers. For Google, it's a chance to outperform Amazon's AWS platform. It will be interesting to see how the two very different cultures of Google and Looker merge.

No matter how small the company, every company has IP rights in the form of trademarks on the name of the business or product, copyrights on advertising design, patents on its product, or trade secrets such as its customer list or business plan. In this chapter, you learn how to navigate the challenging but exciting waters of intellectual property.

As important as it is, intellectual property does have a downside, especially when it comes to knowledge assets. If your company owns a physical asset like a building, you can be fairly comfortable that no one is going to steal it. By contrast, you can't be certain that no one is going to steal your software code. Similarly, you can usually get at least some return on your investment with a hard asset like a building. But preserving the value of your knowledge assets is a totally different story. That's what I talk about in this chapter — strategies for protecting your brilliant entrepreneurial inventions, from the better mousetrap (at last!) to the perfect company logo.

Protecting Your Better Mousetrap with a Patent

What exactly is a patent? A patent grants an inventor a property right — the right to *exclude others* from making, using, offering for sale, or selling the invention in the United States or importing it into the United States — for 20 years from the date on which the application for the patent was filed in the United States. A patent does *not* grant a right to make, use, sell, or import, and that is an important distinction. You gain the right to prevent others from making, using, or selling your patented product. Consequently, once you have a patent, you must enforce it without the help of the USPTO (U.S. Patent and Trademark Office). That means if someone infringes your patent, you need to bring a lawsuit and prove that you have the patent and have paid the required maintenance fees during the time you've held it. At the end of the 20-year period, the patent goes into public domain, and anyone may produce and sell it. Patent grants are only good within the United States, U.S. territories, and U.S. possessions.

Today, patents are enjoying a tremendous resurgence of interest. Everyone, it seems, is trying to patent something. One woman tried to patent her own genes. (She didn't succeed because you can't patent things that naturally occur.) Even the U.S. Patent and Trademark Office (PTO) has gone patent crazy, issuing to itself Patent 5,885,098 for a "spiral patent office," which is the new patent office that looks something like New York's Guggenheim Museum.

Do you have any idea which invention receives more patent applications than any other? Why, it's that better mousetrap, of course. The first patent for a mousetrap was issued in 1903. Even today, the PTO receives at least 40 applications a year for patents on the mousetrap; but of the 4,400 patents issued, only the original inventor has made a profit off a mousetrap patent.

Being able to patent your product, an aspect of your product, your process, or your business model (how you make money) gives you a distinct competitive advantage for a time because it theoretically creates a clear field for you to introduce your product and establish your brand before others can copy what you did. As the rest of the chapter explains, however, what is theoretically true and lawful isn't always what happens in practice.

Timing is everything

Many inventors and entrepreneurs wait until they're ready to file for a patent to document and protect their inventions. That's a big mistake. From the first day you conceive an invention, it is vital that you date, sign, and state the purpose of any documents related to that invention. Having your signature witnessed also adds strength to your claim. Keeping any records that can assist in proving your first-to-invent claim in a safe place is a good idea. In fact, I recommend (as does the PTO) keeping your records in a bound document.

Avoid leaving blanks in your descriptions, and try to avoid erasures and line-out mistakes. If you're working on a computer, make sure that everything you do is date-stamped by the computer and shows the progression of your work. You may also want to print out a hard copy, sign it, date it, and have it witnessed, because you can change dates on computer-generated documents, and they would be difficult to use as evidence to prove your first-to-invent status.

Why is it so important to start documenting your invention before you've even decided to apply for a patent? The reason is something called "prior art." You can't get a patent if someone has invented what you invented and can prove that their invention predates yours. Only an inventor or a person the inventor has assigned the invention may apply for a patent. Your investors, if they have only provided funding, cannot be listed on the patent.

America Invents Act

In 2012, Congress enacted the America Invents Act (AIA), which represented the most sweeping changes in patent law in 40 years. The purpose was to bring the United States into harmony with the practices and procedures of most other countries. One of the biggest changes was the move from a "first to invent" system to a "first to file" system. Under the old system, you were granted a patent if you could prove that you were the first to invent a novel concept and reduce it to practice by demonstrating a fully functional embodiment (prototype) of the idea. Anyone who filed after you for the same invention would not receive a patent.

Under the AIA, inventors are pressed to file quickly since their status as first to invent no longer matters with one exception. Suppose Inventor A invents a novel widget and publishes the invention (makes it publicly known), but delays filing. Inventor B invents the same widget and files for a patent immediately. If Inventor A files within a year of publishing the invention, they may still be able to obtain patent rights over the first filer if Inventor A can prove they were first to invent. However, if Inventor B can prove an invention date prior to that disclosed by Inventor A, then Inventor B's widget becomes prior art for Inventor A's widget and Inventor B may be granted the patent.

The AIA also introduced a new post-grant review where a non-patent owner can file within 9 months after a patent grant a petition to cause the review of a granted patent based on at least one claim that is being challenged. Never before has the public been allowed to challenge patent grants. So an entrepreneur who has been granted a patent must be prepared for a challenge within nine months. So far, it appears that most challenges to patents are for non-obviousness (it was not unique in any of its claims), and the Patent Trial and Appeal Board (PTAB) has found for the petitioner in about 60 percent of those cases. What this illustrates is that patent protection is more easily defended when the uniqueness of the product is clearly articulated in the application in addition to proof that the claims are not the next obvious step that is well known by practitioners in the field of practice being claimed.

Is it patentable?

Your invention must meet several strict criteria before the PTO will consider it for a patent.

>> **Inventions require classification.** An invention must fall into one of five classes:

- Process type or method (industrial or technical)

- Machine

- Articles of manufacture

- Composition of matter (chemical compositions and new compounds)

- New and useful improvement of any of the preceding four classifications

Combined, these classes include almost everything made by humans and the processes to make those things. You cannot patent laws of nature, physical phenomena, or abstract ideas.

>> **The invention must be new and not contain prior art.** You cannot patent your invention if it was known or used by others, or patented, or described in a printed publication anywhere in the world before you invented it or more than one year before you applied for a patent. So, the bottom line is that if you're going to talk about or use your invention in public, filing for a patent immediately helps you avoid the risk of not being able to file at all.

>> **The invention must not be obvious.** An invention must be sufficiently different from what has been used by (or described to) someone having ordinary skills in the area of technology related to the invention. For example, you can't patent an invention that merely substitutes one material for another or makes meaningless changes in dimensions.

>> **The invention must have utility.** This means that your invention must be useful. It can't be whimsical.

Types of patents

In general, the patent office grants three types of patents: utility, design, and plant. Utility patents are the more common type and offer more protection than the other types. They protect the functional parts of machines or processes in addition to software that drives machines. Some examples are toys, film processing, protective coatings, tools, and cleaning implements. A utility patent is valid for 20 years from the date of application.

Design patents cover ornamental designs for an article of manufacture and protect only the appearance of an article, not its structural or functional features. The design patent is valid for 14 years from grant and, unlike a utility patent, requires no fees to maintain. It is, however, more difficult to defend because it's fairly easy to modify a design so that it becomes a new design.

The U.S. Patent Office also recognizes plant patents, which are granted to anyone who has invented or discovered and asexually reproduced a distinct and new variety of plant. The patent is granted for the entire plant for up to 25 years.

With the huge increase in technology businesses, especially Internet-based businesses, the USPTO began to recognize business methods in a special subject matter area called *Technology Center 3600*. It grants patents on data processing, business practice, management and cost/price determination processes. When two Internet companies unveiled their patents in August 1998, shock waves went through the business world. It wasn't the mere fact that they had the patents as much as it was the nature of those patents. Priceline.com and Cyber Gold Inc. hadn't patented technology or products; they had patented their business models. In essence, Priceline and Cyber Gold said that they had invented new ways of doing business, and that if anyone wanted to use them, their companies had to receive a royalty. Priceline claims that it created the first reverse auction for airline tickets. Cyber Gold Inc. developed a system that automatically paid consumers to look at advertising.

Business method patents are essentially utility patents on a business process. However, your business method can't simply take a well-known business process and put it on a computer or the Internet. According to current case law, it must offer significantly more than that and be associated with underlying technology, hardware, or equipment, although the underlying technology is not eligible for a patent. Since most business methods patents are for software, you need to describe in detail what your software does that is of value and provides a useful, concrete, and tangible result. Essentially, the business model patent covers the interaction of a method or way of doing business with a technology. The combination of the two should produce a unique result.

The patent process

The patent process is well defined on the USPTO website at www.uspto.gov/patents/basics/patent-process-overview#step1, so following it on your own is an option. In fact, plenty of books show you how to patent your own invention, including *Patents, Copyrights & Trademarks For Dummies*. But I don't recommend that you tackle this on your own. The examiners and attorneys at the PTO speak a language that only a patent attorney can decipher. When you consider that the issuance of a patent depends on how well you state your claims in the patent application, hiring a good patent attorney to help you through the process is worth your time and money.

TIP

Patent attorneys are specialists, so don't hire your basic business attorney to file your patent application. Furthermore, if you intend to file for foreign patents, know that requirements vary from country to country, and typically, only a specialist in patent law is able to successfully wade through the morass.

Your first order of business is to make sure that you have invented something novel. Generally, you want to do a patent search on the claims you're making for the uniqueness of your invention. You are searching for prior art, anything that matches the claims in the patent application you intend to submit. You can do an initial search on Google patents or the USPTO site to see if anything pops up. Don't forget to look for foreign patents as well. The USPTO has a Seven-Step Strategy and an online tutorial for doing a search, which is found through the link at the beginning of this section. It's definitely worth a read.

If you want to increase your chances of not missing something, you can hire a professional to do the search, but it will be expensive and gives you no guarantee that all prior art was found. Your patent examiner will also conduct research. The examiner is typically an expert in a certain field of practice, so they pretty much know what's happening in that field. Keep in mind that you will have to disclose any prior art you've found when you file your patent application.

Once you file your application (a provisional application for patent — PPA or non-provisional) and pay your fees, it's now a waiting game. If the PTO finds deficiencies in your application, they will give you some time to correct them and, of course, charge you a surcharge. Only when your application is compliant and complete will it be assigned to an examiner. It is not uncommon for the patent claims to be rejected in their entirety the first time they're submitted. You can appeal the PTO's decisions, but if your application is rejected twice, you will need to appeal to the Patent Trial and Appeal Board. If you are represented by an attorney, it will be your attorney who communicates with the PTAB. You, as the inventor, cannot speak directly to the PTAB.

You can expect it to take up to two years or more from the patent application filing date to the date of final disposition, for a patent to be issued or abandoned. The USPTO does have an accelerated examination process, which is difficult to qualify for. It is based on applicant's health or age or the application falls under a special category related to environmental quality, energy, HIV/AIDS and cancer, countering terrorism, and biotechnology applications filed by small entities. You can find more information about this program at www.uspto.gov/patents/initiatives/accelerated-examination.

The provisional patent application

Beginning in 1995, the PTO began offering the option of filing a *provisional application for patent (PPA)*. This kind of patent application protects small inventions whose inventors need more time to talk with manufacturers about building a working prototype. The PPA is less costly and much easier to file than a regular patent. It also establishes an early effective filing date in a patent application and lets you use the term *Patent Pending* on the invention in your disclosures. The date on which the PTO receives your written description of the invention, drawings, and your name determines the filing date.

The advantage to a PPA (beyond the ease of filing and lower cost) is that it gives you an additional year on the term of your patent. The PPA is abandoned by law 12 months after the filing date, so you must file an application for a nonprovisional patent within that time. Be aware that you can't file a PPA on a design invention. You should also note that for a PPA to serve as the official filing date for first-to-file purposes, your application and description of the invention should be complete so that the subsequent nonprovisional filing does not deviate significantly from the description in the PPA.

Filing a provisional patent application

As discussed in the previous section, filing a PPA with the PTO establishes a date of invention that becomes part of your patent record in case your invention receives a challenge later.

WARNING

Don't rely on the old advice about mailing a dated description of the invention to yourself by certified mail. That tactic has no value to the PTO. You *must* follow their rules.

Many attorneys today advise inventors to file a PPA as soon as possible. The PPA requires an elaborate description of your invention such that someone could replicate what you've done by reading the patent. Filing the PPA allows you to use the words *Patent Pending* or *Patent Applied For,* which gives notice to others that you can exclude them from making or selling an invention like yours.

The cost for filing a PPA depends on the size of your business. A small business pays $160 while a normal sized business pays $320. You can add $400 to each of those if you file by paper rather than electronically. Remember that you have to file your nonprovisional patent application within 12 months of filing the PPA or you'll lose the early filing date on the PPA.

The advantage of filing a PPA first and then a nonprovisional application 12 months later is that you effectively extend the patent term endpoint by as much as 12 months. By contrast, if you file a PPA and then request a conversion from the PPA to a nonprovisional application, your term for the patent begins on the date of the PPA conversion filing.

WARNING

If you disclose your invention through publication, public use, or offer for sale more than one year before you file the PPA, you lose your right to patent in the United States. Furthermore, disclosing publicly before filing may preclude your filing in many foreign countries that don't give a one-year grace period. It is important to learn the requirements of the countries in which you plan to do business.

CASE STUDY

How does a high school student from Harlem end up in the National Inventors Hall of Fame, co-founder of the American Institute for the Prevention of Blindness, an ophthalmologist, and a leader in the African American community? For one thing, her parents taught her that education was the path out of poverty. Living in segregated Harlem, Patricia Bath was surrounded by people who worked simple jobs as well as people who were doctors, lawyers, and accountants who served as her role models. At the age of 16, Bath was doing well in her STEM classes, was nominated by one of her teachers and won a National Science Foundation grant to attend the Summer Institute in Biomedical Science at Yeshiva University. Upon completing high school, she attended Hunter College in New York

City and then Howard University's College of Medicine in Washington D.C. By then it was the 1960s, a time of social unrest. Feeling called to serve the underserved, she volunteered her medical services to a poor people's protest encampment on the National Mall. After graduating medical school, she returned to New York for her internship at Harlem Hospital. It was here that she became aware of the large number of blind or visually impaired patients, most of whom were African Americans. She decided to learn more about this anomaly. Her research led to co-founding the American Institute for the Prevention of Blindness in 1976 to provide health information and preventable care to the community she knew so well. Along her journey, Bath faced many challenges and barriers, but her superpowers were persistence and a need to get the job done. While on the faculty of UCLA's School of Medicine's Jules Stein Eye Institute, she caught the attention of Dr. Daniele Aron-Rosa, an ophthalmologist and pioneer in the use of lasers. Dr Aron-Rosa invited Bath to work in her lab in Paris while she was on sabbatical in 1978. This was Bath's chance to devote herself to research into laser cataract surgery. Her work paid off. In 1981, she developed the Laserphaco Probe that enabled lasers to be used in a less invasive and less painful way to remove cataracts. In 1988, she was awarded U.S. Patent No. 4,744,360 for "an apparatus for ablating and removing cataract lenses." She was the first African American woman to receive a patent for a medical device. Today her device and method are used throughout the world. She claimed that her best life moment was in North Africa where she restored the sight of a woman who had been blind for more than 30 years.

Filing a nonprovisional patent application

The nonprovisional patent application has very specific requirements about what to submit. These requirements are as follows:

>> A specification that includes a description and a claim or claims regarding the invention. (A claim is what you consider unique.)

>> Drawings, if necessary.

>> An oath or declaration.

>> The prescribed filing, search, and examination fees.

The specification must contain a complete description of the invention, what it does, and how it uniquely differs from anything currently or previously existing. The application requires you to furnish a drawing of the invention that must show every feature that you specify in your claims — unless your invention deals with compositions of matter or some processes.

In the claims section of the application, you describe in detail (specific enough to demonstrate the invention's uniqueness, but broad enough to make it difficult for others to circumvent the patent) the parts of the invention on which you want patents. This is perhaps the most important section, and you'll want a good IP attorney to write it.

After receiving the application, the PTO conducts a search of its patent records for prior art, which can take about 15 months to respond with a first office action. During that time, the public does not have access to your application, so your invention secrets are protected.

The PTO contacts you when it completes the records search, stating whether it accepts all the claims, accepts only some of the claims, or denies the application completely. You can appeal a denial.

REMEMBER

Most inventions receive a denial of at least one claim on the first round. You may then rewrite that claim, addressing the issues raised by the PTO before resubmitting it.

While the PTO is processing your patent application, you may display *Patent Pending* or *Patent Applied For* on your invention, but understand that these phrases have no legal effect. They simply give notice that you have filed for a patent. Full patent protection doesn't begin until the PTO examiner accepts all the claims and issues a patent.

As a side note, patent examiners specialize in certain categories of inventions, so they're usually familiar with the prior art in their areas of expertise. For example, I met a patent examiner whose specialty was inventions related to hydraulics, and that's all this examiner did.

If your patent application is rejected, even after modifications, you can appeal to a board of patent appeals within the PTO. If your appeal doesn't succeed before the board, you can appeal to the U.S. Court of Appeals for the Federal Circuit. Of course, the appeals process can take years, and by then, you may have lost the window of opportunity to commercialize your invention. Failing to obtain a patent doesn't mean that your product doesn't have market potential; it means that intellectual property will not be one of your competitive advantages.

Once your patent is issued, you must mark your product with the word *Patent* and the number of the patent. If you fail to do so, you may not be able to recover damages from an infringer. On the other hand, if you mark a product as patented or patent pending when it isn't, you have broken the law and are subject to penalties.

REMEMBER

Be aware that once your patent is issued, it becomes a powerful document that you must protect against infringers. If you allow people to infringe your patent, you can lose it. I discuss infringement of intellectual property rights later in this chapter.

Protecting your rights in foreign countries

If you're planning to export your product and want patent protection outside the United States, you need to file applications in each of the countries in which you plan to do business. Your U.S. patent is not valid outside the United States. Patent laws in other countries differ in many respects from U.S. laws. For example, if you publicly discuss your invention prior to filing a patent application, even in the United States, you may be barred from filing for a patent in a foreign country. In addition, most countries require that the product be manufactured in that country after three years.

Under the Patent Cooperation Treaty (PCT), signed by 191 countries, if you file an international application within 12 months of when you first filed for a patent in the United States or another country, that date becomes your earliest filing date for purposes of prior art. You also enjoy first right to file in any of the other member countries. Check with a patent attorney who's experienced in international agreements when you are first considering patenting your invention and keep in mind that because every country in the PCT has different laws and fees, an attorney experienced in international patents is essential.

Patents aren't the only assets you will want to protect. The chapter turns now to some of the more common IP protections you will want to seek.

Copyrighting Your Original Work of Authorship

Copyrights protect original works of authors, composers, screenwriters, and computer programmers, published and unpublished. In general, a copyright does not protect the idea itself but only the tangible form in which it appears. This is a critical point. For example, if you compose a piece of music but don't put it down on paper or record it on some tangible medium like a computer hard drive, it isn't protected because it's essentially just in your mind.

The Copyright Act gives the owner of copyrighted material the exclusive right to reproduce, prepare derivative works, distribute copies of the work, or perform or display the work publicly. Copyrights are registered by the Copyright Office of the Library of Congress. Effective January 1, 1978, a copyright lasts for the life of the holder plus 70 years, after which it goes into public domain. If the material was co-authored, the term is 70 years after the death of the last author. Works made for hire or anonymous works are protected for 95 years from publication or 120 years from creation, whichever is shorter.

Claiming copyright

To protect your original works of authorship, the work must be in a fixed and tangible form and contain a copyright notice (although the latter is not required by law) so that a potential violator cannot claim innocence because there was no notice. Your notice should contain the word *copyright* or the symbol © and provide the year of the copyright along with the complete name of the copyright holder, as in "© 2023 John Doe."

You are not required to register with the Copyright Office to obtain full protection under the law, but doing so is a good idea. To do so, you need to submit an application, the required fee, and a complete copy of an unpublished work or two complete copies of a published work. Although not required, there are some clear advantages to registering your copyright:

>> It establishes a public record of your copyright.

>> Before you can file an infringement suit, the copyright must be registered.

>> If you register before or within five years of publication, your registration will establish evidence in court of the validity of the copyright and of the facts you've presented in the certificate.

>> If you register within three months after publication of your work or prior to an infringement of your work, you will be able to claim statutory damages and attorney's fees in court.

Things you can't copyright

According to the Copyright Office of the Library of Congress, www.copyright.gov, the following items cannot be copyrighted:

>> Works that have *not* been fixed in a tangible form of expression (for example, choreographic works that have not been notated or recorded, or improvisational speeches or performances that have not been written or recorded)

>> Titles, names, short phrases, and slogans; familiar symbols or designs; mere variations of typographic ornamentation, lettering, or coloring; or mere listings of ingredients or contents

>> Ideas, procedures, methods, systems, processes, concepts, principles, discoveries, or devices, as distinguished from a description, explanation, or illustration

>> Works consisting *entirely* of information that is common property and containing no original authorship (for example, standard calendars, height and weight charts, tape measures and rulers, and lists or tables taken from public documents)

The courts have not comfortably settled the scope of copyrights for software. Originally, copyright protection extended to the "structure, sequence and organization" of a software program — in other words, its look and feel. But in cases stemming back to 1992, the courts allowed people to copy program flow, intermodular relationships, parameter lists, macros, and lists of services. In fact, in one case it was held that you could copy a complete program if doing so was the only way to get at the unprotected ideas inside the program.

Well, that opened up a can of worms, and by 1997, the courts were effectively reversing some of their earlier rulings. In April 1999, the courts said that Connectix Corp. had infringed on the copyright of Sony Computer Entertainment Inc. when it copied the PlayStation software code to extract the unprotectable content, which is another example of the importance of registering your copyright *before* an infringement occurs.

Protecting Your Logo with a Trademark

A *trademark* is a symbol, word, or design used to identify a business or a product. For example, Apple Computer uses a picture of an apple with a bite out it followed by the symbol ®, which means *registered trademark.* You may have also seen the term *service mark.* This term identifies the source of a service rather than a product. Throughout the chapter, I use the term *trademark,* but the discussion applies equally to service marks.

As examples of possible categories of trademarks, some famous slogans like "got milk" or "where's the beef" have trademarks. In some cases, a company such as Coca Cola has trademarked the shape of their bottle. Just remember that your slogan has to be available — that is, not trademarked by another company — and it must also be used in connection with the sale of goods, products, or services.

Owning a trademark gives you the right to prevent others from using a confusingly similar mark; however, you do not have the right to prevent others from making or selling the same goods and services under a different mark. Only a patent can provide that level of protection.

You can claim trademark rights after using the mark or filing the proper application to register the mark with the PTO. The application states that you intend to use the mark in commerce. Like copyrights, you don't have to register to establish your rights or begin using a mark, but federal registration provides benefits beyond those of merely using the mark. A federal registration entitles you to use the mark nationwide and presumes that you are the owner.

You can apply for federal registration by

>> Filing a use application if you began using a mark in commerce beforehand.

>> Filing an intent-to-use application if you haven't used the mark in commerce, entitling you to put TM after the name you are trademarking until you register the mark.

Two rights are associated with trademarks — the right to register and the right to use. In general, if you are first to use a mark in commerce, or you file an application with the PTO, then you have the right to register the mark. The right to use a particular mark is more complex. If two people use the same mark in commerce and neither has registered it, only the courts can decide which party has the right to use the mark.

CASE STUDY

THE SPECIAL CASE OF DOMAIN NAMES

Since about 1995, the United States Patent and Trademark Office (PTO) has received an increasing number of applications for marks composed of domain names — the letters and numbers identifying computers on the Internet — mainly from computer services and Internet content providers. When you apply to register your domain name as a trademark or service mark, you are subject to the same requirements as any trademark applicant.

When you apply to trademark a domain name, neither the URL nor the TLD is included, because both are universal to all domain names. You can register a domain name only if it functions as a "source indicator;" that is, it doesn't serve merely as an address to access a website, but actually identifies the services provided or the product being sold, like wine.com or booksforkids.com.

The game company, Hasbro Games, was glad it trademarked its famous game Candyland. They eventually discovered someone using that trademark for a domain name candyland.com, which happened to be an adult entertainment site, not exactly the image they were going for. Hasbro won on the basis of trademark dilution because the domain name confused and offended Hasbro's customers.

Trademark rights can last indefinitely if you continue to use the mark and pay the fees, but the actual term is ten years. You can renew the registration as many times as you like if you continue using it. In the application, you are asked to identify the goods or services for which you will use the trademark. In your maintenance document, you evaluate the usage of the trademark and delete any use you no longer need. You must file accurate maintenance documents or risk jeopardizing your registration. You are expected to show evidence of trademark use in the specific categories on your registration. Note that you pay fees for every category you claim on your registration, so it's important to think carefully about where and how you will use the trademark. The USPTO does not mess around. If you don't pay your regular maintenance fees on time, you will lose your registration. On the USPTO site, you'll find the required filings for each year you must file. For example, between the fifth and sixth years after your registration date, you need to file a Declaration of Use and/or Excusable Nonuse under Section 8.

Like other intellectual property, federal registration protections apply only in the United States and its territories. Protecting your mark outside the United States means registering it in all the countries in which you want protection and following their rules.

Protecting Your Trade Secrets

Trade secrets generally include sensitive company information that can't be covered by patents, trademarks, and copyrights. Trade secrets include recipes, ingredients, source codes for computer chips, customer discounts, manufacturer costs, business plans, software algorithms, and so forth. They are generally information that gives your company a competitive advantage. The only method of protecting trade secrets is through contracts and nondisclosure agreements that specifically detail the trade secret to be protected. No other legal form of protection exists under the Uniform Trade Secrets Act.

Some familiar examples of trade secrets include the Google search algorithm, McDonald's Big Mac special sauce, and WD-40, the well-known lubricant and corrosion prevention formula. In fact, the WD-40 formula is stored in a bank vault and the product is mixed in three different cities to guard against reverse engineering. Many companies choose to not patent their secret processes, but rather hold them as trade secrets. Recall that when a patent is issued, anyone can look it up and determine how it was made.

To protect your trade secrets and maintain them in the event of a case of infringement, you must take reasonable steps to prevent them from being revealed. That means you must ensure that you and your employees are careful about conversations in elevators, airports, and restaurants. If you disclose a trade secret in these situations and it is overheard by someone, you could lose your trade secret rights.

Contracts

A *contract* simply is an offer or a promise to do something or refrain from doing something in exchange for consideration, which is the promise to supply or give up something in return. For example, you are asking your employees to not reveal your company's trade secrets in exchange for having a job there (and not getting sued if they do reveal them).

In addition to using contracts with employees and others who have access to your trade secrets, make sure that no one has all the components of your trade secret. For example, suppose you develop a new barbecue sauce that you intend to brand and market to specialty shops. If you're producing the sauce at scale, you obviously can't do all the work yourself, so you hire others to help. To avoid letting them know how to reproduce your complete, unique barbecue sauce, you can do three things:

>> Execute a contract with them binding them to not disclose what they know about your recipe.

>> Provide them with premixed herbs and spices so they don't know exactly what's in the recipe and in what quantities.

>> Give each person a different portion of the sauce to prepare.

Protecting trade secrets isn't easy. You may not realize it, but your feasibility study and business plan are trade secrets. The forms in which you present them are copyrightable, but the actual ideas are not, so they are trade secrets.

Nondisclosure agreements

Many entrepreneurs try protecting their ideas through a *nondisclosure agreement (NDA)*. An NDA is a document that announces the confidentiality of the material being shared with someone and specifies that the person or persons cannot disclose anything identified by the NDA to other parties or personally use the information for any purpose. Providing an NDA to anyone you are speaking to in confidence about your invention, business plan, or any trade secret is a good idea. Without it, you have no evidence that you provided your proprietary information in confidence; therefore, the PTO will consider it a public disclosure; that is, no longer confidential.

You definitely want to work with an attorney when you construct your NDA, because it must fit your situation. Generic NDAs do not exist. If you want an NDA to be valid for evidentiary purposes, it must include:

» Consideration, or what is being given in exchange for signing the document and refraining from revealing the confidentiality

» A description of what is being covered (be sure this is not too vague or broad)

» A procedure describing how the other party can use or not use the confidential information

What persons should you have sign an NDA? Anyone who will become privy to your trade secret.

» **Immediate family.** Spouses, children, and parents do not usually require NDAs, but it wouldn't be a bad idea to have them sign one anyway so they understand the importance of not disclosing this information.

» **Extended family and friends who will not be doing business with you.** To meet the consideration requirement for the NDA, you typically offer $1 in compensation.

» **Business associates or companies with which you might do business.** Consideration in this case is the opportunity to do business with you. For example, if you show your business plan to a manufacturer who might produce your product for you, the consideration is the potential of producing the product and receiving associated compensation.

» **Buyers.** Buyers typically don't sign nondisclosures because doing so may preclude them from developing something similar, or they may already be working on a similar concept. For example, toy manufacturer Mattel Inc. will not sign NDAs from inventors because they have a large R&D department that continually works on new ideas for toys. Chances are they're working on something that will be similar enough to potentially infringe on an inventor's product.

» **Investors**. Investors frequently avoid signing NDAs because they are privy to so many startup business plans that they might inadvertently put themselves in legal jeopardy.

The truth is, an NDA is only as good (and reliable) as the person who signs it. Fighting a violation of an NDA in the courts is difficult and expensive; so you must be cautious about the people you talk with. If someone does misappropriate your trade secret, you can bring a lawsuit in civil court and potentially be entitled to several remedies as listed here:

>> **Injunctive relief**. This is simply the court ordering the defendant to stop violating your trade secrets.

>> **Damages**. If you can prove economic harm, the court may order that the defendant pay damages. If those damages were willful or intentional, you may also receive punitive damages, which are typically more than actual damages.

>> **Attorney's fees**. If the defendant acted maliciously, the court may order that the defendant pay your attorney fees. However, if the court finds that you, the plaintiff, acted in bad faith by filing the lawsuit, you may be ordered to pay the defendant's attorney fees.

WARNING

Going to court is never a complete win for either side. It's expensive, time consuming, and may put reputations at risk. The best strategy is to place all protections possible on your trade secrets, so it's too difficult for a potential infringer to attempt to misappropriate them.

Strategies for Protecting Your IP

As of 2018, patent-licensing revenues to U.S. companies that performed or funded R&D exceeded $54 billion. The top companies with the largest market share in IP licensing include Walt Disney Co, Warner Media, LLC, McDonald's Corporation, and Marriott International. No wonder so many entrepreneurs are looking for ways to exploit their intellectual property to get a competitive advantage!

This new way of thinking about IP differs from the past, when companies managed their IP by defending their rights from infringement and making sure they kept up the maintenance fees so they wouldn't lose their patents. They didn't really think about how to leverage their IP to create revenue streams. By the mid-1990s, however, we saw investments in intangible assets such as computer software and brand development overtake investments in tangible assets. In 2019, IP-intensive industries generated 41 percent of U.S. GDP and accounted for 33 percent of all employment. Many acquisitions and mergers can trace their origin to acquiring critical intellectual property. Today, defense contractors license technology to toy manufacturers, and NASA technology has wound up in multiple consumer products. The potential is limitless. In this section, you discover why you should consider intellectual property an asset to promote and defend.

Offensive strategies

One of the more important offensive strategies that you can tap is licensing your intellectual property to other companies or in-licensing from other companies intellectual property that your company needs to fulfill its strategies. A *license* is a contract between parties that permits the use of IP in exchange for money or other consideration. Sounds like a contract, doesn't it? It is essentially the link between an inventor and a revenue stream from the commercialization of the technology. I'll consider licensing from two perspectives: acquiring and marketing IP licenses.

IP acquisition

You may have several reasons for acquiring the IP that someone else owns.

>> **You need their IP to enter a market that you wouldn't be able to enter otherwise.** For example, you want to create a business of memorabilia based on blockbuster films. You need to license the rights to use the brands and characters of those films before you can do business.

>> **Your technology needs exceed your resources.** Why reinvent the wheel? If someone else owns a technology that you need to carry out your business concept, try licensing it. Doing so is a lot less expensive than trying to invent around it.

>> **You need another company's technology to supplement your own.** Patent pooling is becoming a major thrust today in high-technology industries where you can't do what you want to do without inadvertently trampling on someone else's rights. For example, when PCs use audio and video signals beyond conventional text and graphics, companies will find themselves stepping on technologies originally invented in the electronics industry. Many industries, especially in the new media area, are finding that they may have to resort to patent pooling to untangle the web of IP.

When you acquire IP from someone else, it's similar to buying a house. You definitely need to check on the licensor's ability to transfer the IP; in other words, do they own it? Does the licensor have experience with licensing IP, and what is their overall track record in licensing IP? You may want to consider talking with other licensees to see how their relationships with the licensor went. If you're the first licensee for this IP, you ought to be able to get some concessions to compensate for added risk. Critical questions you want to address include the following:

>> Does the IP meet your needs?

>> Does the IP work as claimed?

>> Is the IP owned completely by the licensor? (You want to make sure this won't be a sublicense — the licensor has licensed it from yet another party.)

>> How much of an upfront fee and royalty will you have to pay?

>> What will the estimated manufacturing costs be?

>> How critical is time to market? Will the licensing process cause any delays?

>> Are there any performance guarantees?

Licensing your own IP

When you're planning to license your own intellectual property, consider how you're going to market it so that companies know it's available. Here are some actions you want to take:

>> Begin by documenting exactly what you're licensing so that the licensee has no misconceptions about what is included.

>> Decide how to value your IP. How much money is it worth for you to license it? Look for a professional who has experience valuing license agreements, so you don't lose any money in the process.

>> Who is more likely to license your IP and why? This is the "Who is your customer?" question.

>> What is your liability? If your product doesn't perform as predicted, what are you liable for?

Always conduct extensive background checks on any potential licensees, including credit checks, security clearances, and ability to perform.

REMEMBER

Your licensee represents your company indirectly by using your IP. Make sure to choose wisely; a poor choice will come back to bite you.

The license agreement

The license agreement (much like a partnership agreement) is an essential part of any licensing arrangement. In general, a license agreement spells out the terms under which the agreement will be executed — the duties and responsibilities of the parties involved. Here are some of the components of a good license agreement:

>> **Grant clause:** This clause states what specifically is being delivered and discusses issues of immunity, exclusivity, and the right to sublicense.

>> **Support services:** Definitions of what, if any, support services will be provided by either party should be included. Your licensee may need the help of one of your engineers or programmers to fill in missing information on your technology — this is tacit knowledge that can only be protected by contract.

>> **Confidentiality clause:** This clause defines the term for secrecy, the period during which royalties will be paid, any restrictions and permissions, how the agreement might be terminated, and issues related to the transfer of information to foreign governments.

>> **Payments and fees:** You have several choices for how to get paid for your license. You can receive a lump sum up front based on the usable life of the IP, or, preferably, you receive an upfront payment and a royalty as a percentage of sales. Royalties are better because judging the life of IP and estimating sales several years down the road are difficult, if not almost impossible. Other forms of payment include equity, which is usually tied to an initial public offering (IPO), cross-licensing, and most favorable licensee.

>> **Grant-forward and grant-back clauses:** A grant-forward clause provides that any improvements you make on your IP are automatically provided to your licensee. Likewise, any improvements your licensee makes are also available to you in a grant-back clause.

TIP

Many other issues are dealt with in the license agreement. You definitely want to consult an IP attorney with experience in licensing agreements, because putting such an agreement together is not something you should do on your own.

Defensive strategies

In an earlier section of this chapter, I explained that you must defend your intellectual property (prosecute infringers) or risk losing it. If someone doesn't have the right to make and sell your invention or other form of IP but does so anyway, that person has infringed upon your IP rights. Be aware that the government is not going to defend you under any circumstances. IP rights do not protect you from infringement; they give you the right to sue the infringer and enjoin or close down the infringer's operation. A court of law decides infringement cases, and you'll be happy to know that courts generally tend to side with the small inventor, particularly in cases where the infringer is a large company.

Beyond the obvious, how do you know when someone has legally infringed your patent? You look at the claims on which your patent is based and compare them point by point to the accused infringer's device or process. If they match, bingo! The courts can also find an infringement under the *doctrine of equivalents*, which states that if the infringing device or process is sufficiently equivalent in what it does to a patented device or process, an infringement has occurred.

If your infringement case is successful, the federal court will either enjoin the infringer, preventing further sales of the device by them, or mediate an agreement between you and the infringer that gives you royalties in exchange for allowing the infringer to sell the device.

TIP

Look into insurance that can help you pay the costs of fighting an infringement case. If you're protecting a lot of IP, it's worth considering.

Yet another problem that forces inventors into protecting their rights is a company that licenses an invention but doesn't use it, essentially keeping it out of the marketplace, usually to protect its own invention from competition. To protect against this form of infringement, set specific performance targets in your license agreement. Doing so makes the licensee achieve a certain agreed-upon level of sales by a certain point in time or face losing the license. Performance targets also prevent the licensee from keeping your invention out of the marketplace, which in turn helps you to maintain your patent.

International strategies

It is rare today that a company sells its products in only one country. Because of the expense of securing IP in every country, it's a good idea to prioritize based on which markets are most receptive and which respect IP rights. International trademark protection comes under the Madrid Protocol. Some countries, such as the UK, accept a trademark as valid even if unregistered. However, don't use that as an excuse to be lazy about your trademark protections. If you're looking to secure an EU trademark, you can find it at the offices of the EUIPO (the European Union Intellectual Property Office).

Well, you now know more than you probably ever wanted to know about intellectual property. When you start a business, you start with IP that needs to be protected. We live in a litigious world, so identifying an excellent IP attorney is the first step. I cannot stress this enough. This chapter is perhaps the most technical in the book, but you made it. Let's now move on to talk about putting together your founding team.

Chapter 9

Putting Together Your Founding Team

A s an entrepreneur, you bring your concept and skills to the table. It's rare that you would have all the skills and experience required to launch and grow a new business. That's why the most successful new ventures start with a founding team with diverse knowhow.

A Little Science Behind Founding Teams

The fact that teams are associated with successful startups is supported by a large body of research for reasons such as the following:

» You can share the enormous effort it takes to start the business.

» The business can continue even if one team member leaves.

» If your founding team covers all the primary functions in the business — marketing, finance, and operations — you go farther faster before bringing others on board.

» You gain more credibility with lenders, investors, and others if you have a team.

>> You make better decisions as a team than as a solo entrepreneur, especially if your team benefits from diverse experiences and modes of thinking.

The bottom line: Research has found that startups founded by heterogeneous teams are more successful than those founded by a solo entrepreneur.

Who's on First?

The longitudinal research of Noam Wasserman has provided us with a lot of useful insights into what makes for a great founding team. He studied 10,000 founders over a decade and was able to identify the typical challenges they faced.

Those challenges fell into three broad categories: relationships, roles, and rewards. This translates into who is on the team, what their responsibilities are, and why they want to be on the team. When using a team to start your venture, the first place entrepreneurs look for members is among people they know (friends, family, and so on). That tactic can work, but it is also problematic. You obviously need to know your team members well so you can trust them — and your friends and family may fit that criterion. You also want to choose people who bring the skills and expertise you need to the mix.

REMEMBER

The bias to choose people who are like us is a common phenomenon known as *homophily.* It means that humans naturally gravitate to like-minded people. That may work in the short term, but over the long term, homogenous teams tend to underperform because they have sacrificed finding the best talent for someone who is a friend. It's also true that with friends you tend to make suboptimal choices because you want to keep everyone happy.

Starting a new business can be a stressful and tiring experience even with family members and close friends to share the burden. If things start going wrong, you may lose more than your business; you may lose a friend.

Having said that, I started three successful businesses with my husband (and he's still my husband) and one with a close friend (and he's still a close friend), so it can work out if you know the rules, which are covered in the next section. For most founding teams, it's best to create a team with the following characteristics:

>> Similar values

>> Diverse skills and experience

>> Diverse social networks

>> Reasonable geographic constraints

The rules with family and friends

When going into business with family or friends, you have to compartmentalize your efforts. In other words, leave business issues in the workplace and personal issues at home. Here are some tips for deciding whether to include friends and family on your startup team:

>> Choose friends or family members because they have special skills and expertise as well as the values you need and contacts that can help make the business successful.

>> Make sure that you all have the same or similar work ethics. If one of you is a Type A workaholic and the other a slacker, you're not going to work well together.

>> If a friend or family member isn't working out as you had hoped, then it's time to bring in a third party who can either help you resolve the issue or be the one to suggest that this person needs to leave the business. That way, you at least have a chance of saving the personal relationship.

Covering all the bases

Your goal is to put together a multi-functional team of about three people with a variety of strengths and skills. Ideally, members of the core founding team must have skills in the three major functional areas of any business: finance, marketing, and operations. Having access to a network that crosses these three disciplines is a distinct advantage for your venture, significantly increasing your overall information and resources. You will also have three personal financial statements to rely on when you need to borrow money or talk to investors.

No matter what type of legal organization you end up with (see more about legal forms of organization in Chapter 15), members of your founding team are essentially your partners. Choose wisely. Considering that you'll spend more than half of your time each day with these people, you better like, respect, and trust them.

Naturally, fielding the perfect team from the start isn't always possible. Maybe you haven't found the right person, or you have but they aren't available yet or may cost too much to bring on board before the company's revenues reach a certain level. In the latter case, staying in touch with that person is a wise choice. Time goes by quickly, and good people are hard to find. Besides, if your company's making an aggressive start and doing well, the person you've been eyeing may surprise you and come on board sooner than you expected by taking less money in salary for an equity stake in your venture.

Putting everything in writing

I can't tell you how often I see entrepreneurs go into business with people they like and trust only to have things go sideways for one reason or another. None of us can predict what life may throw at us. That's why, no matter your legal form, I always recommend signing a partnership agreement. Treating your business relationship in a business manner helps you avoid the pain that lurks down the road.

Just like prenuptial agreements, you may flinch at requiring a written agreement from a spouse, friend, or family member, but do it anyway, especially if you're not equal partners in the venture. I talk more about the details of partnership agreements in Chapter 15, but for now just accept that you should have one. In the agreement, you may detail the role this person will play in the organization. Normally, you should have a discussion with anyone who will serve in a role that might affect ownership of the business. Try to avoid using big company titles like CEO, CFO, and so forth. When your business is in its infancy, those titles don't make sense. Unfortunately, people want those titles for their perceived prestige; but the fact is that most startups don't start as corporations, so the titles are actually inappropriate. More on that later. If you're starting as equals, that is, the idea was developed by two or more people working together, you may encounter an argument about who is the CEO because again, it's perceived as the most prestigious position. In practice, the CEO has arguably the worst job of all because they are the face of the company. If you're the CEO, it's your job to raise the money needed to start and grow the company and make sure your product is developed and ready for the market in time.

Beside the title argument, cofounders will also need a serious discussion about ownership stakes. Too often the team wants to allocate stakes too early in the process. Furthermore, it's often argued that everyone on the founding team should receive equal stakes. That's a mistake because no team has founders that contribute equally to the effort. If you decide who gets what too early, you miss the opportunity to see how a team member performs. In addition to giving the team a chance to demonstrate their capabilities, think about the following:

>> What is each founding member bringing to the business? Bringing a patent or significant money should rank higher than simply bringing an idea and a willingness to work.

>> What is each member putting at risk or sacrificing to be part of the startup? Has anybody left a job or mortgaged their house? Keep in mind that investors will want the answers to these questions as well.

>> At what date did each member officially become part of the founding team?

>> What are the most important contributions this member will be expected to bring?

The founding team is typically comprised of two or three people. These are the people who make things happen and have the critical skills needed to launch the company. When you have a larger group of say four to six founders, it might suggest that the lead founder does not have enough strength to carry the ball. The designation of "founder" is important because it means that you receive founders' stock, which comes with a vesting schedule. If you want to get a feel for how equity stakes might look, check out the site Foundrs.com where you'll find a free equity calculator. Answer a few questions and it will tell you how the equity should be split. Note that the equity numbers assume a four-year vesting with no cliff and no big salary for any of the cofounders.

TIP

Vesting means receiving full ownership rights to the shares. It is more typical to see a one-year cliff, which means that the founders do not get vested on any shares until the first anniversary of the stock issuance. So, in practice, you get no vesting in the first year, 25 percent vesting at the 12th month, and then 1/48th (2.08 percent) vesting each month until you complete the vesting in the 48th month. If you leave in the first year, you get nothing. If you leave after three years, you get 75 percent of the total shares you were granted. In general, no value is attached to shares in the earliest stages of the company because the company itself has little to no value yet. However, when the company does achieve some future value, shareholders of record will know the percentage of that valuation that belongs to them.

The discussion around equity splits is one of the most difficult you will have. It pays to bring in an outside advisor with experience in startups to offer an objective opinion. That person can help you prepare for the fact that when you eventually take on funding, your percentage of ownership will decline.

REMEMBER

If the founding team starts with C-level titles, the only direction they can go is down when you decide to bring in a professional executive or two to take the company to the next level.

Benchmarking the perfect team

So what does the perfect team look like? Compare your team against the following benchmarks or criteria. Keep in mind that these are super nice-to-have criteria. It's doubtful that you'll be able to check off all of them.

>> You have covered the bases with expertise in marketing, finance, and operations.

>> Someone on the founding team has experience within the industry in which you'll work and preferably in a similar business.

>> The team members have good credit ratings.

>> At least one person on the team has been an entrepreneur with a successful business.

>> The team has a network of contacts that include money and industry sources.

>> The team members are focused on the startup and passionately dedicated to making it happen.

>> The team members have considered all of their personal obligations — mortgage, spouse, children, debt — and are financially sound enough to get through the early stages of the business without a salary.

How did you do? A very low score would suggest that you need to spend more time building the best team possible.

Forming a Diverse Board of Advisors

In the beginning, you typically don't have all the resources necessary to hire all the expertise you need. You certainly can't afford an in-house attorney or accountant, and you may be relying on Uncle Jim or Aunt Jane, who are willing to donate services for a time. A board of advisors comes in handy in these situations, bringing together people who believe in you and in what you're trying to do. The advisors provide experience, guidance, information, and services, and many times play devil's advocate, pointing out potential flaws in what you're doing. They are, essentially, your reality check.

In general, your advisory board consists of attorneys, accountants, bankers, professors, consultants in various specialties, and others outside the company giving you needed advice and helping you find the people and resources you need to tap.

More than ever before, you can't always rely on the ideas and opinions of a bunch of insiders. If chosen well, your board of advisors serves as your eyes and ears to the broader world outside your business. This will be an important experience to prepare you for having a formal board of directors, which is discussed later in the chapter.

The following sections of this chapter look at various professionals your business needs to tap for advice or to hire for professional expertise.

Yes, you need attorneys

When choosing an attorney, pick one for their legal (not business) expertise. Attorneys are professionals who typically specialize in certain areas of the law:

tax, intellectual property, real estate, corporate, and so forth. Because every new business is affected by the law, an attorney is an enormously valuable asset to have on your board of advisors and as an expert your company needs to hire from time to time. Benefiting your company, an attorney can

>> Advise you on the best legal form of organization for your business, whether it's a partnership, some form of corporation, or a limited liability company. Find out more about legal forms in Chapter 15.

>> Advise you and help you prepare the necessary documents for intellectual property rights acquisition — patents, trademarks, and so forth.

>> Prepare and negotiate contracts in a variety of areas.

>> Help you comply with federal, state, and local laws and regulations.

>> Represent you in any legal actions.

Keep in mind that lawyers specialize, so you may not find one who is willing to cover everything in this list. Finding a good attorney takes time. The best way to find the right one for your business is by asking people you trust for referrals, particularly those who own businesses and work with attorneys in areas where you'll need advice. After compiling a list of the attorneys who sound promising, arrange a time for an interview. Yes, I said interview them. You are looking for someone with whom you expect to have a long-term relationship, so finding an attorney with an understanding of your business and who's compatible with your style is important. Likewise, because your business is in the startup phase, select an attorney who is willing to listen to you and spend the necessary time with you, while offering flexible fees.

Entrepreneurs often ask whether going with a small law firm (one to three people) is better than a mid-size or large prestigious firm. If your business concept shows tremendous promise of becoming a large, highly successful business, a larger firm may take you on in the beginning, recognizing that the real benefit to them will come over time as your company grows. But you probably won't work with the partners (the owners) in the early stages. Instead, they'll probably assign you to a young attorney with less experience. The advantage of a larger firm, however, is that chances are it's a full-service law firm that can handle most of your special-ized needs.

A small law firm, on the other hand, may be more energized by your business and its potential and less intimidating to deal with. Small firms may even be more flexible about fees, but they can't be all things to all people. Smaller firms are limited, and better service is not guaranteed, because the one to three partners at smaller firms do all the work. You do, however, work with the most experienced people.

A third option is a firm like New Venture Law Group, which is featured in the side-bar "When Your Lawyer Thinks Like an Entrepreneur," later in this chapter. They are used to working with startups with limited resources and are willing to work on an as-needed basis to keep fees low.

Unless you're willing to change lawyers as your company grows, and companies often do, consider the following when choosing a good attorney:

>> Pick a firm with an excellent reputation.

>> Pick a firm that can grow with your company and its changing needs.

>> Pick a firm that is well connected in all the specialties within the law, so that even if they do not handle, for example, intellectual property law in-house, they have a strategic alliance with another law firm that specializes in IP law.

TIP

Make sure the attorney has malpractice insurance. Every good firm does. You just never know what the future may hold.

Accountants can help you survive

While your lawyer is your advocate and does what you want (short of breaking the law), your accountant is bound by principles and ethics (Generally Accepted Accounting Principles, or GAAP) that do not permit advocacy. Accountants deal with a vital area of your business — its financial health. Before your business starts, your accountant helps you set up your books and periodically maintains those books. Because accountants are expensive, entrepreneurs typically hire a bookkeeper to record daily transactions and do payroll. They visit their accountants quarterly or at tax preparation time.

In addition, your accountant sets up systems and controls in your business and alerts you to responsibilities such as tax withholding, federal deposits, and reporting requirements. Activities, tasks, systems, and controls that your accountant can assist you with include the following:

>> Keeping employee records

>> Preparing stockholder reports

>> Preparing budgets

>> Establishing inventory controls

>> Issuing invoices

>> Making collections

- ❯❯ Providing referrals for professional services
- ❯❯ Making payroll tax deposits
- ❯❯ Preparing financial statements
- ❯❯ Filing yearly tax returns
- ❯❯ Balancing the checking account
- ❯❯ Writing checks
- ❯❯ Verifying and posting bills

Once your business survives on its own — achieving a positive cash flow and beginning to make a profit — you may want your accountant to do an annual audit, making sure that your accounting and control procedures are working properly. During that time, you may need a physical inventory. If your audit accountant finds that everything is in order, they issue a letter to that effect. If you ever decide to take your company public (do an initial public stock offering, or IPO) or sell it to a larger company, having at least three years of audited financial statements is essential.

When choosing an accountant, just like your attorney, find one who is used to working with entrepreneurs. They understand your needs and limitations and can be more flexible in terms of fees and time spent explaining things to you. The accountant who suits your needs will grow with your company and put you in touch with people who can help you. Check out online payroll and bookkeeping services such as Bookkeeper.com and Bookkeeper 360. They typically operate on a monthly charge starting at about $200 per month.

Your banker can dispense advice, if not money

An old saying goes that bankers will give you money only when you don't need it. Many entrepreneurs have found that to be true. It's no surprise that bankers are not risk takers and new, unproven ventures have a poor track record when it comes to success. Most startups seek loans well under $500,000 and it costs a bank just as much to underwrite a large loan of a million or more as it does to underwrite a loan of $50,000, with more risk. So your startup needs to be very convincing. It's a good idea to shop around. Community banks often have less onerous lending requirements and are willing to take a risk on a local business with great promise. Some banks offer special lending packages for franchise owners of operating businesses because the business model is proven.

WHEN YOUR LAWYER THINKS LIKE AN ENTREPRENEUR

Attorneys aren't often thought of as highly creative thinkers, because they work within relatively strict boundaries. But once in a while a law firm comes along whose partners think like entrepreneurs, recognizing a big niche in the market that no one has tapped. One such lawyer/entrepreneur is Susan Rickard Hansen, who founded New Venture Law Group with the purpose of providing partner-level legal advice at affordable rates. The company prides itself on being able to offer quick response times using virtual technology. The company can also be a startup's outsourced general counsel. They have done this for many tech companies where they handle the day-to-day legal needs. When you consider that every aspect of your new business is touched by the law in some manner, ready access to an attorney for advice is a real advantage. Here is a short list of some of the areas of your business for which you will need legal advice.

- **Employment services**: Agreements, employment agreements, termination agreements, and compliance with federal and state laws.

- **Privacy and data security**: Policies and notices for customers, employees, and vendors.

- **Contracts**: Negotiation and drafting.

- **Real estate services**: Contracts for purchase or sale, negotiation of leases, and partnerships and joint ventures.

New Venture Law Group has tapped a lucrative niche in the market where it can work with startups and guide their journey to success.

Despite this, every business needs a banking relationship, because your banker is a vital source of information and may be able to refer you to other professionals. With a community bank, you may be able to establish a personal relationship with a banker. Most larger banks have moved many of their services online, where it's hard to establish that kind of relationship.

Bankers advise you on your financial statements and help you make your capital requirement decisions. Again, be as careful about selecting your banker as you are about your attorney and accountant. Here are some steps to take in selecting the best banker for your business.

>> Start by defining a list of criteria for your banker based on your business's needs.

>> Talk to other entrepreneurs about which banks provide the best services for small businesses. Often that is a community bank, as opposed to a bank with

branches all over the country. A community bank generally is more predisposed to working with entrepreneurs, understanding the nature of entrepreneurial risk and more willing to participate with the entrepreneur in growing the business.

>> Talk to your other professional advisors and ask for referrals to banks with which they have good relationships.

>> If you have a good relationship with the bank in which you hold your personal finances, savings, and such, you may have more leverage in obtaining funding.

>> When it comes time to interview your banker, find an officer with a rank of assistant vice president or higher, because that person is usually the one who deals with small businesses on a regular basis. They also have a certain level of authority to make decisions quickly.

Don't forget your insurance broker

I can't tell you how many entrepreneurs forget about insurance when they're starting their businesses. Catastrophes and problems are not what you're focused on when you're trying to get a business up and running. But the fact remains that you will need several of the following types of insurance:

>> Property and casualty

>> Bonding (to protect against not completing a job — common in construction)

>> Product liability if you're selling a product you manufactured

>> Personal liability

>> Auto on your company's vehicles

>> Unemployment

>> Medical

>> Errors and omissions

>> Life insurance on key management

>> Workers' compensation

>> Cybersecurity if you have a consumer-facing online business and store customers' personal data

Your choice of insurance companies is between major firms like State Farm or Allstate, and an independent broker who finds you the best deal among a variety of different insurance companies. Essentially, an insurance broker is an intermediary who helps you find the policies that best serve your needs. Most large name-brand insurance companies carry the mainstream insurance — life, property and casualty, personal liability, and auto — but they may refer you to specialists for coverages like bonding, product liability, and cybersecurity insurance. It's also important to realize that independent insurance agents represent insurance companies, not you. Brokers represent the buyer and can access any company.

REMEMBER

Your insurance needs are likely to change as your business matures, so establishing a relationship with an insurance broker you trust is a good idea. A good broker looks out for your company, finding ways to save you money on insurance. Make sure you understand their commission rates and other fees before hiring them.

Forming a Board of Directors

Boards of advisors counsel the founders but have no voting power when it comes to major company decisions and the hiring and firing of executives and officers. Likewise, advisory board members are not in the same position as directors of having to protect the interests of shareholders.

Whether or not to have a board of directors is largely a function of the legal structure of your business. If you have a corporation, a board is required, and it's elected by the shareholders. A board is also necessary if you plan to seek venture capital. It's important to distinguish between boards in privately owned companies and those in publicly traded companies.

In privately owned corporations, the founders typically own the majority of the stock in the beginning, so the directors essentially serve at the pleasure of the entrepreneur. In a publicly traded company, directors have designated power to hire and fire the named officers, oversee the operations of the company, and be responsible for its failures. They are elected by the shareholders to represent the shareholders' interests.

Getting people on your board

Here's a strategy for approaching a potential board of directors member:

1. **Identify the kinds of people you need on your board.** For example, you may want to find a strategic thinker who can help you draft your business and growth plans. You may need a specialist in *angel funding* (funds that come from a private investor — see Chapter 14) who can get you into that network. Or, if your business is labor intensive, you may need a human resource expert.

2. **Interview candidates by telephone.** Present candidates with what you're looking for. The interview also adds a personal touch to your request.

3. **Follow the phone interview with a letter.** Give the candidate overviews of your company and the board and its responsibilities.

4. **Follow the letter with a telephone invitation.** Ask the prospective board member to visit your company (and meet other board members).

When you finally meet face-to-face with a board member, find out what really motivates that person to serve on your board. Listening to the kinds of questions they ask is one way to get at what you really want to know — the candidate who spends a lot of time being concerned with how much you're going to pay may be doing it just for the money.

If you happen to be lucky enough to find a candidate who barrages you with questions about the company and shows genuine enthusiasm for the possibility of working with you, grab that person. Such candidates are rare. Likewise, the candidate who challenges you with difficult questions and makes you squirm a little is worth grabbing up. Board members help you and your company grow. You don't want a bunch of "yes" people.

A board of directors, composed primarily of outsiders, is similar in some ways to an advisory board but quite different in others. A board of directors provides advice and counsel, but its main job is holding management accountable for creating shareholder value and reaching established goals.

Deciding when you need a formal board

Several reasons point to why only about 5 percent of private companies have outside boards; that is, directors who are independent of the company. Many entrepreneurs don't like having "outsiders" evaluating their businesses and telling them what to do. In addition, a board of directors is an expensive proposition for a new company with limited resources.

As mentioned, if your company organizes as a corporation, you are required to have a board of directors. Typically, however, that board consists of the founders and maybe their attorney or accountant — pretty much an *insider* board composed of people who are owners or (in the case of the attorney and accountant) independent contractors hired to advise the company.

Some entrepreneurs create a board if they expect to go through a challenging period and need significant advice, when they're raising venture capital, or when they're preparing for an initial public offering (IPO). Others know that their companies are quickly growing; therefore, having a board of directors in place from the beginning is important.

REMEMBER

Communication is the most important factor in the success of any board. Being privy to what's going on, the board moves the company forward. Your board of directors keeps your business on track if you choose wisely; but if you're too afraid of losing control of your company, you may end up choosing friends and family members or not having a board at all. Either approach can prove costly to your company.

A great board of directors with strong and respected people on it builds your company's credibility in the marketplace. A good board helps your business reach the capital markets and make its way through all the challenges of growth. Here are some factors to consider when establishing a board of directors for your business:

» Make at least 75 percent of your board outsiders

» Find people who have a rapport with each other

» Find people who have broad networks of contacts

» Look for people who complement the insiders' strengths and fill in the gaps in experience

» Make sure that your directors do you proud because your board represents your company to the outside world

» Find honest people who have good problem-solving skills and integrity

Founders sometimes are burdened, especially during rapid growth, with operational details, the need to generate sales, and the problem of maintaining positive cash flow — all at the same time. Setting up a new board of directors under those circumstances may be difficult, so doing it before your business starts to rapidly grow is good advice.

Getting people to serve on your board today isn't easy, because boards often are sued for decisions made by management that shareholders don't like, and the frequency with which boards are being sued is increasing. Carrying directors and officers liability insurance (D&O) is a benefit that most board candidates expect and deserve.

Paying directors a flat fee quarterly is typical, so the average board member may make about $35,000 a year. In addition, expenses are covered; and once your company is beyond a startup, board members will probably expect grants of restricted stock.

Once you have a board of directors, you may no longer need an advisory board. However, if your company is working in science and technology, you might consider a science advisory board or technology advisory board to guide your product development.

Creating a Personal Board: Your Mentors

One type of board that many entrepreneurs neglect to establish is a personal mentor board. The top of the company, the CEO, is a lonely place and you need to have someone you can confide in. At least as important as any other board, the personal board is a very small, handpicked group of people who advise you on your career and personal growth. The people on this board are the mentors and role models who represent what you want to become in your life. Mentors are people you trust, who hold what you discuss with them in the strictest of confidence. Your mentors let you know honestly when you're out of balance, micromanaging your business instead of delegating, and stuck in the mud instead of moving forward. One of the most difficult tasks a CEO has is managing people. That is a skill that is mastered over time. In the meantime, your mentors provide a safe place to talk things through before addressing your board of directors or business advisory board.

TIP

Put together a personal mentor board — two or three people at most who are role models for you and who can be your mentors. Then take them to lunch!

Pulling Yourself Up by the Bootstraps

So you don't have the resources to hire the management staff you need to run your business. You're probably doing what most entrepreneurs do — *bootstrapping*. Begging, borrowing, or renting everything you need so you can get your business going, bootstrapping consists of all the creative techniques entrepreneurs use to start their businesses on limited resources.

Outsourcing savvy

One way to avoid having to hire so many expensive employees is to outsource your needs to other businesses that have established expertise. Independent contractors own their own businesses; you hire them to do a specific job. They're responsible to you only for the results of their work, not the means by which they do it. Hiring good independent contractors can save you money because you pay them a flat fee and they are responsible for their own taxes, medical benefits, unemployment insurance, and Social Security tax. All these taxes and benefits combined amount to as much as 32 percent or more of a base salary for an employee.

Whether inadvertently or not, some entrepreneurs have run afoul of the IRS by calling workers independent contractors when they are in fact treated like employees. The Federal Government has very specific rules for who can be considered an independent contractor. See the sidebar, "The Rules for Independent

Contractors," later in this chapter. If you want to use independent contractors instead of employees, you should:

>> Get the advice of an attorney who can make sure you're following the law (see the next section).

>> Execute a contract with the independent contractor specifically stating that this person is not an employee for state and federal tax purposes.

>> Make sure that the independent contractor carries workers' compensation insurance and has the necessary licenses for the work they do.

REMEMBER

If the IRS declares that your independent contractor is really an employee, you will be subject to back taxes, interest, and penalties. If the revenue folks are in a really bad mood, they may charge you with fraud.

THE RULES FOR INDEPENDENT CONTRACTORS

The Internal Revenue Service (IRS) has specific rules that you must adhere to when using independent contractors. A 20-point test for independent contractors spells out the ways you know that a worker is an employee. Make sure that your independent contractor isn't doing any of these things. You should know, however, that even if you follow the rules to the letter, the IRS can still challenge you. Too many business owners have violated the rules, so the IRS is on the lookout. Here are the 20 points.

Workers are employees if they

- Must follow your instructions about how to do the work.

- Receive training from you.

- Provide services that are integrated into the business.

- Provide services that must be rendered personally.

- Cannot hire, supervise, or pay their own assistants.

- Have a continuing relationship with you.

- Must follow set hours of work.

- Work full-time for you.

- Do the work on your premises.

- Must do the work in a sequence you set.

- Must submit regular reports to you.

- Are paid regularly for time worked.

- Receive reimbursements for expenses.

- Rely on the tools and materials you supply.

- Have no major investment in facilities to perform the service.

- Cannot make a profit or suffer a loss.

- Work for one employer at a time.

- Do not offer their services to the general public.

- Can be fired at will by you.

- May quit work at any time without incurring liability.

As you can see, the determination of employee versus independent contractor can be murky, so tripping up and putting your company at risk is pretty easy. Recognizing that, the "Safe Harbor Rules" in the IRS Code provide a bit of relief. Basically they say that a worker will not be considered an employee if

- You have never treated the worker as an employee for tax purposes.

- You filed all the employment tax and information forms needed to establish an independent contractor relationship.

- You have a reasonable basis for treating the worker as an independent contractor (longstanding industry practice, past IRS audit that verified it, judicial precedent).

Leasing your staff

One of the newest ways to get the personnel you need for your business is leasing them through a Professional Employer Organization (PEO). This tactic is different from using a temporary service. The leasing company essentially becomes your human resource department, assuming responsibility for payroll, insurance, and so forth. Your employees actually work for the PEO for tax purposes. The PEO provides this service for a fee that ranges between 3 percent and 6 percent of the gross payroll. You submit a lump sum to the leasing company each pay period that includes the payroll plus the fee.

By leasing your staff, you not only reduce your costs, but you also avoid many personnel headaches, including time spent on employee-related paperwork. The latter is a real benefit, considering that the average small business owner spends more than 25 percent of their time on paperwork related to employees.

Before deciding to use a PEO, ask yourself these questions:

>> Will the PEO help my business achieve its goals?

>> Is the company easy to work with?

>> Is the PEO a member of important industry watchdog organizations: The National Association of Professional Employer Organizations (NAPEO) and the Institute of Accreditation for Professional Employer Organizations?

>> What is the PEO's financial track record?

>> Can the PEO give client references?

>> How are employee benefits funded? Are insurance coverages met?

When you review the agreement with the PEO, be sure that it allows you to cancel with a 30- to 90-day notice. You don't have to go all in with a PEO. You can choose to use one of the many reputable companies that will do the payroll work for you.

WARNING

Even when you lease your staff, you bear the ultimate responsibility for any unpaid payroll taxes, and you could be determined to be the actual employer if you determine salaries, choose your contract employees, or fire your contract employees. Hands off is the name of the game.

FORMING STRATEGIC ALLIANCES

Strategic alliances are quite different from outsourcing with independent contractors. Independent contractor is an IRS designation for tax purposes and is essentially a worker for hire who owns their own business. By contrast, a strategic alliance is not an IRS designation but is a more formal and closer relationship between two companies. It is a type of partnership that can be implied through the way it works or through a legal arrangement with a formal partnership agreement. Your strategic partners can be suppliers, manufacturers, or customers. Reducing expenditures for marketing, raw materials, R&D, and so forth, or joining together to do a specific project, are reasons for forming such a partnership.

In strategic alliances, the partners are stakeholders — regardless of whether they hold stock in each other's company — because each partner invests time and money into the partnership. If the project or arrangement fails, the partners stand to lose, so strategic partners are subject to significant risk. For that reason, choosing partners who can bear the risk is necessary. Before approaching a potential strategic partner, do your homework and make sure that your candidate has the following:

- **Excess capacity**. In other words, your partner shouldn't be working to the limit of their capacity relative to personnel and equipment. They should have room to grow.

- **Experience in strategic alliances**. If your partner has experience with a few strategic alliances, that company will be a better partner because they will know what works and what doesn't.

- **A diversified portfolio**. When a partner's capabilities and investments are narrowly focused — they have all their eggs in one basket — they likely can't bear the risk of investment in your company and the partnership. Diversity limits risks so that if one investment goes bad, it doesn't bring the whole company down.

- **Relative strength**. Choose a partner that is at least as strong a company as yours, preferably stronger.

We can find lots of reasons for strategic alliances, but some of the most successful have involved two companies that didn't seem to go together. For example, the Ford Motor Company partnered with Eddie Bauer, an outdoor clothing manufacturer, to produce the Ford Explorer Eddie Bauer edition, which filled the need of consumers for an upscale sports utility vehicle produced in the United States.

As you can see, a startup team can be formed in many ways, depending on your unique situation and needs. In fact, if you have a carefully chosen founding team, your advisory board and professional advisors can take you far before you need to incur the expense of additional employees. Now might be a good time to review Chapters 5 and 6. A deep understanding of your industry and your customers enables you to forecast the talent you need to get the business launched and running well.

Chapter **10**

Getting Solutions to Customers: The Supply Chain

I n 2022, everyone learned what a supply chain is and what can happen when a supply chain is disrupted. The things you purchased online don't arrive when they're supposed to, if at all. Store shelves are empty of necessities like food. Supply chains are so tightly configured that relatively minor delays upstream in the channel compound to become serious issues downstream. This chapter examines the major aspects of the supply chain and looks at how to think about your supply chain strategically. After all, it's important that you get your solutions to your customers as quickly and reliably as possible.

Understanding Supply Chains, Logistics, and Distribution Channels

Let's start by distinguishing a supply chain from a value chain. Picture a river that starts in the mountains and flows down to the sea. Along that river are all the activities involved in taking your solution from design through product development, material sourcing, production, and delivery to the final customer. When the solution goes through several intermediaries on its way to the customer, it's called an *indirect channel*. Look at Figure 10-1, which depicts two channel options for a solution that involves the manufacture of furniture. The supply chain is represented by the various intermediaries in the chain.

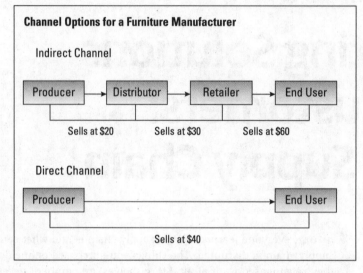

FIGURE 10-1: Comparing the costs of two distribution options for a furniture manufacturer.

Now overlay the value chain onto the supply chain. The value chain depicts the cooperation among all the participants to add value at each point in the supply chain contributing to the final solution. In a direct channel model, the seller bypasses the intermediaries and sells direct to the end user, so typically the price will be less than with an indirect channel.

The Internet has precipitated massive consolidation in many industries by getting rid of intermediaries and collapsing distribution channels. Intermediaries are distributors, wholesalers, and retailers who come between producer and consumer resulting in an indirect distribution channel. Because the Internet is an open channel of communication with access to information at its source, customers connect directly with the source rather than paying to access the source through an intermediary.

The traditional supply chain is essentially linear, moving from raw materials through the distribution channel to the consumer. Today, because of technology, we now have a modern supply chain (SCM) multi-focused on logistics management, partnerships, customers, and speed of service. Supply chains integrate supply and demand, while distribution channels are focused on the demand chain.

An increase in the popularity of low-cost distribution methods is another reason that distribution as a strategy is gaining such prominence. Companies like Walmart and Costco pioneered a price-based distribution model, forcing manufacturers to change their operations so that they produce at lower costs and still make a profit. To many manufacturers, particularly those that deal in commodity products, survival means going direct to their customers via warehouse, factory direct, or e-commerce versions of themselves. Even companies that deal in information as their products are now compelled to position themselves as the low-cost providers, which is never an ideal competitive position.

Looking at Logistics

Distribution is all about *logistics* — the movement of products and services from producers to buyers. Logistics consists of transportation, storage, and materials handling. But distribution is also about the way you market your product or service within your *distribution channel* — deciding, for example, how much of the channel you want to reach.

If you are a manufacturer, do you want to reach every possible distributor of your product? That approach is called *intensive coverage*. Alternatively, do you want to reach only retailers in a defined geographic area? That approach is called *selective coverage*. In addition, you can break selective down even further. For example, if your product is intended for the luxury market, you might limit distribution initially to upscale boutiques, period. Although you can't escape decisions about your distribution channels, you can probably sidestep many of the details involved in logistics, at least for a while.

For most startups, having their own shipping department and distribution center is not within the realm of possibility because of prohibitive costs. Consequently, most startups outsource their logistics needs to companies that specialize in providing that service like UPS. It's surprising how many entrepreneurs who sell online forget the importance of fulfillment, packing, and shipping products. It's a huge job, especially at peak buying times during the year.

Working with a good logistics service provider can ensure that you get the best rates and the most reliable carriers. Your customers will expect that.

Today, finding all the major carriers online and accessing logistics portals such as iShip and Logistics Portal can help you discover your options. When it comes time to decide on a firm, ask yourself these questions:

>> Can the company provide the services you need when you need them?

>> How do this company's costs compare with other companies in the industry?

>> What kinds of services do they provide?

>> Does the company already deal with products like yours?

>> What kinds of guarantees does the company provide to ensure that your products arrive at their destination in good shape?

Distributing through Consumer and Industrial Market Channels

Depending on the nature of your business, you will be using either a consumer market channel or an industrial market channel, or sometimes both.

Businesses selling to end users, or people who purchase goods and services at the wholesale or retail levels, are in the consumer market channel (B2C). Businesses that market goods and services to other businesses deliver products through industrial channels (B2B). An office supply company can access both B2B and B2C channels.

Consumer channels

Let's explore consumer channels first. Within consumer channels, you can reach your customer in a variety of ways.

Selling direct to customers

As discussed in the introduction to this chapter, selling direct means that no intermediaries come between you and your customers, and you take on all the responsibilities of typical intermediaries. Service businesses are usually direct sellers; but more and more, especially with the advent of the Internet, manufacturers are becoming direct sellers. You've probably visited factory-direct outlet malls where furniture, apparel, household, and other types of manufacturers sell goods to customers without going through intermediaries. The same occurs online.

In general, manufacturers start by establishing traditional channel relationships with intermediaries, building brand-name recognition. That way, when they open direct outlets, they don't have to do much in the way of advertising to get people to visit. The Gap, an apparel manufacturer, is a good example of this strategy. It uses outlets for getting rid of excess inventory, slightly defective merchandise, and out-of-season merchandise. That way, its direct outlets don't compete against its retail outlets.

Using retailers to reach customers

Retailers are the most common outlets for getting manufacturers' products to their customers. Attracting customers through their own marketing and promotional strategies is the retailers' responsibility. Of course, manufacturers must also support their retailers with special discounts and manufacturer promotions. But retailers incur the costs of a sales force and stocking enough product to meet demand.

When setting up a retail distribution system, manufacturers either use an in-house sales staff or hire independent sales representatives who work on commission. The job of these sales representatives is locating the appropriate retailers and arranging for product distribution.

Using wholesalers and distributors to reach customers

The terms *wholesaler* and *distributor* are interchangeable in common usage, so for simplicity, I use *wholesaler* in this discussion. Wholesalers typically buy product in bulk from producers and then locate outlets to sell those products, freeing up the manufacturers for other tasks. Wholesalers are probably better at finding the best outlets because that's their core competency. Choosing a good wholesaler is still the job of the manufacturer, however. Remembering that you are entrusting the success of your product to this wholesaler shows you what an important choice that is. Wholesalers provide many services, including

» Warehousing your products

» Advertising and promoting your products to retailers and/or end users

» Providing special packaging and displays to outlets

» Training the retail sales staff

» Arranging transportation of goods to retail outlets and other customers

» Providing warranty or backup services

» Restocking retailer shelves as needed

Talking with your customers, suppliers, business consultants, and bankers who work with wholesalers can make the chore of finding a good one easier. Getting a referral from a knowledgeable source enhances your chances of making a good decision and selecting a company that is trustworthy, reliable, and interested in seeing your company succeed.

Hiring manufacturer reps to find customers

Manufacturer reps are independent contractors whose job is finding outlets for manufacturers' products. They differ from wholesalers in that they don't purchase the products or warehouse them; instead, they act much like brokers or agents by bringing producers and retailers or other types of sales outlets together. They earn a commission on any sales they make. The manufacturer-rep relationship is not transaction based, however. Reps often work with a manufacturer for years, developing a territory. Usually a rep is responsible for that specific territory, so a manufacturer typically has several reps covering all the geographic markets it reaches.

Industrial channels

With retail channels as the exception, businesses using industrial channels have the same options as those using consumer channels when selling direct or using the various types of intermediaries. The difference is that with industrial channels, goods typically sell at wholesale prices and not direct to consumers.

You've no doubt noticed how powerful the business-to-business side of e-commerce on the Internet is. Today businesses purchase most of their supplies and raw materials online, saving time and money. If you're not doing business online, you may lose customers fast. Because customers can more easily shop and compare prices and services, your strategy for the online channel must consider prices and value-added services, thereby distinguishing your company from others.

Using intermediaries

I talked a bit about intermediaries in the channel options section of this chapter, but now I want to address intermediaries from a strategic point of view. Intermediaries inhabit most distribution channels, even on the Internet. A portal site even serves as an intermediary between the producer and end user. The essential service that intermediaries provide is assuming tasks that don't fall within the core competency of the manufacturer. At the same time, they're also serving retailers by finding products that their customers need and want.

Here are the four primary ways you can use intermediaries as part of your distribution strategy:

>> **Sharing the risk of distribution.** When a wholesaler purchases a product from the manufacturer and holds it in inventory for resale, the wholesaler is assuming the risk that it may not be able to sell all of the product it purchases.

>> **Placing products into a line under a single product category.** For example, if your product is a new branded barbecue sauce, you may want it placed with a wholesaler who handles specialty food items. In that way, retailers that sell specialty food items are finding your particular product when they're purchasing other similar products from that wholesaler.

>> **Breaking bulk.** Wholesalers usually purchase a product from manufacturers or suppliers in bulk. They then provide the value-added service of breaking the bulk product into quantities that their customers typically buy.

>> **Being a source of customer/market information for the manufacturer.** You certainly don't want to produce more product than the market wants, yet you want to be ready if demand suddenly increases. Your wholesaler and other intermediaries can be a tremendous source of information about customer needs and preferences on a regular basis, because they're on the front lines when it comes to dealing with those customers and changing demand.

Evaluating Your Channel

Choosing the best distribution strategy for your company is a critical decision that you should consider carefully. In general, the best distribution strategy for your company will include:

>> Reaching your customers in the most effective way

>> Providing an appropriate final price for your product or service

>> Providing service or backup service for customers

>> Allowing you to focus on your core competencies

Although limiting yourself to one distribution channel isn't essential (having more than one is common), you don't want to cannibalize one channel by introducing a competing one. For example, if you sell your product through a wholesaler in a particular city, you don't want to open your retail outlet in that city, because doing so jeopardizes your wholesaler's sales. When looking at the attractiveness of a particular channel, be sure you consider whether customers readily use that channel and whether you can make a profit using that channel.

You determine the feasibility of a particular distribution channel in much the same way you determine the feasibility of a new venture. You want to see whether the channel creates a niche in the market, whether you can afford to use this channel, whether your customers will use it, and whether you can get your products to your customers quickly through this channel.

No one disputes that the profitability of a channel is important, but you need to look at the channel in terms of maintaining a high profit margin while selling your product at a price customers are willing to pay. If the margins in the channel you choose are slim, then that channel must produce a higher volume of sales for you to make enough money to cover your overhead and still make a profit.

The cost of the channel

The costs of your distribution channel consist of all the expenses related to marketing and distributing your product. Referring to Figure 10-1, you can see that although the cost of production may not change, the price to the customer changes based on how the producer chooses to reach the customer.

The manufacturer charges the wholesaler a price that enables the manufacturer to cover the direct cost of producing the product plus an amount for overhead and profit. The wholesaler adds in its costs when it sells to the retailer, and the retailer typically keystones, or doubles (at a minimum), its costs to the end user. If you know that your end user will pay only $50 for your product, and your intent is to use the indirect channel depicted in Figure 10-1, then you've got a problem. Using that channel raises the price to the end user to $60, and chances are you cannot reduce the cost of the product, so you risk profit margin and jeopardize your business.

Cutting out one of the intermediaries or going direct to the customer may bring the final price more in line with what the market says it will pay, but you won't be able to reduce the price to $20. Cutting out the intermediaries means that you now pay for marketing to the end user and taking on tasks of the wholesaler and retailer. But you still may be able to bring the price in line.

Channel coverage

When you have a startup company, using intermediaries may be your wisest choice, because their expertise and contacts with customers help you expand more quickly into the market. Selling your products to just three distributors opens your access to hundreds of outlets at the retail level without increasing your staff or marketing budget, considering what you might spend marketing and distributing your product to those hundreds of retail outlets individually. The bottom line is that wholesalers help your company achieve better coverage in appropriate markets than you can do on your own.

DISTRIBUTING TO THE SUPERSTORES

Many entrepreneurs find homes for their products with superstores and discount outlets like Walmart, Home Depot, and Costco. If you sign a contract with one of these stores, you almost instantly have national, and in some cases international, distribution for your product. These mass merchandisers account for more than 40 percent of all U.S. retail sales, which is amazing considering that they comprise only about 3 percent of all retail outlets. So these megastores are important outlets for small entrepreneurial companies looking to grow quickly. In 2020, Walmart was the leading mass merchandiser over Amazon, Costco, and Target, by more than $200 billion.

But getting a contract with a superstore isn't easy. It takes more than a great product; it takes a plan. Here's a four-step strategy that may help you get a foot in the door with your favorite superstore:

1. **Find and talk to the right person**. Don't waste your time talking to just anyone about your company and products. Find out who the decision maker (usually the buyer) is in your product area.

2. **Get a buyer to return your call**. If you're having trouble getting a buyer to return your phone call, try using a rep or participating in a trade show where the superstores look for new products. The Expo Guide website (www.expo-guide.com) helps you find international trade shows in your industry and market.

3. **Prepare your pitch carefully**. You must convince the buyer that you understand who the consumer is, who the competition is, how your product beats the competition, and how well the product sells.

4. **Prepare to deliver on your claims**. You must deliver on your claims if you do get a contract. The superstore may test your product in a few of its stores first; but if it does well, you may have to ramp up quickly, providing products for all the stores across the country. Being prepared for that means your systems and controls and the resources you need to produce that much volume must be in place. Other costs that you can consider here include where to locate. For example, if you decide to sell direct to retailers, then you may want to locate the manufacturing facility or distribution warehouses near major transportation hubs. Doing so helps in delivering products to customers quickly and as inexpensively as possible. On the other hand, if you are using wholesalers, your manufacturing plant can be located anywhere because you're shipping to a central distribution point.

Distribution control

Basing your choice of distribution channels on the amount of control that you want to exert over your product once it leaves your site is important. If you have a product that requires a unique marketing strategy or demonstrations to convince customers to buy it, you don't want to use intermediaries who aren't willing to perform those tasks.

That very situation occurred with the industrial machine my husband and I produced, discussed in Chapter 7 in the sidebar entitled "Genesis of a Product." We initially introduced the product through equipment rental outlets that were excited about it and were sure they would rent it often. Unfortunately, equipment dealers have the attitude that the customer will come to them because they need a certain product, so they don't do much in the way of advertising or promotion. When you have a brand new product that customers aren't familiar with, they aren't going to come asking for it. Adding to the dilemma, ours was a product that wows people once they've seen it work, and equipment companies aren't used to demonstrating new products they have on the showroom floor. In short, your distributor has to be able to meet the needs of your product. If that's not possible, you have to find another route to the final customer.

REMEMBER

Today, supply chain management (SCM) is a critical function for any organization, even a startup. If you manage your supply chain effectively, you'll be better able to forecast demand for your products and services and, therefore, make sure you have sufficient inventory to meet demand. You can then create backup strategies in case of supply chain disruptions.

When Your Supply Chain Is International

When the first edition of this book was published, it was common to outsource manufacturing overseas to places like Southeast Asia, India, and China. Those entrepreneurs who had done that will tell you that it's not as easy as simply finding the right partner and handing off your product. In some cases, the intricacies of dealing overseas increase the cost of doing business by quite a lot. The following are some things to consider before deciding to outsource internationally:

>> Before you make the decision to manufacture overseas, do your homework. Talk to as many people as possible who have experience in that country, particularly in the manufacturing sector. If would be especially valuable to talk to entrepreneurs who have outsourced to the facility you plan to use for production.

» Choose production tasks that are straight-forward and can be handled easily. A very complex production product is probably best manufactured domestically.

» If your product or service is regulated, you will want to find out if you can manufacture overseas.

» It's difficult to stay on top of things through email or even telephone. You will want to weigh the costs of traveling back and forth to the country of manufacture versus having someone from your team on-site in the country for the duration of manufacturing.

» Be prepared for problems, especially when you start. That means a slower process initially that you need to compensate for.

Keep in mind that where distribution channels focus on the customer and generating demand, the supply chain is process focused. The goal is to improve efficiency, reduce steps in the many parts of the chain, and generally make the process as smooth as possible.

Chapter **11**

Developing and Testing Your Business Model

B uilding a successful new business takes a great team, customers, a value proposition, a product or service, resources, and a business model that can create and capture value for the company. In simple terms, you need to find a way to make money. It's exciting to come up with a new idea for a business, but it's essential to figure out a way to make money from that idea. Will customers actually pay for what you're offering? That's the critical question that must be answered before you invest time and money in trying to launch your venture.

Understanding Business Models

The business model reflects all the strategic decisions and trade-offs entrepreneurs make to generate a profit for their company. The components of the business model begin with the problem/solution, the unique value proposition offered, the unfair advantage, and the customer segments being addressed. These serve as the basis for developing the cost structure and revenue streams the business model will generate. In the simplest terms, the business model answers the question, "how does this company make money?" The various ways to generate revenue can be grouped into the following general categories:

» **Subscription or membership**. Customers pay a set amount monthly or annually.

>> **Volume or unit-based**. Customers pay a fixed amount per unit with a discount on volume purchases.

>> **Licensing and syndication**. Customers pay to use or resell the product, service, or intellectual property.

>> **Transaction fee**. Customers pay a fee for services, perhaps hourly or project based.

>> **Advertising**. The customer is the advertiser, which is a common revenue model for many online businesses.

Having more than one business model is advantageous, and in the following section you find examples of such businesses. But first let's look at a very effective framework for building your business model. It's called the *business model canvas*.

The business model canvas approach

Table 11-1 is an example of a business model canvas, which is simply a popular way to describe, visualize, and assess your proposed business model. It contains all the elements that affect how you make money.

TABLE 11-1 **The Business Model Canvas**

Problem	Solution	Unique Value Proposition (UVP)	Unfair Advantage	Customer Segments
Top three you're addressing; job to be done.	Top features and associated benefits that demonstrate the UVP	How are you different from everyone else?	What cannot be copied or bought? What is unique?	First customer Secondary markets
	Key Metrics Key business activities to measure		**Channels and strategic partners** How to reach the customer	

Cost Drivers	**Revenue Streams**
Customer acquisition costs	Lifetime value of a customer
Distribution and inventory costs	Gross margin
Manufacturing costs	
Support center costs	

This version of the canvas is adapted from Alex Osterwalder's canvas licensed under Creative Commons and the Lean Startup Canvas by Ash Maurya. Let's look at each of major elements of the canvas.

Notice that the top half of the canvas focuses on the customer's problem, the solution, and the value proposition (key benefit). The bottom half are the key activities associated with capturing value or monetizing the solution. Let's examine each quadrant a bit more.

» **Problem**: Every business model starts with a problem you've identified in a market. For example, how to help farmers get their products into local restaurants.

» **Solution**: What are the most important features and benefits you're offering with your solution.

» **Unique value proposition**: What is your unique competitive advantage? What are you offering that is very different from your competitors?

» **Unfair advantage**: What are you offering that can't be copied by others? What advantage do you have over everyone else?

» **Customer segmentation**: Who is your first customer? What additional segments will you pursue? Remember that your customer is the one who pays you, so the customer is not always the end user.

» **Key metrics**: These will depend on where your company lies in the value chain. If you're upstream in the value chain, you may track time to customer. You will probably measure customer buying patterns among other metrics.

» **Channels and strategic partners**: How do you plan to reach your customer and will you need to develop any strategic partnerships such as for manufacturing or logistics?

» **Cost drivers**: To figure out how much money you can make with this business, you need to determine the costs associated with doing business such as the cost to acquire a customer, the cost to get your solution to the customer, and the cost to build your solution. These costs dictate how much revenue must be generated.

» **Revenue streams:** How will you be able to generate revenue? What is the value of your customers over a lifetime? Can you maintain sufficiently large gross margins? You'll learn more about margins in Chapter 12. For now, some of the more common ways to generate revenue for your business are from subscriptions or memberships, volume or unit-based selling, licensing, advertising, and transaction fees, such as those for services.

Keep in mind that all the elements of the business model work together. In the beginning, one element may receive more attention than the others for a time; but over time, they will all come into play. The canvas gives you a clear picture of the components of your business model. When you change one element, be sure to look to see if it affects another element in the canvas.

REMEMBER

One important thing to understand about business models is that they're not static over the life of the business. On the contrary, when customer needs change, your business model will change. For example, Starbucks's business model changed to give the company a needed refresh. It began offering healthy juices and selling downloads of the music it played in its stores. And for the full Starbucks experience in your home or office, you could purchase one of its proprietary coffee makers. Even a highly successful company needs to stay in touch with customer needs and preferences, lest a competitor does the job for them.

A software company business model

Suppose you've come up with a new software program that helps small business owners manage all the activities of their businesses just like the big companies do with enterprise management software. You can offer the customer a choice of business model in one of the following ways:

>> The customer uses the program free of charge, but a small window in the lower-left corner of the computer screen displays advertising while the program is running. In other words, in this model, your end user isn't your actual customer. The companies that display their advertisements are your customers, and you receive your revenues from them. Many app companies have started with embedded advertising and the option for the user to pay to remove the ads.

>> The customer purchases the program for a one-time fee that entitles them to download it from your website, the Google App Store, or the Apple app store.

>> The customer subscribes to the program, which entitles them to add-ons and additional support. You can continually come up with new enhancements and more programs, so you encourage customers to purchase more from you, giving you another stream of revenue.

Going one step further with this example, let's say you also establish a website for users of your program or app. There they can find additional information and entertaining features. So how do you make money off that? Well, you can make it an e-commerce site where customers can purchase items, but you can also charge a membership fee that puts your users into an elite club, perhaps giving them access to information and services that they can't get anywhere else. These are a just a few ways to generate revenue. With a little creativity and a deep understanding of your customers, I'm sure you can discover more business models.

Your restaurant business model

Suppose you own a restaurant featuring Southwestern cuisine at reasonable prices in an atmosphere worthy of a much more expensive restaurant. Your customers like eating there not only because the food is great, but also because members of your waitstaff have charming personalities and you, the owner, enjoy walking around the restaurant greeting customers by name. Let's see how you can build some business models around this concept.

>> The obvious model is selling food and beverages; but if you have a bar, you will have a good revenue stream off that. In most restaurants, alcoholic beverages, rather than food, bring in the most money because they have the highest margins.

>> You provide a catering service, serving your cuisine at banquets and other events.

>> You rent out your entire restaurant for special occasions and private parties.

>> You offer a limited take-out menu and maybe a delivery service partnering with one of the many existing delivery services like Uber Eats, DoorDash, and Grubhub. If your restaurant uses a point of sales platform (POS), you can save money by integrating it with the delivery platform. You can then process the orders and sales through your in-store POS system and you won't have to pay commissions to a delivery service.

Additional business models create new revenue streams for your business. Suppose you have a signature drink that you concoct. You can arrange to produce and market that drink in bottles to supermarkets. You can develop a line of frozen foods from your repertoire and distribute them through specialty stores like Trader Joes. You can also charge for cooking lessons you conduct while your restaurant is closed to the public. As you can see, if you let your mind wander, you can come up with even better business models for restaurants.

WARNING

If your restaurant is upscale, offering unique foods and presentation, you will want to protect your luxury brand so that it doesn't become a commodity. Some of the business models will work — closing for private events, for example. But avoid diluting the value of your brand by associating it with too many different products and services.

The best business models have the easiest time getting funded, and that's important when you consider that most businesses seek outside sources of capital at some point as they grow. So what is the common denominator among the best business models? They provide consumable products and services so customers need to purchase them again and again. This strategy has been referred to as the "Gillette Method" after the famous manufacturer of razors and other products. The aim is to sell the base product — the razor — relatively cheaply or even give it away. Then customers who want to continue to use the razor must purchase razor blades that are not so cheap. Hewlett-Packard uses this strategy with its printers — selling them at low prices and making up the difference on printer cartridges and service contracts.

The best business models also provide for *multiple streams of revenue,* which means that your company makes money on a product or service that it sells through several different channels to different customers. The more revenue streams, the better, because if one dries up, you still have others you can rely on and your business won't be hurt.

This chapter discusses a variety of business models that are in use today. Each has advantages and disadvantages. Only you can determine which is the best model for your business, but remember, you don't have to limit yourself to one when more is better.

A retail business model

Believe it or not, something positive can be said today about starting with a traditional offline business, whether it's a kiosk or a full-fledged store. Many people still enjoy shopping the old-fashioned way, trying on clothes, leafing through books, and wandering around furniture stores. Recent events prove that having a traditional business in place — whether a retail or service business — and establishing your brand before offering products and services on the Internet has many advantages.

>> Your business has instant name recognition when it launches its website.

>> Your business systems — accounting, purchasing, inventory, fulfillment, and so forth — are in place and proven.

>> You already have a reliable revenue stream that carries you until your site becomes profitable.

>> You already have proven advertising and promotional strategies in place that you can leverage letting people know that you also conduct your business online.

Remember Courtney Miller and her boutique P.Cottontail from Chapter 1? Her store is a fixture in the quaint tourist area of downtown Half Moon Bay, CA. During the pandemic, rather than close her business and risk its future, she developed a website so her loyal customers could still buy from her. Today her online sales exceed her in-store sales, and the physical store now serves double duty as a warehouse for clothes and toys that are bought online.

In the following two sections, entitled "Providing a service with an upside" and "Making money while you sleep," I talk about some business models for services and products that are sold through offline businesses.

Providing a service with an upside

Until now, we've been focused on product businesses. Let's turn now to business models for service companies, which typically involve the entrepreneur doing the bulk of the work. In a service company, people are hiring you to do something for them, whether that is consulting or remodeling a house. Service implies some human contact, so this is not a business model that lets you make money while you sleep. *Making money while you sleep* means that your business can generate revenue when you're not there, essentially 24 hours a day, seven days a week (the model I talk about next in the "Making money while you sleep" section). Unfortunately, most entrepreneurs with service models don't often think in those terms, so they build their businesses entirely on what they and a few trusted employees or partners are able physically to do or provide during normal business hours, and that's fairly limited.

However, we're beginning to see service entrepreneurs creating new business models that let them earn more than just their hourly wages or flat-fee arrangements. The following case study illustrates one such company.

CASE STUDY

The industrial design business is competitive, particularly in places like Silicon Valley and Route 128 in Massachusetts. One company that does contract work for major companies such as Silicon Graphics, Hewlett-Packard, and Motorola found that its margins were shrinking as more and more companies entered the field and as the cost of staying current with new technology skyrocketed. The old business model was not going to work much longer. As they began brainstorming new ways to generate revenue, this group of design partners came to the conclusion that they had been spending a lot of their time advising startup ventures — they were essentially acting like venture capitalists without the equity stake. That's when the idea for a new business model hit them.

Why not secure an equity stake in the startups they were serving rather than just receive a fee for service? They were about to discover the power of the multiple. For example, $1 received from a client for a service will never be more than $1, and once you subtract all the expenses associated with providing the service, your profit is probably pennies. But if you take stock in a growing company, betting on their future success, that $1 can turn into $20 or more. For these imaginative entrepreneurs, that was the way to go. And so far, it has worked well. Initially about 90 percent of their work remained fee-for-service (a flat fee based on the service provided); it's now down to 60 percent, yet their revenues have gone up substantially. Without changing the work they were doing, they discovered a way to create more value for their service.

Taking stock in your customers' companies does more than merely increase the value of what you do. You are now partners with your customers. You have a stake in the success of their company, so your customer probably gets more value as well from your services because by nature you're more inclined to protect your equity stake. It's a win-win for you and your customer.

You can take this strategy one step further. You can originate ideas for new products inside your design firm and bring them to your customers as partners to take those products to market. Now you're an incubator for new products, which gives your customers a resource they couldn't otherwise afford. Many industries — engineering firms, consultants, public relations firms, and the furniture and toy industries, among others — use this equity stake business model. So how can you assess your service company to determine if this business model is right for you? Here are some tips:

>> Study your industry carefully, identifying the business models that others are using. If no one uses the equity stake model, ask why. It may be that your type of business is not appropriate for this model, or it may simply mean that no one has tried it yet.

>> Connect with a startup or rapidly growing venture. These companies are probably straining for resources and may be willing to give up equity rather than cash for what you can provide.

>> Determine if what you offer makes a significant contribution to the product or service your client is producing. For example, if your company provides bookkeeping or janitorial services, you're not likely to get stock because no matter how well your firm performs, it won't determine the success or failure of the client's firm.

>> Create a network of talented people in your service area that you can tap when you want to produce a new product or provide a service to your clients. The entertainment industry uses this model because teams never seem to stay together for the long term. You can do bigger, more difficult, and more rewarding projects this way.

>> Do your homework before you take an equity stake in a new venture. Don't let your excitement over equity cause you to make poor investment decisions.

>> Don't take all stock. Be sure you also get some cash. Your customers respect your work more if they have to pay something each month.

>> Make sure that your current business model is healthy enough to enable you to use the equity stake model.

Using the equity stake model has its risks. Before you jump in, ask yourself these questions:

>> Is the market for the client's product as big as the client says it is? Does it really exist?

>> Is the product meeting a real need in the market?

>> Can the team make it happen? Do team members have the right skills, experience, and drive?

>> How will you harvest your investment?

Producing multiple products and services

Service entrepreneurs often limit themselves to thinking about various services they provide and they forget the variety of products they can also offer their customers. Today, you want to think of your business as an information center for your customers. You want them looking to your business for as many of their needs as possible. So, your overall business model must apply multiple models generating many different streams of revenue. The first section of this chapter provided you with examples of various types of businesses and how you can produce multiple models from one product or service. Now I want you to start thinking about how many different products and services you can produce from one business concept, because each product and service can turn into several business models and revenue streams.

TIP

No matter what type of business you start, you will be able to find more than one business model to launch it if you're solving a real problem that customers have.

Making money while you sleep

The best of all worlds is a business that continues without you, freeing you to work on what you want to when you want. Product businesses are more often suitable for this type of business model, because owners don't usually do all the work, and once your product is out in various outlets, the cash registers can literally ring while you're asleep. That doesn't normally happen with a service company.

Serial entrepreneur Wayne Huizenga, the only person in history to build three Fortune 1000 companies from scratch — Waste Management, Blockbuster Entertainment, and AutoNation — was the consummate entrepreneur. Many years ago when he visited our entrepreneurship center at USC, he told me that he preferred a business model that provided a regular income, a rental income, for example. After establishing an initial inventory, you rent that inventory over and over again, recovering your costs quickly. The rest is profit.

Huizenga was no stranger to the need to change business models. His first model was earning rents off videos in his shops called Blockbuster Video. Later he included DVD-by-mail, streaming, video on demand, and even cinema theater. At the height of its success, Blockbuster had 9,000 stores globally, but changing times and the rise of Netflix eventually forced the company into bankruptcy. By 2014, all of its corporate-owned stores had closed, and the locally owned stores were left to struggle on their own. One by one, they too closed, except for the Blockbuster in Bend, Oregon, which, famously, became the subject of a Netflix film in 2017, a year before Huizenga passed away. Suddenly, people came out of nowhere to support the store out of feelings of nostalgia for the place where they had hung out on Saturday nights. People from all over the world began to send flowers to the shop and ordered T-shirts, hats and such, all made by local businesses in Bend. The owners of "last Blockbuster shop" have no plans to close and are enjoying their newfound fame since the Netflix streaming release in March of 2021. An interesting side story is that Huizenga had the opportunity to purchase Netflix years ago when Netflix was still a mail-order DVD service. He passed on the opportunity because he thought it was too niche, and Netflix went on to transform itself into a dominant streaming service. Even seasoned entrepreneurs sometimes misjudge opportunities.

With a product business, you can create additional revenue streams by adding services to your model. Now you can see why the boundaries between product and service companies have disappeared. You need to provide both to have a successful business today.

Evolving Digital Business Models

You're already part of the Internet world as a user, so you — like so many other people — may be asking yourself, "How can I make money on the Internet?" You read about others doing it all the time.

Well, here's the secret. The question isn't "How can I make money on the Internet," it's "How can I make money with my business?" The Internet is merely a vehicle, a tool, in the process of delivering your product or service, nothing more. And for some entrepreneurs, that thought conjures up a great place to start a business, but it doesn't really deliver. One entrepreneur who loves collectibles thought it might be fun to make money selling unique items over the Internet. What a simple business concept — set up a great site, take orders, and you're in business, watching the money roll in. Right? Wrong!

What this enthusiastic entrepreneur didn't realize is how costly, complex, and time-consuming inventory management and order fulfillment (packaging and shipping) can be. They found that their manufacturers had long lead times and most fulfillment companies were automated and set up for huge volumes, something they didn't have. Moreover, the fulfillment houses wanted about $9 a package to handle an order, and at that rate, they couldn't make any money and their customers would balk at the high price of shipping. In the short term, they solved the problem by hiring students to pack and ship their products through UPS; however, they knew that solution wouldn't work for long.

This entrepreneur is no exception to the rule. The fact is that many e-tailers are not able to make money because their fulfillment costs are too high. And making money is something you have to do. Fortunately, there are entrepreneurs like the founders of Etsy who provide a global marketplace for tiny businesses. They help their community of sellers become successful businesses by connecting them to millions of buyers looking for something special that can't be found anywhere else. Etsy uses a combination of in-house fulfillment and third-party services such as ShipBuddies and Amazon fulfillment (FBA), which lets sellers access the service even if they aren't selling through Amazon.

REMEMBER

To make money with a business you need customers, a great team, a value proposition, a good product or service, money, and a business model that works. Let's look at some examples of ways you can do that with a digital business.

Using an advertising model

The first business model on the Internet was probably the *clicks and hits* model where the company derived all its revenues from advertising. That was in the good old days when advertisers didn't know any better and thought that people clicking onto a site actually read the banner ads, buttons, and so forth. Of course, now we know that, for the most part, they don't, which explains why this business model isn't successful in attracting investors or customers.

With millions of websites competing for visitors, the number of visitors to any one site has proportionally decreased.

This means that the advertising model has become the proverbial vicious circle. To entice advertisers to purchase space on your website (providing you your revenue stream), you have to show that you're attracting the number of hits they require. To do that, you have to attract visitors, and that means you have to spend a lot of money advertising both online and offline. Thus, the bulk of your investor money goes to customer acquisition.

But, remember, it isn't merely about hits, it's about click-throughs, or customers who actually click on the banner or button and link to the advertiser's site. If that isn't happening, advertisers are not interested in your site. The amount of time a user spends on a website is a function of what the consumer is looking for and the content and functionality of the website. You may want to track your own organic website traffic over time. That way you can determine if any paid advertising is working — that is, keeping people longer on your website.

TIP

If you still want to use advertising as a business model, make sure it isn't your primary business model, but rather one of several.

Using a subscription-based model

The subscription model has proven successful for some companies and is growing in popularity. With this model, your customer pays a fee to access your site and use its services. It's similar to gaining access to a private club, giving you the right and privilege to use information that only members have. Fees typically are charged monthly, but, for example, *The Wall Street Journal* charges an annual fee to access its online journal and archives. In general, sites like WSJ are perceived as having a higher quality of target content and services than the average site. If your customers really need what you're offering, they are more likely to pay to gain access. However, with this model, you had better know your customer's needs.

Not everyone is willing to pay for even the best information. As a result, entrepreneurs must change business models to survive. One such case is illustrated in the sidebar "Someone has to pay for it."

Growing a hybrid model

Many Internet ventures that originally were virtual e-commerce companies selling products but carrying no inventory (they outsourced their warehouse and fulfillment functions to offline companies) are now being forced to become a combination Internet and traditional offline company. For example, when Amazon.com first launched, it was designed as a totally virtual company that linked with book publishers and distribution houses as its source of supply. Essentially, the publishers and distributors would drop-ship orders to Amazon's customers (that means the books would go directly from the publisher or distributor to the customer). But when an offline competitor, Barnes & Noble, decided to get into the e-commerce game, the game changed. Amazon could no longer compete on fulfillment with Barnes & Noble's well-established warehouse and distribution system, so it was forced to invest in warehouse/distribution centers of its own.

SOMEONE HAS TO PAY FOR IT

You may have the greatest idea in the world, but if people aren't willing to pay you for it, you have no business — your business model doesn't work. One Internet firm provided healthcare information to people with specific diseases through a subscription service. The focus was on serious chronic illnesses. Subscribers received personalized feedback based on information they provided the company about their disease. Essentially, each illness had a community site. The problem wasn't getting people to the site — customers loved the information they received and liked being able to communicate with others who shared the same disease. The problem was getting them to subscribe to the service — less than 5 percent of the firm's trial customers subscribed, and it was about to run out of cash from initial investment capital.

With the status of the company in such dire straits, its founders decided to radically change the business model. They really didn't have a choice. After some brainstorming, the founders realized that they had collected valuable information about their subscribers. What if they dropped the subscription service and, with the permission of their customers, started selling real-time aggregated market research data on people with specific diseases to healthcare companies and pharmaceutical firms? That would be a new business model, plus they could run advertising for their research customers — yet another source of revenue. They decided to go ahead with it. This new business model has worked so far, but it's too soon to know if the firm can succeed competing against major healthcare providers that are starting to provide similar services. Still, the important lesson to be learned is that if your business model doesn't work, another one is bound to be out there that will. Remember, someone has to pay for what you offer. Of course, in this example, you would not want to sell private information without the consent of your customers, especially healthcare information, which is protected by law.

Another challenge emerging for e-tailers who are trying hard not to become commodity sites whose only value proposition is price is the introduction of *shop-bots*. Known simply as bots, they strike terror in the hearts of e-tailers everywhere. Bots are simply digital robots that search all the stores on the Internet for a given product and compare prices for consumers, producing the lowest price and the site that has it. That means the consumer never visits your site unless the bot shows that you have the best price. Bots force you to compete on price, not on value.

What all this means to an entrepreneur considering this business model is that Internet retailing is not as easy as it once was; distribution is hard. So, you may want to consider these tips for partnering with a good fulfillment company to keep your initial investment down.

>> Get your fulfillment system in place before ever taking your first order. That way you won't disappoint your first customer.

>> Consider your fulfillment needs. Do you have a perishable product? Is it fragile? Are you dealing in multiple products?

>> Do your homework on the costs of setting up a fulfillment system in-house versus outsourcing. Find the best method at the lowest cost.

>> Get referrals from other entrepreneurs on fulfillment houses.

>> If you're outsourcing, choose your fulfillment house carefully. Make sure it's used to dealing with your type of product.

>> Negotiate a deal with the fulfillment house where your costs go down as your volume goes up.

>> Put someone knowledgeable in charge of your fulfillment functions.

>> Always be honest with customers about the length of time it takes for them to receive an order. That means you better have a good relationship with a reliable fulfillment house or do it well yourself.

>> If your products typically go to customers' homes, working with companies that regularly deal with home deliveries is a good option. iShip.com and HomeGrocer.com have good home delivery systems in place. Business shipments and some consumer shipments do well with UPS, FedEx, and DHL. (Amazon uses UPS in addition to their own trucks.)

>> Find a way to add value and trust to your site so customers will purchase from you regardless of whether you also have the lowest price.

TIP

Another way to create value is by building your brand, both online and off, and that means your relationship with your customers so those customers trust you. Right now the e-tailers that are most successful have brand recognition — Amazon, eBay, and Etsy. But smaller companies can gain a wide following with personalization and connecting to their customers. Good examples are Barlow Herbal and Artful Home.

Thinking micro

With the Internet loaded with millions of sites, finding a niche that doesn't have a major player or an established brand is becoming more difficult. Many entrepreneurs are creating business models based on tiny niches — micro niches — in the market and doing quite well. I always say that you don't have to own a big company to bring a lot of money to the bottom line. You just have to find a big enough market that wants what you're offering. One tiny company on the East Coast focused on installing recessed lights in homes and businesses. They wanted to be the best — the go to source for recessed lighting, which has become very popular. One specialty they have is retrofitting existing lighting to recessed lighting. When you decide to go after a niche market with a service like this company, it's best to be located in a large metropolitan area. And that's precisely what this company did. They're betting they can win because they know the area and the market better than anyone — certainly better than a company that's trying to serve the entire country.

Don't be afraid to carve out a tiny piece of a market that someone else is serving. Become the expert in that tiny niche, and you'll know those customers better than your competitors. Interestingly enough, the entire state of Maine has that philosophy about entrepreneurship. For years, politicians and local community leaders have advocated for the support of locally owned micro-niche businesses that understand the Maine culture. In doing so they have successfully fought to keep the major chains at bay.

Testing Your Business Model

By now you should have a good understanding of business models and their importance. Once you've settled on your initial business model, you need to test it. Don't simply assume that your business model will work. Don't assume that the market conditions you identified and assessed during your market research remain relevant.

Go to your business model canvas and make some hypotheses (educated guesses) about what you believe to be true. Now you must decide how you're going to test each of your hypotheses to find out if they are in fact true. Design an experiment that generally involves potential customers. You want their unbiased thoughts. Don't lead them to give you the answer you want. That will only hurt your efforts.

Suppose your business concept involves an app that helps students organize the tasks required for all their courses in addition to other obligations they have. If you assume that because you're a student you have a handle on the needs of your potential customers, you'd be wrong. Not all students are alike, so unless you segment your student population into smaller markets, your business model might not work for everyone you're trying to reach. So, your first hypothesis is wrong, which is not unusual. In fact, entrepreneurs typically find that most of their initial hypotheses are wrong because they haven't spent enough time in the field talking to and observing customers. Chapter 6 covers how to do field research to identify and understand your customers. Among all the questions you seek to answer with feasibility analysis, those related to your customers are the most important, because without customers who need what you're offering, you don't have a business.

For the real-life task app, these entrepreneurs made the mistake of defining their customer market too broadly — all students. Once they started to consider how students might differ, they were able to zero in on the students who most needed the app. As it turns out, those students were found in the school of engineering, where projects are a big part of their studies, so they have a lot of responsibilities to manage, more than the typical student. With a first customer now in hand, they could go on to test other hypotheses and adjust as needed.

Once you've completed testing your hypotheses, you can ask yourself if the conditions are right to move forward with the business or if you need to make additional adjustments or corrections.

Keep in mind that the goal of your feasibility analysis is to reduce the level of uncertainty. When you started the process, you probably had an unacceptable number of unanswered questions — too many to even consider launching the business. After the testing process, you will have reduced the number of unanswered questions. Yes, you'll still have some risk, but it's much more manageable.

One big question left to answer is how much money you need to launch the business and operate it until it delivers a positive cash flow from your business model. We look at that in the next chapter.

Chapter **12**

Assessing Your Initial Financial Needs

You have no doubt read stories about entrepreneurs who secured millions of dollars in investment with financials that projected years of losses before finally turning a profit. Amazon, one of the most successful brands in the world, didn't make a profit for nearly nine years, and their investors were getting quite antsy. Let me emphasize that while this strategy is not uncommon, it is definitely not the norm, so don't expect it to hold true for you. Investors will expect you to lay out a viable plan for making a reasonable profit as quickly as possible.

While a lot of money is available to entrepreneurs with powerful concepts, investors are much smarter and more savvy to the inner workings of e-commerce and what makes a good business investment. They aren't throwing money after concepts that can't demonstrate a solid revenue model or that won't be profitable within a reasonable period of time — the way they once did.

Yes, times have changed, but two things remain constant: you need to create value and you need to make a profit. That doesn't mean you need a lot of money to start a winning business. Some of the legendary and venerable companies you recognize today started on a shoestring. For example, The Clorox Co. started when five men from Oakland, California each threw $100 into a pot to start the company. Lex Wexner borrowed $5,000 from his aunt to open a small retail women's clothing store that eventually became The Limited. Apple Computer, Inc., began with $1,350 that Steve Jobs and Steve Wozniak raised by selling a Volkswagen van and a Hewlett-Packard calculator. Domino's Pizza was started with $900, and the list goes on. The point is, figure out the essentials to operate your business and you might discover that you need less money than you originally thought.

REMEMBER

Don't let money stop your progress this early in the process. In this chapter, you discover ways to calculate how many resources you need and how to potentially reduce the amount of cash you need.

Touring Your Business Virtually

Working with hundreds of new businesses, I have found that one of the most important exercises you can do to understand your resource requirements is to create a process map, which is a virtual tour of your business from the point at which the customer touches the business to the completion of a sale. In other words, you walk your customer through the purchase journey.

Identifying the resource needs of a startup venture requires walking through the business and its various processes and activities in your mind. Without doing this little exercise, you can easily forget important steps that can adversely affect your estimates. So, take a virtual tour of your business and begin mapping out how you want your business to work.

For simplicity's sake, consider a simple, traditional business example that assumes a physical business. Starting at the front door (that could even be the front door of your home), perhaps the first thing you see is a desk with a receptionist answering the phone while typing or dictating something into a desktop computer and printing another document on a nearby printer. Okay, what do you know so far? You know that you need a receptionist, a desk (and a chair — the receptionist has to sit on something), a computer, a printer, a telephone, and various office supplies. And you've just begun! Here's a suggestion for completing the tour:

>> Make your way through the business in the same way that a purchase order moves through it. Who gets the order first, second, and so on?

>> Where each activity takes place, note what that activity is, who performs it, and what equipment and supplies are needed to complete the task.

>> If you are developing a product, consider all the tasks related to that development, including everything that goes into building the prototype and the final product.

>> If you are outsourcing tasks, note that and calculate the costs.

>> Continue the tour through the completion of order-taking, billing, collection, and post-sales services.

>> Don't forget administrative tasks like payroll and accounting, and general expenses like rent and utilities. Those are basic operational tasks for any business.

By now, you have a good sense of the expenses related to startup and to the operating business. Double-check the list, making sure you aren't forgetting something important like telephone service or a high-speed Internet connection.

I always recommend graphing the business process so you can see how everything comes together. Doing so sometimes makes it easier to figure out the best way to run your business. You can do this by creating a flowchart of the various processes in your business (product development, manufacturing, administration, service, and so forth) and how they interrelate. Figure 12-1 shows an example.

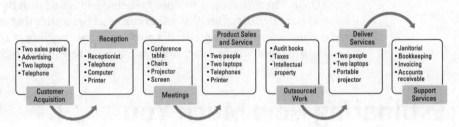

FIGURE 12-1:
A process flowchart for a service business.

The business represented in the flowchart is one that sells business analytics software to small and medium-size businesses. I have categorized it as a service business because it's a software as a service business that requires customer support in the form of training and follow-up.

Once you know the number of people you will need, ask yourself if these people need to be full-time employees, part-time, or perhaps contractors. Usually on the first pass, you will surprise yourself with how many people you think you need. But if you stop to consider whether a particular person can do more than one task, you can usually bring that number down. In this example, the two people who will do sales and service are performing two different tasks. As the customer downloads the software to their computers, the same two people can potentially provide the training and follow-up.

Remember, this is a startup. Even the CEO can help take care of the plants and do some other tasks, and you can outsource some tasks like bookkeeping and janitorial on an as-needed basis. Running a startup is a team effort, so don't make the walls around certain activities too high. This is the time to conserve your resources. Just because you hire someone to sell your product doesn't mean that you will start making money off their work from day one. The reality is that even the best salespeople take months to bring in more revenue than their salary, so plan for it.

One other thing you need to consider once your virtual walkthrough is complete is the equipment and major supplies needed for each activity. Remember that you don't have to buy all your equipment outright. If it's extraordinarily expensive, you might investigate leasing to keep more cash in the business.

Upon completion of the process graph, you should have a better understanding of how your business will look when it's operating. If it looks lean and mean, you've done a good job and positioned your business to survive the rocky early days.

REMEMBER

Now ask yourself one more question. Where is your company positioned in the value chain? The value chain is discussed in Chapter 10. You want to understand what the channel markups are so you can figure out how much profit you can potentially make. In this example, it's a software business, so it's at the top of the value chain. The product is developed in-house and is sold directly to customers so there are no intermediaries. You sell to customers at a price that covers your costs and enables you to make a profit. It's also a price that customers are willing to pay. You learned that important fact from your market research (see Chapter 6).

Estimating How Much You Will Sell: Demand

Estimating demand for a new product or service is difficult. Much of this difficulty is due to the lack of historical demand data and to seasonality and industry discounts, which are often unknown until you're doing business in the industry. To avoid overestimating sales, a common problem, entrepreneurs need to triangulate demand from historical analogies using similar products/service, customer or end user and intermediary feedback, and the entrepreneur's own experience from having conducted field research.

No matter how carefully you research demand, you must be prepared that your numbers will likely change once you're in operation. However, if your forecasted numbers were derived from excellent research, it's likely that you won't be too far off the mark and it will be easy to adjust.

Why do forecasted numbers change, even when you're careful about projecting your demand and expenses? Here are two reasons:

» When designing and developing a new product, calculating accurate demand and cost figures is difficult because you don't yet have a production quality prototype. The prototype typically costs substantially more than the mass-produced product units will cost, but the prototype provides a basis from which to estimate costs of components, parts, labor, and so forth. So, the sooner you have a physical prototype, the closer your estimates will be to the actual production costs when you start the business.

» When you're forming a service company, you typically base demand and cost estimates on other similar companies in the industry. Without inside information, however, getting accurate figures is difficult.

Triangulating to demand

Estimating demand is the first piece of the information puzzle you must solve. I see too many entrepreneurs avoid dealing with demand until the last minute and then doing a shoddy job of it. This estimate is too important to avoid or try to do quickly. Given the difficulty of arriving at accurate estimates, many entrepreneurs use a process called *triangulation*, which means that they approach an estimate of product demand from three vantage points — their industry, their market/customer, and their own knowledge. To develop these estimates, consider this three-pronged approach:

» **Talking to industry watchers, suppliers, distributors, and the like.** Reading trade journals and visiting outlets helps you find out the kind of volume you can expect from your type of product or service. For a service business, you can find out how many clients an outlet sees in a month's time. Sometimes proprietary information like client volume is best estimated through observation or from third parties such as suppliers and competitors.

» **Talking to customers.** I can't emphasize enough how important customers are in developing your business concept and providing valuable information in determining demand for your product or service. You can even talk to customers of your competitors. They are more likely than your competitors to give you the information you need, and you can get a sense of how satisfied these customers are. Ask how often they buy, what they buy, in what quantities, and for what reasons. Make a point of talking to your customers directly to complement information you get from the field.

» **Relying on your own knowledge.** Bring your own knowledge and experience in your industry to bear on your estimates. Become a secret shopper. Visit a competitor's site and observe who the customers are, what they do, and what they purchase.

Using these three sources of information may enable you to arrive at a number for demand that is reasonably close. Once you launch your business, you will be tracking sales on a regular basis to improve your demand estimates.

REMEMBER

No demand estimate survives first contact with the market. Therefore, make your estimates fairly conservative. Now is not the time for overblown estimates that you can't meet.

Forecasting your sales

Because sales impact other numbers in your forecast — namely, your expenditures — calculate them first. If you have done sufficient demand research and you've settled on a winning price point, your job of forecasting sales will be much easier. If you are introducing a new product or service, you must find a suitable substitute product to use as reference for demand. For example, when compact discs were introduced to the market, estimates of demand were based on sales of cassette tapes, because the belief was that customers who bought cassettes would eventually all switch to CDs. Otherwise, if you're introducing a derivative of a product or service currently in the market, you can use that product as your guide. Information that you need to collect includes:

>> *Sell-in* to the retailer (if you're using a retailer). This is the amount of product you sell to the retailer.

>> *Sell-through* to the customer. This is the amount of product that the retailer sells to the customer.

>> Seasonality in the market. Are there certain times of the year when sales are highest or lowest?

>> Growth rates in your product or service based on the market. How fast are sales growing?

>> Innovations that may enable you to charge more for the product or service. Are there cost-effective ways to upgrade your product to increase its value?

>> Innovations that may let you produce the product for less than competitors and therefore charge less.

WARNING

If you choose public or well-established companies as benchmarks for demand, you need to discount your projected volume of sales because you won't have the same brand recognition as these companies or enjoy the economies of scale they do because of their size and experience in the market. Therefore, it's unlikely that you can achieve their demand numbers.

Forecasting How Much You Will Spend

Some of your expenditures vary with sales, so your job is a bit easier. For example, inventory and marketing expenses often vary with sales. Other expenses may vary by season, by the number of employees, or by usage, as in the case of utilities. Some expenses like rent and lease payments are fixed and won't vary, remaining the same each month. Your accountant can help you determine which expenses are fixed and which are variable.

Determining the cost of goods sold

Manufacturing businesses deal with complex issues when forecasting expenditures. One important issue is called the *cost of goods sold* (COGS) — the price you pay to create or acquire your product. This number is critical to calculating your gross profit and gross margin.

Most startup ventures figure the cost per unit to produce a product and then apply that figure (expressed as a percentage) to a more detailed cost accounting model that includes raw materials inventory, work-in-process inventory, finished-goods inventory, total inventory, factory overhead, work-in-process flow in units, and weighted-average cost per unit. The result is a more accurate COGS estimate. But for now, you don't have to worry about all that technical stuff. You just need a ballpark figure for startup purposes.

Here's what a simple COGS calculation looks like:

Selling Price =	$60/unit
COGS	
Raw materials =	$ 4/unit
Direct labor =	$25/unit
Factory overhead =	$10/unit
Total COGS =	$39/unit

You should calculate this breakout whether you create your product or have another company produce it for you.

Forecasting general and administrative expenses

General and administrative expenses include selling expenses like advertising, travel, sales salaries, commissions, and promotional supplies, and fixed expenses like facility, equipment, and administrative and executive salaries. Using a percentage of sales to project G&A expenses isn't smart, because some of these expenses are fixed and others are variable, that is, they change with the volume of sales. To be as accurate as possible, I suggest breaking out the details of each of these expenses in separate statements and transferring the totals to the financial statements, which you learn about later in this chapter. That way, your financial statements don't become cluttered.

Determining taxes

The last thing you'll consider is taxes (everyone tends to leave taxes until the end). You need to account for payroll taxes; state, federal, and in some instances local income taxes; and a variety of other taxes that are payable at varying times of the year, such as property taxes. To calculate your income taxes, you'll prepare an income (profit and loss) statement so you know how much taxable income you have. I deal with the income statement in an upcoming section. In general, figure that taxes can amount to about 40 percent or so of taxable income. Failing to account for taxes may lead to serious cash flow issues. Again, your accountant can advise on which taxes your business will need to pay based on the type of business and where your business is located.

Preparing Financial Statements

For purposes of determining the feasibility of your new venture, the only financial statements that really matter are the income statement and the cash flow statement. Ask any entrepreneur what the most important financial figure is (in any business), and they will tell you that it's cash. The old saying rings true, "You can't pay your bills with profit, only with cash." To determine your estimated cash needed to launch, you need to prepare an income statement, a cash flow statement, and a break-even analysis.

When you prepare any financial statement, you want to include *notes* or *assumptions*, explaining how you arrived at the figures in the statement. You should also explain any unusual or non-recurring expenses, such as the cost of setting up a booth and displaying your products at a tradeshow. In general, every line item in your financial statement references an assumption, explaining the premise for the number. Explaining these assumptions is an excellent way to prepare to talk to investors who will want know how you arrived at your numbers. "It sounded like a reasonable number" is not going to fly. You must explain where the number came from.

Calculating profit and loss — the income statement

The income statement reports the profit or loss made by your business during a specified time. You usually calculate this statement first because you need profit totals (taxable income) to figure taxes for the cash flow statement. Taxes appear on the cash flow statement when they are paid. If your business is a sole proprietorship, Sub-chapter S Corporation, partnership, or Limited Liability Company, you don't show taxes on your cash flow statement because taxable income passes through to the owners to be taxed at their individual rates. I discuss legal ways to structure your business and their tax implications in Chapter 15.

Startup ventures often do not show a profit in the first year or so because generating sales takes time and paying initial startup costs usually puts the business in the red for a time. How much time it takes to make a profit is a function of the type of business and the strategy it uses. So, how do you forecast sales, profits, and cash flow, when you know your business is not going to earn a profit for several years? Many Internet companies face this dilemma, struggling to appear viable while they are burdened with enormous marketing expenses to attract customers to their websites and an inability to generate enough sales to show a profit.

For the most part, investors treat e-commerce a bit differently than traditional businesses. Investors are more interested in the size of the market and whether the concept will *scale*, that is, grow to reach a mass market. So, the value of what you're forecasting is directly related to the size of your potential customer base rather than to the traditional profit projections. In fact, investors in Internet businesses often don't care whether you include financials beyond revenue projections, because they will essentially determine what your financials look like using their own assumptions.

More important perhaps is addressing any uncertainties in your financial projections. Are there any weak points that affect your analysis and estimates? What steps can you take to deal with these weak points? Forecasting sales and expenses as accurately as possible and justifying them is necessary. Figure 12-2 shows an example of a typical manufacturing business's income statement.

The basic formula to calculate profit and loss in a business is

Revenues − Expenses = Net Profit before Taxes

You can see in Figure 12-2 that Perfect Products's revenues ($440,875 for the year) come from sales of its product, Widget 1. The income statement presents the variable costs, or the COGS. I separated out labor within the COGS, showing the addition of one employee in Month 8 to handle the increasing demand projected for the product. This need is determined from the sales forecast (demand).

Variable costs and gross profit

The difference between revenues and variable costs (or COGS) yields a company's gross profit. For the year, Perfect Products expects gross profit of $195,986, representing 44 percent of gross sales for the year ($195,986/$440,875). Understanding gross profit as a percentage of gross sales is important.

About 44 percent of every sales dollar pays the direct costs of making Widget 1, meaning that about 56 percent of every dollar is left over for paying overhead (general and administrative expenses or operating expenses) and making a profit. That is a healthy margin, but you're not finished yet.

Fixed costs

The next section in the statement includes fixed costs, which are operating expenses or overhead that you must pay at a constant rate no matter how much product you're producing. Advertising expenses are a notable exception. There is a fixed percentage of 3 percent that varies with sales. This percentage represents what you found to be typical in your industry for advertising expenses.

This section also includes an entry for depreciation. Improvements that Perfect Products made on its facility became an asset. The cost of that asset can be spread out, or depreciated, over a number of years (typically the useful life of the asset), essentially recovering the cost of the asset. Perfect Products' $10,000 improvement to its rented space depreciates over five years; thus one-fifth of the depreciation expense can be taken in the first year, or $167 per month, the amount that appears on the income statement. I advise you to check with your accountant about the most appropriate depreciation method for a particular asset.

Net profit

You can show three kinds of net profit on your income statement: net profit before taxes, earnings before interest and taxes (EBIT), and earnings before interest, taxes, depreciation, and amortization (EBITDA). For simplicity's sake, I'm indicating earnings before interest and taxes. If you make interest payments and have a corporate entity in which you show taxes, you'll have the following additional lines on your statement.

Perfect Products

	Premise	Month 0	Month 1	Month 2	Month 3	Month 4
Number of units sold			17	30	60	120
Revenues						
Widget 1			2,125	3,750	7,500	15,000
Total Revenues			**2,125**	**3,750**	**7,500**	**15,000**
Variable Costs						
COGS	33% of Sales		701	1,238	2,475	4,950
Labor cost	2 employees @ $16/unit		544	960	1,920	3,840
	1 employee@$16/unit					
Total Variable Costs			1,245	2,198	4,395	8,790
Gross Profit		**0.41**	**880**	**1,553**	**3,105**	**6,210**
Fixed Costs						
Salaries-Principals	1,500 per month each		3,000	3,000	3,000	3,000
Depreciation on improvement			(167)	(167)	(167)	(167)
Gen. & Adm. Expenses			600	600	600	600
Building Rent	Per 1 year lease		1,800	1,800	1,800	1,800
Equipment Lease			2,200	2,200	2,200	2,200
Advertising			64	113	225	450
Insurance			1,600	1,600	1,600	1,600
Utilities			510	510	510	510
Total Fixed Cost			9,607	9,656	9,768	9,993
Total Costs			10,852	11,853	14,163	18,783
Earnings Before Interest and Taxes (EBIT)			(8,727)	(8,103)	(6,663)	(3,783)
Cumulative P & L			(8,727)	(16,831)	(23,494)	(27,277)

FIGURE 12-2:
An income statement reflects a company's revenue and expenses and reports its profits or losses.

>> Interest expense

>> Earnings before taxes

>> Income tax expense

>> Net income

You can see in the sample statement that Perfect Products makes its first profit from operations in Month 9. This statement doesn't, however, include startup costs prior to the business being in operation. So, Perfect Products's *break-even point*, which is the point beyond which a profit is made, requires a higher sales volume because it also accounts for the startup costs.

Forecasting your cash flow

Without a doubt, the most important financial statement for entrepreneurs is the cash flow statement, because it reflects the company's *liquidity* and forecasts when your company will achieve a positive cash flow based on revenues. Cash flow statements are also important to your bankers and investors, because they predict your company's ability to generate the positive cash flows that are needed to meet the company's obligations.

The simplest way to explain the cash flow statement is to imagine it's like your checkbook. In your checkbook you log your deposits, *cash inflows,* from paychecks, clients, and other sources, and the money you spend, *cash outflows,* to pay your expenses. The difference between the two tells you whether you have a positive or negative cash flow. A simple version of a cash flow statement is shown in Figure 12-3.

Perfect Products Pro Forma

	Premise	Month 0	Month 1	Month 2	Month 3	Month 4
	Number of units sold @ $125/ea		17	30	60	120
Sales Forecast						
Widget 1			2,125	3,750	7,500	15,000
Total Sales Forecast			2,125	3,750	7,500	15,000
CASH INFLOWS						
	70% COD		1,488	2,625	5,250	10,500
	30% collection of 30 days		0	638	1,125	2,250
Total Cash Receipts			1,488	3,263	6,375	12,750
CASH OUTFLOWS						
Upfront Cash						
Deposit-Rent	1 month in advance	1,800				
Equipment down-payment		2,200				
Permits		1,737				
Property Improvement		10,000				
Initial Supplies		1,500				
Insurance down-payment		1,600				
Computer		2,500				
Advertising		2,000				
Misc.		1,000				
Total Upfront Cash		24,337				
Variable Costs						
COGP	33% of Sales		701	1,238	2,475	4,950
Labor cost	2 employees-paid by unit Add 1 employee by unit		544	960	1,920	3,840
Total Variable Costs			1,245	2,198	4,395	8,790
Fixed Cost						
Salaries-Principals	1,500 per month each		3,000	3,000	3,000	3,000
Gen. & Adm. Expenses			600	600	600	600
Building Rent	Per 1 year lease		1,800	1,800	1,800	1,800
Equipment Lease			2,200	2,200	2,200	2,200
Advertising			64	113	225	450
Insurance			1,600	1,600	1,600	1,600
Utilities			510	510	510	510
Total Fixed Cost			6,774	6,823	6,935	7,160
Total Cash Expenditures			8,019	9,020	11,330	15,950
Net Cash In / Out per Month			(6,532)	(5,758)	(4,955)	(3,200)
Cash Balance-Beg. of Month		0	0	(30,869)	(36,626)	(41,581)
Cumulative Cash Balance		(24,337)	(30,869)	(36,626)	(41,581)	(44,781)

Text boxes:
In "Month zero", before operations commence, Perfect Products has big cash outlays. Capital needs will total $64,222. (See Fig. 11-5)

30% of sales will be on 30-day terms, slowing cash flow.

Separate "break-out" statements provide details on all these items.

FIGURE 12-3: This cash flow statement depicts the cash inflows (revenues) to the business and the cash outflows (expenses).

Cash Flow Statement (Unfunded)

Month 5	Month 6	Month 7	Month 8	Month 9	Month 10	Month 11	Month 12	TOTAL
200	250	300	350	400	500	600	700	3,527
25,000	31,250	37,500	43,750	50,000	62,500	75,000	87,500	440,875
25,000	31,250	37,500	43,750	50,000	62,500	75,000	87,500	440,875
17,500	21,875	26,250	30,625	35,000	43,750	52,500	61,250	308,613
4,500	7,500	9,375	11,250	13,125	15,000	18,750	22,500	106,013
22,000	**29,375**	**35,625**	**41,875**	**48,125**	**58,750**	**71,250**	**83,750**	→ **414,625**
								1,800
								2,200
								1,737
								10,000
								1,500
								2,500
								2,000
								1,000
								24,337
8,250	10,313	12,375	14,438	16,500	20,625	24,750	28,875	145,489
6,400	8,000	9,600	7,504	8,576	10,720	12,864	15,008	85,936
			1,848	2,112	2,640	3,168	3,696	13,464
14,650	**18,313**	**21,975**	**23,790**	**27,188**	**33,985**	**40,782**	**47,579**	**244,889**
3,000	3,000	3,000	3,000	3,000	3,000	3,000	3,000	36,000
600	600	600	600	600	600	600	600	7,200
1,800	1,800	1,800	1,800	1,800	1,800	1,800	1,800	21,600
2,200	2,200	2,200	2,200	2,200	2,200	2,200	2,200	26,400
750	938	1,125	1,313	1,500	1,875	2,250	2,625	13,226
1,600	1,600	1,600	1,600	1,600	1,600	1,600	1,600	19,200
510	510	510	510	510	510	510	510	6,120
7,460	**7,648**	**7,835**	**8,023**	**8,210**	**8,585**	**8,960**	**9,335**	**93,746**
22,110	**25,960**	**29,810**	**31,812**	**35,398**	**42,570**	**49,742**	**56,914**	**338,635**
(110)	**3,415**	**5,815**	**10,063**	**12,727**	**16,180**	**21,508**	**26,836**	→ **51,653**
(44,781)	(44,891)	(41,476)	(35,661)	(25,598)	(12,871)	3,309	24,817	
(44,891)	(41,476)	(35,661)	(25,598)	(12,871)	→ 3,309	24,817	51,653	

Callout boxes:

- Cash receipts lag forecast because of accounts receivable.
- First year, positive cash flow of $51,653 – not bad!
- Second employee hired to help meet growing demand for Widget 1.
- Perfect Products breaks out of the red, makes first profit in Month 10!

FIGURE 12-3: (continued)

REMEMBER

One important difference between a cash flow statement and an income statement is that you record cash inflows and outflows when they occur. So, if you make a sale in January but you receive payment in March, the cash inflow is recorded in March. By contrast, recall from earlier in this chapter, in the income statement you record expenses when they're incurred and revenues when they accrue (are earned). So, if you made the sale in January, it is recorded in January's income statement, even though you may not receive the cash until March. Perfect Products's cash flow statement is a good example.

Cash inflows

You record cash inflows — all the money coming into the business from various sources — first in the top section of the cash flow statement. Multi- product companies may separately record revenues from each product, providing a better picture of how each is doing. Cash inflows consist of:

>> **Gross receipts on sales.** This is the total amount you receive from all sources during the accounting period.

>> **Dividend and interest income.** This is money from savings accounts or other securities.

>> **Invested capital.** This is money that the owners or others invest in the company.

Because we are trying to calculate startup needs, the cash flow statement of Perfect Products is considered unfunded, which means that investment capital isn't included. Perfect Products produces one product — Widget 1 — and sells 3,527 units at $125 a piece in the first year, for total sales revenue of $440,875. Notice, however, that total sales received are only $414,625. Why the difference? Well, 70 percent of sales are for cash, and 30 percent are collected within 30 days, thus creating accounts receivable. You must show the cash when it's received, so in Month 1, you see that the company receives $1,488 on sales of 17 products, but the remaining 30 percent, or $638, is collected in Month 2, along with 70 percent of Month 2's sales revenue.

Cash outflows

The next section of the cash flow statement records operating cash outflows (your disbursements or expenses). You notice several differences about this section, including a Month 0 column, which includes all the *startup costs* you incurred — everything that you put into the enterprise before ever opening the doors. I explain these startup expenses later in this chapter.

Variable costs, expenses that vary with sales or the volume of product you're producing, appear next. The COGS is a variable cost, describing what you produce in any given month in terms of inventory. This figure likely differs from the *cost of goods sold* (COGS) figure on your income statement because COGS includes sales out of inventory (products you have already produced and paid for) but not the cost of products that you add to your inventory. For example, if Perfect Products reduces its inventory by $3,000 this period, its COGS is $3,000 less than its COGS on its income statement.

Other entries to look for in cash flow statements include:

>> **Sales, general, and administrative expenses (SG&A).** SG&A include salaries, rent, equipment expense, utilities, and so forth. Remember that providing key totals in your statement and referring to a breakout statement for details won't clutter your financial statement or make it difficult to read. Likewise, remember that you list only expenses you have actually paid each period.

>> **Interest expense.** What you actually pay out in interest. Perfect Products carries no interest expense.

>> **Capital expenditures (buildings, major equipment, machinery).** When you purchase something major like a piece of equipment, you generally don't pay cash for it, so your cash flow statement reflects your monthly payments, while your income statement shows a depreciation expense because you trade cash for another asset, the equipment, that must be depreciated. See my discussion of income statements earlier in this chapter to understand depreciation.

>> **Long-term debt reduction.** If your company takes out a loan, you need to pay it back. The interest portion appears in the interest expense section, while the principal reduction appears in long-term debt expenses. Perfect Products has no outstanding loans.

Companies that distribute stock may account for the distribution of dividends to owners in a section of their cash flow statement. Most entrepreneurial companies do not distribute dividends in the first few years because reinvesting their earnings helps the company grow.

What's left

The final section of the cash flow statement displays the net change in cash flow (whether you show a positive or negative cash flow for the period you're describing). In any particular month, net cash flow applies to that month only. Below the line for net change is a cumulative cash flow line showing the cash balances at the beginning and end of the month. The final column displays the net change in cash position. Perfect Products plans to end the first year with a positive net cash flow of $51,653 — not bad for a startup company — provided their assumptions are correct.

Planning to Break Even

One figure you want to know at the feasibility stage is how long it will take the business to break even, or when your sales revenue equals your total expenses. In other words, the break-even point shows when you recover the COGS and pay operating expenses. Dividing the total fixed operating costs by the contribution profit margin per unit gives you the percentage of revenue left to pay your overhead expenses. Dividing revenue by price per unit gives you the number of units you need to sell to break even.

You can see in Figure 12-4 that Perfect Products has total fixed costs of $127,746 for the year and a contribution margin of 56% (100 − 44% COGS), when considered together makes the break-even point at $228,117 in sales, or 1,825 units. What this means is that the company must sell at least 1,825 units before it can begin to pay its overhead and make a profit.

Now you're ready to consider how much capital it will take to start your business and, perhaps equally important, what form that capital will take.

$$\text{Break-Even Point} = \frac{\text{Fixed Cost}}{\text{Contribution Rate}}$$

$$\text{Contribution Rate} = 100\% - 44\% = 56\%$$

$$BE = \frac{127,746}{56\%} \qquad \frac{228,117}{\$125/unit}$$

$$BE = \$228,117 \qquad BE = 1,825 \text{ units}$$

FIGURE 12-4:
Analysis tells you how much product you must sell to begin to make a profit.

Calculating what you need to start

Not everything about starting a business requires actual cash. So, figuring out what your expenditures to start the business are going to be is the first thing you need to do.

Using the financial statements covered in the last section, this section explains how to prepare the cash needs assessment. In general, you prepare your cash flow and income statements without considering any funding from yourself, investors, or other sources. That way you can find out exactly how much money it will take, at a minimum, to start your business.

Understanding types of capital

Money is spent in many different ways as a business starts out. Knowing that you have alternatives when it comes to finding capital to spend for your business is important to an entrepreneur because it gives you more flexibility and makes it easier for you to discover ways to reduce your capital requirements. That may make the difference between being able to start the venture or not. Here are some of the types of expenditures you will encounter.

>> **Capital expenditures.** Simply put, capital expenditures are physical items like plant and equipment that have a useful life longer than a year.

>> **Startup costs.** These are all the costs related to getting your business ready to function in the marketplace. If you are introducing a new product that you developed, your startup costs will include your design, development, and prototyping costs. If you intend to manufacture your product, startup also includes the costs of setting up a facility, installing equipment, and training personnel in production. You also must prepare some initial inventory.

THINKING ABOUT YOUR BUSINESS IN STAGES

Many businesses don't need to have everything in place when they launch. They merely need enough to satisfy the initial customers who already believe in what they're doing.

Knowing your initial customers' needs is why most entrepreneurs start businesses with low overhead, no employees (if possible), and leasing rather than buying equipment. Suppose you're starting a business producing and selling three-dimensional, educational floor maps designed for elementary school children to a company like Rand-McNally (one of my former students did this). You don't have a lot of money, but you do have a customer in hand — the map company — that will pay you as soon as you deliver the first order. With that assurance, you can contract with a manufacturer to produce the product and a packager/shipper to deliver the product, while you can handle the paperwork from your home office.

As you look toward building your customer base or increasing the size of your orders, you must think about the point at which you need to bring in an employee to manage your paperwork. If you're happy with your outsourcing arrangement, you don't ever have to bring all those tasks in-house. But, if you decide to add to your product line, you may want to hire someone who can design new products for you. Increasing the number of employees, bringing in an additional investor, adding equipment, increasing your facility, and so forth, are what I call activation points for changing the resources of your business. If you're forecasting your cash needs for the first year and then doing pro forma (forecasted) financial statements for three years, you need to decide when activation points will occur. You don't need to know exact dates; what you need to know is what will trigger the addition, whether it is a certain sales level or when you enter a new geographic market, for example.

If you are offering a service, setting up an office and training personnel may be necessary. If you're leasing, deposits on utilities and your place of business are needed. If you're in the retail business, your startup costs include preparing your storefront, training salespeople, stocking the store, and announcing the opening with some initial advertising.

In short, you can think of startup costs as all those costs that occur prior to opening the doors of your business.

>> **Operating losses.** Rarely does a startup business operate at a positive cash flow from the first day. Your revenues won't likely be enough in the beginning to cover all your expenses. Calculating just how much you're in the red each month is important because you must find a way to cover that loss eventually.

>> **Fixed costs.** Fixed costs are expenditures that don't vary with sales. They fall under the general category of overhead and include things like rent, salaries, and loan payments. The important thing to remember about fixed expenses is that if your sales decline, these expenses stay the same; therefore, generating enough cash flow is vital to cover your fixed expenses.

Putting It All Together

You now have enough information to assess the amount of capital you need to start and operate your business to a positive cash flow. Consider these steps as one way to do that.

1. **List and total your startup costs.**

Remember that startup costs are the costs you incur prior to starting the business. Group them by capital expenses (plant, equipment, patents, and inventory) and soft costs (deposits, labor expenses, and prepaid expenses).

2. **Find your operating losses.**

Look at the cumulative balance on your unfunded cash flow statement and see if your business reaches a positive cash flow from sales during the first year based on your demand estimations. If it reaches a positive cash flow in, say, Month 8, then you know you need enough cash to cover the losses to Month 8 at a minimum. If your negative cash flow goes into the second year, you need a way to cover all the losses through the point of positive cash flow in the second year.

3. Calculate a safety factor.

Having additional cash on hand is a safety factor that mitigates any miscalculations or unanticipated events that impact your business. How much you add as a cushion depends on your industry and the regularity with which your customers pay. For example, you may choose to add six months of fixed costs as your safety margin.

As an example, Perfect Products's total startup needs are shown in Figure 12-5.

Capital Cost		
Computer	2,500	
Property Improvement	10,000	
		12,500
Soft Cost:		
Equipment Lease Downpayment	2,200	
Deposits	1,800	
Permits	1,737	
Insurance	1,600	
Advertising	2,000	
Misc	1,000	
Initial Supplies	1,500	
		11,837
Upfront Cash		24,337
Start Up Loss		20,554
Safety Factor (6 months fixed costs)		59,799
Total		**$104,690**

FIGURE 12-5: Startup capital requirements for Perfect Products include capital and soft costs, upfront cash, startup losses, and a safety factor.

Perfect Products's startup costs of $104,690 is a substantial sum for most entrepreneurs to come up with. Arriving at that total and knowing that you have no way of raising that kind of money, is there anything you can do? You can first look at your capital expenditures. You're proposing a computer purchase of $2,500 and property improvements amounting to $10,000. In the first instance, you don't have to pay cash up front for the computer. You could lease it or make payments. By making payments of $114 a month, including principal and interest, you can still own the computer within two years. As for the improvements, suppose you decide to sign on for a longer-term lease in exchange for your landlord agreeing to split the cost of improvements with you. That could reduce your cash outlay by $5,000. It's worth a try.

Adjusting your estimates

Now that you have some confidence in reducing your cash outlay, try tackling a more difficult challenge. A majority of lease companies don't charge a down payment. With good credit, you can often sign an equipment lease agreement for no money down and with only monthly payments. At the end of the lease, you can choose to purchase the equipment for an agreed-upon payment.

The safety factor is something else you can adjust. How much you need depends on your industry and your confidence that you can generate sales. Suppose that a bit more research reveals that your projected sales levels are such that you feel comfortable reducing your safety factor to three months of fixed costs. Now have a look at what your new startup capital requirements look like in Figure 12-6.

Capital Cost		
Computer	0	Make payments of $114/mo for 2 years
Property Improvement	5,000	Split with landlord
	5,000	
Soft Cost:		
Equipment Lease Downpayment	0	
Deposits	1,800	
Permits	1,737	
Insurance	1,600	
Advertising	2,000	
Misc	1,000	
Initial Supplies	1,500	
	9,637	
Upfront Cash		14,637
Start Up Loss		20,554
Safety Factor (6 months fixed costs)		29,031
Total		**$64,222**

FIGURE 12-6: Adjustments to purchases, leases, and safety factors considerably reduce capital requirements.

What a difference! You've managed to reduce your startup capital to $64,222. Now you can see the value of breaking out your startup costs into the types of money you will need so you can find creative ways to reduce the actual cash you put out.

The one-minute financial plan

In keeping with the idea that you should always have the most important information about your concept at your fingertips, here are the key factors you should be able to provide to a potential investor, banker, or partner relative to capital needs:

>> Total startup capital required and for what major categories of expenditures

>> When the business will reach a positive cash flow

>> Volume of sales or number of units sold required to break even

You have done a lot of work to reach this point. You have one final important question to ask yourself now that you have a better understanding of your company's financials. Can you make enough money to make this effort worthwhile? If the answer is yes, then ask yourself, can you make more money than you would make working for someone else? If you're not sure, are there areas of your business you can tweak to increase its potential value? Now is the time to consider all these questions. Once you start the business, you won't have time. In the meantime, Chapter 13 explores the business plan and your company's design.

3
Designing a Company

Chapter **13**

Preparing a Business Plan

I n Part 2 of this book, you worked through a feasibility analysis using customer discovery and business model validation. These were important tests to determine whether to move forward with your business concept. Assuming your concept passed the feasibility test — you have a solution customers want and you have a business model that works — you can now look into what it takes to operate and grow your business. We do that through a business plan.

In this chapter, you learn that writing a business plan is a big undertaking, in large part because you need to address your many stakeholders' interests. For all stakeholders, two things must be true:

» You must grab their attention with a compelling story about your business that highlights your unique, competitive advantage.

» You must demonstrate proof of concept with a prototype, purchase orders, and/or customer sales.

Who are your stakeholders at this stage? In general, they are investors, lenders, and strategic partners. Each will have specific needs beyond the two just mentioned. For example, investors will want to know that your business will grow, by how much, and when. They also want to be able to gauge their return on investment, degree of risk, and how you will protect their original equity in your company. Lenders (you likely don't have any traditional lenders) want to know the impact of their loan on the business, the kinds of assets you have that can serve as collateral (pledged as security for the loan), and how you will protect the lender if your business doesn't meet its projections.

Telling a compelling story to grab attention is vital if you're going to be taken seriously. What kinds of things attract attention? How about a unique solution to a very big problem? Or proof that customers are already paying for that solution? Or a founding team with successful, recognized entrepreneurs? Just make sure that you lead with what your stakeholders want to hear to assure them that you know what you're doing.

In this chapter, you build on the results of your feasibility analysis and turn those results into an operating business. The best business plans — the ones that reflect reality — are built after you've run the business for a while. Since it's rare that a business plan survives first contact with the market, it's wise to operate the business and test your assumptions before you plan for the future. You'll be in a better position to undertake the enormous task of putting together a business plan for the future of your company.

Starting with a Feasible Concept

By now, all your research from the feasibility study has probably led to an initial conclusion about whether you want to move forward with the business. I challenge you to ask yourself just a few more questions to ensure that your decision is the right one.

>> Do customers really want what you're offering? How do you know?

>> Can you sell at a price that will enable you to cover your costs and make a profit?

>> Is the market large enough that there's room to grow?

>> Are there additional markets you can tap later?

>> Are your key financial goals achievable?

>> How sensitive are your cash flow numbers to change?

>> Considering capital investment and profit, is there enough money in this venture to make the effort worth doing? In other words, is the return on investment large enough?

At any point along the way, you may conclude that the concept isn't feasible. Maybe the customer base is too small, or your startup costs are higher than expected, or you discover regulations that make it difficult for you to do business the way you want. If any of these is true, you can think about modifying your concept so it is feasible under the current conditions, or you can decide that this concept is not going to fly. On the other hand, even if you have proof of concept, you still must decide under what conditions you're willing to move forward with this new venture.

Planning to Plan

If a feasibility study is your way of testing your business concept, the business plan is the tool that demonstrates how you plan to execute your concept. You don't build a home without a set of blueprints. Similarly, you don't build a business without a plan. You can, but you put yourself at risk of finding out things you didn't know at the most inopportune times.

In addition to including all the conclusions you drew from your feasibility analysis (see Chapter 4), a business plan includes the operational, organizational, and financial management of a new business. In general, a business plan serves four purposes:

>> **It's a reality check for you.** The business plan gets you into the details of the business in a way that a feasibility analysis does not. Sometimes those details reveal previously unforeseen problems. If the problems are significant enough, you may decide (even this early in the project) against starting the business.

>> **It may reveal new opportunities on the operational side of the business.** A feasibility analysis does not focus on the operations of the business the way a business plan does. As you delve into the organizational and operations plan, you may discover innovations that you didn't think of before. In fact, you may find that your concept has more market potential than you thought. In the business plan, you envision the culture of your company — the way the business will operate and the diversity of people and skill sets the business will attract — as even more exciting than the product or service itself. That's not unusual. In fact, the culture you build in your company is a competitive advantage that can't be replicated by someone else.

>> **It's a living guide to your business.** The business plan details all aspects of your business so that anyone reading it has a thorough understanding of how your business works. I call it a living document because it has the capacity to change as it responds to changes in the environment. You must have an open mind to change and prepare to be flexible. At a minimum, I recommend updating your business plan quarterly in the first year and then semiannually thereafter.

>> **It's a statement of intent for others.** The business plan is not just an internal document; it is also of great interest to others — investors, bankers, potential management, strategic partners, suppliers, and lessors. In the next section, I address aspects that are of particular interest to these third parties.

Addressing the needs of your stakeholders

Many different groups of people are interested in seeing your business plan. Remember that each reader looks at your business plan from a different perspective and has different needs that they want to satisfy. Your business plan must address those needs.

Investors

Investors tend to be interested in the quality of the founding team and factors that predict growth. Why? Because they want to increase the value of their investment during the period of time they're invested. In general, they look at your projections for rate of growth (they want fast growth in line with their fund's timetable), return on investment, risk (investors are not risk averse but they do want you to reduce their risk as much as possible), and how their original equity stake will be protected over time as they take on more rounds of funding.

Entrepreneurs often make mistakes with their business plans that investors will be quick to point out. Examples of common mistakes include:

>> **Projecting growth that exceeds the capability of the founding team.** Maybe you're lucky enough (or unlucky enough) to come up with a concept that has the potential for rapid growth at launch. Assuming this kind of growth attracts investors is natural; however, if you don't show how your management team can handle that kind of growth, you actually discourage investors from considering your business. Rapid growth can be a stressful time for a new venture, and even collapse a new venture unless the systems, controls, and professional management are in place to guide the business through that rapid growth phase. Furthermore, projecting high levels of growth and not achieving them make investors unhappy, to say the least.

» **Trying to be a jack-of-all-trades.** While it is understandable that an entrepreneur typically wants to control the launch without a full management team on board, investors will question how a solo entrepreneur can grow the business to the next level. Successfully operating a business requires a variety of skill sets that likely took several years to develop. It is unlikely that the entrepreneur possesses all these skill sets and many entrepreneurs often make the mistake of overestimating their talents. Investors prefer to invest in teams comprised of people who have experience in the major functions of the business.

» **Projecting business performance that exceeds industry averages.** Face it. Why would an investor believe that your new company could outperform existing industry leaders? It just isn't going to happen. Projecting figures that are realistic but support growth and future market share is the better approach, especially if you can provide investors with a strategy to exceed industry averages in the future.

» **Underestimating your need for capital.** Investors can readily recognize when you're trying to do something on too much of a shoestring budget; they've been down that road many times before. They don't see you as being frugal or conservative; they see naiveté on your part.

» **Confusing strategy and tactics.** As you'll see in an upcoming section, strategies define the overall focus of a business. Tactics are the means and methods by which you implement those strategies. So if an investor asks what your strategy is for growing the company at 30 percent per year for the next three years, and you respond with "advertising on the Internet and attending trade shows," you quickly lose that investor's confidence because you responded with tactics.

» **Focusing too much on price.** It is rarely possible for a new venture to compete on price in a market comprised of established players. Building economies of scale in production take time, and you can't lower prices until you cover your costs. Investors know this, so they are more interested in your bundle of competitive advantages as a way of differentiating your business in the market.

» **Being proud of not investing cash in the business.** While I am a big proponent of bootstrapping, you won't attract investors to your business unless you have invested cold, hard cash in it. Sweat equity doesn't count — it's expected. Investors figure that if you invest your life's savings or mortgage your home, you're willing to take a big risk and not likely to take the easy way out and walk away. They also reason that you're probably trying harder to make the business a success.

Bankers/lenders

The needs of bankers and lenders differ considerably from those of investors. Bankers and lenders are more concerned with how you can repay the money they lend you, so they look at your gross margins (revenues – COGS = gross profit/revenues). If your gross margins are slim — 5 to 10 percent — you won't have much room to make errors because only 5 to 10 percent of your sales are available to pay your overhead and make a profit. Bankers also look at your cash flow projections to determine whether you can pay all your expenses and still have money left over at the end of the month.

WARNING

Bankers look at your qualifications and may ask you to personally guarantee any loan they give you. Although you can try to avoid personally guaranteeing a loan, it may not be possible. More and more lenders are asking for personal guarantees from the founding team, no matter how well financed the new venture is.

Here's a checklist of major concerns bankers and other lenders have when dealing with entrepreneurs:

>> **Not supporting the amount of capital required.** You must show specifics about the amount of money you need and how you plan to use it. Justifying the amount with appropriate calculations and forecasts is essential.

>> **Using the loan to pay off old debt.** Bankers, like investors, want to know that the money they're providing is going to have a positive impact on the business and is not just being used to pay off old debt or enable the founders to remove cash from the business.

>> **Not having assets to use as collateral.** Not all assets are equal. Some of your assets may have no value to the bank because they aren't worth anything outside the business in which they're used — for example, custom equipment. Bankers are looking for assets they can quickly and easily convert to cash or another use if your business gets into trouble.

>> **Not demonstrating an ability to repay the loan.** Before approving a loan, lenders must know that your business generates enough cash to repay it. They look closely at your cash flow projections and the market research, determining whether your sales projections make sense.

>> **Not showing the bank how it is protected in case of failure.** Lenders look to see if you have contingency plans for responding to unexpected events or downturns in the market. Again, they want to ensure that you can repay the loan no matter what happens.

>> **Not demonstrating an adequate stake in the business.** Like investors, lenders want to know that you've taken an appropriate cash risk with this venture before they're willing to throw their cash into the pot.

Strategic partners

Strategic partners include suppliers (who provide you with products or services) and distributors (who, depending on your business model, will take your products or services to market) as well as retailers. They will be interested in your business plan because they can assess whether your company is a fit with theirs and how much business they will do with you now and In the future. This is why they are particularly interested in your growth and marketing strategies.

Starting with your proof of concept

Before I discuss the general business plan outline, let me take a minute to talk about the proof of concept (POC), or one-page executive summary, because you will use this as a separate document to introduce your business to stakeholders.

All on one page, the proof of concept sets out the major arguments that validate your business venture. *Proof of concept* is a phrase that traditionally refers to a prototype or experiment that proves that your product can work. I broaden the use of the phrase here to include all those factors proving that your business concept works, and that includes the business model, the way you make money.

You can think of the proof of concept as the way you validate your business's story. You prove it works. For example, with just three questions, you can create your compelling story:

>> What do you do? What problem are you solving and how?

>> Why should people care? Why is this idea compelling?

>> How will you win? (What is your competitive advantage?)

Here's an example of how this might look from a former USC student, Mike Kwon:

> *WhiteCoat is an on-demand house call app that brings healthcare quickly to a patient's home at an affordable price of $50 by using Nurse Practitioners with support of the largest association of nurse practitioners in the United States, called AANP. WhiteCoat will fill the increasing gap left by 40 percent of primary care physicians leaving their practices in the coming years. NPs enable us to drive down costs and the AANP support gives us an advantage in rolling out nationally. NPs can earn twice their normal salary with no administrative responsibilities.*

AN ALL-PURPOSE BUSINESS PLAN OUTLINE

EXPANDED EXECUTIVE SUMMARY (six-page expanded summary as a separate document)

A standard executive summary provides a paragraph on each of the following topics:

- How your business is unique

- The compelling problem your business solves, for whom

- The size of the initial market and your strategy to grow the market and enter new markets.

- People on your team and their experience and skills to execute the plan

- Funding plan. Funding required to meet the first major milestone (usually to achieve positive cash flow) and subsequent milestones. No discussion of equity stakes or ROI as that comes later as part of a negotiation.

I. BUSINESS CONCEPT

- Business concept statement (product/service, customer, benefit, distribution)

- Purpose of the business; why you're in business; goals

- Core values (values that never change)

- Description and uses, unique features/benefits of the solution

- The primary customer (customers who are most in need)

- Spin-off products and services

- Environmental impact (if relevant)

II. MANAGEMENT TEAM

List team members and responsibility

III. MARKET ANALYSIS

- Industry description

- Target market (description and customer segmentation)

- Competitors — competitive grid

- Your product/service differentiation and competitive advantage (also called a "unique selling proposition")

- Pricing

IV. PROCESS ANALYSIS

- Technical description of products/services (core features and benefits; proprietary aspects unique to the product or service and how they're protected — e.g., copyright, trademark)
- Status of product development and related costs
- Distribution channels and physical distribution plan

V. ORGANIZATION PLAN

- Philosophy of management and company culture
- Legal structure of the company
- Organizational chart

VI. MARKETING AND SALES PLAN

- Purpose of marketing plan, business branding
- Plan to reach first customer (unique niche) and target market
- Customer acquisition plan
- Plan to reach subsequent customers
- Sales strategy (direct/indirect; sales channels; how will customers pay you; sales incentives)
- Pricing model
- Distribution channels

VII. FINANCIAL PLAN

- Summary of key metrics and capital requirements
- Needs assessment breakout (hard costs, working capital, startup costs)
- Break-even analysis and payback period
- Narrative assumptions for financial statements
- Plan for ongoing funding

VIII. GROWTH PLAN

- Strategy for growth
- New markets, products, and acquisitions
- Resources required to scale
- Organizational changes resulting from growth

(continued)

(continued)

APPENDIX (organize and separate parts with tabs)

FINANCIAL STATEMENTS

- Assumptions for financial statements

- Proforma financial statements

PROCESS PLAN SUPPORTING DOCUMENTS

- Manufacturing or operating requirements and associated costs

MARKETING PLAN SUPPORTING DOCUMENTS

- Marketing tools

- Media plan

- Marketing budget

ORGANIZATIONAL PLAN SUPPORTING DOCUMENTS

- Compensation programs and incentives

CONTINGENCY PLAN

ADDITIONAL SUPPORTING DOCUMENTS

Think of the POC as a pyramid. At the base of the pyramid is a working prototype. As you work your way up to the apex, you have other types of proof: Letter of intent for beta testing from a customer, final product, purchase order, and customer sales, which are the strongest proof. The "Executive Summary Checklist" sidebar offers ideas to include in your executive summary and, even more concisely, in your proof of concept.

Using an outline

You can find plenty of guidelines for how to create a business plan. Some are more detailed than others, but they all feature the basic components you see in the sidebar, "An All-Purpose Business Plan Outline." You can modify the outline (add things and throw things out that you don't need) to suit your particular purposes. I discuss the guideline/outline components here in more detail. The key point is to keep the plan concise. I discuss the presentation of business plans in a later section.

Starting with the feasibility analysis sections

The front part of the business plan is essentially the feasibility analysis. This component of the plan may require updating as you continue to test the business concept and gather more data. Looking at the example outline (see the "An All-Purpose Business Plan Outline" sidebar), you can see that your work on your feasibility study takes you down to the *process analysis*. The financials you calculated for feasibility are a start, but by the time you prepare them for the business plan, you may have more data to include and you must also produce a balance sheet. Most importantly, if you have achieved sales, you definitely want to put that front and center because it validates your claim that customers want what you're offering.

Process or operational plan

This section of your business plan presents a technical description of your product or service — engineering specifications where appropriate, a description of the prototype, and a depiction of the production process operates (operations). Every business, including service businesses, has processes to design and develop. Chapter 11 helps you think about your business model and the business processes.

Organization plan

This section of your business plan addresses the legal form of organization by which you are structuring your business — sole proprietorship, partnership, corporate form, or limited liability company. Chapter 15 provides you with guidelines for choosing the legal form for organizing your business.

In the organization plan, you discuss your philosophy of management, present key management personnel, and deal with compensation and human resource policies.

Marketing plan

The marketing plan section of your business plan is quite different from the market analysis that you performed for your feasibility analysis. Your market analysis uncovered information about your customers — how they buy, when, where, how much — that will help you structure a marketing strategy to reach those customers. Your marketing plan includes your niche in the market, customers' perceptions of your company, and the tools you plan to use in reaching out to the customer. You can find out more about the marketing plan in Chapter 17.

Financial plan

The financial plan explains the business model and projects gross and net revenues based on sales forecasts. Newer business plan formats provide summary financial figures and ratios within the plan itself and refer to a complete set of financial statements in an appendix. A well-designed financial plan demonstrates that all the claims you make in other sections of the business plan are supported by the financials in a way that supports your business's ability to survive and grow over the long term. Chapter 18 helps you complete this section. This section will also include a plan for ongoing funding.

Growth plan

In this section, you explain how you plan for your business to progress from startup through the various growth phases. The growth plan presents key strategies for growth in the form of new products or services, new customers, or acquisitions. It discusses the resources required to support your growth strategy and the organizational changes that may result. You can find out more about planning for growth in Chapter 16.

Contingency plan

Some entrepreneurs include a contingency plan in their business plan as a way of showing others that you recognize that everything might not go as planned. The contingency plan addresses how your company responds to changing market conditions, for example, what you expect to do if demand for your product is not as strong as projected. You can discover more about the contingency plan in Chapter 19.

Appendixes

Business plans today are more concise. That means that the appendixes, or supporting documents, are longer. Appendixes contain supplementary information that is important but not vital to the business plan, such as resumes, job descriptions, lease agreements, maps, letters of intent, evidence of patents, designs, and complete financial statements.

Executive summary and proof of concept

Although I am discussing the executive summary last (it's difficult to write without first completing the entire business plan), the truth is it may be the most important piece to the business plan puzzle. Most investors, bankers, and other interested parties look at the executive summary first, so you must grab their attention by providing information that clearly and forcefully makes your business case.

In fact, many e-commerce ventures receive funds based on expanded executive summaries (about six pages) that describe concepts, define customers, and establish market sizes, and the ability of businesses to *scale*, which means to grow in size and valuation. These summaries are separate documents that you can provide without handing out your entire business plan. The expanded executive summary is a good way to gauge interest in your company before revealing all the details of your business plan.

TIP

In the executive summary, you must immediately (within the first 30 seconds) capture the reader's attention. Developing a great concept statement that creates excitement and clearly presents your business idea is of utmost importance (if you need to review concept statements, revisit Chapter 4.) Here's an example:

CompanyURL.com builds a connection between online retailers and Internet consumers. Through its propriety software, CompanyURL.com enables customers to establish prepaid purchasing accounts, providing a safer, quicker, more efficient method to purchase goods or services from online merchants when they don't have or don't want to use credit cards online.

You can grab a reader's attention in many ways. As shown in this example, you can use a key selling point or benefit that your business provides. Alternatively, you can introduce a problem and then show how your product or service solves that problem. In this example, the problem is that the most common way of purchasing goods online is to use a credit card; but for many customers, particularly those in the 14–25 age group, credit cards are not always available. The solution to that problem is to set up a secure, prepaid account that the customer can access as needed. Solving a real problem will definitely catch the reader's attention.

REMEMBER

Most people who read business plans see a lot of them. You have to find a way to make yours stand out from the crowd. You can do this by giving your plan a professional appearance, providing a very tight and persuasive executive summary, and creating a plan that is well organized, concise, and supported by good research.

Getting Started with a Vision

If you don't know where you want to go, any path will get you there. In fact, if you don't know where you're going, how will you know when you've arrived? The bottom line is that you must have a vision for your company. A vision is a broad picture of what you see as the future for your company. It's analogous to a rainbow. You can see it in the distance — it's where you want to be — and you keep moving toward it, but you never actually reach it because the vision is aspirational and, if done well, becomes part of the culture of your company. The vision is designed to inspire people and motivate them to be part of your company and contribute to the vision. The Disney Co.'s vision is to "bring happiness to millions." Disney constantly strives to do that and it's a constant effort. Remember that the vision is not only about your customers, but your employees as well.

As the entrepreneur or leader of the organization, it's your job to be the catalyst for a clear and shared vision. Research has found that vision seems to be the critical component to a company that endures over time. It's essentially the glue that holds everything together and gives the business a context and value system in which to make important decisions.

EXECUTIVE SUMMARY CHECKLIST

As you're preparing your executive summary and proof of concept, this checklist helps you make sure you include all the important points. Remember that discussing all these points in detail in your business plan is essential.

- Do you grab the attention of the reader in your opening sentences? Does your concept create excitement? Testing your opening on several people helps you discover its effectiveness.

- Does your business concept section clearly describe the purpose of the business, the customer, the value proposition, and the distribution strategy?

- Does your management team section persuade the reader that you have a team that can successfully implement the business concept?

- Do your industry/market analyses support your business concept and demonstrate demand for your product/service?

- Does your process plan demonstrate how the product/service can be produced and distributed?

- Does the organization plan (legal structure and functions) depict an effective infrastructure to facilitate the achievement of your business goals?

- Does your marketing and sales plan demonstrate how your company can reach its customers and create long-term relationships?

- Does the financial plan convince the reader that your company has long-term potential and can provide a superior return-on-investment for its owners?

- Does the growth plan demonstrate the potential for reaching new markets, developing new products and services, and diversifying the company's offerings?

You are no doubt quite familiar with enduring companies and products such as 3M's Scotch Tape and Post-it Notes, and Disney's animated films. These companies and others with vision survive economic shifts, changing technology, and changes in management because they have a vision that endures through every change, and customers can count on it (most of the time).

The vision for your company comes from your core values — those things you hold to be true and are fundamental beliefs about what's important. Your company's core values reflect what you stand for, who you are, and they rarely change over time. They are your company's code of ethics, what you believe. For example, Nordstrom, one of the nation's top retailers, claims service to the customer above all else and continuous improvement in every aspect of their business. If they hold to their core values, when a situation comes up that involves a customer, they will always come down on the side of the customer because customer service is a core value.

One thing that's important to mention is that the core values of great companies are never about profits. They're always about ideals. Now, you may be thinking that you will be too busy figuring out how to start your business to concern yourself with something as soft and philosophical as core values. But, if you consider that all the number one companies in their respective industries put their core values in writing from the very earliest stages of their ventures, wouldn't you also want to do that?

Here are some suggestions for thinking about core values:

>> Choose five or six at a maximum.

>> Ask yourself, for each of your core values, if you can think of a situation where you may have to change one. If you can, you probably haven't identified a core value.

>> Make sure that your core values are communicated and accepted by everyone in the organization.

Identifying the Big Mission

A mission is a common goal that will bring everyone together to reach it. A mission is a clear and compelling goal that focuses the effort of everyone in the organization. Unlike the vision, the mission is a major goal that is achievable. It's a way of turning the broad purpose (the reason you are in business) into a goal. To have an effective mission, you should meet three requirements:

>> The mission must have an end point. State the date when the mission will be achieved.

>> The mission must be exciting and galvanize the energy of everyone.

>> The mission must be measurable; that is, you must know when you've achieved it.

Here's an example of a good mission statement that worked:

To become a $1 billion company by 1980.

This mission statement belongs to Walmart Stores Inc. Sam Walton, the founder and CEO, set that mission in 1977 and achieved $1.2 billion by 1980.

CASE STUDY

Invisible Children's mission is to end violence and exploitation in the world's most isolated and vulnerable communities. That's a pretty audacious mission. But it tells you where they will compete and how they create value. They didn't set a deadline because this is a very complex problem with lots of moving parts. Every time one of their community-based protection initiatives and peacebuilding tools are put into action, a community in central Africa and the Congo is saved. For example, in February 2021, a woman named Tatiana received word through the Invisible Children's Early Warning System that an armed group was approaching her community, located in a remote area of eastern Central African Republic. The community had an action plan that was immediately put into effect, and they were able to move families to a predetermined safe place and avoid the looting and death that would have occurred. Then trained psychologists provide counseling to begin the process of healing.

ESG for Small Companies

ESG stands for environmental, social, and governance, and it has become a buzz-word usually associated with large public companies that are required to disclose and report on their efforts in these three areas. In the simplest terms, ESG describes the way a company affects the world around it. Let's look at the three categories to see how they might apply to a startup.

Environmental responsibilities

The degree of your company's environmental responsibilities are largely dependent on the type of company you have. For example, if you have an e-commerce startup, you may want to look at your packaging and associated carbon emissions across your supply chain. Is there a way to reduce either of those? Likewise, if you have a manufacturing company, the issues you will monitor include materials sourcing, manufacturing emissions, energy efficiency and waste disposal. If you outsource your manufacturing, you are still responsible for choosing partners who are environmentally responsible. Failure to comply with environmental standards in your industry may expose you to penalties and damage to your company's reputation.

No matter what type of business you have, you are still responsible for making sure that you operate efficiently with minimal waste.

Social responsibilities

Two social factors that affect all startups include the protection of customer data and cybersecurity. You have no doubt heard stories of customer databases being hacked, exposing very private information to thieves and putting the company at risk for lawsuits. Social responsibility also includes making sure your products are ethically and sustainably sourced and that you are inclusive in your hiring practices.

Governance responsibilities

Governance relates to your company's culture and policies, which are important indicators of your reputational risk. You want to work toward a culture that is positive, welcoming, and ethical. One measure of healthy governance is employee satisfaction. In larger companies, it is the board of directors who generally are responsible for governance, but they must be allowed to carry out their oversight duty, which means that management needs to be transparent in its business dealings.

REMEMBER

The primary reason for startups to look at ESG is the fact that you won't be a startup forever. Moreover, investors are using these factors in their investment decisions. It's important to note that today many consumers buy from companies who have good ESG records. Your accountant should be well-versed in ESG and can guide your decisions about where to focus your efforts so that you have impact that counts and that doesn't inhibit your ability to survive and grow.

Looks Count: Preparing and Presenting the Plan

No one gets excited about writing a business plan, because it takes so much time, energy, and effort. Business planning doesn't always work as logically and orderly as I've tried to show. Although you may be looking for industry information first, you're no doubt going to encounter important information to include in other sections of your plan. Don't be disconcerted when you find yourself confounded by information from all parts of your business plan at once. Here are tips for overcoming the toughest hurdle — getting started.

>> **Know where to start.** The task can be daunting and the amount of information you need to collect overwhelming, but finding that first piece of information will lead to the next piece and the next. A hint: Everyone goes to the Internet first. Why not follow their lead?

>> **Don't be discouraged.** Many entrepreneurs become discouraged when a particular piece of information doesn't just jump off the page. Rest assured, finding information tends to mushroom so quickly (sometimes it gets out of hand). You will soon find that you have more information than you can imagine.

>> **Answer key questions.** Organizing that pile of information sitting on your desk is the second hardest part of writing a business plan, so find out how each piece of information answers key questions about every section of the plan. Labeling folders with the key questions and filing the answers as you collect them makes the job go easier.

>> **Always include sources.** Always be sure to include the sources of information you include in your business plan. You don't want someone asking, "Where did you get that statistic?" without the answer.

>> **Use your outline to put the plan together.** Writing in a clear, concise style and making sure that the most important points stand out makes finding things easier for your reader.

Making the plan look good

Looks count when you want someone to pay attention to your business plan. The trick is to create an attractive, professional looking plan that conveys the personality of your business without being too slick. I saw one business plan for an entertainment-based Internet company that was bound, full color on glossy paper. It must have cost thousands of dollars to produce. When I saw it, I had to ask, "If you can afford to create this type of business plan, why do you need me to invest?" Any investor criticizes the misallocation of money when it isn't necessary.

Here are tips for making your business plan look professional and attractive:

>> Spiral-bind your plan (use the good, vinyl coated stuff), so that it lies flat.

>> Use excellent quality white or ecru paper, but do not enclose the paper in plastic — it makes the plan too thick.

>> Use index tabs to separate major sections of the plan, so that it's easier for the reader to find things. Readers don't often start at the beginning of the plan and read to the end. They might want to do a deeper dive into the parts of the plan that matter most to them, so make it easy for them to find information.

>> Use a 12-point font in an easy-to-read character like Times New Roman or Arial.

>> Use boldfaced headings and subheadings so they stand out, and use bulleted lists wherever possible.

>> Put your company logo in the header section of every page.

>> Make sure that you write clearly and concisely. A business plan is not the place for expository writing or expounding on your favorite topic at length. Prune excess words and get someone you trust to read it and do the same. The more people you can have edit the plan the better.

>> Number each copy of your business plan and slip a nondisclosure statement inside that you can hand to your readers.

>> In the footer of every page include the following statement: "Copyright Year (Your Name). All rights reserved. No part of this plan may be copied or used without permission of its author." If you want to find out more about copyrights, see Chapter 8.

Presenting your plan

If you're seeking capital from an investor you don't personally know, or who is from an investor group, don't be surprised about being asked to make a presentation of your business concept. The invitation to make such a presentation typically happens after potential investors read your executive summary. Getting a feel for you and your founding team is the purpose of the presentation. Investors enjoy seeing if you measure up under pressure.

Prepare for your presentation

This is by no means a formal speech, and once you introduce your concept and key arguments for its validity, the presentation typically turns more toward interaction. Here are tips to help you prepare for the presentation.

>> **Check to see how long a presentation your investors are expecting.** Nothing is worse than preparing to speak for a half-hour and finding out you have only 10 minutes. On average, expect to speak uninterrupted for about 20 minutes (And you'll be lucky if you get that long). The main part of the presentation is the question-and-answer period, which will probably last longer than your presentation.

>> **Grab your audience's attention in the first 30 seconds.** Appear genuinely happy for the opportunity when discussing your concept with your hosts. Check with them to see if they can hear you clearly and see your visuals. This will demonstrate your concern that they enjoy your presentation, and they will feel more comfortable with you.

>> **Don't use a lectern to speak!** Using a lectern may make you appear too stiff, and you may find yourself using it as a crutch, clinging to it. As long as you don't pace, walking a bit makes you appear more confident in what you're saying. Use a few visual aids and gestures, and be sure to look people in the eye.

>> **Be careful not to pace or use any kind of repetitive movements.** Doing so may distract your audience from what you're saying, causing them to focus more on what you're doing, which, if it's pacing back and forth, will quickly become annoying, especially if you're moving quickly. The audience will feel like they're watching a ping pong match. Also be careful of repeating a phrase constantly like "you know," which could quickly become the focus of your message.

>> **Whenever possible, demonstrate your product or service.** Product demonstrations create more excitement and make the whole concept more real. One word of caution. Do test your demonstration several times to make sure it works flawlessly every time. Nothing is more embarrassing than a product that doesn't work.

>> **Be sure to involve all the founding team in the presentation.** Strength and safety come in numbers. While the CEO is the primary speaker and the face of the company, you want investors to know that you have a well-rounded and strong team supporting the leader.

>> **Practice, practice, practice.** Practicing in advance for your presentation helps you feel comfortable with the material so you don't have to use notes. You might try videotaping your rehearsal so you can review your presentation from the audience's point of view.

>> **Brainstorm.** Compile a list of questions you think audience members may ask. Answering them helps you avoid being surprised by their inquiries.

>> **Use visual aids but don't overwhelm the audience.** I remember the trouble one entrepreneur got into attempting to set up a computer-actuated, animated slide presentation on a timer so the slides changed automatically while he was speaking. He didn't give himself enough time to breathe, and by the time he finished (ten minutes faster than he thought he would), the combination of his rapid speaking and constant activity on the slide presentation left his audience out of breath, not quite understanding what happened. As an audience member, it was hilarious to watch but was undoubtedly not the result the presenter was going for. At the end of his talk, you could hear an audible sign from the audience. They were exhausted.

Prepare to answer questions

If you're thinking the presentation is the hard part, think again. Many entrepreneurs agree that the Q&A following the presentation is much more stressful, because investors love putting entrepreneurs on the hot seat and seeing how they respond. After all, starting a new business is a stressful activity (fun, but stressful), and investors rightfully want to know if you can handle it. They also like asking questions they've already answered, so they can see if you know what you're talking about.

Watch out for questions requiring precise (impossibly precise) responses or questions that are so broad that you wonder what the question actually is. Asking for clarification if you don't understand the question is far better than appearing ignorant by answering the wrong question.

One question that is most problematic for entrepreneurs is a complex question that contains several underlying assumptions. Here's an example of that type of question:

If you were to look at your venture and its market share before and after this potential investment, how would your market strategy have changed, and how much of your budget would you allocate to that change?

When you find yourself on the hot seat in a situation like this, have courage (maybe take a deep breath) and regroup — fast! You can

>> Attempt to restate the question in your own words, seeking confirmation that you heard it correctly.

>> Ask the questioner to repeat the question, so that you're sure you heard it right. (The question may have been so complex that, chances are, the person may not be able to repeat it.) This will give everyone a chance to take a breath, have a laugh, and start over.

>> If you heard it right, then ask for a bit of time to consider your response. You never have to answer without skipping a beat. Sometimes a pause is more effective, at least making you appear as if you're considering the best way to respond.

>> Decide to respond to only one portion of the question — for example, the part about market share — and not commit to a specific course of action without first taking the time to thoughtfully consider your strategy. This type of response doesn't make you look indecisive; on the contrary, you're likely gaining the respect of your audience because you haven't made a precipitous decision.

REMEMBER

If you're asked a question for which you don't have an answer, don't bluff. It may be a question your audience already has answered, or think they have. Instead, admit graciously that you don't have the answer at your fingertips, but you'll be happy to find it for them after the meeting. Just make sure that the question for which you don't have an answer is not something fundamental about your business that you should know.

If you *are* criticized for any aspect of your business plan (and expect that to happen), don't get defensive or attack your audience — you'll lose their respect immediately and may not be able to regain it. Instead, be gracious and remain cool. This is often a tactic to see if they can get you to become flustered or angry. They also want to learn how coachable you are.

The one-minute business plan

If you had only one minute with an important person who could make or break your new venture, what would you tell that person about your business concept? This is an important exercise for you to master, because you will have many one-minute occasions to grab someone's attention. In fact, you won't often have more time than that. So here are the most important points:

>> Your two-sentence concept statement with the product/service, customer, value proposition, and distribution strategy.

>> Why you, and why now. Why are you the right person or team to do this, and why is the window of opportunity now?

>> How you're going to differentiate your business in the market.

>> How you're going to make money — your business model.

>> How you know there's demand for what you're offering.

By the time you complete your business plan, you will know your business inside and out. But understand that when you actually go into business, you'll quickly find out the weaknesses in your plan (and there will be weaknesses) and you'll need to correct them.

REMEMBER

No business plan survives first contact with the market.

Chapter **14**

Finding Money to Start and Grow Your Venture

" I need money to start a business venture" is usually the opening line when an entrepreneur walks into my office. Most of the time, however, I discover that these entrepreneurs haven't done the homework they need to do before approaching an investor. Once I ask them a series of questions, they soon find out how badly they would have stumbled had they talked to an investor before they were ready.

Two major fallacies about startup funds make successful funding difficult. They are

>> The more money I get, the better. I can use as much as I can get.

>> My business plan numbers are just estimates — the investor will tell me what I need.

If you're thinking along these lines, stop right now! First, why seek more investment money than you absolutely need? Every bit of capital invested in your business costs you some equity (ownership) in your company. Besides, having too much money may lead you to make poor decisions because you don't think as carefully as you should about how you spend it.

Second, although it's true that your business plan financials are estimates, they need to be good estimates based on solid research. Your investor may discount your estimate of rapid sales growth, but they want to know that you've carefully considered all your numbers and that they make sense.

In this chapter, you see how to raise capital to start and grow a business the smart way. As always, you start with a plan.

Starting with a Plan

Before you talk to anyone — even your grandmother — about money, have a plan in place, a set of strategies for targeting the right amount of money from the right sources. Here are some guidelines for putting together a plan that works:

>> Seek what you actually need, not what you think you can raise.

>> Understand what you need from an investor. Financial investors provide capital and maybe a little mentoring, but they're in it for a return. A strategic investor provides capital but also expertise and connections in your business segment.

>> Look at how your company will grow and define the points when you'll most likely need additional capital.

>> Consider the sources of money available to you at each stage of your business.

>> Make sure that the activities of your business let you tap into the correct source of money at the right time. For example, if you know that you are planning an initial public offering (IPO) in three years, start putting in place the systems, controls, and professional management that you'll need before the IPO takes place (I talk about IPOs later in this chapter).

>> Monitor your capital needs as you go so that you don't have to return to the trough too many times. Every time you go back for another round of capital, you give up more stock in your company, so the percentage you own declines.

You can come out a winner if you prepare for your future capital needs. Just follow the lead of one technology company I know that produces custom productivity and e-commerce applications. This company maintains a solid prospect for investment by:

>> Creating value in the form of long-term customers and great products.

>> Running a profitable business.

>> Keeping cash flow positive (see Chapter 18).

If you do these three things, you will not have difficulty raising growth capital whenever you need it. If you have a startup venture, strive to achieve these goals from day one. They may help you source capital while you are still at early stage.

Funding a traditional business

Traditional businesses (non–Internet businesses) typically follow fairly predictable funding cycles. Figure 14-1 shows the stages of funding for a typical business.

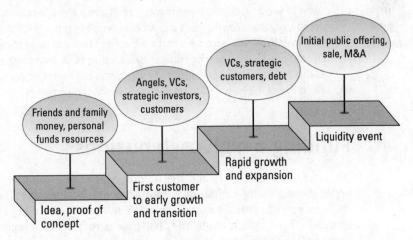

FIGURE 14-1:
Stages of funding a typical business.

Friends and family money, personal funds resources

Angels, VCs, strategic investors, customers

VCs, strategic customers, debt

Initial public offering, sale, M&A

Liquidity event

Rapid growth and expansion

First customer to early growth and transition

Idea, proof of concept

Each of these stages has a specific focus:

>> First-stage funding is about securing seed capital to finish preparing the product and the business for launch. It's also when you begin to seek funding to begin operations and reach a positive cash flow. That funding typically comes from the founders and other friendly money such as family.

>> In the second stage, you're usually looking for early growth capital from sources beyond friends and family. Your business has proven its concept, you have attracted customers, and now you want to grow. Alternatively, your customers have demanded that your company grow to meet their needs (that's a nice thing when it happens). In general, your internal cash flows are usually not sufficient to take the business to the next level. To successfully use second-round financing, you need to be out looking for capital in advance of

needing it. This capital will likely come from angel investors (smaller private investors) or strategic investors with a particular interest in your type of business. They will expect some type of liquidity event in the future, where they can cash out of the business and take their returns.

>> Third-stage funding for rapid growth generally comes from professional venture capitalists (VCs) and it's used to fund rapid growth that results in an acquisition by a larger company or a merger. It's the harvest stage for entrepreneurs who want to take their wealth out of the business and possibly exit, or for investors who want to exit. In general, if you take on venture capital (a professionally managed pool of money), you are probably looking at a buyout or IPO within three to five years. That's because a buyout or IPO provides the cash your investor needs to get out of the investment with the return they expect.

REMEMBER

Keep in mind that not all businesses achieve this rapid growth stage that VCs want to see to justify an investment. If you have a lifestyle business with steady, organic growth, that's a great business, but not a great investment. This eventually will become a mature business that will need to disrupt itself to continue to grow and be competitive. Mature businesses with excellent, stable revenues can seek debt to fund growth, but their owners will likely need to sell the business to harvest any wealth they created.

Funding a high-tech business

It's pretty easy to understand the funding stages of a traditional business, but what about raising capital for nontraditional businesses? The Internet has spawned some business models, especially in the domain of high tech, that don't fit those stages well, if at all. The challenge is to describe a nontraditional business model or innovative concept to an investor.

Your ability to describe your solution to a real and compelling problem and show that you can tap a large market are both crucial here. Drugstore.com is an example of a company that was funded on the concept alone before it went live on the Internet. Investors got it. It was a simple concept with tons of potential growth. By contrast, most ventures require a working prototype and early sales before investors will take the leap.

Grabbing early brand recognition from competitors online takes a lot of money, a professional management team, and the ability to grow in a hurry. If that describes your business, here are some suggestions for maneuvering through the capital maze:

» **Don't take the easy money. You want smart money.** It's okay to fund a traditional business with money from friends and family. However, doing so isn't a good idea, when you're seeking early-stage capital for an Internet or high-tech concept. Who is funding your business is as important as how much they're giving you. Be sure that you associate with people who attract the right kind of money to your venture.

» **Get an introduction to the money source through one of your advisors.** Be sure you exercise due diligence on the investor to find one who has worked with your type of business before and has compatible firms in their portfolio that provide synergies with yours.

» **Don't get married on the first date.** Large quantities of money are available for Internet and high-tech concepts that show potential. If you have such a concept, you may have more term sheets (agreements listing what an investor is willing to do) than you know what to do with. It's tempting to grab the first term sheet under the assumption that the first is always the best. The agreement may be for the most money, maybe not, but the investor may not be the most compatible with your business. Compatibility is even more important than money, because the money source has a lot to say about what happens to your business. So, consider all your options before selecting one. Remember that the most important person to get to know in any potential investment firm is the partner you will be dealing with. If you don't have a good feeling about that person, you may want to look elsewhere.

» **Take the deal that moves you to the next stage.** The biggest deal doesn't always win. What you're looking for is enough money to get you comfortably to the next round of financing and an investment firm that adds value to what you're doing in the form of introductions, contacts, advice, and so forth.

» **Get your website up as quickly as possible.** Get it up and running and start receiving feedback from potential customers as soon as possible. You need to keep the momentum going and collect data on the people who visit your site. This is important information to have when you talk to your potential investors.

» **Buy the best management you can get with your capital.** Investors are practically unanimous: The management team is often more important than the business concept itself. When you obtain money, invest in the best management you can get. If you have to bootstrap with your own funds, seek a strategic alliance with a company whose great management you can leverage. Professional management is critical for a fast-growing company that doesn't permit the founder enough time to learn all the facets of running a business.

Tapping Friendly Money

The majority of entrepreneurs — well over 70 percent — start their businesses with personal savings, credit cards, and other personal assets like the proceeds from second mortgages and the sale of stock portfolios. Why is that? With all the venture capital and private investor money out there for the taking, why do you have to use your own resources? The answer is simple: Your new company is just too big a risk — it's unproven; you don't know for certain if the market will accept it. The only people who'll invest in your business at this point are people who know and believe in you. And you're first in line.

But what if you don't have a network of friends and family willing to give you money, or from whom you prefer not to take money? What do you do then? One thing you do is bootstrap — beg, borrow, and barter for anything that you can from products to services to an office site. (Suggestion: Look at Chapter 12 to see how to reduce your startup capital needs and lessen the frontend load.) One way to bootstrap is to avoid hiring employees as long as possible (employees are typically the single biggest expense of any business). Here are some other tips:

>> Look for an office suite where you can share facilities and equipment with other tenants.

>> Share office space with an established company that is compatible with yours. I know of a public relations firm that shared space with a friend's well-established advertising firm. In exchange for the space, the PR firm referred clients to the ad agency.

>> To reduce cash needs, consider leasing rather than buying equipment.

>> Barter with established companies for services. A friend of mine needed a wardrobe for a media tour when she was starting her business. She talked to a clothing designer and managed to get an entire wardrobe in exchange for promoting the label on her tour.

>> Get your customers to pay as quickly as possible. Sometimes a new company can get customers to pay a deposit up front, providing capital for the raw materials you need to make the product.

>> Ask your suppliers for favorable payment terms, and then pay on time. Those relationships become important to your business as it grows. You may find it necessary to request smaller amounts of credit from several suppliers until you establish your business.

If you do decide to take money from friends and family, do it in a businesslike manner. That is, have an attorney draw up a contract that protects both sides. Investing in a business venture is a risk and should only be undertaken by people who can bear to lose their investment, should that occur.

Family money is the most expensive money you'll ever use because you pay for it for the rest of your life!

Finding an Angel Investor

The second most common source of capital for starting and growing a business is an angel investor, also known as a private investor. Angels are members of the *informal risk capital market* — the largest pool of capital in the United States. So, how do you find one of these gift-givers from heaven? Unfortunately, that's the hard part because angels tend to keep a lower profile than any other type of investor. Entrepreneurs typically find angels through referrals from someone else. That's why networking with people in your industry is so important when you begin thinking about starting a business. You need to build up a personal network to tap when it's time to look for private investment capital. Another place to find angels is at universities that support entrepreneur programs and fund some of the startups coming out of those programs.

What are angel investors?

I described angels differently in my first book about entrepreneurship. For one thing, I said that they were into the investment for the long haul. That was true at the time, but times have changed; angel investors have, too. Today, angel investors look a lot like professional venture capitalists except that the amounts they invest are significantly smaller. Angels typically ask you for the same credentials that a venture capitalist wants:

>> A business plan

>> Milestones — funding and growth

>> A significant equity stake in the business

>> A seat on the board of directors

The similarity between an angel and a venture capitalist came about because of the long bull market in the late 1990s when venture capital funding reached astronomical levels. Flush with cash, the venture capitalist stopped looking at deals that were less than $3 million to $5 million, leaving the playing field wide open for angels to step in and do bigger deals than normal, with the promise of a quicker turnaround and handoff to the VCs. So, angels typically play in the gap between founder resources and venture capital.

Angels used to be characterized as middle-aged, former entrepreneurs who generally operated solo and invested near their homes. They usually funded deals for less than a million dollars and stayed in the investment for several years. Today, angels come in all ages, even turning up among the 20-something Internet crowd who hit it big with their first ventures. Angels also band together to increase the size of their investment pools and take on larger deals.

Networks like The Tech Coast Angels and Berkus Technology Ventures, based in Los Angeles, California, consider themselves to be seed venture capitalists. They have become as sophisticated in their investment methods as any professional venture capitalist — exercising more due diligence and sometimes looking for a quicker return on their investment, often to the dismay of the entrepreneur.

In other words, they need to be cashed out of their investment often before the growing business is in a position to do so. Entrepreneurs typically work with longer growth and performance horizons than venture capitalists and many of the new breed of angels. So their goals are often in conflict.

REMEMBER

The key difference between angels and VCs is that angels invest their own money, while VCs invest other people's money in addition to their own. Angels typically take far less equity even though they are investing at arguably the riskiest time in the life of a new venture.

How to deal with angel investors

In many ways, you deal with angels the same way you deal with professional venture capitalists. You start with a good referral from someone who knows the angel well. Then:

>> **Make sure your goals and your angel's goals are the same.** Otherwise, you may risk the goals you've set for the business. Try to avoid an angel who wants to get in and out in three years or less. You can't build a sustainable business in that timeframe. Besides, you need to find a way to buy out the investor at that point, and that may mean selling the business or offering an IPO, which may not have been your original plan.

>> **Exercise your own due diligence (investigation, background check) on the angel.** Don't be afraid to ask for references from other companies the angel has invested in. Talk to those entrepreneurs to find out what their experience was.

>> **Look for an angel who provides more than money.** You want contacts in the industry, potential board members, and strategic assistance for your business. These things are as important as money.

>> **Get the angel's commitment to help you meet certain business milestones that you both agree on.** Their assistance, advice, and expertise are valuable and you need to take advantage of them.

When It's Time for Venture Capital

Venture capital is a professionally managed pool of funds that usually operates in the form of a limited partnership. The managing general partner pulls together a pool of investors — individual and institutional (pension funds and insurance companies, for example) — whose money they invest on behalf of the partnership. Typically, venture capitalists invest at the second round of funding and are looking for fast growth and a quick turnaround of their investment. Consequently, their goals often conflict with the entrepreneur's goals for the company.

In the late 1990s, it appeared that all the rules about what a good investment is changed as VCs began focusing on Internet companies and investing in ideas rather than in intellectual property. They rushed to invest in companies like Amazon.com, Buy.com, and e-Toys, companies that weren't projecting profits for several years. But as stock valuations of these companies plummeted to near zero levels in late 1999 and early 2000, VCs began rethinking their strategies. They didn't stop investing in Internet companies; they just started doing a better job of evaluating those opportunities.

VCs usually manage large portfolios of perhaps 20 to 100 investments, and the reality is that maybe one big win — an Uber, Google, or Amazon — will cover all the losses in the portfolio and provide fund returns of 10 to 15 times. After a long period of a strong market, VCs are expected to slow their pace of investment moving forward in an uncertain economy, and that will affect their return expectations, although they're still surprisingly optimistic. Here are some typical return expectations based on the stage of investment.

>> **Seed stage**: If VCs invest here, it's like throwing spaghetti at the wall to see what sticks. They have high expectations, perhaps 100 times return on their investment, because the probability of failure is very high.

>> **Series A:** Here the amounts are greater because some of the risk has been reduced and the VC can see an actual product worth around $15-20 million. They are looking for a 10 to 15 times return on their investment.

>> **Series B, C, late stage:** Since investments at this stage are close to an IPO or acquisition, VCs are looking for a three to five times return on their investment of as much as $100 million or more. The probability of success at this stage is high, so even with a five times return in a short timeframe, their internal rate of return (IRR) is good.

What is still true about venture capital is that it funds less than 1 percent of all new ventures, mostly in technology areas — biotechnology, information systems, the Internet, and computer technology. Today we are seeing more women-owned VC firms like True Wealth Ventures, which recently raised a second fund at

$35 million to fund women–led startups. Fairview Capital is an example of a diverse private equity firm that is targeting minority–owned businesses. To see how you may be able to use venture capital to your advantage, you first need to understand the cost of raising capital and the process by which it happens.

GETTING READY TO DEAL

One of the more important rules about negotiation is, "The person with the most information wins." Negotiating the best funding deal really is about understanding the needs of the other party, knowing what you want, and knowing your alternatives if you can't come to an agreement. Here's a checklist of information you should have at your fingertips when you negotiate for funding:

1. How much money do you need for the business years one through five?

2. How will you use the funds?

3. What sources of money will you seek and why?

4. If you seek debt funding, what will you use as collateral?

5. Are you willing to personally guarantee the debt?

6. What funds have been invested to date and by whom? Are these funds debt or equity?

7. If you have received outside investment capital, what did the investor receive in return for the investment (that is, how much equity?)?

8. Which outside investors have you approached, or will you approach? What were the results?

9. Under what legal form is the company organized and how does this help the principals and investors?

10. What tax benefits does the legal structure provide for the company, the principals, and the investors?

11. What is the proposed exit strategy for the investors? The principals?

12. Have your financial projections been reviewed by an accountant?

13. What leases and loan agreements do you currently have?

14. How much equity are you willing to exchange for investment? You may have a sense of where you stand on equity and control, but so does the VC. If you want the capital, you need to be flexible to some degree because the VC will probably stand firm.

15. How much control are you willing to exchange for investment?

Calculating the real cost of money

Raising money for your business, whether private or venture capital, is a time-consuming and costly process. That's why many entrepreneurs in more traditional businesses (non-high-tech or non-Internet) opt for slower growth, using internal cash flows as long as they can. But if you want aggressive growth using outside capital, you need to have reasonable expectations about how that can happen. Here's what you need to know:

>> Raising money always takes longer than planned, at least twice as long. Count on it.

>> Plan to spend several months seeking funds, several more months for the potential investor to agree to fund your venture, and perhaps six more months before the money is actually in your hands.

>> Use financial advisors experienced in raising money.

>> Recognize that raising money takes you away from your business a lot, probably when you most need to be there. So be sure to have a good management team in place to back you up.

TIP

Start looking for money before you need it!

Investors can be fickle

Once you've found what you think is the ideal investor — you're compatible, you have the same goals for the future of the company, and you genuinely like each other — the investor may back out of the deal. That's right, after you've spent months trying to find this investor and even more time exercising due diligence (yours and the investor's), the investor may change their mind. Perhaps the investor stumbled across something unfavorable; more likely, they couldn't pull together the capital needed to fund your deal.

TIP

Always have a backup if you sense that the deal may be going sideways.

Investors often want to buy out your early investors, including your friends and family, typically out of the belief that first-round funders have nothing more to contribute to the venture. Investors also don't want to deal with a bunch of small investors. A buyout like this can turn into an awkward situation if you haven't explained to your early funders that it's a possibility. If you don't agree to the buyout of the first round, your investor may walk away from the deal.

It takes money to make money

It takes money to make money. Truer words were never spoken. The costs of finding your investor, including preparing and printing the business plan, travel, and time, all are paid up front by you. If you're seeking a lot of money — several million — you probably need to have your financials prepared or reviewed by a CPA, and you need to prepare a prospectus, an offering document spelling out the risks and rewards of investing in your business opportunity. Again, these are costs you bear up front.

Once you receive the capital, the cost of maintaining it, ranging from paying interest on loans to keeping investors apprised of what's going on with your business, can usually be paid out of the proceeds. You'll also have *back-end costs* if you are raising capital by selling securities (shares of stock in your corporation). These costs include investment-banking fees, legal fees, marketing costs, brokerage fees, and any fees charged by state and federal authorities. The total cost of raising equity capital can reach 25 percent of the total amount of money you're seeking. You see it definitely takes money to make money.

Getting your plan approved

The first thing venture capitalists do is scrutinize your business plan, particularly to see if you have a strong management team consisting of people experienced in your industry and committed to the launch of this venture. Then they look at your product and market to ensure the opportunity you've defined is substantial and worth their effort and the risk they're taking. If you have a unique product that is protected through patents, you have an important barrier to competitors that is attractive to the venture capitalists, who also look at the market to ensure a significant potential for growth — that's where they make their money, from the growth in value of your business.

If the venture capitalists like what they see, they'll probably call for a meeting at which you may be asked to present your plan. They want to confirm that your team is everything you say it is. (See Chapter 13.) The venture capitalists may or may not discuss initial terms for an agreement at the meeting. It is likely they'll wait until they've exercised due diligence.

Exercising due diligence

If you've made it past the meeting stage, and the venture capitalists feel positive about your concept, it's time for them to exercise due diligence, meaning they thoroughly check out your team and your business concept or business as the case may be. Once they're satisfied that you check out, they'll draw up legal documents detailing the terms of the investment. But don't hold your breath waiting. Some venture capitalists wait until they know they have a good investment opportunity before putting together the partnership that actually funds your venture. Others just take a long time to release the money. In any case, you can certainly ask what the next steps are and how long they'll take.

One more surprise for you: It's unlikely that the money will be released to you in one lump sum. Study your term sheet carefully; it probably states that the money will be released in stages triggered by your achieving certain predefined goals.

Crafting the deal

Always approach a venture capitalist from a position of strength. If you sound and look desperate for money, I guarantee that you won't get a good deal.

REMEMBER

Venture capitalists see many business concepts, but most of them aren't winners. Your power at the negotiating table comes from proving that your concept is one of the winners. The operative word here is *proving*.

Every deal is composed of four parts:

» The amount of capital to be invested

» The timing and use of the money

» The return on investment to the investors

» The level of risk

The amount of capital the venture capitalist provides reflects need. However, it also depends on the risks involved, how the money will be used, and how quickly the venture capitalist can earn a return on the investment (timing). The amount of equity in your company that the venture capitalist demands depends on the risk and the amount of the investment.

Selling Stock to the Public: An IPO

An *IPO* (initial public offering) is the process of selling stock in your company on a public stock exchange. The aura and myths surrounding the IPO have grown with the huge IPOs undertaken by upstart companies that don't have an ounce of profit to their names. The glamour of watching your stock appear on the exchange you've chosen and the attention you get from the media make you forget for a moment all the hard work that led to this point and all the hard work that you can expect to follow as your company strives every quarter to satisfy stockholders and investment analysts that you're doing the right things. I should know. I've had the good fortune to ring the bell at the NYSE twice in my career. It's a surreal experience.

It's no wonder so many naïve entrepreneurs announce their intention to go public within three years (if not sooner). If they knew more about what it's really like to launch a public company, these starry-eyed adventurers may think twice. I can't stress enough the importance of doing your homework — reading, talking to people who have done it — before making the decision to do an IPO. Once you decide to go ahead, you set in motion a series of events that take on a life of their own. Yes, you can stop the IPO up to the night before your company is scheduled to be listed on the stock exchange, but doing so will cost you a lot of money and time, not to mention bad publicity.

An IPO is really just a more complex version of a private offering. You file your intent to sell a portion of your company to the public with the Securities and Exchange Commission (SEC) and list your stock on one of the exchanges. When you complete the IPO, the proceeds go to the company in what is termed a *primary offering*. If, later on, you sell your shares (after restrictions have ceased), those proceeds are termed a *secondary distribution*.

Considering the advantages and disadvantages of going public

The real reason that many entrepreneurs choose to take their companies public is that an IPO provides an enormous source of interest-free capital for growth and expansion. After you've done one offering, you can do additional offerings if you maintain a positive track record. Other general advantages that companies derive from becoming publicly held are

>> Access to the capital market can be cheaper than other sources of funding.

>> More clout with industry types and the financial community.

>> Ability to offer stock to your employees.

>> Ability to form partnerships and negotiate favorable deals with suppliers, customers, and others.

>> Ability to harvest the wealth you have created by selling some of your shares or borrowing against them.

But becoming a public company also has several disadvantages that you should carefully consider. Some of them include:

>> The cost of an IPO exceeds $300,000, and that doesn't include the commission to the underwriter (the investment bank that sells the securities).

>> The process is extremely time consuming, taking most of every week for more than six months.

>> Everything you and your company do becomes public information.

>> You are now responsible first and foremost to your shareholders, not to your customers or employees.

>> You may no longer hold the controlling share of stock in your company.

>> Your stock may lose value because of factors in the economy even if you're running the company well.

>> You face intense pressure to perform in the short term so that revenues and earnings rise, driving up stock prices and dividends to stockholders.

>> The SEC quarterly and annual reporting requirements are a time-consuming and expensive burden.

WARNING

Out of 3,186 firms that went public in the 1980s, only 58 percent were still listed on one of the major exchanges in 2000. As far back as 1993, the stock of only one-third of these companies was selling above its issue price.

Deciding to go for it

If you've weighed all the advantages and disadvantages and still want to go forward with an IPO, you need to have a good understanding of what happens during the months that precede the offering. In general, the process unfolds in a fairly predictable fashion.

Choose the underwriter

You need to choose an underwriter that serves as your guide on this journey and, you hope, sells your securities to enough institutional investors to make the IPO a success. Like meeting a venture capitalist, you need to secure an introduction to a good investment banker through a mutual acquaintance and investigate the reputation and track record of any investment banker you're considering. Many disreputable firms out there are looking for a quick buck. You also want to find an investment banker who'll stay with you after the IPO and look out for the long-term success of the stock.

Once chosen, the investment banker drafts a letter of intent stating the terms and conditions of the agreement. The letter includes a price range for the stock, although this is just an estimate because the going-out price won't be decided until the night before the offering. At that point, if you're unhappy with the price, you can cancel the offering. You will, however, be responsible for some costs incurred.

Satisfy the SEC

You file a registration statement with the SEC. Known as a *red herring*, this prospectus presents all the potential risks of investing in the IPO and is given to anyone interested in investing. Following the filing of the registration statement, you place an advertisement, known as a *tombstone*, in the financial press announcing the offering. Your prospectus is valid for nine months after the tombstone is published.

You need to decide on which stock exchange your company will be listed. Here are the three best known in the United States:

>> American Stock Exchange (AMEX)

>> National Association of Securities Dealers Automated Quotation (NASDAQ)

>> New York Stock Exchange (NYSE)

The NYSE is the most difficult to qualify for listing. The NYSE and AMEX are auction markets where securities are traded on the floor of the exchange so that investors trade directly with one another. By contrast, the NASDAQ is a floorless exchange that trades on the National Market System through a system of broker-dealers from respected securities firms.

You may also want to look at regional exchanges like the Pacific Exchange and the Boston stock exchange. They are generally less expensive alternatives.

Take your show on the road

Many consider the road show to be the high point of the entire IPO process. It is exactly what it sounds like, a whirlwind tour of all the major institutional investors over about two weeks. The entrepreneur and the IPO team present the business and the offering to these potential investors, whom they hope to sign on. The goal is to have the offering oversubscribed so that it can be sold in a day.

One of the more important skills you should develop if you intend to go the IPO route (or seek money from any source) is how to talk to money people. These people have seen so many presentations from so many people begging for their resources that they are jaded. You have to work hard to capture their attention, and that's not an easy thing to do. Here are some suggestions based on the lessons taught by Jerry Weissman, whose company, Suasive (formerly Power Presentations), has been behind some of the most famous IPOs in history — Cisco, Yahoo!, and Compaq, to name a few.

>> **Tell a great story.** Investors want to hear why this is the best investment opportunity they've ever seen. In short, they want to know what's in it for them, their return on investment. Entrepreneurs, by contrast, are generally more focused on what's in it for the customer.

>> **The entrepreneur must tell the story.** Not only must the entrepreneur/CEO tell the story, but they need to write it as well. No one has the passion for the business that the founder does, and that passion means a higher valuation for the business. So, tell your own story, and tell it with energy and passion.

>> **Don't exaggerate your story.** Remember that investors have heard it all, so you need to tell them what makes your company stand out from the crowd and provide proof. Don't hide potential problems or negatives your business may have. Every business has them. Recognize them and then tell investors what you intend to do about them.

>> **Get their attention.** You can grab attention in many ways, but one of the best is to show your audience that you have a solution to a problem they're experiencing. For example, Scott Cook of Intuit (Quicken, QuickBooks) started his story with a question: "How many of you balance your own checkbooks?" Every investor raised their hand. "How many of you like doing it?" Not one hand was raised. He explained that millions of people around the world dislike that task, but he had a product that would solve the problem. That approach definitely caught the investors' attention.

Deal with failure

CASE STUDY

Once in a while, even when you've done all the right things, the IPO can fail. One example is the Texas company that developed a computer that would stand up to the toughest environments — places like machine shops and hot restaurant kitchens. When the founder decided to raise money through a first registered stock offering on the Internet, it was a long and costly undertaking (more than $65,000) to secure the necessary approvals from the SEC. But finally the company began selling shares through its website, its sights set on raising between $1.5 million and $9.9 million. The offering period was 90 days, and at the end of that time the company had raised only about $300,000. Attempts to do a traditional offering failed as well and the company eventually filed for Chapter 7 bankruptcy. The total bill for the IPO was about $250,000, for which the company received nothing.

Just because you start an IPO doesn't guarantee that you'll finish it. Many entrepreneurs cancel their IPOs the night before they come out because they are unable to raise sufficient capital during the road show, meaning they failed to generate sufficient interest in the stock. Those that don't cancel often pay a price. NASDAQ has analyzed companies that have gone public since the 1980s and found that the IPO success rate is only 20 percent. They also found that the majority of IPOs underperformed the market within three years of their IPO date. The bottom line — carefully consider your decision to do a public offering and make sure you get expert advice.

Uber's IPO was a failure because the ride-sharing company didn't meet its expected valuation of $120 billion at the debut. The company was aiming for $45 per share at opening, but it opened at $42 and then closed the day at $41. The market was clearly not as excited about the stock as management or the underwriters were.

Special Purpose Acquisition Companies: SPACs

SPACS are shell companies, which means they are not operating businesses. They are corporations put together for the sole purpose of doing an IPO. Although SPACS have been around since the 1990s, they surged from 59 in 2019 to 247 a year later with $80 billion invested. In 2020, SPACs accounted for more than 50 percent of new publicly listed companies. Why is that?

A SPAC has a two-year life span, during which it must raise the required funds and target an operating business to acquire. The SPAC sponsors pay millions of dollars in non-refundable fees to raise investment capital. If it can't close the deal, all the money raised is returned to the investors and the money for the fees is lost. The SPAC goes through the typical IPO process and is assigned a ticker symbol. Investor money is held in escrow. The money for the SPAC comes mainly from public-equity investors, although unaccredited investors (consumers) can purchase shares in the SPAC before the merger is complete. SPACs compete with late-stage venture capital, private equity, as well as the traditional IPO process.

Although very popular and the source of huge wins for the rich and famous, the actual returns for ordinary SPAC investors are mixed. The median investor lost 53 percent and 63 percent post-merger, according to Michael Batnick of Ritholtz Wealth Management. Some on Wall Street liken SPAC fervor to the dot-com bubble in 2000 and the junk bonds in 1987. A crash may be coming, they warn.

TIP

For entrepreneurs, SPACs represent a way to transition to a publicly traded company with more certain pricing and control over deal terms as compared to a normal IPO.

That doesn't mean they are right for everyone, though. Here are some important aspects of SPACs to keep in mind:

» SPACs prefer to target entrepreneurial companies that are disruptors in the consumer, technology, and biotech industries. Since many of those companies cannot guarantee near-term revenue or even viability, SPACs offer capital that isn't typically available to these companies.

» One troubling aspect of SPACs is that investors can withdraw from a deal even after a target merger company has been announced. These investors can redeem their shares for the amount of cash invested plus interest.

How often does this happen? The *Yale Journal on Regulation* published a study showing that in more than a third of the SPACs they studied from 2019 to the first quarter of 2021, more than 90 percent of investors withdrew from their SPACs. However, in the two years after the study, it appears that the SPAC process has been refined with more high-quality candidates. In fact, *Harvard Business Review* reports that the average stock price for post-merger SPACs is up 47 percent, which is 27 percent higher than the S&P 500. So, it appears they may be here to stay.

» SPAC deals are complex and require dedicated professional staff to coordinate and steer the efforts. While they offer an interesting possibility for going public for less money and more quickly, SPACs require a team of qualified, experienced people to guide the entrepreneur through the process, which typically takes three to five months, far shorter than an IPO. Once the acquisition is complete, the target company is listed on the stock exchange.

In 2021, Richard Branson took Virgin Galactic public through a SPAC, the first space company to do so. The stock has had a bumpy ride since the debut due to Virgin Galactic's problems with its suborbital rocket plane, SpaceShipTwo.

Finding More Ways to Finance Growth

Equity is not the only way to finance the growth of your business. Debt vehicles — IOUs with interest — are another way to acquire the capital you need to grow. When you choose this route, you typically hand over title to a business or personal asset as collateral for a loan bearing a market rate of interest. You normally pay principal and interest on the note until it's paid off. Some arrangements, however, combine debt and equity. For example, a debenture is a debt vehicle that can be converted to common stock at some predetermined time in the future. In the meantime, the holder of the debenture receives interest on their loan to the company. Some angel investors prefer debentures because it increases the overall return on their investment.

Here are some of the more common sources of debt financing for growth.

>> **Commercial banks.** Banks are better sources for growth capital than for startup capital, because by the time you come to them, your company has, in all likelihood, developed a good track record. Banks make loans based on the *Five C's*: character of the entrepreneur, capacity to repay the loan, capital needed, collateral the entrepreneur can provide to secure the loan, and condition of the entrepreneur's overall financial health and situation. For entrepreneurs with new ventures, character and capacity become the overriding factors.

>> **Commercial finance companies.** Also known as asset-based lenders, these companies are typically more expensive to use than commercial banks by as much as 5 percent above the prime interest rate. But they are also more likely to lend to a startup entrepreneur than a commercial bank is. And when you weigh the difference between starting the business and not starting because of money, a commercial lender may not be that expensive.

>> **Small Business Administration.** The SBA guarantees loans up to 90 percent and works with commercial lenders to deliver those loans. Because SBA-funded businesses tend to have a higher success rate than the average business, lenders enjoy working with the SBA. Underrepresented groups should check the SBA website for special programs geared to them.

>> **SBA Express.** SBA Express aims to reduce all the paperwork associated with a traditional SBA loan. If you qualify at a bank, you can borrow up to $150,000 without going through the standard SBA application process. In fact, this program promises to give you a decision within 36 hours. Because the Small Business Administration only guarantees these loans to 50 percent of their face value, not all the SBA-qualified lenders have signed on to the program.

Crowdfunding

In Chapter 7, I talk about crowdfunding as a source for financing product development. It can also be a source when you're thinking about growing your business depending on how much money you need to raise. Growth typically involves adding new products and services to your original offering and that's where crowdfunding can play a role. Consumers enjoy supporting the efforts of entrepreneurs who are innovating, and including the consumer in their designs is a great way to prepare the market for your new offerings.

If you're thinking about crowdfunding, keep in mind that the amounts of money raised on average may be smaller than you'll need. For example, successful crowdfunding campaigns in 2021 raised on average about $28,000. How you do is a function of how well you run your campaign. I recommend doing your own research before committing to this source of funding.

Here are a few tips:

>> Campaigns with videos typically earn twice as much as those without them.

>> Regularly update your followers.

>> Reach out through email to seek pledges. Statistically, more than half will convert to donations.

>> An all-or-nothing campaign where the donors get their money back if you don't succeed attracts more donors.

>> Keep your campaign description to no more than 500 words.

>> Teams have more success than solo entrepreneurs.

Strategic alliances

A strategic alliance is essentially a partnership with another business, whether that partnership is formal or informal. Sometimes you can structure deals with businesses in your supply chain to bring down some of your costs and increase your cash flow for growth. Customers and suppliers are two frequent sources of funding. Suppliers can offer special terms and grant extended timelines for payment. Customers are a more difficult nut to crack but it can be done. Getting customers to pay for preorders of new products is one way to cover production costs. Alternatively, letting customers invest in what you're doing for higher returns than they would normally find in more traditional investments can be another path to success.

Do a little research, add some creative thinking, and you may just come up with a working partnership that can carry your business a long way. If your business has done well, don't forget to talk with your banker. You are probably in much better shape to take on debt than you were at startup.

IN THIS CHAPTER

» Finding the right legal form for your business

» Using the sole proprietorship

» Choosing the partnership

» Electing the corporate form

» Looking for flexible forms

» Selecting the best legal structure as your business grows

Chapter **15**

Starting with the Right Legal Structure

Choosing the legal form for your business is one of the necessary decisions you must make before you can launch the business. Changes in laws have given entrepreneurs more choices over the form of their organization. Your need for capital and protection from liability are just two reasons that understanding the options available to you is so essential.

Those changing laws are also a good reason for seeking the advice of an experienced attorney and CPA to make sure that you're making the best choice for you and your type of business. This chapter gives you a solid background on what you need to think about before choosing a form of organization and what you need to understand about the various forms available to you.

Choosing a Legal Form for Your Business

All companies operate under one of four broad legal classifications: sole proprietorship, partnership, corporation, or limited liability company. Today, only one in three entrepreneurial businesses actually starts as a sole proprietorship, meaning with one owner. If you remember the discussion in Chapter 9, you'll recall that most ventures today start as teams of entrepreneurs, so a sole proprietorship would not be appropriate. Many entrepreneurs assume that the best entity is always one that lets profits pass through to the owners at their personal tax rate reasoning that they will pay lower taxes or not be taxed twice. They further assume that incorporating in their home state is preferable to out-of-state.

These assumptions can be wrong for some entrepreneurs and businesses. For instance, if you know that you want to eventually do an IPO (initial public offering) within a few years, you should probably form as a C Corporation at launch because that is the required form to go public. If you're going to use venture capital, you probably want a C Corporate form as well, and you may want to incorporate in California or Delaware, because those states have a substantial body of law in the area of corporate governance.

WARNING

Choosing the wrong legal entity when speed is of the essence can mean costly delays and lost opportunities.

Understanding the various factors that come into play when you choose a particular legal structure is important. Seven factors typically affect your choice. A summary comparison of these factors appears in Table 15-1. Here they appear in the form of questions you can ask yourself.

1. Who will be the company owners?

If more than one individual owns the company, you can eliminate sole proprietorship as an option. If many people own the company, the C Corporation form is often the choice because it has an unlimited life and free transferability of interests. If you intend to have many employees, the C Corporation also lets you take advantage of pension plans and stock option plans.

2. What level of liability protection do you require, especially for your personal assets?

Some forms protect you; others do not. It's a sad fact that too many businesses ignore the risks they face and don't acquire the correct forms of insurance. Just as you want to seek the advice of an attorney and accountant as you develop your business, you also want to consider the advice of an insurance broker. The corporate form offers the greatest liability protection for reasons you'll learn in an upcoming section.

TABLE 15-1 **Comparison of Legal Forms of Organization**

Issues	Sole Proprietorship	Partnership	S Corp	Limited Liability (LLC)	C Corp
Number of owners	One	No limit	100 or fewer	No limit	No limit
Life of business	Dissolution on death of owner	Dissolution on death of partner unless otherwise specified in agreement	Perpetual existence	Perpetual existence	Continuity of life
Transferability of interest	Owner free to sell or transfer to estate upon death	General partners require consent of other generals, limited subject to agreement	Shareholders free to sell unless restricted by agreement	Permission of majority of members required	Shareholders free to sell unless restricted by agreement
Distribution of profits	Profits go to owner	Profits shared based on partnership agreement	Profits go to owners	Profits go to members	Paid to shareholders as dividends according to agreement and shareholder status
Taxation	Pass-through, taxed at individual level	Pass-through, taxed at individual level	Pass-through, taxed at individual level	Pass-through, taxed at individual level	Tax-paying entity; corporate income is taxed and employee salaries are taxed at individual levels
Liability	Owner liable for all claims against business	General partners liable for all claims; limited partners only to amount of investment	Limited liability	Members liable as in partnership	Shareholders liable to amount invested; officers may be personally liable
Management control	Owner has full control	Shared by general partners according to partnership agreement	Shared by owners/ shareholders	Rests with management committee (owners or named shareholders)	Rests with the board of directors, elected by the shareholders

3. **How do you expect to distribute the company's earnings?**

If you choose an entity allowing pass-through income and losses (partnership, S Corporation, or LLC), your earnings are distributed immediately without additional taxation. But in a C Corporation, only a salary or other forms of compensation are paid out pretax from the company to an owner.

4. **What are the operating requirements of your business and the costs of running the business under the particular form in question?**

If you own a manufacturing company that uses a lot of machinery, you have different liabilities and costs than a service company, and you should take those issues into consideration.

5. **What are your financing plans?**

How attractive is the form to potential investors? Are you able to offer ownership interests to investors and employees? In general, if you're going to use venture capital, you need a corporate form. Most venture capitalists raise their money from tax-exempt entities like pension funds, universities, and charitable organizations. These organizations can't invest in companies that have pass-through tax benefits.

6. **What will be the effect on the company's tax strategy and your personal tax strategy?**

This includes minimizing tax liability, converting ordinary income to capital gain, and avoiding multiple taxation, as well as maximizing the benefits of startup losses.

7. **Do you expect the company to generate a profit or loss in the beginning?**

If you think your company will lose money for the first few years (this is often true with biotech or other companies developing new products), a pass-through option can be justified because you get to deduct your losses on your personal tax return.

Going It Alone: The Sole Proprietorship

Would you be surprised to find out that more than 75 percent of all businesses operating in the United States are sole proprietorships? A sole proprietorship is a business where the owner is essentially the business; that is, they are solely responsible for the activities of the business and are the only one to enjoy the profits and suffer the losses of the business. Why do so many businesses start this way? Sole proprietorship is the easiest, quickest, and least expensive way to form a business. If you're using your own name as the name of the business, all you need is a business license and some business cards, and you're in business!

Deciding to use another name for your business is only slightly more complex. For example, in the case of ABC Associates, you apply for a DBA, which is a *Certificate of Doing Business under an Assumed Name.* You can secure a DBA at your local government office. Securing a DBA ensures that two businesses don't operate in the same county with the same name.

Advantages of sole proprietorships

I already mentioned that sole proprietorship is the easiest to start and least expensive form of organization, but it also gives the owner complete control of the company. You make all the decisions and suffer all the consequences. The income from the business is yours, and you're taxed only once at your personal income tax rate.

Many professionals, like consultants, authors, and home-based business owners, operate as sole proprietors. Chances are the owners of your neighborhood café, pizza parlor, or shoe repair shop are sole proprietors.

Disadvantages of sole proprietorships

For most entrepreneurs, the sole proprietorship form of organization is not satisfactory for several reasons.

>> As a sole proprietor, you have unlimited liability for any claims against the business. In other words, you are putting your personal assets at risk — your home, car, bank accounts, and any other assets you may have. So, having business liability and errors and omissions insurance is extremely important. If you're producing a product, you'll need product liability insurance to protect you against lawsuits over defective products. If your company does certain types of work such as renovations and construction, and you do the work for clients, you may be required to have bonding insurance to ensure that you complete the work specified in your contract. Because there are so many areas of liability and so many different types of insurance, you should talk to an insurance broker who has the right products for small business.

>> Raising capital is much more difficult because you're relying solely on your financial statement. You are, for all intents and purposes, the business, and most investors don't like that situation.

>> You probably won't have a management team with diverse skills helping you grow your business. You may have employees, but that isn't really the same thing. Putting together an advisory board of people with skills you need helps compensate for the skills you lack. To find out more about advisory boards, see Chapter 9.

>> The survival of your company depends on you being there. Legally, if the sole proprietor dies, so does the business, unless its assets are willed to someone who can take over the business.

Choosing the Partnership Form

A partnership is two or more people deciding to share the assets, liabilities, and profits of their business. Partnering is an improvement over the sole proprietorship because more people are sharing the responsibilities of the business and bouncing ideas off each other. Additionally, you now have multiple financial statements on which to rely and an entity that can survive if one of the partners dies or leaves.

In terms of liability, however, you're raising the stakes, because each partner becomes liable for the obligations incurred by other partners in the course of doing business. This *doctrine of ostensible authority* works like this: Suppose one of your partners enters into a contract on behalf of the partnership, purchasing certain goods from a supplier. That partner has just bound the partnership to make good on a contract even if the rest of the partners knew nothing about it. You can see what a problem that could become and why it's important to pick your partners carefully. Fortunately, the one major exception to the doctrine is that personal debts of an individual partner cannot attach to the rest of the partners.

On the positive side, each partner uses any property owned by the partnership and shares in the profits and losses of the partnership unless otherwise stated in the partnership agreement. Partners don't have to share equally in the profits and losses. Ownership in the partnership can be divided in any manner the partners choose.

The biggest issue with partnerships is that they often are fraught with conflict in much the same way family businesses are. However, when you think about it, any business that includes a team of entrepreneurs, whether a corporation or limited liability company, has similar issues. The partnership agreement, therefore, becomes important from the beginning. I talk about partnership agreements in an upcoming section.

Forming a partnership

You don't have to have a written agreement when forming a partnership; a simple oral agreement works. In fact, in some cases, the conduct of the parties involved implies a legal partnership. Just as when doing business with family members, I strongly encourage you to have an attorney write up a partnership agreement.

WARNING

Accepting a share of the profits of a business is *prima facie* (legally sufficient) evidence that you are a partner in the business, meaning that you may also be liable for its losses and other obligations.

Partnerships come in several types. In most partnerships, entrepreneurs are *general partners*, meaning they share in the profits, losses, and responsibilities, and are personally liable for actions of the partnership. But, you can have other types of partners who have more limited liability, including:

>> **Limited partners:** These partners' liability generally is limited to the amount of their investment.

>> **Secret partners:** These partners are active in the venture but are unknown to the public.

>> **Silent partners:** These partners are usually inactive with only a financial interest in the partnership.

The partnership agreement

I cannot emphasize strongly enough the importance of a partnership agreement. I often see people who claim, "We've been the best of friends for years; we know what we're doing," or "How can I ask my father to sign a partnership agreement?" How can you not? You must separate business from friendship and family, at least when it comes to structuring your company. This is a serious deal. No matter how well you know your partner, you probably haven't worked with them in this particular kind of situation. You have no way of predicting all the things that can cause a disagreement with your partner. The partnership agreement gives you an unbiased mechanism for resolving disagreements or dissolving the partnership, if it comes to that.

Of course, consulting an attorney is necessary when drawing up an agreement, so that you're not inadvertently causing yourself further problems because of the way a phrase is worded in the agreement or something important is omitted. The partnership agreement addresses the following:

>> The legal name of the partnership.

>> The nature of your business.

>> How long the partnership is to last. Just like any contract, it needs an end date.

>> What each of the partners is contributing to the partnership — capital, in-kind goods, services, and so forth. This is the *initial capitalization*.

>> Any sales, loans, or leases to the partnership.

>> Who is responsible for what — the management of the partnership.

>> The sale of a partnership interest. This clause restricts a partner's right to sell their interest to third parties. It provides, however, a method by which a partner can divest their interest in the partnership.

>> How the partnership can be dissolved.

>> What happens if a partner leaves or dies.

>> How disputes will be resolved.

REMEMBER

If you don't execute a partnership agreement, all partners are equal under the law. Do not form a partnership without the help of an attorney, especially if your partners are friends. You need the objective advice of a professional who will make sure that you've covered all the bases in the unlikely event that something goes wrong.

The Corporation

A corporation is a different animal entirely from the other forms of legal organization, because it is a legal entity under the law. That means it can survive the death or separation of all of its owners. It can also sue, be sued, acquire, and sell real property, and lend money. Essentially a corporation can do everything a person can.

Corporation owners are stockholders who invest capital into the corporation and receive shares of stock usually proportionate to the level of their investment. Much like limited partners, shareholders are not responsible for the debts of the corporation (unless they have personally guaranteed them). In any case, their investment amount is the limit of their liability.

I address two major types of corporations in this chapter — the C Corporation (closely held, close, and public) and the S Corporation, which I discuss in the next section. Most corporations are *closely held corporations*, which means that their stock is held privately by a few individuals. A closely held corporation operates as any type of corporation — general, professional, or nonprofit. In a close corporation, by contrast, the number of shareholders you may have may be restricted, usually to between 30 and 50 shareholders. In addition, holding directors meetings is not required. Such meetings are a requirement for a general corporation.

The close corporation is not available in every state and does not permit you to conduct an initial public offering. Basically, a close corporation operates much like a partnership or other pass-through entity. While you have fewer reporting requirements and shareholders to deal with, you will not be as free to sell your shares. Additionally, since all the capital comes from the owners, you could find yourself in a bind should you decide to expand the business.

Doctors, lawyers, accountants, and other similar professionals, who previously were not allowed to incorporate, now often use professional corporations that must be incorporated within the state where the professional is practicing. Shareholders' personal assets are protected from liability for debts incurred by the corporation. You should be aware that only members of the specific profession can be shareholders in the professional corporation. To be taxed at a federal flat rate of 35 percent, 95 percent of the business activities of the corporation must be within the area of specialization of the professionals, so for doctors that would be medical practice. Unlike a non-professional corporation, which is taxed based on net income, a professional corporation is taxed based on revenue.

WARNING

In a professional corporation, the shareholders may be liable for negligent or wrongful acts (malpractice) of any shareholder, depending on the governing laws of their state. Be sure to check the tax rates and liability burden for professional corporations in your state or province.

Up until now, we have been talking about private corporations. But if you at some point elect to do an IPO, your company will become a public corporation, where stock is traded on a securities exchange like the New York Stock Exchange, and the company generally has thousands (in some cases, millions) of shareholders. Chapter 14 discusses the IPO in more detail.

Three groups of individuals — shareholders, directors, and officers — make up the public corporate structure. Shareholders own the corporation but they don't manage it. Shareholders exert influence through the directors they elect to serve and represent them on the board. The board of directors, in turn provides oversight for the affairs of the corporation at a policy level and hires and fires the officers who are responsible for the day-to-day management of the company.

What is surprising to many is that corporations comprise only about 17 percent of all businesses, yet they generate 87 percent of all sales. Part of this surprising picture is attributable to the fact that most entrepreneurs who intend to grow their companies choose the corporate form for its many benefits.

Enjoying the benefits

The advantages of a corporate form definitely outweigh the disadvantages. In another section, I mention that the owners enjoy limited liability to the extent of their investment (the one important exception is payroll taxes that haven't been paid to the IRS). By selecting the corporate form, you also can

>> **Raise capital through the sale of stock in the company.**

>> **Own a corporation without the public being aware of your involvement.** So, if you want anonymity, it's the way to go. Just don't take the company public through an IPO because information about management will be public.

>> **Create different classes of stock to help you meet the various needs of investors.** For example, you may need to issue non-voting *preferred stock* to early conservative investors wanting to be first to recoup their investment in the event the business fails. Most stock issued is *common stock,* whose owners enjoy voting rights and share in the profits after the preferred stockholders have been satisfied.

>> **Easily transfer ownership.** In a private corporation, you want assurances that your shareholders can't sell their stock to just anyone. In other words, you want to know who owns your stock. You can protect yourself by including a buy-sell clause in the stockholder's agreement. Usually, this clause specifies that the stock must first be offered to the corporation at an agreed-upon price.

>> **Enter into corporate contracts and sue or be sued without the signatures of the owners.**

>> **Enjoy more status in the business world than other legal forms because corporations survive apart from their owners.**

>> **Enjoy the benefits of setting up retirement funds, Keogh and defined-contribution plans, profit sharing, and stock option plans.** The corporation deducts these fringe benefits as expenses that are not taxable to the employee.

Weighing the risks

Every legal form has disadvantages and risks, and the corporation is no exception. Here are risks worth considering when contemplating this form.

>> Corporations are much more complex, cumbersome, and expensive to set up.

>> Corporations are subject to more government regulation.

>> A corporation pays taxes on profits regardless of whether they are distributed as dividends to stockholders. Most early-stage companies don't pay dividends, as they need the cash for growth.

» Shareholders of corporations do not receive the tax benefits of company losses.

» By selling shares of stock in your corporation, you're effectively giving up a measure of control to a board of directors. The reality, however, is that, in general, the entrepreneur determines who sits on that board of directors in privately held corporations.

» You must keep your personal finances and the corporation's finances completely separate. You must conduct directors' meetings, and maintain minutes from those meetings. If you don't, you may leave your company open to what is known as *piercing the corporate veil,* which makes you and your officers liable personally for the company's obligations.

Where and how to incorporate

You create a corporation by filing a certificate of incorporation with the state in which you plan to do business and issue stock, making your company a *domestic corporation.* If you incorporate in a state other than the one in which you do business, your company is considered a *foreign corporation.*

In general, you want to incorporate in the state where you're planning to locate the business so that you don't find yourself working under the regulations of two states. When deciding where to incorporate, consider

» **The cost difference of incorporating in your home state versus doing business as a foreign corporation in another state.** In general, if you're doing business mostly in your home state, incorporating there won't subject you to taxes and annual report fees from both states.

» **The advantages and disadvantages of the other state's corporate laws and tax structure.** For example, in California, a corporation pays a minimum state tax regardless of whether it makes a profit. Colorado has no minimum state tax. Likewise, if you're incorporating anywhere other than your home state, and find yourself defending a lawsuit in the state of incorporation, you may incur the expense of travel back and forth during that time.

» **The fact that corporations pay taxes on the profits they earn, and the owners (shareholders) pay taxes on the dividends they receive.** This is what is referred to as "double taxation." However, if you draw a salary, the corporation will deduct that as an expense of the company, and you will be taxed at your personal income tax rate.

CHOOSING THE RIGHT LEGAL FORM

Choosing the best legal form of organization can be a relatively simple task if you consider the type of business you have and what its needs are. Let's look at a hypothetical example.

Suppose your spouse is a highly paid executive for a major corporation, making possible your pursuit of developing a product you've been playing around with. You decide to set up a small business with a shop near your home. Because you're already covered for medical insurance by your spouse's company, you don't have this worry. However, you need to limit your liability, because you and your spouse have acquired a number of valuable assets. You realize that in any business dealing with products, some liability issues crop up and you want to make sure you're covered.

In the beginning, you expect losses as you purchase equipment, build your prototypes, and test them in the market. You expect losses to continue once you launch your product, as you will have marketing expenses and will be hiring employees. But you have big plans for this business; in fact, within a year of introducing the product, you expect to need venture capital to be able to grow as fast as the market demands. You also see an IPO in your future.

The question is: What type of legal form should you choose?

Analysis: Developing a new product takes time, during which you are not bringing in any cash to the business, but you are spending money. Working out of your garage as a sole proprietor is the least costly form of organization and you can deduct your losses on your personal income tax. Your liability at this point is minimal because your product is not yet available for sale. But once you move to an office and hire staff, the situation changes. You may still be incurring losses but you've increased your liability substantially. Because you don't yet have any revenues, however, you won't have to worry about taxes. At this stage, you may be considering the S Corporation form, which provides you with the liability protection you need but allows you to pass the losses through to be used against your family income on your personal tax return. Although you can keep this form throughout the time that you're incurring losses right after you launch, don't forget that if you intend to seek venture capital, you must switch to a C Corporate form, the preferred form for investment purposes that is also required for an IPO.

Looking for Flexibility: The S Corporation and the LLC

A number of different legal organizational forms offer flexibility for entrepreneurs in a variety of ways. In this section, we look at two: the S Corporation and the LLC. The next section covers the nonprofit. All the criteria used for deciding which form to choose that we discussed previously applies here.

Sizing up the S Corporation

Don't let the term "corporation" fool you. An S Corporation, for the most part, is nothing like a C Corporation. It is not a legal entity and does not pay taxes as a legal entity. Basically, S Corporations are financial vehicles for passing company profits and losses through to owners who pay income taxes at their personal tax rates. As a shareholder in an S Corporation, you may deduct any losses of the corporation on your personal income tax return, up to the amount you invested in the corporation. If you sell the assets of your S Corporation, you pay a tax on the amount of appreciation of those assets.

An S Corporation can provide employee benefits and deferred compensation plans. To qualify for S Corporation status, you must

1. **Form your corporation with no more than 100 shareholders, none of whom can be nonresident aliens, a trust, or another corporation.**

2. **Issue only one class of stock.**

3. **Ensure no more than 25 percent of the corporate income is derived from passive investments like dividends, rent, and capital gains.**

In addition, your S Corporation cannot be a financial institution, a foreign corporation, or a subsidiary of a parent corporation. If you elect to change from an S Corporation to a C Corporate form, you cannot go back to being an S Corporation form for five years.

WARNING

S Corporations work if your business generates a lot of cash. If it doesn't, you can easily create a situation where you owe taxes on your profits, while the business isn't generating any cash to pay them.

In general, S Corporations work best

>> When you expect to experience a loss in the first year or two, and owners have other income they can shelter with that loss.

>> Where shareholders have low tax brackets (lower than the corporate rate), so the profits can be distributed as dividends without double taxation.

>> Where your business may incur an accumulated earnings penalty tax for failure to pay out its profits as dividends.

It's important to check the rules in your state, as the S corporation is not recognized in all states.

Comparing the S Corporation to the LLC

The Limited Liability Company (LLC) is the newest legal form of business organization, and while gaining in popularity for many entrepreneurs, it adds another layer of complexity to the many choices in structuring their companies. The LLC combines the best of partnerships (pass-through earnings) with the best of the corporate form (limited liability). LLCs have grown in popularity because they offer something for just about anyone. LLCs:

>> Limit liability for business debts up to the amount invested.

>> Offer flexible management structure that allows members (the equivalent of shareholders in a corporation), or nonmembers they hire, to manage the organization.

>> Allow the choice of being treated as a partnership with the benefits of pass-through earnings or as a corporation, whichever provides the lowest tax liability.

>> Enable flexible distribution of profits and losses, meaning that you can divide them up any way you want among the members.

So what differences exist between an LLC and an S Corporation? Why would you choose one over the other?

>> An LLC provides for an unlimited number of owners, whereas the S Corporation limits you to 100.

>> An LLC permits you to include nonresident aliens, pension plans, partnerships, and corporations as members, whereas the S Corporation does not.

>> LLCs can have different classes of stock (preferred, common), whereas an S Corporation is generally limited to one class.

You need two members to form an LLC in California, the District of Columbia, and Massachusetts. Expect other states to raise the number of members they require from one to two.

The members of an LLC are analogous to partners in a partnership or shareholders in a corporation. If the members self-manage, then the members act more like partners than shareholders, because they have a direct say in what happens within the organization. Stock in an LLC is known as interest. With an LLC, you have an operating agreement, which is much like the bylaws in a corporation.

WARNING

The primary disadvantages of an LLC come from fees and taxes. Although the owners (members) avoid double taxation, they are required to pay self-employment taxes — twice! This is because the owner is both an employee and an employer. In addition, some states like California charge an annual franchise tax of $800 that increases as net income increases. If you are considering operating internationally, be aware that some countries like Canada don't recognize the LLC form, so your company will be treated as a corporation and be subject to those rules.

If you're looking for more flexibility in what you're able to do, choose an LLC over an S Corporation. However, as always, check the specific rules in your state or country before making any decision and do consult an attorney.

What about a B corporation?

A B corporation is a benefit corporation, a for-profit entity with a social mission. It must consider the impact of all its decisions on its stakeholders — workers, shareholders, communities, customers, suppliers, and the environment. In other words, profit cannot be the sole basis for a decision. Your company must pursue a general public benefit alongside any social or environmental benefit. Note that each state has its own requirements that you should review to make sure this is what you want to do.

Whether or not you choose to become a B corporation, it is wise to look at what the certification groups are targeting as controversial in case you find yourself in their crosshairs. For example, suppose you are offering online education in entrepreneurship in the belief that many people can't easily go to college while working full time. The B certifiers note that for-profit education is controversial because of its business models, recruiting practices, and educational quality.

Some examples of successful B corps include Patagonia (outdoor clothing), Allbirds (casual shoes), and Prose (customized hair products). In each case, the company is doing good at many levels. Patagonia, for example, gives 100 percent of its Black Friday profits to grassroots nonprofits working to protect air, water, and soil quality. Allbirds makes all its shoes from sustainable materials. Prose focuses on clean, sustainably sourced ingredients for its made-to-order products.

If you want to make money and do good at the same time, it might be worth your time to investigate B certification further. Many investors are focusing their investments on startups that are doing good, especially for the environment.

Making Profits in a Nonprofit Organization

Let's dispel the biggest myth about nonprofit organizations first. You can make a profit in a nonprofit company; in fact, doing so is a good idea because it signals that your business is healthy. What you can't do is distribute those your profits in the form of dividends or capital gains to the owners the way other legal forms do. A nonprofit, or *not-for-profit corporation,* is required to be formed for charitable, public (scientific, literary, or educational), religious, or mutual benefit (as in trade associations) purposes.

Like the C Corporation, the nonprofit is a legal entity with a life of its own and offers its members limited liability. Profits that it generates from its nonprofit activities are not taxed as long as the company meets the state and federal require-ments for exemption from taxes under IRS 501(c)(3). When you form a nonprofit, you actually give up proprietary interest in the corporation and dedicate all the assets and resources to tax-exempt activities. If you choose to dissolve the corpo-ration, you must distribute those assets to another tax-exempt organization — you can't take them with you. Any profits you make from for-profit activities unrelated to your core business are taxed the same as any other corporation.

Nonprofit organizations derive their revenues from a variety of sources. They receive donations from corporations (these donations are tax deductible to the corporation) and individuals. They conduct activities to raise money, or sell services (a for-profit activity). As entrepreneurs, founders of nonprofit, tax-exempt corporations can pay themselves a salary typical of a similar company in the for-profit sector, be provided with a car, and generally do the kinds of things you would do within a normal corporation (within reason), except distribute profits or assets.

CASE STUDY

Most entrepreneurs who start nonprofits do so for reasons other than money — for example, a driving need to give back to the community. James Blackman founded the Civic Light Opera of South Bay Cities, Redondo Beach, California in 1999, providing a cultural arts center for the community. The opera became the third largest musical theater in California and has won many awards. As part of his mission, Blackman's company also provides opportunities for physically and mentally challenged children to experience music and the theater arts. Blackman recently expanded his reach by acquiring the trademark "Los Angeles Civic Light Opera," which had not been in use since 1977. He has also been invited to join with the Warner Grand Theater in San Pedro, a city that is undergoing extensive renovation and is well located to serve a broader base of customers.

Benchmarking the Right Choice

TIP

Now that you have a good overview of what's available, Figure 15-1 offers a method for choosing the best legal form for your new business. Starting with the first question, work your way down, mapping an easy way to consider your alternatives and organize your business.

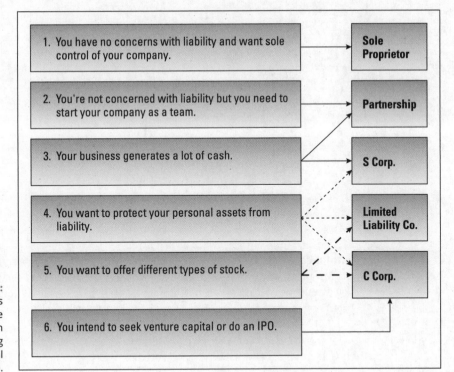

FIGURE 15-1:
Six questions point you in the right direction for choosing your legal organization.

1. You have no concerns with liability and want sole control of your company. → Sole Proprietor

2. You're not concerned with liability but you need to start your company as a team. → Partnership

3. Your business generates a lot of cash. → S Corp.

4. You want to protect your personal assets from liability. → Limited Liability Co.

5. You want to offer different types of stock. → C Corp.

6. You intend to seek venture capital or do an IPO.

Keep in mind that the legal form of your organization does not have to be a static decision; rather, it is based on the needs of your company at startup and at critical milestones in the future.

Choosing the legal structure is one of the most important decisions you will make, so get the advice of a good attorney and talk to other entrepreneurs to be better informed. Your legal structure will affect your tax strategy for years to come, so it's definitely worth spending some time now to consider all the possibilities.

4

Growing a Company

Chapter **16**

Planning for Growth

f you're thinking the birth of a company and its early stages are the most perilous, I have news for you. They're not. I say that because if you plan for the launch of your business and do all of the things we've talked about in other chapters of this book, you better your odds for success. Moreover, you'll likely set your business up for rapid growth. Growth causes the kinds of problems that make the startup phase look relatively easy by comparison. One reason is that the problems associated with growth can be difficult to predict. New business owners simply don't know how to plan for them.

Growth is an inevitable outcome of a successful startup, so why don't entrepreneurs plan for it? The main reason is that they are so busy with the day-to-day effort of running their businesses that they don't pause to raise their periscope and see what's coming their way. Consequently, demand smacks them in the face and they don't have the systems and personnel in place to handle it.

The lesson here is that the skills you need to bring resources together to start your business aren't the same as the skills you need to take your business to the next level. You may find that you need to bring in more talent to make it to the next stage, and that costs money you probably don't have.

A good growth plan includes your goals, the strategies to reach those goals, and the tactics you will use to execute those strategies. In this chapter, you learn some effective growth strategies. You also learn more about how to scale your operations so that they match your growth trajectory. Let's get started.

Identifying Factors That Affect Growth

When designing an effective growth plan, you first must understand all the factors that affect your company's ability to grow. They start with:

>> **Your intentions about your business.** You may be surprised to discover that business owners don't always want to grow to the next Disney or Amazon. Sometimes they're perfectly happy running their little shop just the way they are, thank you. But probe a little deeper, you may find that the decision not to grow is rooted in fear. With a small business, you can pretty much control everything; but when your business grows rapidly, you need to rely on other people. For some entrepreneurs, delegating authority for their businesses to others is hard, like handing your child over to the care of someone else. Before your business can grow, you must want it to grow; it doesn't normally happen by itself.

>> **Your ability to pull together the right team for growth.** No matter how much you believe in your growth strategy, you can't do it alone. You need a team of people as committed to your business as you are. Conveying your vision of company growth and convincing everyone to buy into it is critical to the successful execution of your growth plan.

>> **What your target market looks like.** How much your company can grow is a function of the size of your market and the buying power of your customers. If your market is small and not showing signs of growth, achieving high levels of growth may be unachievable. On the other hand, if your product or service has global potential, substantial growth is definitely within the realm of possibility if you plan for it.

>> **What your competition looks like.** Why would anyone enter a market where giants play? Going toe-to-toe with the big guys is not a good strategic plan in most cases, unless you can create a unique niche in that market that no one else is serving. That way you can gain a foothold before the big companies find you. Competing against established brands is tough unless you introduce an innovative product or new technology.

>> **How innovative the industry is.** If your industry isn't known for being innovative, your business may have a competitive advantage by introducing something new. On the other hand, if you're in a highly innovative industry

like software, you must quickly produce a constant stream of innovations to grow.

>> **The importance of intellectual property rights.** Not many industries exist today where intellectual property isn't critical to long-term success. Owning patents, trademarks, and copyrights is the key to entering some industries and providing barriers to entry for others. If you can't gain access to the intellectual property you need through licensing, it may be difficult to grow.

>> **How predictable the industry is.** If you're in a predictable industry, differentiating your business from the rest can be more difficult. In an unpredictable industry like high tech, you have more opportunities to find untapped niches in the market.

>> **Barriers to entry.** Your ability to grow your company is also affected by barriers to entry that others in the industry set up to keep you out. Those barriers can take the form of intense research and development, heavy expenditures in plant and equipment, contracts with key supply channels, or regulations, to name a few.

If you performed a thorough industry analysis as discussed in Chapter 5, you can check what you learned against the factors that affect your ability to grow.

Starting with a Basic Growth Strategy

Companies grow at different rates because of the factors discussed in the previous section, but two common patterns describe most businesses — the normal growth rate and the accelerated growth rates seen in high-technology companies. In this section, we look at the normal growth curve. Accelerated growth is covered in "Growing as a High-Tech Company" later in this chapter.

Refer to Figure 14-1 in Chapter 14, where you see the normal growth path for most businesses depicted in four phases. The length of time a business spends in any one phase varies. Some businesses spend a long time in startup, trying to reach enough critical mass to enable them to grow. Others start growing rapidly almost from the beginning. Some businesses never reach what we would call *high growth*; they simply continue growing at a relatively stable pace, generally because of the market they're in or sometimes because entrepreneurs put brakes on their businesses to keep them from growing faster than their resources can handle. That's okay if you're meeting customer demand; but if demand far exceeds your ability or desire to meet it, you could be shooting yourself in the foot.

At each stage of growth, you and your business face differing issues and activities. The defining issues you find in each of the four phases of growth are

1. **Startup:**

   Your concerns center on securing sufficient startup capital, seeking customers, and designing an effective way to deliver your product or service. Your role is that of doing almost everything (including, sometimes, the janitorial work). Cash is important, because you never have enough of it.

2. **Initial Growth:**

   You know you've made it through the first phase if you have enough customers to keep your business running with a positive cash flow. Now the question becomes, do you have enough cash flow to sustain the business while it's growing? Although your business is still small during this phase, you're still doing a lot of the work because you're keeping employees to a minimum. Nevertheless, it's stable, and if you wanted to, you could actually keep it running this way indefinitely.

3. **High Growth:**

   If you're an ambitious entrepreneur, you probably won't be satisfied maintaining your business at the level of initial growth, which is essentially where most small, lifestyle businesses remain. You probably want to expand and grow the business to the next level, but that takes a much more intense level of growth. Attaining high growth usually doesn't happen using internal cash flows alone, so you must consider finding the resources you need to do it. (See Chapter 14, for suggestions on where to find financing for growth.) You also must:

   - Plan carefully for this type of growth, because it can quickly get away from you, depleting your resources before you achieve your goals.

   - Delegate more responsibility and perhaps even bring professional management on board. In a high-growth business, it's common to find a management team in place that is different from the one that founded the company. Your job is to get product to the customer quickly and without problems. You don't have time for much else.

4. **Stable Growth:**

   If you succeed in passing through the high-growth phase, your company can probably achieve a more or less predictable level of stable growth. Your company now has all the systems and controls found in a larger company. The danger at this point is complacency and your assumption that stable growth can continue indefinitely. Unfortunately, the market will torpedo that assumption. If your company isn't in a relatively constant state of change, responding to and leading in the market, it may begin to lose market share. Companies can and do fail at this stage.

Growing within Your Current Market

In general, most new businesses attempt to grow as much as possible within their current markets before taking on new markets. That kind of growth makes sense financially. Growing within your current market means increasing the number of customers and volume of sales to those customers. Let's look at the methods for doing that.

Building your customer base

One of the first growth strategies that businesses use is *market penetration*. You increase sales to current customers by doing a better job of advertising and promotion, a topic covered in Chapter 17. You're gradually increasing the number and types of customers you serve. Suppose, for example, that you own a company that provides technology services to small businesses. You may extend your services to mid-size companies or extend your reach beyond your current geographical area. After solidifying each customer group, you move on to the next group.

Another way of achieving market penetration is by finding additional uses for your product, luring customers away from your competitors, and educating non-users about the benefits of your product or service. You have a lot you can do before you think about the next strategy for growth.

Developing your market

When you use *market development* as your growth strategy, you're expanding your product or service market into a broader geographic area. For example, if your company starts on the West Coast, you may begin moving into the Midwest. One of the more popular and rapid ways of growing geographically is by franchising. You're no doubt familiar with the popularity of this strategy considering such famous franchises as Kentucky Fried Chicken, Golf USA, and Kragen.

Franchising

With franchising, you sell the right to do business under a particular name as well as the right to the product, process, or service. You provide training and assistance to your franchisees in setting up their businesses. Your franchisees pay you an upfront fee and royalties on sales. Some franchisors also charge a monthly marketing fee of about 2.5 percent of the franchisee's net revenue.

In exchange for the fees you charge, you provide your franchisee:

>> A product or service with a proven market

>> Trademarks

>> A patented design, process, or formula

>> An accounting and financial control system

>> A marketing plan

>> Volume purchasing and advertising

Franchising isn't without risks, because it's essentially like starting a new business all over again. You need to document all the processes and procedures of your business in a manual for franchisees and offer training and field coaching. You also must be careful about whom you select as your franchisees, because they represent you and your business's reputation. Franchises are costly propositions because of legal, accounting, consulting, and training expenses, and they generally take about five years to show a profit. It's a wise idea to explore the kinds of businesses that are best suited to franchising to see if yours is a fit.

Not every business is suitable for franchising. While assessing your business, benchmark it against the following criteria:

>> Do you have a successful prototype operation (preferably multiple outlets) with a good reputation and proven profitability?

>> Do you have registered trademarks or other forms of intellectual property?

>> Is your business easily systematized and replicated?

>> Can your product or service be sold in many different geographic regions?

You need sufficient resources, many times in excess of $150,000, to develop an effective franchise program, and you must create

>> A prospectus that details the franchisee's rights, responsibilities, and risks.

>> An operations manual that explains in detail how the business works.

>> A training and support system for your franchisees before they open their franchise, and an ongoing system after launch.

>> Site selection criteria and architectural standards.

WARNING

You should always consult an attorney when setting up a franchise program to avoid errors that could result in litigation.

Licensing

Licensing is another effective way to develop your market without having to invest in additional sites yourself. Licensing works when you have intellectual property — patents or trademarks — that has value in the marketplace. You can license the right to use that intellectual property to others. For example, suppose you develop and patent a new kind of vacuum cleaner that revolutionizes the way people clean. You set up a company to produce a machine under your brand. But to grow, you also license the right to manufacture and distribute the technology outside the United States to one or more vacuum cleaner manufacturers that are doing business in other countries. That way you don't have to set up additional manufacturing facilities. Licensing is discussed in depth in Chapter 8.

Developing your product

A third way to grow the current market is developing new products and services for the customers you have. The goal is selling more to your current customers because they are the easiest sales you can achieve. The computer hardware and software industries are a classic example of this strategy. They regularly upgrade their products to newer versions, fixing bugs in earlier versions and installing new bells and whistles to entice their customers to purchase the upgrades.

Your customers are the best source of ideas for product and service innovations. Most of these ideas come in the form of improvements to existing products (*incremental innovation*), but once in a while you uncover an idea for an entirely new product that can be a tremendous source of growth for your company. These *breakthrough* products are not something you can plan for. They usually surface during intense brainstorming sessions or when customers, suppliers, or employees suggest them. Breakthrough products usually require a much longer product development cycle and cost more to develop than incremental products, but the return on investment can be huge.

Branding your company

One of your more important products — and many entrepreneurs don't realize this — is your company and what it stands for. Too many entrepreneurs focus exclusively on promoting their products and services and forget that their company images — their brands — are far more valuable assets than any products or services. If you establish brand recognition for your company, marketing any new products or services that you develop is by far easier. When customers associate your company name with quality, service, reliability, and great products and services, that brand becomes an umbrella under which you can add new ways of serving the customer.

The classic examples of the effectiveness of branding are apparel companies that don't design their own clothes but put their branding on articles of clothing they purchase from a commodity apparel manufacturer. Nike and Mossimo, among many others, purchase T-shirts from apparel manufacturers such as Hanes and print their logos on them. These companies find that customers pay more for the same T-shirt with a Nike design on it than for the same T-shirt with no design or the design of a lesser-known company.

Creating a brand is an essential part of developing new products and services. Actions you can take to start creating brand recognition for your company include:

>> **Identifying the things your company does well.** What is special about your company? Outstanding quality and service? Agility? Remarkable and diverse pool of talent? Do you offer the highest quality products? Do you have an outstanding company culture? Are you dominating a niche that competitors aren't serving so you can build rapid brand recognition?

>> **Selecting two or three of your biggest strengths to serve as the focus of all of your marketing efforts.** Make sure customers see the strengths associated with your company's name again and again so that the two become synonymous. For example, Indeed, founded in 2004, is now the largest job website in the world. And when it comes to finding jobs, size matters. Indeed provides listings in every industry at every level from entry to executive. On their site you can read reviews on prospective employers, which is helpful before you accept an offer. Its competitors like FlexJobs focus on niche markets such as work-from-home opportunities and in that way, they can differentiate themselves from the biggest players, Indeed and Monster.

>> **Deciding how your brand name will be used.** In a sense, you must create rules for the consistent use of your brand name. For example, make sure that the company name is always displayed with the product or service that you're promoting. If you want your company to be associated with the highest quality, you probably won't promote it in an environment that is not perceived as such, for example, in a discount catalog.

>> **Getting feedback from your customers.** Conduct blind tests with customers to see how they're responding to your branding efforts. Then adjust your strategy based on what you learn.

Growing within Your Industry

Growing within your industry means expanding by acquiring or teaming with other companies in the industry and in your distribution channel. In this section, we look at three ways to take advantage of growth opportunities inside your industry.

Moving vertically in your channel

Your distribution channel offers opportunities for moving upstream or downstream in a movement known as *vertical integration.* (If you need to find out more about distribution channels, see Chapter 10.) When you move upstream in your channel, (vertical integration) you gain control of your suppliers by acquiring them, by securing exclusive contracts, or by starting a supply outlet of your own. Gaining control of upstream activities in your channel is popular with companies using a just-in-time approach to production. Doing so enables them to receive raw materials and supplies exactly when they are needed without carrying an inventory. This control saves time and money and significantly reduces the cost of production. Entrepreneurs often consider vertical integration because they're not big enough to be a priority for manufacturers, so they're don't get the best pricing or production speed. But, there are some serious downsides to vertical integration. You have to learn a new industry (e.g., manufacturing) while you're trying to grow your business with lean resources. The long-term benefits and increased profit margins make this a strategy you might come back to when the timing is right, and you have the ability to execute on the strategy.

When gaining control of downstream activities in your channel, you're controlling the distribution of your product by either selling directly to the customer — for example, you purchase a retail or wholesale outlet or sell online — or acquiring the distributors of your products.

What you can control is a function of where you are located in the distribution channel. As a retailer, for example, you already control the downstream portion because you sell directly to the consumer. If you're a distributor, you can decide to purchase retail outlets or sell directly to consumers through a warehouse type operation (Costco did this). If you're a supplier, you can look at distributors and/or retailers to control your channels of distribution. Most entrepreneurs with products ready to sell choose online channels because they're the least expensive and you deal directly with your end customer — the consumer or business that pays you.

Moving horizontally in your channel

You can also grow within your industry through *horizontal integration,* or by acquiring your competitors or starting a competing business. Suppose you own a theme restaurant catering to customers who like sports. Your restaurant is located in the northern part of the city. One way you can grow into other areas of the city is to acquire one or more of your competitors that are located where you want to be.

Another way to grow horizontally in your channel is to manufacture your product under another label, reaching a different customer segment without compromising the image of your core product. For example, some established high-end apparel designers reach the mass markets by producing a line of apparel under a different label, a strategy that also is common in the major appliance and grocery industries. Major retailers such as Safeway, Kroger, and Costco regularly put their brand names (often a surrogate name—i.e., Signature for Safeway) on products made by others expressly for that purpose.

Creating a network in your industry

One effective way to grow as a small company is to develop strategic alliances with other companies in your industry, so that you focus on what you do best and rely on your network for everything else you need. These alliances enable you to work with the best suppliers and distributors, grow more rapidly, keep your unit costs down, and develop new products more quickly. Another benefit is that because investing heavily in fixed assets no longer is a necessity, you can devote those resources to finding new competitive advantages.

Even if you have a service business, you can take advantage of this strategy by forming strategic alliances with companies that are the best in accounting, payroll, telemarketing, and data processing, to name a few.

Diversifying Outside Your Industry

Intuition probably tells you that you need to exploit all the opportunities in your current market and industry before jumping outside to foreign territory in the form of a new industry. However, entrepreneurs have succeeded in using a diversification strategy early in the growth process in the same way that great venture capitalists diversify their portfolios by investing in several industries to reduce risk from any one industry. Situations in which such a strategy makes the most sense include these:

>> You have excess capacity or spare resources that aren't in use. Making use of them provides a new revenue stream for the company.

>> Your customers are asking you to provide them with products or services that are outside of your current industry.

>> You foresee major changes in your industry forcing you to look outside for your growth.

Capitalizing on the synergy of like businesses

The easiest way of diversifying so that you make the most of what you already have is to find products or businesses that are technologically similar or, better yet, complementary to your business. This is called *synergistic diversification*. For example, a restaurant chain may acquire a bakery to bring down the costs of supplying baked goods to its chain. A sporting goods store may acquire a batting cage business as a promotional opportunity for its baseball equipment and apparel.

Acquiring an unrelated business

When you acquire businesses that have no relationship to your core business, it's called *conglomerate diversification*. That's a mouthful that may give you pause before you try it. You do not want to become a conglomerate without ensuring your core business is in a healthy position, because no synergies exist between the two businesses; they operate as two completely different entities. So, why try conglomerate diversification? Sometimes, it enables entrepreneurs to gain control of a business function that can ultimately help them. Examples of conglomerate diversification are

>> Purchasing the building in which you have your offices and becoming a landlord to other businesses to which you lease your excess space.

>> Acquiring a travel agency to manage all of the travel plans of all of your busy sales people, saving money by bringing that function in-house and possibly offering this new service to others.

Whenever you acquire another business, particularly one that is completely different from yours, working with someone who's experienced in mergers and acquisitions is a necessity. You'll also want to ask

>> Are the cultures of the two companies compatible? Don't focus only on financial and operational synergies.

>> Are the leadership styles of management compatible?

>> Will you be better off a year from now having acquired this business?

Going Global to Grow

The truth is that you don't have to take your business global to be a success, but in today's marketplace, avoiding global influences is pretty hard. And if you do business on the Internet, you've become a global business whether you wanted to or not. So, I would say that the question isn't "Should you go global?" but rather "When should you go global?" Several reasons why you need to consider the global marketplace in your growth planning are

>> The Internet brings the world to your doorstep. You may find that your best suppliers, distributors, and customers are located in other countries.

>> The Internet also brings your competitors to your doorstep. Today, even if you have a local business, your competitors can pounce on your market from anywhere in the world with the click of a mouse button and the overnight delivery capability of companies like FedEx and UPS.

>> Shortened product lives and costly research and development force your company to enter more than one major market to start out just so you recap the costs of product development more quickly. The global marketplace is a major supporter of businesses introducing new products.

>> You may find new markets for your products that are losing their luster in the United States. You may also find complementary products produced in other countries that you can add to your product line.

>> Exporting to countries governed by the USMCA (United States-Mexico-Canada Agreement) is attractive because of the elimination of trade barriers. Similarly, the Uruguay Round of GATT (the General Agreement on Tariffs and Trade) reduces or eliminates tariffs among 117 countries and improves patent and copyright protections.

Deciding if you're ready

Most new businesses don't begin exporting until they establish their businesses domestically, because global markets present entirely new issues that must be dealt with. Likewise, most entrepreneurs with startups are busy enough just establishing their products and services in the domestic market. In the case of my company and its generator/compressor product, we saw a huge potential in the international market; but before taking that leap, we realized that the machine's components would have to be redesigned to meet electrical and other requirements in different regions of the world. Doing that at startup would take important resources away from the need to build presence in the domestic market.

Research points to certain business attributes that serve as precursors of greater success for businesses deciding to go global. Ask yourself whether you or your business has the following attributes:

>> You've had a global vision from the inception of your business.

>> You have a management team with international experience.

>> You have a strong international network of contacts you can tap.

>> You have a new technology that other countries don't have.

>> You have a unique, intangible asset in your business such as knowhow that no one else has.

>> You can derive additional products and services from your core technology.

>> You have systems and controls in place that will work in the international environment.

WARNING

You also need to know that exporting is a long-term commitment. You may not make money for some time, so you must be in a position to suffer the losses for a while.

Finding great global markets

The world is a big place when you're figuring out where to sell your products and services. Some countries are friendlier to U.S. products than others. In general, here are three indicators you might want to evaluate about any country in which you want to sell your products or services.

>> **Gross domestic product**. You want a country with a growing GDP where inflation is not a problem. I note ironically that the United States would not fare well by this metric in 2022.

>> **Employment indicators**. Determine how productive and wealthy a nation's citizens are and how much money they have to spend on goods and services.

>> **Import restrictions.** Such restrictions will very likely raise the price of goods.

In general, the easiest countries to deal with are Canada, the UK, and Australia. But you need to look at countries where your customers live, which of course depends on what you're selling.

TIP

One good way of starting your search is consulting the *World Trade Statistical Review*, `www.wto.org/english/res_e/statis_e/wts2021_e/wts2021_e.pdf`. This is the main publication of the World Trade Organization, which deals with the global rules of trade among nations. Using the SITC (Standard Industrial Trade Classification) 4-digit codes found in their book, you can find information about demand in specific countries for your type of product or service.

When looking at demand for U.S. products in general, you want to find countries where the demand for U.S. products exceeds 5 percent.

Getting help

Moving into the global market is not something that happens without a great deal of planning and effort. Most companies wisely put all their systems and controls into place before they venture into international waters.

REMEMBER

U.S. brands, while familiar to people in the United States, are not always recognizable in other countries. Couple that with desires and preferences of foreign buyers that can be different from those of U.S. buyers, and you see that you need plenty of research on the purchasing habits of the customers in the region you're trying to reach.

Many resources are available to companies wanting to export goods abroad. A few of them are

>> **Trade missions.** Trade missions are tours of particular regions of the world that are organized by the U.S. Department of Commerce to help U.S. companies find good connections with trading partners and customers in other countries. These tours are a great way to make first contacts with the right people. The DOC provides several types of trade missions to businesses.

- **Specialized trade missions** focus on specific product lines and are designed for producers of those products.

- **Seminar missions** provide technical presentations for companies with technological or sophisticated products that need to connect with appropriate representatives in the foreign country.

- **Matchmaker trade delegations** are for exporters or companies new to the world of international trade. Lasting a week, company representatives typically visit two foreign countries where they meet with customers, distributors, and so forth.

>> **Trade fairs and exhibitions.** International trade fairs are a good way to test your products in an international environment without leaving the United States. They are also a good way to meet potential distributors and suppliers.

>> **Catalog shows and video catalog exhibitions.** This is the least expensive way to promote your products in the international arena. You send your product literature to the appropriate Department of Commerce agency, and it displays the material at exhibitions in U.S. embassies and consulates. The video catalog is excellent for machinery and other products that cost a lot to ship to a normal trade fair.

Uncle Sam's interest in helping you export your products overseas is evident in the wealth of resources available to exporters. A portion of that wealth includes:

>> **The Export-Import Bank of the United States** (`www.exim.gov`). Provides loans to small businesses, helping them extend credit to potential foreign customers and provides insurance to protect exporters if a foreign customer defaults on a purchase contract.

>> **The U.S. Trade and Development Agency** (`https://ustda.gov/`). Pays companies to develop business plans for foreign development projects that benefit American exporters. The goal is to create markets for U.S. exports. If your company has a product or service with export potential, read *Pipeline* at the agency's website. Summaries of project feasibility studies are available there.

>> **The Department of Commerce** (`www.doc.gov`). Helps you find the most appropriate region of the world for your products and set up booths at selected trade shows frequented by agents for various industries and countries.

>> **U.S. International Development Finance Corporation** (`www.dfc.gov`). A federal agency offering political risk insurance and loans to help U.S. businesses of all sizes invest and compete in 140 emerging markets and developing nations worldwide.

>> **International Trade Administration** (`www.trade.gov`). A global network of trade professionals helping business owners reach their international goals. It's sponsored by the Department of Commerce.

Using the Internet to go global

The Internet gives every business with a website an instant global presence. No quicker way of reaching another country with information about your company and its products and services exists, but that doesn't mean that you'll instantly attract those customers to your site. Furthermore, even if you attract them to your site, how do you deal with customers who are not fluent in English? Ask yourself the following two questions if you decide to go global via the Internet:

>> How will I know if I'm attracting potential global customers to the site?

>> How can I make my site more user friendly to the global community?

Technology has made answering the first question easy. Your server statistics reports (your Internet Service Provider provides these to you or will give you the tools and password to access them yourself) can tell you what's happening at your site, helping you determine whether you're getting global visitors. For example, looking at the Domain Report tells you that visitors with .com, .org, .net, or .edu extensions to their domain names usually (but not always) are based in the United States. When you start seeing extensions like .ca (Canada) and .uk (United Kingdom), you know that you're reaching the rest of the world. That's a start and it may give you some clues as to which countries you should focus on. If you want to reach the international market, you need to invest some time and money into designing a globally user–friendly site. But, in the meantime, you can immediately encourage international visitors to consider doing business with you by:

>> Including your contact information: toll-free and direct phone lines (be sure to include the country code and area code. For the United States, the code is 1), and email.

>> Including your customer service hours on the site. Don't forget the time zone. Spell it out in full (PST=Pacific Standard Time), because not everyone is familiar with U.S. time zone acronyms.

>> Remembering to write your dates, the way most of the world writes dates — as day-month-year. To avoid problems, write out the date as February 5, 2023 or 5-Feb-2023 to avoid confusion.

>> Stating clearly on your site whether you sell products only in domestic markets so you don't confuse or disappoint your international visitors when they learn that you will not ship to their country. If you are planning to sell internationally in the future, let your international customers know that their visits to your site and their feedback are appreciated and will speed up your ability to justify selling internationally.

Even doing just a few of these things, you can take baby steps toward becoming a global enterprise.

Growing as a High-Tech Company

As I said at the beginning of this chapter, the growth pattern of high-technology businesses often differs from that of other businesses because their technology is often new to the world, so the adoption pattern is very different from a company whose technology is a natural outgrowth of a previous technology. Disrupters are pioneers within their industries and this section focuses on them. Their goal is to make their technology the industry standard, so that everyone will adopt it.

Finding early adopters

The first stage in the life cycle of a technology business is defined by the introduction of the product to the early adopter market. These are consumers or businesses who are eager to purchase new technology products that solve their problems or give them a competitive advantage. Because they typically follow a company doing research in a particular industry, such as AI (artificial intelligence), they may be asked to serve as beta testers (beta refers to a second-stage prototype — alpha is the first stage) for a new product, giving their feedback to the company in exchange for benefits or discounts.

Although the early adopters are a very small group, certainly not large enough to sustain a company in terms of sales, they provide an important opportunity for the company to work out the bugs before demand increases. The company can't stay in this stage too long, however, before it must gain mainstream acceptance of the technology.

Getting to mainstream adoption

Geoffrey Moore, author of *Crossing the Chasm* and *Inside the Tornado*, asserts that somewhere between the early adopter and mainstream adoption stages of technology lies what he has coined as *the chasm* — when early adopters have used the technology long enough to grow tired of it, but mainstream customers are still not comfortable with it. Crossing the chasm to have a chance at mainstream adoption, a company needs to create a bunch of niche markets in which the technology is adopted. The goal is to rack up as many niche markets as it takes to gain enough momentum to drive the product into what Moore calls *the tornado*.

The tornado is a period of mass-market adoption — when everyone finally decides that your technology is the best and they all switch to it. The tornado produces a flood of demand that can't be met. This situation is quite unlike what faces most entrepreneurs, who are always looking for ways to *create* demand. In this case, everyone wants what you have, so you can set marketing aside for the moment and focus on production and distribution. At this point, process is what counts. You can worry about developing customer relations later. Right now, all customers want is the product.

Surviving mainstream adoption

If your company makes it through the tornado, it must shift gears again, becoming more customer focused and looking for ways to sell more products to the customers you gained from the tornado. Now, marketing comes back into play. Consider these important rules about coping with a hypergrowth situation:

>> You must be willing to attack the competition ruthlessly. Your goal is to become the industry standard. It's a life or death situation. There is no choice here. If you don't become the standard, someone else will, and then the game is over.

>> You can only become the market leader by expanding quickly, even at the expense of the customer. Remember that prices on technology always come down, so you have to increase volume to make money, and that comes from selling to every type of outlet possible.

>> You must focus on process above everything else, making sure you have your partners, and production and shipping mechanisms in place before hypergrowth occurs. Once you've hit hypergrowth, it's all about execution.

>> You must always drive to the next lower price point. Hewlett-Packard executes this strategy brilliantly, always becoming the first to hit a new lower price point on a product. That way they gain customers who are waiting for that price point first. If you don't play the lead in grabbing the lower price point, you'll lose customers to your competitors.

WARNING

Customer excitement can quickly overwhelm a young company that isn't prepared for it. When large, established players enter the market, it's much easier for them to claim the standard and win over the entire market of customers, precisely because they have more resources, and their brands are recognizable. This may lead you to believe that revolutionary technology is quickly recognized and adopted. Nothing could be further from the truth. For instance, smartphones, first marketed in the mid-1990s, took ten years to achieve a 40 percent penetration in the market. Contrast that with the telephone, which took about 80 years to be in wide adoption. Planning for rapid growth goes hand-in-hand with product adoption by customers.

NOT EVERYONE SURVIVES A TORNADO

Not every company that experiences a tornado of mass market adoption survives it. For example, the company Pebble made waves in 2012 when it became the most funded Kickstarter campaign ever, raising $10.3 million for its first smartwatch product. In 2013, it began selling its smartwatches and was sold out in a matter of days. By 2014, it had sold a million watches, and in 2015, it launched two more smartwatches. Quite a run for the tiny company. But the company struggled financially — hypergrowth is very costly — and unfortunately for Pebble, the wearable industry and market matured very quickly and the young company found itself in direct competition with Apple and Android, that had far more resources to market their smartwatches. Ultimately, Pebble had to refund its backers on Kickstarter, and in 2016 the company was forced to close. However, it did hold intellectual property that was ultimately acquired by Fitbit.

Moving from Founding Team to Professional Management

The success of your growth strategy depends on your ability to move your operations from founding team to professional management. Changing doesn't mean that you leave your entrepreneurial spirit behind — far from it. What changing to professional management means is you recognize that the skills you need to rapidly grow your company are quite different from the skills you needed to gather resources and start your company.

REMEMBER

Most entrepreneurs don't have strong enough professional management skills; rather, they are by nature resource gathers, when what the company needs most as it grows are people who can manage resources. The reality is many entrepreneurs don't enjoy the management aspect of the business, so they leave it to others who are better at it. Table 16-1 is a snapshot of the two points of view: entrepreneurial and managerial.

As you see from Table 16-1, entrepreneurs are driven by an opportunistic attitude, while managers are generally driven by the need to manage resources. Managers are typically given a budget within which they must strive to stay. By contrast, entrepreneurs don't limit themselves to the resources they currently have because they know they can find more if needed.

Similarly, entrepreneurs tend to break rules and create new ways of doing things. Managers, for the most part, work in a more evolutionary fashion, building on what already exists, improving and refining it.

TABLE 16-1

Entrepreneurial versus Managerial View

Entrepreneurial View	Managerial View
Motivated by opportunity — resource acquisition	Motivated by resources — resource management
Risk taking	Risk management
Revolutionary — breakthrough, disruptive actions	Evolutionary — derivative actions
Unpredictable environment with limited resources	More predictable environment with committed resources
Rented, leased, borrowed resources	Owned or employed resources
Flat organizational structure — team based structure	Hierarchical organizational structure — chain of command

Entrepreneurial organizations are generally flat, which means that they don't involve multiple layers of management. Everyone works together as a team, quite unlike the layers of management found in most larger organizations.

If you're making the transition from entrepreneurship to professional management:

>> Recognize that a change in your management structure must take place before growth begins. You won't have time to make the change when rapid growth hits.

>> Get help putting formal decision systems in place that give more people authority and responsibility over major decisions for the company. Bottom line: Be prepared to give up some control.

>> Make sure that any functions of your business that are critical (life and death) to the success of the business are not in the hands of only one person. Consider the consequences if that person were to leave.

>> Carefully evaluate your growth strategy and make sure that the systems and procedures you have put in place match your strategies.

>> Establish a board of directors if you don't already have one. They can offer critical advice at this important time in your company's life.

Identifying your company's culture

Every company has a personality, a distinct way of doing things that you recognize the minute you spend any time at all inside that company. This distinct personality is known as corporate culture, and it has become an important competitive advantage for most businesses. While you describe a company culture in your handbook or allude to it in your promotional activities, you see it mainly in the daily interactions of the people who work in your company.

Culture is important for two reasons:

>> It gives people in your company a sense of purpose and connection and motivates them to achieve the company's goals.

>> It reflects the implementation of your company's vision.

I once worked with a manufacturer that epitomizes the benefits of a strong corporate culture. This company is fanatically customer driven. Walk onto the floor of its assembly plant, pick out anyone to talk to, and I'll bet that within one minute you'll hear the word *customer* from that person. Everyone in that organization, from the janitor to the CEO knows what they do to contribute to customer satisfaction. They all know that it's the customer who pays them.

That kind of deep loyalty to culture is found in many successful companies, including Southwest Airlines, UPS, and Intel Corp., to name a few. When employees are committed to the vision and culture of the company, they can accomplish nearly impossible feats. For example, one company's product development team had to develop an innovative new computer to try to save their company from a financial crisis. During the process, the team discovered that the programming of the software piece for the computer's operating system was far behind schedule and might cost them their market opportunity. The three engineers assigned to the project spent an entire night trying to resolve the software problem. They succeeded in completing two or three months of work in one night. That kind of effort doesn't happen without a commitment to the company.

Asking yourself and your employees the following questions can help you think about the kind of culture you have:

>> Does your company work in teams or individually?

>> How does your company deal with change?

>> How does your company deal with failure?

>> How does your company make decisions? Who makes the critical decisions?

>> How do you prioritize work?

>> How do you share information inside and outside your company?

>> Do you take a long-term or short-term view of decision-making?

>> How do you make sure you have competent employees?

>> How do you encourage diversity of experience and thought?

>> How are employees treated? What does your company's vision say about employees?

Your company's culture is a big part of its competitive advantage. Employees as well as customers need to recognize and promote your company's culture and competitive advantages. If it's strong like the culture at Southwest Airlines, which makes up for its no-frills service with wacky, irreverent flight attendants and ground crew, customers may choose to deal with your company just because of its customer-oriented culture.

Developing a human resource policy

The human capital side of your business affects everything your business does; it is the heart and soul of the business. Your vision, culture, core values, and goals affect policies that you develop to guide human resource decision-making. While a detailed discussion of all the new principles of management (check out *Managing For Dummies*) isn't possible here, key management principles for the new marketplace promote:

>> Using self-directed, multi-functional teams rather than departments, functions, or specific tasks. This strategy empowers employees and focuses everyone's energies on company goals.

>> Focusing on core competencies — those things the company does to create value.

>> Including the customer in everything the business does, from product design to marketing to service. Everyone in the organization needs to know the customer.

>> Providing rewards for team effort above rewards based solely on individual effort if that is what you're trying to achieve. If you reward individuals when you're trying to encourage teamwork, your employees become confused.

>> Sharing company information with employees so they can use it to provide input and feel a vested interest in the success of the company.

>> Keeping lines of communication with upper management open.

THE TRUTH ABOUT SUCCESSFUL COMPANIES

Think you know what makes a successful company? Answer these five true/false questions to test your knowledge.

1. In general, the greatest and most enduring companies started with a great idea.
2. Great companies have charismatic leaders.
3. The driving force in great companies is shareholder wealth or profit.
4. Great companies do not take big risks.
5. Most people would be comfortable working for a great company.

Sorry, but all five are false. If you answered true to some, you're not alone. These statements represent five of the biggest myths about what makes a great company. In their research, which became part of their best-selling book, *Built to Last,* Jim Collins and Jerry Porras studied the number one companies in every industry, comparing them against the number twos. They discovered

1. Few of the great companies started with a great idea; in fact, most were not even successful in the beginning. Sony Corp. started by producing rice cookers and failed at several products before beginning a stream of breakthrough products like the magnetic tape recorder in 1950, the first all-transistor radio in 1955, and the Sony Walkman in 1979, to name only a few.

2. The great companies did not have charismatic leaders heading their teams; instead, they had entrepreneurs who wanted to build a great and enduring company. How many readers would recognize the name of William L. McKnight — probably few if any. Yet, he was at the helm of one of the most innovative manufacturing companies of all time for 17 years — 3M Corp.

3. The driving force in the great companies is adherence to their purpose and core values above shareholder wealth or profit. Every one of the great companies had written vision statements and clearly articulated core values that they held to rigorously.

4. The great companies didn't plan for everything. They took risks when their intuition told them it was time.

5. In general, the great companies hold so firmly to their core beliefs and the company culture that arises from them that anyone who doesn't fit into that culture has a difficult time surviving in the organization.

These management principles are well-suited for entrepreneurial businesses with limited resources working in this fast-paced market. In fact, they are more successfully implemented in startup companies where you can hire the right people for your company's culture from the beginning rather than trying to achieve a cultural fit with legacy hires.

Organizing for Speed and Flexibility

Throughout this book, I talk about the importance of planning, of having a plan for startup, for growth, and later on, for your exit from the company. But having a plan doesn't mean that you know what the future will bring. It's pretty obvious today that we don't know what the future has in store except perhaps more of the same — change. So how do you plan for change? For one thing, you build a flexible organization that can quickly respond to change.

More and more, new business models that never existed before have entrepreneurs looking for new ways to do old business and taking advantage of the low overhead and speed of doing business on the Internet. These new models require a different way of organizing when examples of these new organizational structures aren't always out there to guide innovation. So, in the true spirit of what they're all about, entrepreneurs must make things up as they go.

To build a company that can respond to whatever is thrown at it, you must

>> **Invest in technology that can handle a big surge in growth.** Don't invest only for what you need right now.

>> **Train your current employees how to orient new employees.** That way, if you have to hire many people quickly, they can be assimilated into your business culture without disrupting workflow.

>> **Not take success for granted.** Be paranoid. Keep your periscope up and constantly scanning the horizon for competitors, for a change in demand, or for a shift in market conditions.

>> **Design an organization that operates in a constant state of change.** That way, you'll never have to completely reinvent it, and you'll always be ahead of the game.

Organizing around teams

CASE STUDY

Teams are a vital part of any company, whether the business has just opened or has existed for 50 years. Studies show that organizations learn and grow at the team level, not at the individual level. That's because teams that work in collegial environments, where they share a company vision, become aligned in their purposes and goals, which benefits the company and results in more team satisfaction.

Promoting team interaction is often easier with a startup company, because you can't get the company going unless everyone shares their knowledge. If you're not careful, however, as the company grows you can lose some of that entrepreneurial team spirit, and getting it back is hard work.

One entrepreneur avoids that trap by documenting her company's best practices so that she can bring everyone — including new hires — rapidly up to speed. She identifies four documents that detail the company's best practices and ensure that employees are able to work together as a team. They are:

>> **The training document.** This document spells out for everyone what their knowledge-sharing obligations are to everyone else in the organization. The job of managers is to set performance benchmarks, reward achievement, and provide to employees the resources they need to do their jobs, while the job of employees is to take charge of designing and implementing training programs.

>> **The vision statement.** The vision statement indicates that everything the company does must make a positive contribution to great food, great service, and great finance. All the decisions that employees make are guided by the vision.

>> **The training questionnaire.** This survey helps management target training efforts by identifying the expectations of employees and understanding the metrics for determining when and how those expectations are met.

>> **The training skills document.** This document outlines skills an individual employee must acquire by designated points in time. It also discusses the resources, help, and training that the company provides to assist the employee in achieving their skills targets. The training passport is a record of that achievement.

Finding and keeping great people

Ask any company owner what the most difficult issue they face is and you'll hear, "finding and retaining good employees." In a volatile marketplace, especially post pandemic, great employees come at a premium, and keeping those employees can be almost a daily task in some industries like high tech. Yet, many entrepreneurs aren't effective at recruiting and hiring top talent because during startup, they usually had a closely knit team that satisfied all the functions of the organization and worked well together under a common goal. Bringing new people on board is sort of a shock to the system because these new people don't always fit neatly into the culture and ways things are done. But, bringing new people into the organization doesn't have to be such a culture shock if you spend the necessary time and effort to find the right people and prepare them.

The question of when to add new people to the team is paramount. Some companies take the approach of doing it when it becomes obvious that they have to — when it's clear that it's time to delegate authority and bring in professional management to give the organization some structure.

One company founded by a husband–and–wife team decided it was time to bring in help when their employees began working upwards of 80-hour weeks just to keep up. Because the company was established and had a good reputation as an employer, it was in a great position to hire the best people.

Another strategy is to start your company with a professional management team. In other words, you hire the best people you can — those who have had experience running larger companies — with the resources you have, then add more later. One software company did this by hiring key management to handle all the major functions of the business. They kept their flat structure and entrepreneurial spirit by making sure that no one reported directly to any of these management people.

Many high-tech and Internet companies start with a professional management team in place because they seek significant venture capital at an early stage and expect to do an IPO. In both cases, professional management is critical.

Your need to bring on additional management is a function of:

>> Your ability to delegate responsibility and authority

>> The resources you have for hiring the best

>> Your company's need for more structure and the skills of professional management

Recruiting the right people

Recruiting is the task among all the aspects of the hiring process on which entrepreneurs probably spend the least amount of time. And that is surprising, because the recruiting process determines whether you ultimately get the right person for the position you want to fill. Entrepreneurs often find someone to fill a job rather than someone with the potential to fit in well and grow with the organization. Part of the fault for that slipup lies in the way they announce the opening for the position. If you describe a position solely in terms of skill requirements and function, you'll probably find someone who's looking for a job rather than a career.

Young entrepreneurial companies need people who can perform several functions and work as a team. The following tips can help you find the right people for your needs:

» **Have a marketing plan for attracting talent.** Just like your marketing plan creates awareness by customers for your business, you need a marketing plan to catch the attention of the best candidates for the positions you want to fill. That plan spells out your strategy for going after the type of people you need — in simple terms — what kind of person you're looking for and where you can find and engage that person.

» **Identify the talents and skills that describe your best employees.** Most entrepreneurs can profile their best customers, but can they profile their best employees? Knowing the characteristics, skills, experience, and attitude of your best employees helps you look for those traits in your new hires. If you know what you're going after, you're more likely to find it.

» **Be creative about where you find talent.** Some companies are so concerned about hiring new people who immediately fit in with their corporate culture that the first place they look is through their current employees. That's not a bad idea. Put the word out about the positions you're trying to fill. Chances are people who are recommended to you by your current employees are in a better position to fit right in from day one because your employees know exactly what you're looking for and probably won't recommend someone who doesn't fit your needs. Other places to look are professional associations, personal recommendations from your professional advisors, universities, and recruiters.

» **Define what makes your company and the open position unique.** Remember, you're marketing this new position so a potential candidate understands the benefits of coming to work for your company. Are you offering: Better pay? More flexible work hours? Opportunities for advancement? A company culture second to none? If you want to ensure that you position your company correctly, research what job seekers in your industry value.

» **Establish a talent channel.** Over time you'll discover the best sources for recruiting, so keep in touch with them even when you're not recruiting. You also need to keep your company name in the limelight by associating with the local college or university, sponsoring community activities, and writing articles for trade journals.

» **Look at other companies.** Your best candidates are not those who respond to an ad. The best candidates are working for someone else. So how do you reach them? You need to develop relationships with universities, recruiters, and executive search firms. Encourage your employees to recommend people and to participate in industry associations and conferences, which are excellent sources of candidates.

» **Hire for strengths.** For whatever purpose you need the person, they should already have the right skills and talent. You want employees who are ready to go on day one.

» **Check references carefully and do background checks when appropriate.** Background checks, which are normally done by third parties, can verify academic credentials, previous employment, credit checks, drug screenings, and criminal background checks if they are typical in your industry. If you side-step some of these checks, keep in mind that if the person you hire harms another employee, you may be held responsible for not adequately screening them. It is well known that job candidates tend to embellish their accomplishments on resumes. That's why it's important to check them out.

Developing an effective job description

Before beginning your search for a candidate, you need a good job description — essentially guidelines for you and a potential candidate about the requirements for a particular position. Some of the things you may want to include in your job description are:

» What level of education and work experience do you need? I recommend that you state these as "desired" levels rather than "required." You will still screen out candidates who don't come close, but you also have the opportunity to look at people who may not have the exact education and experience you seek but may, nevertheless, be best suited for the position based on experience and character.

» A list of the duties and responsibilities of the position so that the candidate knows what's expected. Be careful, however, not to be so precise that you neglect to leave open the possibility for more flexibility in tasks.

» The name of the person to whom the candidate will report.

» An explanation of the personal characteristics that you're looking for, including such things as communication skills, self-motivation, ability to work in a team, and so forth.

WARNING

As you design your job description, keep in mind that the Equal Employment Opportunity laws prohibit discrimination based on age, sex, color, race, national origin, religion, and so forth during the recruiting and hiring processes. For example, your job description or application can't require a photograph of the applicant, unless the position requires certain physical characteristics essential for the job (usually this would be for a job such as modeling or acting, not most business situations). Know the laws and follow them! (See the sidebar "Employment Laws You Need to Know," for more about this important issue.)

Choosing the right candidate

Your selection of the best person for the position is the result of studying a job application form and resume and conducting an interview. The application and resume are good screening tools, but exercise caution because applicants tend to overstate their qualifications and achievements on resumes. Factors to check out in a resume are

>> The length of time an applicant spent in any one previous position. Does it seem reasonable to you or did the applicant seem to move around a lot? Keep in mind that younger employees do tend to move around a lot, and they tend to want more flexible working conditions.

>> Does the applicant's prior work experience match your needs?

>> Does the appearance of the resume suggest that the applicant is serious about their career? If a resume is poorly prepared and contains spelling and grammatical errors, I won't consider the candidate. If the jobseeker can't take the time to produce a clean resume, which involves attention to detail when the stakes are high, what level of care and attention will they bring to their duties?

>> Did the candidate emphasize skills and experience that are relevant to the position?

Contacting the references provided with an application and finding out more about the candidate is important before conducting an interview. However, your final decision about a candidate may come during an interview when you can observe their nonverbal and verbal skills. In person, you have the opportunity to sense whether the candidate fits in with your company culture.

TIP

During the interview, ask questions that explore whether the person can provide the skills your company needs and can work well with others. Be sure to spend the majority of the interview, however, asking questions that probe the candidate's character. Putting candidates into a hypothetical situation forces them to make decisions that reveal character. For example, "You become aware that someone on your team has been revealing critical information to a friend in a competing company. What would you do about it?" Or, "What do you like to do in your spare time?"

EMPLOYMENT LAWS YOU NEED TO KNOW

You need to be aware of important employment laws when you recruit and hire new employees. Eight of the more important laws to know about are:

- You must pay women and men the same for the same work (Equal Pay Act of 1963). In other words, you are paying for a specific set of skills and responsibilities and the amount should never vary by sex, race, color, religion, national origin, age, disability, or retaliation.

- You cannot refuse to hire, promote, train, or increase pay based on race, color, sex, or national origin (Civil Rights Act of 1964 — applies to companies with more than 15 employees).

- You cannot discriminate against persons between the ages of 40 and 70 (Age Discrimination Act of 1973).

- If you have a federal government contract of $50,000 or more, and 50 or more employees, you must actively recruit and hire the handicapped (Vocational Rehabilitation Act of 1973).

- If you have a federal contract in excess of $10,000, you must make an effort to employ and advance qualified disabled veterans (Vietnam Era Veterans Readjustment Act of 1974).

- You must examine documents of all candidates to ensure that you don't hire illegal aliens (Immigration Law of 1986).

- If you have 15 or more employees, you can't do any testing to screen out the disabled or someone related to a disabled person (Americans with Disabilities Act of 1990).

- You must prove that any seemingly discriminatory practices in which you may engage are job related and required to operate your business (Civil Rights Act of 1991).

Knowing about and adhering to these laws is important. In a time of increasing litigation and regulation, not doing so can be costly to your business. Besides, treating everyone fairly is the right thing to do.

AVOID ASKING THESE QUESTIONS

The EEOC (Equal Employment Opportunity Commission) has released the following guidelines regarding questions that may not be asked before hiring someone.

- What is your age? Only in the case of a young applicant can the employer ask if the person can prove they are legal age after hiring. In other cases, age questions like "When did you graduate from high school?" are not permitted.

- What church do you attend? No questions regarding religion of the applicant or the applicant's family are allowed.

- Do you have children or plan to get pregnant? Questions regarding personal family plans or living arrangements are not permitted.

- Have you ever been arrested? This is not a permissible question to ask. "Have you ever been convicted of a crime?" is permissible.

- How is your health? This general question is not permitted. "Do you have any condition that would prevent you from doing your job?" is permissible.

- You have beautiful skin; where are your ancestors from? Questions about ancestry, heritage, culture, and so forth are not permitted.

Note that if your candidate is in a wheelchair, for example, you may ask what accommodations are necessary to hire this person.

Getting someone to talk about their life outside of work, as long as the question doesn't get into personal issues such as living arrangements and pregnancy plans, often reveals a lot about their values and how they spend their time. Someone who has a lot of outside activities that take a lot of time may not be willing to work the long hours you may expect. Be sure to observe the candidate's body language as they respond to questions like these. It is often said that 90 percent of communication is nonverbal.

You must be careful not to ask questions that are illegal to ask prior to the point of hiring someone. The sidebar "Avoid Asking These Questions" lists what some of those questions are.

When You Need an Experienced CEO

Today's Internet environment calls for changes in the way founding teams are put together. Many new e-businesses are started by young entrepreneurs in their early 20s who know technology and may have great business concepts, but they are not seasoned enough to take a venture through venture capital funding and an IPO and come out successfully on the other side. Compensating for their lack of experience, these young entrepreneurs often seek out veteran CEOs, but successful company leaders are in short supply because of high demand by technology companies. If you're starting a tech business and need an experienced CEO, the more important characteristics that describe the candidate you need are that the potential candidate is

>> **A visionary.** In other words, the CEO candidate must see clearly where the company needs to be heading and must convey the confidence that this vision is right for the company.

>> **Adaptable to change.** The environment for tech businesses is volatile and in a constant state of flux. A good CEO must be ready and able to quickly and effectively change the direction of the company when conditions call for it.

>> **Market driven.** Technology companies often fail because they focus on the technology instead of the solution the customers want (how the technology solves the problem). Customers must understand how to use your products and services, or they will not purchase them.

>> **Experienced.** The CEO must demonstrate an understanding of the market and be able to effectively lead the company.

>> **Well-connected.** In other words, they should have good contacts at high levels in the industry. Who you know matters more today than ever before, because today's marketplace is a collaborative one in which competitors sometimes have to work together.

Founding a successful technology business is about having a great professional management team in place. It can literally make the difference between a venture that grows successfully and one that languishes. Many founders have continued in the CEO role post launch and early growth and have done so successfully. They are the problem solvers who are always thinking strategically about what the company needs to do next and they're able to offer possible solutions. They maintain a 360-degree view of the company while having a deep understanding of operations. These founders know how to create a professional environment that respects everyone and engenders a sense of trust and integrity.

CASE STUDY

Oura Ring (see https://ouraring.com/) is a great example of a small company that has exploded with a five-year growth rate of 4,000 percent. Started in 2013 in the small city of Oulu, Finland, the founding trio developed a small, unobtrusive wearable ring that accurately monitors heart rate 24/7, sleeping patterns, and body temperature and reports to the user via a smartphone app. (Full disclosure: I wear one and swear by it.) They raised $148 million in a Series C round and have received rave reviews for their design and accurate data. Succeeding in the crowded wearable market is no easy trick (as evidenced by Pebble, discussed earlier in this chapter), but this team really understands their customers' needs, so they were able to hit it out of the park.

Get your business ready for rapid growth before that growth happens. Trust me. You'll be glad you did.

Chapter **17**

Developing a Marketing Strategy

The traditional role of marketing as the primary conduit to the customer has radically changed. Because technology has provided many more ways to reach customers, marketing is no longer an activity isolated in one department of a business; on the contrary, you find aspects of marketing in every functional area of the business, from research and development to operations and finance. This change came about because companies now increasingly understand the value of being completely customer focused.

Training everyone within an organization to listen to the customer puts the company in a stronger position to serve their customers. Customers are the best source of information for the most appropriate channels to reach them as well for the particular product features and benefits that matter to them.

Marketing has changed for other reasons as well. Today, customers are more market savvy; they have more choices than ever before, and it's easier than ever to compare prices. Today's customers demand choice, quality, and superior levels of service; they expect businesses to respond quickly to their fickle changes in tastes and preferences. They also demand customized and personalized products and services, which means today, you must market to specific customers in the way they want. Your goal should be to satisfy their particular needs how and when they want them satisfied. What's more, with the ubiquitous use of Amazon Alexa and Google Home, you now face the challenge of marketing to a device rather than a human.

In this chapter, you discover how to build a marketing plan for your business that recognizes all these changes. You also find out how important branding is to your business's success in a marketplace where it's easy to get lost in the cacophony of competing products. Let's start by learning how customers adopt new products and services.

Understanding Product/Service Adoption Patterns

To accurately forecast revenues, demand, customer acquisition costs, and even personnel requirements, you need a good understanding of your product/service adoption patterns as well as typical growth patterns in your industry.

Many entrepreneurs rely on the adoption/diffusion curve as a tool to manage demand. In fact, the curve was developed in Iowa in 1957 to help the agriculture industry identify patterns in how farmers adopted new hybrid seed corn techniques. What they learned was the basis for Everett Rogers's graphic a version of which is shown in Figure 17-1.

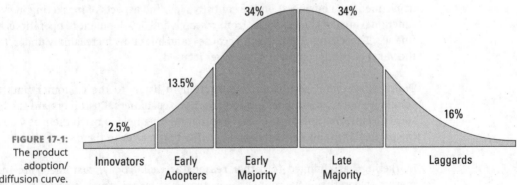

FIGURE 17-1:
The product adoption/ diffusion curve.

Much later, Rogers's adoption/diffusion curve became Geoffrey Moore's famous technology adoption/diffusion curve, which provides more insight into how customers choose to adopt new technologies. Chapter 16 covers this unique adoption cycle for tech companies.

The customer journey from awareness to purchase

Your first customers typically comprise a tiny base of visionaries who can see product benefits that others don't see. They are essentially the customers for whom you developed the solution and who will give you critical feedback along the development path before you go to a wider market.

Your true first customers are the next group, the early adopters, who are willing to pay for the product. These are optimistic customers who have money to spend and who only require that your product solve about 80 percent of their problem. The third group is the early majority. These customers are more pragmatic; that is, they want to be sure that your product solves their problem. They typically watch what happens with the early adopters before making the leap to buy.

The fourth group is the late majority, customers older in age who are price conscious. They typically wait until the price comes down before they buy. The final group are the laggards. These are customers who buy something only if they absolutely have to. They want cheap solutions that are easy to use and replace what they're currently using.

Creating a marketing strategy based on adoption patterns

It's critical that you understand the size of each of these market segments so you can plan your marketing strategy accordingly. At launch, you need to focus on the groups that will get you to mass adoption of your solution, and those are the early adopters and the early majority. Unlike the later groups, these two groups are not motivated to buy based on price, but by whether you've solved their problem. You want to avoid having to reduce the price to gain more customers as long as possible.

The success of your market introduction efforts across various customer segments is a function of some key factors:

>> Recognition of the benefit

>> Usability

>> Acceptance of your promotional efforts

>> The intensity of your distribution efforts

>> The learning curve to adopt your product

>> Switching costs from the current solution to the new one

>> Ability to test the product before purchase

>> Price commensurate with the benefits provided

Marketing to Customers, One at a Time

Organizing around customers should be the goal of your marketing strategy. That means you cannot treat every customer the same; instead, you must create a relationship with each customer and strive to keep all your customers for life. Well, it isn't quite as simple as that, but companies everywhere have learned the value of what is known as *relationship marketing*.

CASE STUDY

For example, Federal Express learned that it could save money and benefit its customers by using the Internet to enable customers to track their own shipments. When a customer calls FedEx to inquire about a shipment, it costs the company $2–$3 to handle that call. But if customers use the website to check on packages using the tracking number, they get an instant response. FedEx makes money by reducing costs. A win-win situation for both.

Despite everything else your business may have (including money), customers are its most important asset. If you don't have customers, you don't have a business. So, you need to build an environment where customers and your company can share information and create value for each other. Developing these relationships takes a long time, so don't expect a quick return on your investment.

If you want your business to be successful at marketing, you need to understand your consumers' core expectations. Here are three of them:

>> Consumers want a unique experience tailored to their needs.

>> Consumers don't want to climb a learning curve to understand what you're offering. They shouldn't have to work hard to understand your product/service.

>> Consumers want to interact with your business anytime, anywhere, and that includes with a human.

A major side benefit to building customer relationships is that your customers won't automatically shift their allegiance to someone else when your company runs into a problem. Having customers see your business through a rare negative experience can actually strengthen the relationship because they are not accustomed to having businesses care about them enough to try to solve a problem. Your business will thrive if you stop thinking of customers as transactions and treat them like the assets they are.

Creating a Marketing Plan

Marketing includes everything you do to create awareness of your business and its products and services — the name you give your business, the features and benefits of your products and services, the way you deliver those products and services, where you locate your business, and the advertising and promotion tactics you use to get customers and keep them.

Think of your marketing plan as a living guide to your customer relationships. It contains the goals, strategies, and tactics that you use to build your customer base. With a new venture, your goal may be creating awareness for your company and capturing those initial customers. Later on, you can create a marketing plan designed to grow your business to the next level.

WARNING

One big reason marketing plans fail is that their creators don't stick with them long enough to see the results. Most marketing strategies don't provide immediate results. Expect them to take some time.

Preparing to plan

An effective marketing plan is the result of preparation — not a lot, but some is necessary. You should begin by identifying the points at which you interact with your customers along their journey from awareness to purchase to the end of the product life cycle. Then put yourself in the shoes of your customers and take that journey to see how satisfied you are with each interaction. A typical journey map includes the following touchpoints. Depending on your business, you may come up with more.

>> Learning about the product the first time

>> Gathering information and getting questions answered

>> Deciding to purchase

>> Making the purchase

>> After-sales service

For each of the touchpoints, you need to find out how customers view the business, how they rate the interaction with your business, and what new opportunities came out of the interaction.

The point of all this is to keep ahead of your customers so they're pleasantly surprised at the experience. Once you've completed the journey assessment, follow these important steps:

1. **List your marketing options.** Because so many ways of marketing to your customers exist, you must explore all the possibilities. Don't limit yourself to what you already know or what your industry already does. Talk with other business owners, customers, and suppliers. Check out books, articles, and videos on successful marketing strategies that others have used. A strategy that worked well in another industry may also work in your industry.

2. **Start to think like your customers.** Take a look at your business and what you're offering from the customer's point of view. What would entice *you* to make a purchase? Richard Branson, the founder of Virgin Airways, looked at his service from the point of view of a passenger and designed his planes to meet their needs.

3. **Know your competition as well as you know your own business.** You have to know what others in your industry are doing so that you can identify the gaps that your business can fill. In fact, one of the best tactics you can use is to become your competitors' customer.

4. **Rank the pros and cons of your options.** Of the many options you've collected, start by eliminating those that aren't feasible right now, usually because you can't afford them. Then rank your top ten choices based on how well they enable you to reach your customers.

Once you complete these steps, you're ready to begin writing your marketing plan.

Writing a one-paragraph marketing plan

One of the best ways to begin preparing a marketing plan is to write one paragraph that includes all the elements of a complete plan. The advantage of writing a one-paragraph plan is that it forces you to focus on what's important and to determine what your key benefits are — those things that will grab your customers' attention. A good one-paragraph marketing plan looks like the following:

KosmoTrade assists furniture traders around the world by using an Internet-based portal. This marketing plan creates company awareness and name recognition in the marketplace where the target customer is any organization dealing with furniture. The plan specifically targets small exporters needing buyers in other countries or outlets for excess inventory and importers seeking new vendors under competitive conditions. This value-added e-solution reduces time and risk in finding new customers or suppliers. The company serves a niche market that targets smaller companies wanting access to worldwide business opportunities. Stakeholders view KosmoTrade as a professional, innovative, and customer-focused company with a quality-driven service. Initial marketing tactics include personal selling at industry events, partnering with similar organizations to exchange links and banner ads, listing with major search engines, developing a public relations strategy to create publicity, and generating traffic by providing useful information to the customers. The company uses an average 16 percent of sales to implement the marketing strategy.

(Authors of this marketing plan: Christopher Besmer and Veronica Havranek, Top Ten Business Plan 2000, Greif Entrepreneurship Center, University of Southern California)

Let's take this one-paragraph plan apart to see the details:

>> **The purpose of the plan:** What does the plan accomplish? In this case, the plan creates awareness for the company and brand recognition in the marketplace.

>> **The benefits of the product/service:** How does the product or service satisfy a need or help the customer? The KosmoTrade solution reduces the time and resources consumed in finding new customers or suppliers.

>> **The customer:** Who is the primary customer? In this example, the primary customer is any organization dealing with furniture, specifically small exporters needing buyers in other countries or outlets for excess inventory.

>> **The company's identity and product position:** How does the customer view the company and the product? In this case, customers see KosmoTrade as a professional, innovative, and customer-focused company with a quality-driven service.

>> **The market niche:** What niche has the company defined? How does the company differentiate itself? KosmoTrade positions itself in a niche targeting smaller companies that want access to business opportunities worldwide.

>> **The marketing tactics:** What specific tools can be used to create awareness and build customer relationships? KosmoTrade's initial marketing tactics include personal selling at industry events, partnering with similar organizations to exchange links and banner ads, listing on major search engines, developing a public relations strategy, and generating traffic by providing useful information to customers.

» The budget: What percentage of sales does marketing represent: KosmoTrade spends an average of 16 percent of sales to implement the marketing plan.

Each of these parts can be explored and discussed more fully in your marketing plan.

Defining your customer

In developing your marketing plan, you discover as much as you can about your customer. The more you know, the better you're able to provide what your customer wants. In traditional market research, you generally look at demographics and psychographics.

Demographics are characteristics such as age, income and education levels, and race, while *psychographics* include attitudes, intentions, values, and lifestyles. Companies like Mediamark Research, Inc., www.mediamark.com, and Simmons Market Research Bureau, www.smrb.com, conduct this type of research by taking random samples of the population to segment markets. Segmenting a market makes it easier to focus on the particular slice of the market that your company intends to serve. In general, the four market segments are

- **» Product:** Certain products appeal to certain types of customers.

- **» Geography:** Different regions have customers with distinct buying habits or tastes and preferences.

- **» Psychographic characteristics:** Knowing that your typical customer has a specific trait, like a propensity to take risks, helps you design your marketing strategy to reach those particular customers.

- **» Demographics:** You can segment the market down to the exact neighborhood in terms of what customers purchase, how often, when, and so forth.

TIP

You can also segment a market based on the bundle of benefits that you're providing the customer. For example, perhaps your customers look for the highest quality; moreover, they're willing to pay for it. That customer segment differs from customers who seek out the product to save as much money as possible.

Doing your market research

The best information you can receive about the customer is the information you gather by getting out and talking to potential customers. Chapter 6 discusses the techniques for researching your customers. Doing your own market research means that you get exactly the type of information you want when you want it.

Besides gathering information about your customers, you gain a sense of how customers view your product or service in relation to those of your competitors. Is your product more or less expensive or of higher or lower quality? Product positioning defines the product in terms of its benefits to the customer.

Testing your product positioning with your customer is important, because you want to ensure that your customer sees your company and its product in the same light you see it. Test your product positioning statement with several different groups, including:

>> **Peers:** Ask people you know to give you their opinions about your positioning statement and how they think the product will do. Keep in mind that their responses are not typically the most objective.

>> **Members of your distribution channel:** Talk to suppliers, distributors, retailers, and salespeople, who usually have definite opinions about product positioning.

>> **Focus groups:** Get feedback from customers through focus groups. Make sure these customers aren't the same ones who participated in the design and development of your product. You want unbiased opinions.

>> **Test markets:** Check your product positioning by test marketing your product in a specific geographic area. Launching your product in a specific geographic area is a common practice and you will find that the feedback you get will vary based on the geographic area you define. For example, you may choose a rural area to find out how your product is received and compare it to an urban area with similar demographics.

Building and protecting your brand

Building brand loyalty today is a difficult but not insurmountable task as long as you build your brand around your company's values rather than around an image of your products. For example, associating your products with young, sexy, 20-something people doing exciting things may sell products initially; but when you're building a brand for the long term, you don't want to fight a war of images. Companies like Kabbage, which helps fund small businesses, and Black Rifle Coffee, which supports veterans, communicate the values of their companies that make them stand out from the crowd, breaking with the tradition of image advertising.

Values are more enduring than images, and customers who buy based on a company's values tend to be more loyal.

As you establish a brand name, you need to protect it. Of course, you want to trademark it (see Chapter 8 for more about trademarks). But that's just the beginning; you must protect it from people who misuse or use it incorrectly. Make sure that the media correctly refer to your brand. And when you're selecting your brand name, test it to make sure it does what you want it to do and isn't too similar to existing trade names.

Package it to perk up profits

Packaging is a form of branding and marketing, particularly when you sell consumer products. Carefully designing and testing your packaging can mean the difference between a product that sells and one that languishes on the shelf.

As an example, declining sales pointed one gourmet cookie company in the South to its customers — major retailers like Neiman Marcus — who thought the packaging didn't fit in well with the rest of their gift items. The cookie company hired a design firm, spent $250,000, and as a return on their investment, saw their sales increase by 50 percent. Packaging tips that can help promote your products suggest that you:

>> Create packaging that quickly and easily identifies the product, including its features, directions for use, ingredients, remedies for misuse, quality, and warranty.

>> Make sure its key benefits stand out, including convenience, price, quality, and so forth.

>> Put your company philosophy on the package. For example, *customers are our most important assets.*

>> Make sure the customer recognizes the product from the package alone, without having to read anything.

Price it right

No matter how great your product or how well you package and promote it, if the price isn't right, it won't sell. Who determines the price of your product? The customer, of course. Customer perception of the value of the product or service ultimately decides the price. Of course, other aspects affect price. Let's look at how this happens:

>> **Demand is greater than supply.** When you can't supply all the demand for your product, you can price the product higher than the market price and then reduce the price as your ability to meet demand increases.

>> **Price doesn't matter.** If people need or want your product and purchase it regardless of the price, you can charge more. Generally, these are products for which there is no real substitute.

>> **You have a great deal of competition.** In this case, you reduce your price to meet or beat your competition.

>> **Your product has unique features.** You may be able to charge a higher price if your product is unique.

>> **Your product introduces new technology.** Here you want to charge a higher price initially and then reduce the price as competitors enter the market.

>> **Your product positioning associates your product with a particular price.** For example, if you position your product as the do-it-yourself alternative, customers expect a lower price point.

TIP

When considering the price of your product or service, take into account the level of sales and profit margin you want to achieve. Look at your costs to produce the product and what the market says the price should be, and then find a point that covers your costs, allows you to make a profit, and offers a correct perception in the marketplace. Examples of common pricing strategies include:

>> **Cost-based pricing.** In this strategy, you add the costs of production and business operations to a profit margin, arriving at a market price. This doesn't work if the market doesn't agree with the price you came up with.

>> **Sliding on the demand curve.** You introduce the product at a high price, and as you begin to achieve economies of scale and your costs decline, you reduce the price accordingly.

>> **Skimming.** When you have a product that no one else has and demand for it is high, you can enter the market at a high price until competitors force the price down.

>> **Demand-based pricing.** Through market research, you find out what customers are willing to pay for the product and price accordingly.

>> **Penetration.** When you must grab as much of the market as you can quickly, you introduce the product at a low price with minimal profit and promote the heck out of it. Once you have achieved the market share you're after, you can gradually increase the price to match the rest of the market. Be aware that this is a costly strategy in terms of advertising and promotion and should only be used to achieve a specific goal in a specific amount of time.

>> **Competition-based pricing.** With this strategy, you price your product in line with your competition, or higher if you are offering a valued-added service or feature.

>> **Psychological pricing.** Your pricing position reflects an odd-even strategy. If you price your product at $10.99, customers perceive it as a bargain; if you price it at $11.00, they perceive it as more expensive. Luxury items rarely use .99 pricing.

>> **Loss leader pricing.** You price your older products below cost to attract customers to your newer products.

WARNING

You will soon face pricing problems if your prices are always based on costs or always follow the competition, if your new prices are always a percentage increase over the previous year's prices, or if your prices to all your customers are the same. Pricing strategy must be flexible to meet changing market conditions. Failing to modify prices when necessary can result in lost profits.

Using Customers to Check Your Market Strategy

Your customers are the best source of feedback on your branding strategy. Consider the following:

>> **Make sure your company positioning is based on how you want customers to view your company and its products and services.** Identical products, for example, can be perceived differently depending on who's marketing them. That's why, for example, customers will pay much more for a branded shampoo than for a generic, even though each might contain the same ingredients. The reputation and integrity of the company behind the product sells the product.

>> **Build credibility for your company and its brand.** Invest in quality, service, and customer satisfaction to reap referrals from satisfied customers. Build trust with your customers by always delivering what you say you will.

>> **Use mass customizing with your key customers.** One entrepreneur I know supplies the products and services needed for developing resorts worldwide. He points out that if he understands the specific needs of a resort developer in the Middle East, he can suggest the best products and services and create a level of customer satisfaction that can't be attained with more standardized products.

>> **Find out who your best customers are and make sure you keep them.** Good customers are worth their weight in gold — literally. Keep in mind that the cost of customer maintenance goes down the longer that you keep your customers.

Using Technology to Build Your Market Strategy

The Internet isn't the only technology affecting the way companies market their goods and services. All sorts of technology — from database marketing to social media and video — shape marketing strategies. You must look at all possible touchpoints with customers. We know that consumers base their decisions more often on the quality of the experience than on the price.

As a result, the emphasis in marketing shifts from products to information and solutions. Rather than selling mere products to customers, companies search for ways to solve customer problems with a bundle of products, information, and services to provide a complete solution. The value of this strategy is that product acceptance increases, and costly redesign is often avoided.

Additional ways you can use technology to market more effectively include:

>> Using email to communicate rapidly and easily with customers, suppliers, and partners around the world. Yes, personalized emails have come back into fashion.

>> Using the teleconferencing or video conferencing capabilities of an application such as Zoom or Microsoft Teams. This can help personalize the relationship.

>> Providing connectivity, laptops, and tablets to your employees, so they can work virtually from anywhere in the world. This increases productivity and brings your company closer to your customers.

>> Using voice mail and live chat services such as Ruby to answer the phone, receive messages when you're not in the office, and obtain customer feedback. This can be a boon to a small company trying to grow.

>> Receiving updated information about equipment, supplies, and other industry information through direct links to your suppliers. This can be a handy way to locate items that aren't normally carried in stock.

When you think about technology, remember that it isn't merely a tool to improve the way you do business or to free up your time to focus on the customer, it's also a driver of innovation and competitive advantage. However, it can't replace personal contact with your customers, which is essential, and it can't replace your unique ability to make sense of a lot of customer information.

Using the Internet to Build Your Market Strategy

The world of marketing online turns the traditional precepts of marketing strategy upside down. You can't sell *to* customers on the Internet; they sell themselves. After all, customers can easily comparison shop for consumer and business products online and decide for themselves what they want. The hard-sell, close-the-deal kind of salesmanship that prevailed for years in the traditional marketplace is alien on the Internet. If that sounds like a problem for entrepreneurs trying to market their products and services, think again. Yes, you approach marketing from a different perspective, but you also reap greater benefits, because Internet customers tend to be more loyal once they've successfully done business with you.

Remember that Internet customers still experience considerable fear and anxiety about purchasing online. They've heard too many stories about credit card identities being snatched from their owners by hackers tapping into online transactions. So, they're more likely to stay with a company they trust, where they are confident that their private information is secure. Consider the following four marketing strategies and examples from successful companies doing business online.

Using information to brand your company

In traditional marketing terms, when you want to increase sales, you create a pitch and broadcast it to the masses. On the Internet, however, that gets you nowhere. Most people don't read those ads, so you need to provide information that enables customers to make their own choices. For example, look at CarMax, www.carmax.com, which links used-car buyers with sellers. You start with a budget for the car you want, search by the type of car, and CarMax finds your dream car, tells you the wholesale price (no negotiations), and essentially gives you all the information you need to make an informed decision. It even goes one step further to gain your trust. You get to take the car home for 24 hours to test drive it and you get a 30-day return option. So, as a company marketing online, you don't have to make a hard-sell pitch to win a happy customer; you just give them what they want.

Creating positive public relations

Some companies excel at using their sites to generate positive public relations for their companies by satisfying not only their customers but their suppliers, shareholders, and other stakeholders. MiniMed, `www.minimed.com`, acquired by Medtronic, has good reason to celebrate what it does. This medical device company provides website visitors with the latest about how to deal with the chronic illness Type 1 diabetes. Its devices help patients manage their insulin needs and monitor glucose levels. On the site, shareholders stay in touch with how the company is doing financially, and physicians learn about the latest therapies.

So successful was this startup in its niche market that it was acquired for $3.28 billion in 2001 by the world's largest medical device company, Medtronic, an Alfred E. Mann company. For Medtronic, the acquisition provided new top-line growth and a solid position in the rapidly growing chronic disease market.

Providing customer service

Under the old marketing paradigm, you provided customer service within the limits of your resources. On the Internet, by contrast, customers want their needs satisfied immediately. In 2018, PricewaterhouseCoopers conducted a customer experience survey. What it found is important for every entrepreneur to understand. Here are some of their findings:

>> 80 percent of consumers want speed, convenience, and knowledgeable help when they have a question.

>> Many customers will pay a bit more for a great customer experience.

>> Unsatisfied customers are more likely to share their negative experience through social media.

>> Your customer service team must be knowledgeable and ready to answer any question quickly and accurately.

>> You must personalize your customer service, so customers feel the company knows who they are.

>> Don't make your customers wait for an unreasonable amount of time to get service.

>> Only make promises you can keep.

>> Listen to your customers. Don't mentally work on a solution while your customer is describing the problem. You may miss the most important point.

>> About 40 percent of consumers prefer self-service over human contact. Be sure to spend time understanding which customer needs can be satisfied with self-service and which customer needs require human support.

TIP

Savvy entrepreneurs are developing tools to help small businesses deal with the role of social media and customer service. Companies such as Freshdesk, `freshdesk.com`, are helping entrepreneurs engage in meaningful relationships with their customers across every channel.

Creating your image

People will visit your website if it's entertaining, lively, interactive, and regularly updated. One of the better examples is the Primal Kitchen site at `www.primalkitchen.com`. Its founder, Mark Sisson, started the company in 2015 with a simple, but powerful mission: to change the way the world eats. His products include salad dressings, mayo, and ketchup, all made with healthy, organic ingredients. On the site, customers can buy products, locate local stores that carry those products, try recipes that use the products, and learn about their nutritional philosophy, which focuses on real food, no dairy, no artificial sweeteners, and good fats such as avocado. Today the company has disrupted the condiment industry at a time when more people are switching to whole foods, particularly plants.

WARNING

Once you have established your image, be very careful to protect it. One site I subscribed to produced excellent short documentary films designed to educate people on topics of general interest and societal importance. However, once they succeeded in increasing their customer base, which had developed certain expectations, they began sending out hyperbolic headlines based on fear and trying to sell all sorts of products to deal with the fear they had generated. Customers are not stupid. They eventually figure out what you're doing, and they will feel taken advantage of. Be sure you understand the image your customers have of your company; don't deviate from that image without support from your customers.

Understanding Customer Acquisition Costs (CACs)

Entrepreneurs, at their peril, often forget to calculate the cost of acquiring a customer. Depending on the industry in which you're doing business, that per customer number could range from $7 (as in the travel industry) to $395 (as in the software industry). This cost includes such things as advertising expenses, time spent in contacting leads, salaries, and so forth.

Besides the obvious reason, why is it important to know your CAC? Well, if you know how much it costs to acquire one customer, you can more easily evaluate the cost of your growth strategy against the lifetime value that the customer brings to your business.

Retaining customers

The lifetime value (LTV) is found by multiplying the monthly revenue generated by a single customer by the gross margin and dividing the sum by the customer *churn rate*; that is, how often customers leave your business.

You can calculate the churn rate, in turn, by dividing your total number of customers in a specific period by the number of churned customers in that same period. Keep in mind that your results are a function of how you define "churned customers" and "total customers," which isn't as easy as it sounds.

In general, a customer is defined as *churned* when their subscription ends and they don't renew or when they proactively cancel a subscription to your product or service. Which is the best scenario? If the customer has cancelled before their subscription has run out, you still have the opportunity to win them back. The chances are higher than if the subscription has run out, signaling that the customer was just not interested or didn't understand the terms of the subscription. Worse, they may not have known that they signed up for a subscription.

Do make sure you are consistent in how you promote a subscription so you don't confuse your customer. Another scenario is a customer who buys a product that has refills and they stop buying refills. Now you don't know if the customer churned because they don't like the product or because they buy refills at a lower price somewhere else. As you can see, customer churn is a big deal. Make sure you understand it.

What can you do to keep acquisition costs down and customer loyalty up? Here are some tips:

>> **Build your brand quickly.** The sooner you gain brand recognition, the sooner your marketing costs, as a percentage of revenue, typically come down. Don't just try to build your brand on the Internet. You must create awareness in offline situations as well. Today, retail sales from physical stores are nearly equal to their digital sales. Entrepreneurs are investing in omni channels (multiple channels) so they can sell anywhere. To put things in perspective,

China generates $351 billion in revenue from online sales through social media. That is ten times more than the United States generates.

>> **Encourage referrals.** Referrals are the least expensive way to get new customers who are more likely to purchase and remain customers over the long term. Referrals also bring down your CAC.

>> **Respect your customers' privacy.** You can no longer collect first-party data from your customers without their approval. Some companies use quizzes and gated content (you need to give the company a piece of information before you're allowed to see the content you're trying to see). But, under current privacy laws, that is no long possible. If you are marketing globally, you need to be aware of GDPR (General Data Protection Regulation) laws in the EU, as they affect any company that transacts in the EU. It is the toughest privacy and security law in the world with requirements for what information you can collect and how you must handle it. And you must consider data protection in the design of any new product or activity. Furthermore, there are strict rules about consent from a data subject for processing their information. We're in a whole new world when it comes to data privacy, so be prepared.

Many entrepreneurs make the mistake of devoting too much time seeking new customers and forgetting to take care of the ones they already have. That's a big mistake. Although it's true that you have to build your customer base when your company is new, at the same time, you must work equally hard to keep the good customers you acquire. Here's why. Most companies lose about 25 percent of their customers annually. If you figure that acquiring a new customer costs about five times as much as maintaining an existing one, you realize a lot of money is going down the drain. About 65 percent of an average company's business comes from current, satisfied customers. In this section, you find out a variety of techniques for keeping great customers.

Creating your promotional mix

Promotion is the creative side of marketing. It deals with guerrilla advertising, publicity, sales, and personal selling tactics. Your choice of tactics is called the *promotional mix*, which differs from company to company, depending first and foremost on your budget but also on the type of business you have, your goals, and your target market.

Your promotional mix must include the input of everyone in your company. The tactics that convey benefits to the customer should be paramount. Advertising and publicity are two of those tactics.

Advertising

Advertising creates product and company awareness. Advertising is everywhere you look, from the sign in a store window to the billboard along the highway, from the drive-time radio spot to the prime-time TV slot. Advertising creates awareness but can't guarantee sales, because most customers aren't as swayed by advertising the way they used to be.

Moreover, most entrepreneurial startups can't afford to compete in the advertising arena with bigger companies, so they often revert to what are called *guerrilla tactics*, less expensive methods that target specific customers. In general, any advertising you do must

» Target your specific customer.

» Convey a positive image of your company.

» Reflect the vision and culture of your company.

» Ask for the sale.

Asking for the sale is one advertising accomplishment that many entrepreneurs forget about. You can do everything else right, but if you don't convince the potential customer to commit to the purchase, you have achieved nothing.

Social media

It's hard to ignore the pervasive influence of social media in a company's marketing strategy. Social media marketing includes a number of categories and each serves a different purpose.

» **Blogs, twitter, email, and e-newsletters.** These serve as effective ways to communicate your company's expertise and stance on relevant issues of the day.

» **Podcasts and YouTube.** These are increasingly popular ways to get customers to subscribe to your channel and share what they've seen with others. In particular, YouTube has become the source of viral videos that could give your company wide reach quickly and cheaply if you're able to come up with something that catches people's attention enough to want to share it. And let's hope it's something positive.

» **Facebook, Instagram, and Pinterest.** These are effective ways to reach a younger audience that relies on social media for information. Offering free products and services is always a winning strategy, but depending on what you're selling, that may not be possible.

When using social media, you need to make sure that your servers can handle the increased traffic that might result from a successful campaign. It's a good idea to study what other companies are doing to determine which approaches have the best chance for success and, more importantly, which are likely to fail.

Publicity

Perhaps the best way to promote your company is through free publicity, which is basically free advertising for a product or business through various forms of media. The key to getting free publicity is having a product or company that is newsworthy, that has a great story. Ben & Jerry's, the ice cream producer, won millions of dollars' worth of free publicity early on with their tale of a company that issued a public offering for the people in its home state of Vermont. If you believe that your company has an important story to tell, try

>> Contacting a reporter suggesting the idea and then following up with a phone call. It's better if you initially get to that reporter through a referral.

>> Issuing a press release that answers who, what, where, when, and why.

>> Building a press kit that contains a press release, bios of the founding team, photos of the key people in the story, background information, and any other media about the business. By making the reporters' job easier, you're more likely to get them to write something about your company. If an article is written, be sure to get reprints that you can use in your advertising and promotion.

>> If you have a story that is book worthy, writing a book is a good way to get on a news show or podcast. One thing you should never do is spam a lot of media outlets with the same message. It's a small community and they don't like being part of a crowd.

>> Start a blog or podcast, but don't use it to just promote your business. Use it to provide useful information or to tell the personal stories and struggles you had starting your business.

Building relationships

To build relationships with customers, you need more than a mere collection of information. You need a dialogue with your customers — by phone, by email, interactively over the Internet or via social media, or in person. The point is that the dialogue must be a two-way conversation if you're going to obtain any useful information. For making your relationship-building efforts more effective:

>> Do not attempt to sell every time you talk to your customer. Let them know that sometimes you call just to see how they enjoy their dealings with your company. Be sure to find out if they're okay with these calls. Some customers, no matter how much they like your business, don't want to have ongoing conversations with you.

>> Be sure to provide voice mail, so customers can leave messages or voice complaints after business hours.

>> Include a place on your website where customers can post or send you their ideas and thoughts.

Develop a customer information file

One of the more important support components of any customer relationship program is the customer information file (CIF). It contains information you collect over time about your customers. Besides the normal contact information, you'll want to include:

>> How recently the customer made a purchase

>> How often the customer purchases

>> How much the customer spends on average per purchase

>> How much the customer spent during the past six months or year

>> Where purchases were made and how

>> Any purchases returned and why

>> Method of payment and debt history

>> Types and dates of promotions the company sent to the customer

>> Information gathered through dialoguing with the customer

>> Customers' perceptions about the company's products, versus competitors

All this information will help you to calculate the lifetime value of this customer to your company.

Reward your best customers

Don't expect to build long-term one-on-one relationships with all your customers once the number of those customers becomes large. Do your best, but remember that as few as 24 percent of your customers account for 95 percent of your revenues, so you really want to make sure that you're taking care of that precious 24 percent. At the same time, you want to identify your worst customers, those that cost you time and money but never buy from you on a regular basis or those with a poor debt history. If you're keeping good CIFs — especially if you're using a relational database — finding the best and worst customers won't be difficult.

CASE STUDY

GETTING YOUR COMPANY NOTICED

Guerrilla advertising approaches help your company become noticed in an ever-increasing crowd of competitors. It is a creative way to drive publicity and brand awareness in ways that are surprising or even shocking. Guerrilla tactics include:

- **Sponsoring a special event.** For example, one company presents a business-after-hours event, displaying its products to an invited group of professionals who can enjoy drinks and hors d'oeuvres. Another company sponsors a Little League baseball team, providing team shirts and trophies.

- **Demonstrating your expertise in a particular area.** One public relations firm creates awareness by developing a newsletter that focuses on women who work in large organizations. Taking a humorous approach, the newsletter captures a lot of attention.

- **Giving your products away to people who can get you free publicity like celebrities, social media influencers, and others with access to the media.**

- **Offering free information on your website.** This can attract visitors and keep your current customers coming back.

These are some conservative examples, but guerrilla marketing is known for its more unconventional approaches. When Gold Toe, the sock company, wanted to promote the launch of its new line of underwear, it decided to make a splash by putting the underwear on statues throughout New York City. For example, the iconic charging bull statue (the bull of Wall Street) was seen wearing an enormous pair of briefs.

The *event ambush* is another guerrilla tactic that takes advantage of an audience at an in-progress event, such as a concert or sporting event, to promote a product or service in a very noticeable way without the permission of the event sponsors. Fiji Water did this at the 2019 Golden Globes by strategically placing models dressed in blue and carrying trays of water around to the attendees. One adventurous model photo bombed high-profile celebrities by positioning herself in the background of the photo shoots. Soon people noticed that she was appearing in all the photos and fans began calling her #FijiGirl. Without being the focus of the event, she managed to make the Fiji Water brand stand out and get everyone talking about her.

Two proven ways to reward your best customers so they'll keep coming back and referring other customers to your business are

>> **Frequency programs or VIP clubs.** If you fly, you are no doubt familiar with frequency programs in which you receive mileage credits each time you fly. You can redeem the credits for airline tickets when you've accumulated enough. Because rewards increase with use, you have an incentive to continue using that airline. Other businesses successfully use frequency programs. For example, many drugstores use cosmetic cards that give the holder a discount after they purchase a certain number of cosmetics. Pizza parlors often offer frequent user cards that entitle the holder to a free pizza after they purchase a certain number of pizzas. Still other businesses offer memberships that entitle members to special discounts and other benefits that regular purchasers don't receive.

>> **Just-in-time programs.** Many businesses keep track of dates and special occasions that are important to their customers. Many program their databases to automatically send a message to the customer on a particular date (in other words, a birthday, anniversary, and so forth) or remind the customer of a special sale on something they typically buy. If you keep an up-to-date CIF, you have a good idea what your customer usually purchases.

GIVE YOURSELF A TEST

Even if you think you're doing everything right when it comes to taking care of your customers, ask yourself these questions:

1. Do you treat all your customers the same?

2. Do you have a learning relationship with your customers? Do you learn from them and they from you?

3. Do you keep your customers?

4. Is your business organized around its customers?

If you treat all your customers the same, you're wasting time and money. It is a common fact that about 24 percent of your customers provide 95 percent of your revenues. So, spend most of your marketing dollars on that 24 percent who are driving your revenues. That doesn't mean you ignore the rest. But your primary goal should be to keep your best customers happy so they want to refer their friends. Those friends will likely join the ranks of your best customers, so it's time well spent.

(continued)

(continued)

You create a learning relationship with your customers by listening to them and learning their needs and requirements. For example, successful computer companies like Dell are interested in knowing *why* you need a computer before they ever get to the question of how fast you want that computer to be.

Try never letting your customers go to someone else to satisfy their needs. You should have a huge network of contacts, so that once your customers have purchased from you, you can refer them to one of your strategic partners when they need something that you might not carry. That way, your customers think of you no matter what they need.

Make sure that everyone in your company understands the needs of the customer and how they can help to satisfy them. In that way, your company becomes customer focused.

As you can see, marketing to customers is not simply a matter of getting your message out. Marketing needs to be a two-way street that ends in a relationship with your best customers. The strategy with the greatest return for your business is, hands down, referrals from loyal customers.

Chapter **18**

Making and Using Money Wisely: The Financial Plan

To turn your business into a reality requires understanding how you will capitalize it and find the money and resources to grow it. In short, you need a financial plan.

Some successful businesses have launched with back-of-the envelope calculations. They may even have succeeded for a time. But this casual strategy will not sit well with investors or bankers, who need to understand how you arrived at your numbers (and they'll ask you), because it gives them insight into your growth plans and also into whether you know your business or are just faking it.

If you're thinking that this process is too frustrating and time consuming, keep this in mind: It's not what you discover from the results of the process that matter the most; it's what you discover from going through the process of planning your company's finances that's so valuable. Don't make the mistake of burying yourself in the daily activities of your businesses to the exclusion of never taking stock of where the business is and where it's headed. Going through the process of planning your financial future organizes and focuses you on important factors about your business that you might not be aware of otherwise.

Another important reason for planning your company's financial future is to help your business deal with change. When you take time to evaluate your company's strengths and weaknesses, what's happening in your market and industry, and what your competition is doing, you put your company in a better position to discover new opportunities and avoid unexpected problems.

One scenario I've run across too many times involves business owners who are concerned about cash flow; in short, there's not enough. It's difficult to solve a problem like this when you don't know what what's causing it. Are costs increasing? Are accounts receivable in decline? These are just two of the many questions that should be asked to get at the root of the problem and solve it.

In this chapter, you discover the steps needed to create a successful financial plan and ways to manage your cash flow so that your business stays healthy.

Identifying the Components of a Successful Financial Plan

Let's start by looking at the story of Janice, a solo entrepreneur with a small retail outlet who experienced three consecutive years of losses after turning a marginal profit in her second year. After financing the business with as much as she was able to scrounge up, the declining cash flow alone led her to conclude that the business was not worth saving.

Not surprisingly, Janice didn't have a financial plan. You probably guessed that was coming. A proper financial plan would have given her insights into why her business began to suffer losses and enable her to focus her problem-solving efforts.

Before giving up, Janice obtained the helpful advice of a *turnaround consultant* (someone who specializes in saving failing businesses), who put together *pro forma* (projected) cash flow and income statements in addition to preparing a break-even analysis. The break-even analysis showed Janice how much product she had to sell and by how much she needed to reduce operating expenses to be cash-flow positive. With this new information in hand, Janice set achievable short-term goals and tracked cash flow on a daily basis. These efforts ultimately led to stability and a business that is profitable to this day.

Starting with goals

Every good plan starts with setting of short-term, mid-range, and long-term financial goals. Once you have these, you can develop strategies or ways to achieve those goals. Only when you have your strategies pinned down should you consider tactics or tasks that you need to do to implement the strategies. Table 18-1 provides a basic example of how this works.

TABLE 18-1

Royal York Property Management's Goals, Strategies, and Tactics

Goal	Founded in 2010 in Ontario, Canada, it now has 29 global office locations and more than 12,000 properties under management. Its goal is to become the global innovation platform leader for property owners and tenants.
Strategy	Expand to 38 office locations across Europe and the Middle East by implementing new technologies focused on security and integration of property management tasks to guarantee rental income for property owners.
Tactic	Employ a franchising model to grow more quickly,

Having goals focuses the energy and enthusiasm of an organization on specific targets and helps a company make better decisions. For example, if you're considering investing in a particular new product but it doesn't help you meet your overall goal, you may decide to forego the investment for the time being. It's important to be focused.

REMEMBER

The key to successful goals is acceptance. Everyone in the company should support the company goals so that focus and energy are not dissipated.

Many business goals take the form of sales or revenue numbers, numbers of SKUs (stock keeping units), or gross/net margins. These are good jumping-off points, because you can easily identify when you achieve them; however, they must be combined with strategies for achieving them. Your company may be great at setting goals and defining outcomes for the organization, but if you never talk about how you're going to achieve those outcomes, everyone will have a different idea about strategy. And, in the confusion, the goals won't be achieved. It's always best to associate a goal with a specific strategy.

Budgeting for capital expenditures (CAPEX)

A *capital* budget looks at what you plan to spend on assets like plant, equipment, and office space. It helps you achieve your company's objectives through proper allocation of resources among the many investments that you need to make.

In creating capital budgets, you consider alternatives to determine the best use of your funds, so that you can optimize the returns for your investors. You also look at the *cost of capital,* which is generally the amount of interest, equity, or return on investment charged by the various sources from which you acquire the money.

Preparing your capital expenditures budget essentially sets up a plan to acquire and manage longer-term assets. You may have bootstrapped the startup of your company with few or no assets; but over time, you will likely need to add equipment or technology, hire staff, increase your office or plant space, or expand your product line.

Capital expenditures differ from current expenses because the company benefits from capex for more than a year (or one fiscal period if the company's business year isn't based on a calendar year). Here are some questions you should ask as you define your capital expenditures:

>> To lease or purchase a new truck — which is more financially prudent?

>> Is it better for the company to invest in an automated assembly system or outsource to another manufacturer?

>> Which projects should the company fund, given its limited resources?

>> How many projects can the company take on at one time?

Because capital expenditures require more time and effort in the decision-making process, having an evaluation system in place for making such decisions is a good idea. You must weigh the cost of investing in, say, a piece of equipment, the length of time required to recoup the cost, the return on investment, and the alternatives to making a purchase. In general, you will aim to spend your precious dollars on capex with the highest return on investment.

Budgeting for operations

The *operating budget* is a group of several budgets that all relate to the operations of the business. Depending on your business, these budgets may include the following:

>> Sales budget

>> Production budget

>> Direct materials budget

>> Direct labor budget

>> Factory overhead

These sub-budgets allow you to analyze business performance and uncover existing or potential problem areas. Let's take a deeper dive into these five operating sub-budgets.

Sales budget

The *sales budget* presents a forecast for your company's sales levels over the period that you're focused on — usually a year. This budget is normally prepared first because sales as a reflection of demand affect every other budget. The steps you use to prepare a sales budget are

1. **Estimate the number of units you think you'll sell during the forecast period.**

2. **Estimate the sales price per unit.**

3. **Multiply the number of units to be sold by the price per unit to arrive at an estimate of your sales revenue.**

You estimate sales price and units separately because they are correlated, meaning that as the number of units you produce increases, the price per unit often (but not always) comes down, and vice versa. If you want to remind yourself of ways to estimate sales, check out Chapter 12. See Table 18-2 for an example of what a sales budget looks like.

TABLE 18-2 **Sample Sales Budget**

	Year 1	Year 2	Year 3
Projected Sales in Units	10,000	15,000	20,000
Sales Price per Unit	$16	$14	$12
Total Sales	$160,000	$210,000	$240,000

Production budget

The *production budget* describes your company's output measured in units of products you're producing or purchasing for resale. The production budget is derived from the sales budget and projected demand. Typically, you have to account for adjustments that are the result of overproduction or underproduction. Those adjustments are expressed in the inventory budget. Table 18-3 is an example of a production budget based on the sales budget you saw in Table 18-2.

The first thing to note is that management is forecasting increasing sales of 50 percent year over year for the first three years. You can assume this estimate is based on market research (I hope it is). Next look at the current stock of finished goods or beginning inventory. The logic is that beginning inventory will increase by at least 50 percent each year to keep up with forecasted sales.

TABLE 18-3

Sample Production Budget

	Year 1	Year 2	Year 3
Projected Sales in Units (Forecasted)	10,000	15,000	20,000
Beginning Inventory (Opening Stock of Finished Goods)	1,500	2,500	4,000
Units in Production	11,000	-16,500	10,000
Ending Inventory (Closing Stock Assuming Projected Sales Occurred)	2,500	4,000	-6,000

Now, the first decision is how many units to produce in Year 1? Management has decided to produce the demand (10,000 units) plus a small increase of 1,000 units to be safe. So you finish Year 1 with an ending inventory of 2,500 units (1,500 + 11,000 – 10,000 sold). Now look at Year 2. Keep in mind that projected sales are just that — projected. They're an estimate, so the actual number will likely come in above or below that target.

In Year 2, you start with finished goods of 2,500. By management's formula, you should put 16,500 units into production in Year 2 (a 50 percent increase over Year 1). If you then add the finished goods units to the units in production and subtract the total from the forecast, you end up with a closing stock of 4,000 units. Keep in mind that management can revise their decisions based on new data, for example, and decide to put fewer units into production in Year 2. It's all a function of the cost of holding inventory and whether it's important to smooth out production costs over time.

In Year 3, let's say that management decides to put fewer units into production — perhaps 10,000 units — because the economy is showing weakness that could affect sales, so they don't want to trust their demand forecast and overproduce. You add the 10,000 units to the beginning inventory of 4,000 units and subtract the total from the forecast. You can see that you are short 6,000 units, so the ending inventory is negative. You didn't produce enough to meet demand, which, surprisingly, stayed as predicted. Oops!

This exercise illustrates how valuable scenario planning is in that it leads to more informed decisions. If you start this process with a goal of keeping inventory levels low, that will be a key factor in how you create your budget. Don't forget that inventory affects how quickly your customers can get your product. Be careful of skimping too much.

Direct materials budget

Using the production budget, you can estimate the direct materials you need and the cost of those materials. If you are producing several products, you want to separate them so that you can track each one to determine which are doing well and which aren't. The *direct materials budget* includes:

>> Production in units

>> Material needed per unit

>> Total amount of material needed (units × material per unit)

>> Cost per unit of material

>> Total projected materials cost

Direct labor budget

In the *direct labor budget*, you determine the cost of labor required to produce your products. Start by estimating hours of work per unit produced and then the dollar amount per labor hour. Multiply the two and you get the total direct labor cost.

Factory overhead

The last budget you build depicts the costs related to *factory overhead*, including management salaries and facility costs — all the costs that you can't trace directly to the production of the product. These costs aren't as easy to break out by specific product, so they're often allocated in a way that makes sense for the particular type of business you're in. Remember that if you outsource your production, you're still paying factory overhead somewhere in your costs, so be sure to get that number from your strategic partner.

Running financial forecasts and ratios

Your financial plan includes a complete set of financial statements:

>> Cash flow statement

>> Income statement

>> Balance sheet

The cash flow statement is vital because it reflects the true financial health of the business — in other words, its ability to pay its obligations. The income statement tells you if your business made a profit or suffered a loss during the period. Keep in mind that you don't pay your bills with profit. You pay them with cash, so the cash flow statement is arguably the most important, especially in the early stages of the business. The balance sheet gives you a snapshot of the business's net worth and overall health at a specific point in time. It describes the assets, debts, and owners' equity. You can find out how to build these financial statements in the next section.

Another important component of your financial plan is the ability to calculate ratios that provide you with a better understanding of what's going on in your business. Ratios tell you something about your company's financial health and stability over time or relative to other companies in your industry. In the section entitled "Using Financial Ratios to Judge Performance," you find out how to calculate several important ratios.

Building the Financial Statements

Financial statements provide a great deal of information about the financial condition of a company. Everyone, from investors to lenders to employees, managers, suppliers, customers, and in some cases, the Securities and Exchange Commission, is interested in your financial statements. The information in financial statements helps someone who is interested decide whether to invest in your company, make a loan, or take a management position.

REMEMBER

Your company will normally complete a set of financial statements quarterly. The process is fairly straightforward. First, you record all your financial transactions in a journal (this is typically done online using accounting software). Then you post the journal transactions to their respective ledger (accounts receivable, payable, interest paid, and so on). Then you create a trial balance from the ledger balances and, unless figures require clarification, you build the financial statements.

Looking at deviations from expected financial performance and differences from period to period also produces important information that will help you catch a problem early. The information that key decision-makers within your organization require influences financial reports. For example, your marketing manager may want to see sales levels per salesperson to spot problems. Your production manager may use financial reports to evaluate the potential purchase of a piece of equipment designed to save time and money over the long term. At a higher level, the CEO may want to know how the company's international sales stack up relative to the total revenue picture.

Building the income statement

In Chapter 12, I talk about how to develop an income statement. In the simplest terms, the formula for the income statement is

Revenues – Expenses = Net Profit or Net Loss

See Figure 18-1 for an example of an income statement.

The income statement in Figure 18-1 shows that this sample company became profitable in 2022, but it doesn't say how healthy the company is in terms of cash flow. The Cash Flow from Operations Statement provides that information. Looking at the differences between the two years can reveal potential problems. For example, sales increased by $150,000 but advertising declined by $2,000, which is counterintuitive and gives rise to questions such as the following: Does this reflect more targeted and cost-efficient advertising tactics? Did the company focus more on selling more products to its current customers than on acquiring new customers, bringing acquisition costs down? The answers require further research.

	2021	2022	Difference
Net Sales	500,000	650,000	150,000
Cost of Sales	350,000	420,000	70,000
Gross Profit	150,000	230,000	80,000
Operating Expenses:			
Wages & Salaries	55,000	59,000	4,000
Rent & Lease Payments	9,000	9,000	0
Utilities	7,800	8,403	603
Insurance	15,000	18,000	3,000
Advertising	12,000	10,000	(2,000)
Vehicle Operation/Maint.	35,000	35,000	0
Accounting & Legal	4,000	2,500	(1,500)
Payroll Taxes	7,600	8,900	1,300
Depreciation	2,970	3,300	330
Total Operating Expenses	148,370	154,103	5,733
Net Operating Income	1,630	75,897	74,267
Less: Interest Expense	(4,620)	(5,445)	(825)
Net Taxable Income	(2,990)	70,452	73,442
Less: Income Taxes	(31,925)	(34,209)	(2,284)
Net Income	(34,915)	36,243	71,158

FIGURE 18-1: This sample income statement details how sales and expenses result in a company's net income.

Total operating expenses increased by about 4 percent, while gross profit increased by 53 percent, which combined may be a good sign that the company is keeping its overhead under control while it grows. However, it can also be a signal that if the company continues to grow at its current pace, it must prepare for increases in overhead, such as hiring more talent or increasing production.

Developing the balance sheet

The balance sheet tells you what the company owns and owes as well as the amount of shareholder investment at a particular point in time. It takes into account the assets of the company, such as equipment, inventory, cash, accounts receivable, property, and patents. It also shows the liabilities or obligations the company has entered into, such as notes payable, accounts payable, wages and taxes payable, and installment loans. The owners' equity section presents the shareholders' residual interest in the company after the liabilities are subtracted from the assets. Shareholders' residual interest is reported in the form of common stock, preferred stock, and retained earnings. The basic formula of a balance sheet is

Assets = Liabilities + Owners' Equity

It is normally prepared at the end of a financial year. Take a look at Figure 18-2 for an example of a balance sheet.

The first section of the balance sheet covers the assets, which represent the actual cost of the items listed. Current assets, those consumed within a year, are considered liquid. Fixed assets or non-current assets are tangible items such as equipment and facilities or intangibles such as patents and licenses. Fixed assets, except for land, are displayed less depreciation. The value of land is not depreciated. For example, if you started a retail store and bought $20,000 in inventory to start, that inventory will show up on the balance sheet as a current asset. By contrast, if you take out a long-term loan, that will appear as a non-current liability on your balance sheet.

The important thing to remember about a balance sheet is that it must balance! In other words, the asset side of the balance sheet must equal the liabilities plus owners' equity side. Again, comparing balance sheets from one year to the next provides you with valuable information, because you find out

>> If accounts receivable and inventory increased or decreased relative to sales during the same period.

>> If debt financing increased or decreased during the period.

>> If accounts payable were at an appropriate level relative to sales.

>> If sales increased to such an extent that additional investment in equipment is necessary.

	2021	2022
Assets		
Current Assets:		
Cash	21,450	44,025
Accounts Receivable	42,533	90,090
Inventory	39,875	92,606
Prepaid Expenses	0	8,250
Total Current Assets	103,858	234,971
Fixed Assets:		
Land	49,500	49,500
Building	247,500	247,500
Vehicles	52,800	57,750
Equipment	33,000	37,950
Less: Accumulated Depreciation	(34,650)	(37,950)
Total Net Fixed Assets	348,150	354,750
Total Assets	**452,008**	**589,721**
Liabilities & Owner's Equity		
Current Liabilities		
Notes Payable	34,831	62,700
Accounts Payable	20,130	27,904
Accruals Payable	3,762	6,088
Total Current Liabilities	58,723	96,692
Long-term Liabilities		
Installment Loan Payable	0	42,354
Mortgage Payable	181,500	174,900
Total Long-term Liabilities	181,500	217,254
Total Liabilities	**240,223**	**313,946**
Owner's Equity:		
Capital Stock	49,500	88,575
Retained Earnings	162,285	187,200
Total Owner's Equity	**211,785**	**275,775**
Total Liabilities & Owner's Equity	**452,008**	**589,721**

FIGURE 18-2: This sample balance sheet depicts the basic accounting equation — Assets = Liabilities + Owners' Equity.

Creating the cash flow from an operations statement

Chapter 12 explains how building a simple cash flow statement helps you figure out how much capital you need to start a business. Equally important is the ability to plan and manage for cash and other assets, both now and into the future. This section demonstrates how to prepare an operating cash flow statement for a growing business.

Summarizing the process, the cash flow statement reports on the cash flow from operations, financing, and investing activities of the company for a specific period. Important factors to remember when you're thinking about cash flow are

>> You must make sure that your company has enough cash to meet all its obligations.

>> You must identify alternative sources of cash for times when it's needed, along with the forms and terms associated with using those sources.

>> You need to forecast and plan for the financial requirements of your company's operations into the future.

REMEMBER

Cash flow is not a measure of your company's performance; it's a measure of your company's health and ability to meet its obligations. You can have a healthy cash flow and not have a company that's growing and performing well within its market. Similarly, profit is a measure of performance but not necessarily of health and ability to meet obligations, since you can have a profitable company that doesn't have the cash to pay its taxes.

Determine your cash flow needs

When planning for future cash needs, you need to look both at short-term and long-term needs. Short-term needs usually focus on the timing and the amount of cash flow. So short-term planning is about managing regular cash inflows and outflows.

The typical planning horizon for short-term goals is one month. Some companies find, however, that because of the nature of their businesses, they prefer to manage cash flow daily. Maintaining sufficient cash on hand to cover shortfalls is a wise choice for these businesses, as well as for those for which the size of cash inflows and outflows is difficult to predict.

Long-term needs are usually related to the acquisition of capital assets like equipment and facilities and are based on long-term goals for the growth of the company.

Cash inflows include such things as cash sales and collected accounts receivable, while cash outflows consist of payments for inventory, payments of accounts payable, and payments associated with payroll taxes, rent, utilities, and so forth. All are activities related to operations. Non-operating cash flows come from bank loans, additional investments by owners, the sale of assets, payment of principal or interest on debt, dividend distribution, or the purchase of fixed assets.

Prepare the statement

Once you prepare and begin operating with a cash flow statement in your business, you will eventually want to link the income statement items with changes in balance sheet items arising from normal operations from one period to the next. Take a look at Figure 18-3 for an example of this statement. It's linked to the income statements and balance sheets that were discussed in the two previous sections.

Net Sales	650,000	
Less Increase in Accounts Receivable	(47,557)	
Net Sales Adjusted to a Cash Basis		602,443
Cost of Sales	320,925	
Plus: Increase in Inventory	52,731	
Less: Increase in Accounts Payable	(7,774)	
Cost of Sales Adjusted to a Cash Basis		(365,881)
Operating Expenses	155,704	
Less: Depreciation Expense	(3,300)	
Less: Increase in Accruals	(2,326)	
Plus: Increase in Prepaids	8,250	
Less: Operating Expenses Adjusted to a Cash Basis		158,328
Taxes Paid		(34,209)
Cash Flow (Cash Drain) From Operations		44,025

FIGURE 18-3: Cash inflows and outflows result in a company's cash flow from operations.

If your eyes are crossing now from all these new financial terms and calculations, you may want to skip this next part, but be sure to discuss it with your financial advisor, because the cash flow statement is vital to your business's health.

For those readers who are ready to tackle the preparation of a cash flow from the operations statement, I recommend that you have a calculator handy and make copies of Figures 18–1 through 18–3 so you can easily refer to them.

Let's look at the steps you need to take to prepare this statement.

1. Adjust sales to a cash basis.

Note that sales for 2022 were $650,000, but they were not all cash sales; some were made on credit. On the balance sheet, you find that accounts receivable increased from $42,533 in 2021 to $90,090 in 2022, so it appears that the company extended significantly more credit in 2022. Extending that credit results in a cash drain for revenues the company didn't collect. Although sales increased, cash flow from sales did not. So you need to adjust sales down by the amount of increase in receivables.

2. Adjust the cost of sales.

Your cost of sales is the cost of goods you actually sold in the accounting period. It is affected by changes in the level of inventory, which is reflected in the current assets on the balance sheet and by changes in accounts payable and current liabilities on the balance sheet. Notice in Figure 18-1 (the income statement), that in 2022, the company had a cost of sales of $420,000. Figure 18-2 indicates that inventory increased by $52,731 and accounts payable by $7,774 (on the balance sheet). The increase in inventory is a cash outflow that doesn't show up in the income statement, so it must be added to the cost of sales. The increase in accounts payable means that the company was using supplier credit and keeping more of their cash. This increase is deducted from the cost of sales.

3. Adjust the operating expenses.

Because depreciation is a non-cash expense that reduces revenue, operating expenses don't appear to be as much on the cash flow statement as they appear on the income statement. Similarly, accruals are unpaid obligations and are a current liability on the balance sheet, because they represent money retained in the company. So you must deduct the increase from the operating expenses. On the other hand, prepaid expenses are cash outflows that increase operating expenses. You must add the increase in prepaids to the operating expense figure.

The results of these calculations show that the company was in a relatively healthy cash position. However, increases in the company's accounts receivable reduced its sales revenues for the period (the amount of cash it took in).

WARNING

Whenever both inventory and accounts receivable grow at a faster rate than sales, the company needs to pay attention, because such situations signal a future problem.

Here is a summary of the steps used to prepare a cash flow statement.

>> An increase in accounts receivable reduces cash flow from sales.

>> A decrease in accounts receivable increases cash flow from sales.

>> An increase in inventory uses cash, while a decrease in inventory decreases the cost of sales.

>> An increase in accounts payable decreases the cost of sales.

>> A decrease in payables means that you've paid obligations, so your cost of sales has increased.

The bottom line on cash

Regardless of whether you plowed through the calculations on the sample cash flow from operations statement, here are a few simple rules to follow to ensure that your company's cash flow stays in the black:

>> **Tighten up credit and collections.** Follow up immediately if a customer is late on a payment.

>> **Set up a cash reserve for bad debts.** Have a cash fund to mediate the effect of unpaid receivables.

>> **Take advantage of your suppliers' credit terms.** Always pay your bills on time, but don't pay too early. For example, if you're given 30 days to pay, don't pay on day 5. Keep your money on hand until close to the 30th day.

>> **Offer cash discounts.** Provide cash discounts to customers for prompt payment.

>> **Manage your inventory carefully.** Inventory you don't need costs you money. If you find that some inventory is not selling, cut prices and move it out to turn it back into cash.

>> **Make cash surpluses work for you.** When you have more cash than you need (above your reserve for contingencies), invest it in a short-term certificate of deposit or in the stock market in reliable funds to earn money on it.

>> **Keep payroll under control.** Having more people on hand than you absolutely need takes a lot of cash. Consider outsourcing some of your tasks to retain more of your cash.

>> **Cut expenses.** Be careful not to spend freely when you do have a cash surplus; the bills follow quickly. Keep overhead expenses down because they are expenses you continue to pay even when sales decline.

Using Financial Ratios to Judge Performance

Fortunately, many tools can help you further analyze your company's health and even see how your company's performance stacks up against others in your industry or against your own company's performance from period to period. When analyzing financials, you'll generally focus on:

>> Sales growth

>> Profitability

>> Gross margin (revenue less cost of goods sold, divided by revenue — bigger is better)

>> Selling, general, and administrative expenses as a percentage of revenue

>> Profit earned on the asset base (how much you earn per dollar of investment)

>> Debt-equity ratio

>> Seasonality

>> Liquidity

Ratios provide a way of interpreting information from your financial statements in all the areas just listed. But, they are useful *only* if they compare one company with another or compare periods within one company to look for patterns of change. Although it's possible to produce many ratios from the financials, that would be a waste of time. You want to produce only those ratios that have the most value for your company within your industry. I categorize them into the three most common groups — liquidity ratios, profitability ratios, and leverage ratios — to give you a good start on your analysis.

WARNING

When you compare your company against another in your industry, you'll probably be comparing it with a public corporation, because companies on the stock exchange are the only ones required to publish their financial statements. If you have a small business such a comparison will not be appropriate, because economies of scale and productivity levels are different for large, public companies.

For this reason, it is more likely that you'll use ratios to judge how your business is doing from one month, quarter, or year to the next, which is valuable in itself.

Liquidity ratios

Liquidity ratios help you understand your company's ability to meet its short-term debt obligations and maintain normal operations — in other words, stay alive. The more liquid assets your company has, the better, because liquid assets convert easily to cash, and cash is what your business needs. Let's look at two easy-to-use liquidity ratios:

>> **Current Ratio:** The current ratio is your total current assets divided by your total current liabilities. So, if your business produces a current ratio of 2.00, it means that for every $1 in liabilities, you have $2 in current assets. You can pay your debts two times over. That's good, because the higher the number, the more liquid your company is. Over time, you want to look for patterns of change in liquidity, so you can catch potential problems early.

>> **Acid Test:** This is a popular and tougher test for measuring a company's ability to meet its current liabilities with its current assets. The reason this test is tougher is that it removes inventory (which is often difficult to convert to cash, especially if it's obsolete). To calculate this ratio, subtract inventory from your current assets and divide the remainder by your current liabilities. Again, the higher the ratio the better, although the minimum rule of thumb is a 1:1 ratio.

Profitability ratios

With profitability ratios, you are evaluating the company's ability to generate net income (profit) from revenues. Here are two profitability ratios:

>> **Gross Profit Margin:** With this ratio, you use net sales from your income statement to figure out the dollar amount that remains after subtracting all costs of operations from sales revenues. This is called "cost of goods sold" (COGS). Essentially, you learn how much you'll retain from revenues to pay for the costs of production and service. You find the gross profit margin taking net sales (gross revenue minus returns, allowances, and discounts) and subtracting COGS. Normally, the margin is expressed as a percentage, so divide your gross profit margin by gross sales. Now you can compare the percentage you come up with against other similar businesses in your industry to determine whether you're operating your business efficiently.

In Figure 18-1, the gross profit for 2022 is $230,000, which we divide by net revenues, $650,000. We arrive at a net margin of .35. That's pretty decent, but it would be important to compare it to industry margins to make sure you're at least in the ballpark.

>> **Return on Investment:** Using net income from the income statement and shareholder equity from the balance sheet, you divide net income by shareholders' equity to arrive at a percentage that represents the number of dollars of income earned per dollar of capital invested in the business. The higher the number, the greater the return. In the example, net income is $36,243 in 2022, which you divide by $275,775 (balance sheet) to arrive at .13. So the return on investment is 13 percent.

Leverage ratios

Leverage ratios measure the level of debt the company maintains. Usually, a high number suggests a riskier situation, because even though the earnings for the company can increase or decline, the debt payments normally remain constant. Three leverage ratios that you can use to analyze your company's debt position are

>> **Interest Coverage:** This ratio looks at earnings from operating income generated to meet interest charges on debt. The greater the earnings relative to the interest expense, the less risky the company is, and the happier your lender will be. To calculate this ratio, divide earnings before interest and taxes by interest expense. If you get a number like 16, it means that earnings are 16 times interest expense, which is a healthy result. Watching this number over time helps signal potential problems.

>> **Debt to Asset:** This balance sheet ratio measures the percentage of your company's assets that are covered by creditors versus the percentage that are covered by the owners of the company. You calculate this ratio by dividing total debt by total assets. For example, most manufacturers have debt to asset ratios between 0.30 and 0.70. Look at industry averages to see if your company is in the same ballpark as the industry.

>> **Inventory Turnover:** This is a critical ratio if you produce products that you carry in inventory. It is found by dividing average inventory over a period into cost of goods sold. If you get an answer such as 5.5, it means that you sell your inventory 5.5 times per year. The higher the number the better, because you then reduce storage and other holding costs.

Cash Planning: Managing Your Working Capital

Working capital is the money you need to run your business and pay your employees on a regular basis even when your revenues aren't received or collected on a regular basis. Cash planning is vital to your business, especially when you're in the growth mode. The biggest reasons you want to plan ahead for your cash needs are so that you can predict when you might experience a shortfall and plan to tap resources outside your business to cover you until the revenues you expect materialize.

If you don't plan for cash needs and instead react when something happens, you put your company in a dangerous position. By that time, you may be too far into a cash crisis to recover. Besides, when you stop paying your suppliers because you're low on cash (and suppliers are one of the first groups small business owners neglect when things get tight), you discover that you've actually shot yourself in the foot. Suppliers who don't get paid usually delay shipments or put your company on a cash-only basis, and that only exacerbates the situation. And if you choose the route of trying to get emergency funding from your friendly banker, you send up a huge red flag that you don't manage your business's finances very well. The bottom line: You need to manage your working capital better and plan ahead for your needs.

Planning for accounts receivable

You have accounts receivable in your business when you choose to extend credit to your customers, which is something most businesses do. When you extend credit, you allow the customers to keep their cash longer, but you have to wait longer for yours — 30, 60, or 90 days is typical.

TIP

The secrets to successful accounts receivable management are watching deadlines carefully and being consistent and careful about collecting payments.

Mismanagement of accounts receivable can send a business into a tailspin from which it is difficult to recover. You can manage your accounts receivable effectively if you:

» Minimize the time between shipping, invoicing, and sending billing notices, so you *start the payment clock* as quickly as possible.

» Regularly review your customers' credit histories with your company, so you can spot problems before they cause irreparable harm. *Age your accounts receivable* on a monthly basis at a minimum (aging is looking at the status of each account in terms of whether the customer is late on payments and by how much).

>> Make sure you get credit applications from all new customers. Provide incentives to pay early. This is typical in business-to-business transactions. You provide a discount for an early payment and an interest charge for a delinquent payment.

>> Develop a policy for collecting overdue accounts.

>> Avoid having account receivables in the first place. If you accept credit cards from customers, you hand off the accounts receivable problem to the credit card company (but remember the credit card company charges you for the pleasure of doing that task).

Developing a credit policy

Having an effective credit policy in place makes life much easier and makes handling credit situations more routine. A credit policy includes four parts:

>> The conditions under which your company extends credit

>> The criteria your company has for extending credit

>> The length of time for which you will grant credit (in other words, 30 days, 60 days, and so forth)

>> A collections policy for customers who fail to comply with your credit policy

Judging a customer's creditworthiness

The following are examples of standards used by companies to judge the credit-worthiness of a potential customer:

>> Current debt is free of delinquent payments

>> If consumer credit, the applicant has a full-time job

>> Income level greater than your minimum requirement

>> If consumer credit, applicant has a valid credit card

>> If business credit, a Dun & Bradstreet rating of A or better

>> A credit bureau report showing no delinquencies

Collecting your accounts

On the collections side, you want to establish a policy and procedure that you use consistently without discriminating. The following example of a collection policy, which prescribes actions from mild to severe, is only a suggestion:

>> When the account is ten days overdue, mail a reminder statement.

>> When the account is 30 days overdue, mail another past-due statement.

>> When the account is 45 days past due, call the customer.

>> When the account is 60 days past due, notify the customer in writing that the account will be turned over to a collection agency if payment is not received within 15 days.

The important thing about this process is that, in addition to treating everyone the same, it keeps the matter in the forefront, minimizing the chances that the unpaid amount will become a bad debt write-off. Ultimately, you must make the decision as to what the best course of action is for your business, but for the business to stay healthy, you must collect your debts.

Borrowing against your accounts receivable

Many businesses that deal with accounts receivable resort to borrowing against them to speed up the cash flow from those receivables. Commercial banks and finance companies offer two major types of receivables financing:

>> **Collateral:** In this type of financing, you pledge your accounts receivable as collateral against a loan that the bank grants to you. Then your customers' payments are sent directly to the bank.

>> **Factoring:** In this type of financing, you sell your accounts receivable at a discount to a factor (finance company). The factor then collects on them and gives you the money collected minus a fee.

Setting up a revolving line of credit

The least expensive way of getting outside help is through a revolving line of credit from your bank. Assuming your business has at least a small track record of success, this may be a good source for you. How do you know how much to request when you go to your banker to ask for a credit line? To answer that question, you need to calculate your cash conversion cycle. Here's how you do that.

1. **Figure out how many days it takes your customers to pay you.**

2. **Calculate the number of days it takes to make your product.**

3. **Count the number of days your product sits in inventory before being sold.**

REMEMBER

A seasonal business typically requires more cash during the busy season and less at other times, so you will need to work that out with your banker as well.

TIP

Although it's possible to seek a line of credit at any time, bankers prefer to see you after your first profitable year.

Managing your accounts payable

Managing your accounts payable is an essential part of total cash management. It involves timing and negotiation. When your business finds itself in a cash crisis, you may need to request an extension of an obligation to a vendor or lender. If that creditor agrees to the extension, you are not released from the obligation, but your cash at least temporarily becomes available. Through that extension, you have received *trade credit*, which carries with it terms that usually involve a cash discount — for example, *3/10, net 30*, meaning you get a 3 percent discount if you pay within 10 days; otherwise, you must pay the full amount within 30 days.

Let's look at this situation in real terms. Suppose you purchase something for $30,000. You have a choice. You can pay $29,100 on any day from 1 through 10 or the full amount of $30,000 on days 11 to 30.

If you can take advantage of the discount, pay on the 10th day, but no earlier. If you can't pay until after the 10th day, then pay on the 30th day, so you have an additional 20 days to use your money.

TIP

Vendors have bills to pay as well, and it's smart to establish a good relationship with them because it helps you in the end. Ways you can take advantage of trade credit include:

>> Paying early whenever you can and taking advantage of discounts.

>> Paying COD (cash on delivery) whenever you can and then asking for an additional discount.

>> Choosing quality vendors that can extend flexible terms.

>> Contacting the vendor immediately when you find out you can't pay a bill on time. Your vendor will probably work with you if you don't ignore the situation.

>> Staying on top of cash flow management even if it means doing it on a daily basis. You must make sure that you can meet all your business's obligations in a timely manner.

This chapter gives you lots of things to think about and do, but I assure you, these tips will help you keep your business in shape. Discovering problems early is always the best approach. Fellow entrepreneurs will advise you to "know your numbers." Take that advice to the bank.

Chapter **19**

Planning for Things That Go Bump in the Night

N o matter how well you manage your business, the unforeseeable will happen. A key employee gives you notice they are leaving. You get slapped with a lawsuit from a former employee who says they were wrongfully terminated. A Black Swan event (completely unpredictable), such as the pandemic of 2020-22, results in massive business shutdowns. The list goes on and on.

Surprises aren't the only thing you'll face as a business owner. Another certainty is that at some point in the future you will want to harvest the wealth you've created by selling your business. Making a graceful exit takes planning so that you don't hurt your business and you're able to reap the full rewards of what you've created. You find out how to do that in this chapter. Graceful exits, however, are not always possible; so you will also discover ways to terminate your business in a manner that is least harmful to you, your investors, and your creditors.

It certainly isn't my intent in this chapter to frighten you away from entrepreneurship. Life is full of change, so why should business be any different? After all, with change comes opportunity, and that's a good thing.

Preparing for the Unknown: When Bad Things Happen to Good Companies

When I encourage you to prepare for the unknown, I'm not suggesting that you need to think about all the things that can possibly go wrong with your business. That would be a waste of time. Instead, you want to consider the most likely threats and focus on ways to deal with them. In this section, I take a positive look at some of the more common threats to your business and give you some tips for coping with them.

Before we do that, however, let's consider what you can do short of having a specific plan. Research has found that entrepreneurs use a type of thinking that researcher Sara Sarasvathy has termed *effectual reasoning*. With this type of thinking, you start from the position that the future is unpredictable and look at what's available to you right now. This is called *The Bird in Hand* principle and it states that everyone possesses three basic resources: who you are, what you know, and whom you know. Start here.

Then move on to the principle of *affordable loss*. This includes the resources available and how much you are willing to lose. It's a good way to quickly eliminate ideas that don't fit your risk tolerance.

The third principle is *lemonade*, which is about the element of surprise and your willingness to welcome surprises as opportunities. For example, test some ideas that, on the surface, may seem incompatible with your business. Thinking about your business from this new perspective just might surprise you with a great idea.

The fourth principle is called *patchwork quilt*, which is creating partnerships to move a project forward more quickly. This principle is also about building trust. The final principle is called *pilot-in-the-plane*, which means focusing on activities within your control. It makes no sense to spend time worrying about something over which you have no control; for example, the war in Ukraine and its aftermath. This principle is based on the belief that entrepreneurs create the future they want through the process of effectuation. Solve the problems that are in your control and leave the rest to a higher power.

Once you have a contingency plan worked out, make sure it answers some basic questions (these come from the what-you-know exercise):

>> In a downturn, which of your suppliers would be willing to extend credit beyond their normal repayment time?

- » What non-essential assets does your business own that could be turned into cash rapidly?
- » Can you secure additional capital from your investors?
- » Will any of your customers prepay or order ahead of schedule?
- » Can your banker help you get through this problem?

Identifying Potential Risks and Their Impact

Before tackling specific types of problems, let's identify the categories of potential risks your business might face. In general, they are:

- » Supply chain disruption, which makes materials more expensive and harder to get when you need them. Your production schedules are also affected, and you are likely to face unhappy customers who are not getting your products on time.
- » Tax increases and new regulations that add layers of cost.
- » Intellectual property offense and defense.
- » Product liability claims.
- » Cybersecurity risks.
- » Succession planning.
- » Sudden sales decline.

Doing a risk assessment and impact analysis

For any business, the risk associated with each of these categories will be different and the impact of that risk on the business will be different as well. A simple equation helps you estimate the probability of a particular risk for your business.

Risk of Loss = (Probability X Cost X Significance of Impact)

Let's say you've identified that you have a 50 percent risk of losing a critical employee and you expect the cost to search for a new employee to amount to about

$6,000. On a scale of 1 to 100 percent for the importance of this loss, you rate it at 80 percent. Putting these figures into the equation, we get

Overall Risk of Loss = (.50 X $6,000 X .80) = $2,400

Now let's say the importance of the loss of this employee was only 25 percent, meaning that on-boarding a new hire will not be too much of a challenge. Put these new numbers into the equation.

Overall Risk of Loss = (.50 X $6,000 X .25) = $750

You will no doubt look at this situation very differently from the previous one.

If you look at all your risks in this manner, it will be easier to judge where you should focus your immediate contingency planning efforts. Keep in mind that these numbers are only educated guesses, so make sure you take your time and not just pull them out of thin air.

Now let's look at some of the typical types of problems businesses face and should plan for.

Protecting your company from lawsuits

I'm sure you're aware of the litigious society we live in. Hardly a day passes that you don't hear about some company being sued by customers, shareholders, other companies, or the government.

To add fuel to the fire, your own employees may be your greatest threat. Employee lawsuits against former and current employers have increased dramatically. One reason for the increase is that employees can sue without it costing them any money. They hire an attorney who works on a contingency basis (the attorney is paid only if they win the case), so they're not out any money upfront. But they stand to gain a lot, particularly because many of these cases ultimately settle out of court. Even when a claim is frivolous, employers end up weighing the risks of going to court, spending thousands of dollars and hundreds of hours of time, and having the business suffer from bad publicity versus settling the lawsuit and moving on.

As you can see, fighting or even settling a lawsuit can be a costly proposition for a small business. But you can put your company in a better position to avoid lawsuits by doing the following:

>> Carrying the appropriate liability insurance so that if you are sued, at least you're covered financially and won't risk throwing your business into a crisis from which it may not recover. Instead of worrying about money, you'll make better decisions.

>> Being extremely careful about the people you hire. The most important characteristics you need to look for in an employee are trustworthiness and character. Call the references you are given, and check out education and experience claims, which often are embellished or falsified.

>> Keeping an accurate and current file on each employee. Your employee files must document all the events related to individual employees, including promotions, raises, performance evaluations, training, and infractions of company policy. Write in an objective and factual style because the file may be viewed as evidence in court. For objectivity, more than one person needs to contribute to the file. Other contributors can include the employee's immediate supervisor, a manager in the employee's area, your human resources person, or anyone in regular contact with the employee.

>> Putting in writing any communications that you have with your employees about job performance, regardless of whether it's good or bad. Be sure to note the dates and times when these communications occurred; and more important, obtain a signed receipt from the employee confirming that they have seen your written communication.

>> Showing care for your employees by watching for signs of fatigue, failing mental health, addictions, anxiety and stress, or aggressive behavior that is affecting the work environment, which may signal a need to intercede.

>> Taking seriously any complaints you receive about an employee and thoroughly investigating those complaints.

>> Consulting your labor attorney before taking the step of firing an employee. The attorney will examine the employee's file to make sure that you are able to effect the termination and can defend the company against a potential lawsuit. You can also be sued for negligence for not firing an employee if that employee presents a danger to other employees.

While your chances of being sued may seem too much of a risk, companies do manage to avoid lawsuits. The key is that even when you must let an employee go for cause, that employee leaves feeling as though they were treated fairly.

Handling a sharp, sudden decline in sales

Your company does well for several months when suddenly (or even worse, so gradually that you don't notice until it's too late) sales drop so low that you can't cover your overhead. Many business owners react by slowing down payments to vendors and other creditors to conserve declining cash; laying people off as the situation worsens; and refusing to answer the phone when creditors and vendors start calling to ask when they'll see their money. At this point, the owner is panic stricken and makes poor decisions about the use of dwindling resources. They are thinking, "If I can just hold on for a little bit longer, things will get better." Unfortunately, what the owner has done is made the situation exponentially worse.

You can deal with an abrupt decline in sales, because it is within your control. Here are some tips to help you put your company in a good position to survive and even turn around a sudden decline in sales:

>> You need to view a weekly sales report so you can identify sales patterns for your business. This practice makes you more aware of sales volumes and cycles and enables you to immediately detect the signs of a decline. Search for the source of that decline and make necessary changes immediately.

>> Do not reduce your prices. If you create products and services that your customers perceive as a fair exchange of value, reducing prices will only puzzle customers. The decline in sales may have nothing to do with price. Don't forget to warn vendors you deal with if you intend to be slower than normal in making payments for a while. Work out an arrangement with them in advance, so you don't lose their confidence.

>> Talk to your customers. They're your best source of information and clues to why sales are declining.

>> Be on the lookout for competitors that have entered the market without your knowledge.

>> Make sure that the quality of your products still exceeds industry averages.

>> Control your overhead costs and reduce them where possible, especially where the expense does not produce revenue for the company. For example, are you able to sublease any portion of your office or plant space to another company? This will not only reduce your overhead but also give you another source of revenue. It's unfortunate, but the quickest way to reduce your overhead is to reduce the number of employees you have. Make sure, though, that you don't compromise your ability to produce and deliver your product or service when demand returns.

>> Make liquidity a top priority; that alone helps you ride out many bumps in your business life.

>> If you haven't already done so, put a contingency plan in place that you trigger when you see the start of a downturn in sales.

>> If you're too late to forestall a cash crisis, consult a debt negotiation company, crisis management consultant, or attorney who can help you work through problems with your creditors.

Surviving the loss of a key employee

You must prepare for the fact that other businesses may try to entice your most talented personnel over to their side. If you have a high-tech company, employee turnover can become a way of life, particularly if you're located in an area populated with many of your competitors — Silicon Valley and the Research Triangle Park in North Carolina are examples. In those tech areas, key employees don't have to make a major move to change employers. That's one reason why Microsoft Corp. located its headquarters in Redmond, Washington, far away from the technology belts, where it wasn't under all the pressure of headhunters. Microsoft reasoned that it's more difficult for a key employee to decide to move if it means selling a home and relocating to a different state.

Demand for talent is one way to lose an employee, but you can lose key employees in plenty of other ways, such as in a fatal accident, sudden heart attack, or the onset of chronic disease. Have I made my point for succession planning?

Preparing your business for the loss of a critical employee means

>> Carrying key-person insurance on vital people in your organization. Doing so helps you cover the cost of replacing that person quickly at a time when it may be financially difficult to do so. This type of insurance also helps to replace lost profits; provide the funds to recruit, hire, and train a suitable replacement; and pay a tax-deductible death benefit to the employee's family. How much you need depends on how many of these needs you want to cover and the type of business you have. Talk to your insurance broker about suitable coverage.

>> Having your company's key employees train their replacements inside the company. That way if something happens to one of them, the trainee who is familiar with the position is ready to step in.

>> Conducting an exit interview to find out why a key employee has chosen to leave. Perhaps, as a result, you can prevent the same thing from happening in the future.

Dealing with the economy and Uncle Sam

Always count on the economy and good old Uncle Sam to create situations that you, as a business owner, must deal with. Fortunately, most of these events (recessions, military conflicts, economic volatility) have leading indicators that warn you to prepare for hard times. Some events, however, move so fast it seems like you have no warning.

Even in cases where you have a warning, how many times have you heard business owners complain that their business failed because of a recession? Does that mean that the business otherwise was destined to become a roaring success? That notion is just plain wrong. Recessions don't happen overnight — you have plenty of warning if you know what you're looking for. If you go to the U.S. Department of Commerce site at www.doc.gov, you'll find the latest economic indicators right on the homepage. Many of them decline several months before the onset of a recession, which means that if you start to recognize the typical signs of recession in the national and regional statistics, as well as those in your industry, you have some time to prepare.

TIP

If you have great employees who have been with you since you launched the company, you won't find reducing the number of employees an attractive response to unhealthy economic conditions. Nor should you. Over time, employees in a smaller company become like family, so you should do whatever you can to keep them. If this is your situation, you need to look at other expenses of the business where you can cut back a bit. Encourage your employees to help find ways to cut expenses for a while. Employees' ideas for where to cut, especially if it means a small cut in everyone's salary for a specific length of time, will be more palatable to them if they suggest it.

Coping with product liability

As a manufacturer or business owner associated with the production of a product, you'll probably be sued at some point in your business life. The courts increasingly appear to have shifted accountability for product liability away from the user and onto the manufacturer, a serious problem for business. Even if your product is of high quality, completely safe, and comes with all the required warning labels ("Don't put your hand into the machine." "Don't run the machine in water."), someone is bound to carelessly misuse and abuse it and then blame the resulting injuries on you and everyone else in the distribution channel. Ways to avoid and prepare for product liability issues include:

>> Making sure that you provide appropriate instruction manuals for your product, detailing how to correctly use and service it.

- » Applying the required warning labels for your type of product. A good place to start is with the Occupational Health and Safety Administration (OSHA), the government agency that monitors workplace safety. The OSHA website is located at www.osha.gov.

- » Making sure that you train dealers, distributors, and reps in the correct use of the product, so they can pass that training along to your customer outlets.

- » Responding immediately to complaints from customers about your product and resolving those complaints so that your customer isn't inclined to take legal action.

- » Promptly notifying customers if you discover a problem with your product that can result in liability. If there's a quick solution that's easy for the customer to do, pass that along immediately.

- » Establishing a safety panel responsible for reviewing safety requirements and establishing new ones as your business grows. The panel maintains records on all decisions about product design, testing, and evaluation, as well as any problems that occur.

- » Exercising care not to claim anything in your advertising and promotions that implies a level of safety that your product does not have.

- » Carrying product liability insurance, which covers your defense and any personal injury or property damage, but does not cover lost sales or the cost of redesigning the product.

- » Finding an experienced and qualified attorney you can go to if a product liability issue arises.

- » If any of your products or their components come from other manufacturers, make sure you get warranties from them. Also, talk to your attorney about your risk for liability from these supply chain partners.

Harvesting the Wealth with a Graceful Exit

Talking about an exit strategy may seem strange in a book about starting a company, but an exit or harvest plan is part of the overall strategic planning for your business. In fact, knowing where you want to end up informs the decisions you will make from the first day forward. Some entrepreneurs plan to never leave their businesses; others just enjoy the startup phase and like to leave the management to other people. Still others take the business to a certain stage and then move on. Whatever you decide is right for you, I assure you that at some point you'll want to harvest the wealth that your efforts and your company have created. You have many alternatives for doing this, and I'm giving you two of the best.

Selling your business

If you're ready to move on or you're ready to make a change in your life or where you live, selling your business may be right for you. Doing so leaves you free mentally and financially to do whatever you want. But don't think that selling the business that you sweated blood over and cried real tears to create will be easy. On the contrary, selling is one of the more difficult decisions you'll ever make about your business. Some entrepreneurs experience a sense of loss much like losing a loved one. Others experience a sense of exhilaration from the freedom of not having to think about the business every day, but then they realize they've lost their focus and don't know what to do next.

TIP

Much like the decision to retire, never sell your business without knowing what you're going to do the next day, and the next, and the next.

In a perfect world, you know from the day you start your business that you intend to sell it at some point in the future. That way you make decisions that place your business in the best position possible to be sold at the appropriate time. You make sure that your business is profitable and sustainable (instead of showing no profit to avoid taxes, which devalues your business), and that you have dependable employees, solid customer and vendor contracts, superior sales people, lots of goodwill, and so forth. Knowing that you're going to sell, you want to build as much value as possible, so you have more to harvest from the sale and your company will be more attractive to potential buyers.

Who can help you?

With so many ways to sell their businesses, many small business owners rely on the services of a business broker or business opportunity broker who takes a commission from the sale just like a real estate broker. Owners of larger or high-tech businesses are more likely to rely on an investment banking firm that specializes in the sale of these types of ventures. Expect to pay a retainer for the services of an investment banker, which may not apply against the final fee for the sale of your business.

Using brokers isn't a necessity. You can advertise in your local paper if your business is more localized or in *The Wall Street Journal* if it has national or international appeal. However, much like finding a business you want to buy, the best buyers are found by networking with your attorney, accountant, and banker. Those professionals hear about buyers for particular types of businesses all the time.

What do you sell?

You don't have to sell all the assets of your business. For example, you may sell all the equipment but choose to maintain ownership of the building and lease it to the new owner who will run the business. Your buyer may not want to purchase all the equipment you have, so you'll have to find another buyer for surplus equipment. Accounts receivable, inventory, and accounts payable are negotiable items, too. Never assume anything. Include an inventory of what you're selling to eliminate any possibility for error.

Be sure to check out your buyer, making sure they have the skills and financial resources to purchase your business and keep it operating at the same level of quality that you established. These factors are particularly important if your name has been on the business for a long time.

CASE STUDY

An entrepreneur friend of mine experienced difficulties when she sold her successful chain of healthy food stores that bore her name to a larger company. The new owner, a big corporation, didn't treat the customers with the same care and attention that my friend had insisted on when the company was hers. It isn't easy to see your name on something that no longer represents your values. So do your homework. She found out after the sale, she didn't even own her name anymore. If your personal name is the business's name, consider excluding your name from the sale.

Selling out but staying involved

You may reach a point when you want to take some of your investment out of the business to enjoy things you've always wanted to do; yet, you're not ready to completely leave the business. You can accomplish this in several different ways.

Selling your stock

One choice you have is selling some or all the stock you hold in your company. Remember that selling stock applies only to corporations and limited liability companies. If you're in a partnership, you can sell your interest back to the partnership. If your company is privately held, you're probably governed by a shareholders' agreement that was drawn up when you formed the company, specifying how much of your stock you can sell at a given time, to whom you can sell it, and how its value is determined. A similar situation exists for limited liability companies whose members have interests rather than shares (see Chapter 15 for a review of legal forms of business organization).

WARNING

If you succeed in creating a viable and profitable company, your equity increases substantially, which means a big tax liability when you sell your stock. Be sure to discuss your strategy with a tax attorney or accountant with expertise in this area.

Restructuring your company

Many entrepreneurs envision turning over leadership of their companies to a son or daughter and cashing out a rather significant portion of their investment. You can do this by splitting the original company into two businesses. For example, suppose you own a restaurant, but you no longer want to spend your days running the business. You give the ownership of the restaurant (the name, the operations, the employees, and so forth) to your daughter while you continue to own the building and the equipment, which you lease to her. Now you derive an income from the lease and you're still somewhat involved in the business without the pressures of day-to-day management.

Doing a phased sale

You've decided. You want to sell the business. You can make the sale less shocking to your system by phasing it out over a specified period, in say, two phases. Here's how it works:

>> **Phase I:** Sell a portion of the business but remain in control of operations and continue growing the company to an agreed-upon point.

>> **Phase II:** Finish the sale of the business at the prearranged price. The entrepreneur (seller) may stay on for the transition in ownership or leave as agreed upon.

A phased sale has advantages for the buyer and for the seller. You, the seller, stay on with the business, making sure it keeps moving in the direction you wanted it to go and getting your equity back so you have cash to do other things. The buyer, on the other hand, benefits from not immediately having to come up with all the cash to buy the business and from keeping you on board during the transition to ease typically nervous employees through a change in ownership. The buyer has the added advantage of being introduced by you to all the people they need to know to run the business successfully.

REMEMBER

Always involve an attorney in a phased sale because it is more complex than a straight sale. Your attorney will ensure that you have a proper buy-sell agreement that specifies the terms of the purchase, the amount of control your buyer can exert during the time you're still in the business, and the amount and type of proprietary information that you must share with the buyer before the sale is complete.

Being acquired

In the past decade, mergers and acquisitions (M&A) have soared to an all-time high in 2021 of $5.9 trillion. If your business has innovative technology or a customer base that a larger company might want, you may be a target for an acquisition. In general, acquirers come in two types:

>> **Financial acquirers,** such as hedge funds or private equity, that provide growth capital to get the business to the place where they can sell it for a profit.

>> **Strategic acquirers**, such as large public companies, looking to diversify or expand their offerings or acquire expert talent.

Acquisition is not an easy path because you are essentially merging one company into another, each with its own culture and ways of doing things. Nevertheless, today being acquired is probably the most common way that entrepreneurs harvest the wealth they have created, especially if you have a tech company.

When You Can't Exit Gracefully

The fact that most entrepreneurs refuse to even consider failure as a possibility proves they are the eternal optimists of the world. What you won't find when looking at most books about entrepreneurship is the slightest hint of a discussion of the topic of failure. The problem isn't failure — that's an integral part of entrepreneurship; the problem is failing to know when to walk away. The shame is not in having a business fail; rather, it's in taking your family down with it, all because your pride would not allow you to quit. Failure is an option, and sometimes it's the only option.

If you read this book all the way through, you increase your chances of avoiding failure — I can't guarantee you'll never fail, but I can say with some degree of certainty that you won't experience failure in the same way as the entrepreneurs who don't plan their ventures well.

It's wise to learn what your options are if, for any reason, your business finds itself on the brink of failure. We talk about those options here.

Facing bankruptcy

The term *bankruptcy* sends shivers up the spines of entrepreneurs, because they want to avoid it at all costs, and for good reason. Contrary to the popular notion that you can solve all your problems by bankrupting out of your company and walking away, it just isn't that easy. Besides, if you have any ethics, you don't want to leave your vendors and shareholders high and dry, because it really is a small world, and you may need their help in the future.

What causes a business to reach the point of considering bankruptcy is not easy to identify. Typically, the immediately precipitating cause is the inability to pay off debt because of a lack of cash. But that lack of funds is only a symptom of a much deeper and more complex problem. I have a dear consultant colleague who always said, "A tree grows from the bottom up, but it dies from the top down." How right he is. Whenever a business suffers or dies, the root cause of a bankruptcy is always poor management.

The bankruptcy code contains several sections. The two that relate to businesses are Chapters 11 and Chapter 7. Each is quite different in its approach.

Reorganizing: Chapter 11

Chapter 11 isn't really a bankruptcy in the most common sense of the word. Rather it is a reorganization of the finances of a business with the agreement of its creditors so the business can continue to operate and pay off its debts. In cases where the creditors are confident that the entrepreneur intends to pay all debts, the entrepreneur can manage the reorganization without a court-appointed trustee. Here's how a Chapter 11 works.

The business owner files for reorganization and:

>> Within 30 days, the owner and the creditors must meet to consider the status of the company and the steps it must take to reorganize so it can pay its debts and become viable again.

>> The court appoints a committee, which includes the owner, to develop a plan for the reorganization.

>> The reorganization plan must be submitted to the court within 120 days.

>> Out of the total number of creditors affected by the reorganization, at least half must accept the plan.

>> Once the court accepts the plan, the entrepreneur is discharged from any debts not listed in the plan.

Chapter 11 bankruptcy is the avenue you choose if you know you have the ability, given some time, to recover and pay off your debts.

Liquidating: Chapter 7

When your business doesn't have the resources to pay its debts or any hope of securing them anytime soon, you'll probably resort to liquidating all the assets of the business and discharging most of your debt that way. I say most of your debt because you can't bankrupt out of payroll taxes that you failed to pay. They become your personal obligation until they are paid in full.

When you file a Chapter 7 petition, you request an *order for relief*. The court appoints a trustee to manage the liquidation of the business with the goal of reducing everything to cash and disbursing the cash to the creditors in order of priority. In general, secured creditors get paid first and then the priority claimants (administrative expenses related to the bankruptcy, wages, salaries, commissions, employee benefits, and so forth). Anything that remains after distribution to everyone who has a right to be paid goes to the entrepreneur. The entrepreneur's only exemptions from the bankruptcy are

>> Interest in any accrued dividends up to the legal amount.

>> The right to social security benefits, unemployment compensation, public assistance, veterans' benefits, and disability benefits.

>> The rights to stock bonuses, pensions, or profit sharing.

Avoiding bankruptcy

Business owners have more control over a possible bankruptcy than you may think, because creditors naturally would rather be paid, and they usually fare better in a restructuring of the debt than they do in a liquidation.

If you want to try your best to avoid bankruptcy, follow these tips:

>> Don't rely on one major customer to generate most of your revenue — in other words, don't put all your eggs in one basket.

>> Keep your overhead down to the essentials — those things that result in revenue.

>> Stay as liquid as possible. A good rule-of-thumb is to have several months of overhead expenses on hand.

>> Pay attention to your relationships with your creditors. Be honest and forthright with them.

>> Before you consider taking the bankruptcy route, seek the advice of a turnaround consultant who specializes in bringing businesses back from the brink of disaster.

Stepping Back from the Brink

Turnaround consultants specialize in making unhealthy — even dying — businesses healthy again. They are true magicians who find positives in your business that you never knew you had. They put you on a diet, help you establish small goals, and make sure you stay on track. From the experiences of turnaround consultants I've talked to, some tips for facing failure with grace (so that you can start again with dignity) suggest that you:

>> **Find entrepreneurs who have *been on the brink* and get their *"done that"* advice.** Unfortunately, when your business is failing, your family and friends are probably the last people who can help you. So you need to talk with people who've gone through what you're experiencing. Ask around. In general, entrepreneurs who fail and come back to experience success are more willing to talk about what they found out and to help you get back on your feet.

>> **Fail fast.** If things go badly, don't drag it out. I know of entrepreneurs who stuck with a dying business for years while it sucked the life out of their families, friends, and their own health. You must focus on the fact that the business failed, that you did not, and that you still have the talent and skills to start again. That's important.

>> **Give yourself a deadline.** Tell yourself that if your business isn't making a profit or generating a positive cash flow by next year, you're going to quit. That isn't easy to do, because entrepreneurs, you remember, are optimists, always thinking that the market will shift and a big order is just around the corner. But when the numbers don't add up (go back to your financial statements and ratios to check this), give yourself a deadline and stick to it.

>> **Never mess with the government.** Unless you want to risk losing your personal assets and have a debt follow you for the rest of your life, follow this guideline. Too many entrepreneurs in distress borrow funds from their payroll-tax and sales-tax accounts. Resist those temptations. Don't do it!

>> **Keep your eyes on the next prize.** Opportunity is out there, and you already know how to take advantage of it. This business was not your last opportunity, so start looking. I always say that things happen for a reason. Sometimes your best opportunity comes along because you were willing to leave behind a business that was draining you.

>> **Do whatever it takes to pay back your investors.** They took the risk, yes, but if you pay them back, even if it takes a long time, they'll respect you and perhaps be there for you the next time you need them to fund an opportunity.

No business avoids the unexpected. However, the suggestions in this chapter can help you better plan for the unexpected and deal with it when it happens.

5

The Part of Tens

Chapter **20**

Ten Reasons Not to Start a Business

Judging by the popularity of *Shark Tank* and *Dragons' Den*, people have dreams about running their own business. After all, wouldn't it be great to work for yourself or to be rich? I'm here to tell you that it's not that easy. Consider these ten reasons not to start a business.

Because Everyone Is Doing It

It does seem as though everyone is starting a business, from the paper boy down the street who just opened a web-design shop to the paper boy's mom who finally started that public relations firm. While there's nothing wrong with wishing and hoping, bear in mind that *talking* about starting a business is easy; actually *starting* a business is hard work. There is no such thing as work-life balance with entrepreneurs. If you're feeling pressure from all the newly minted entrepreneurs out there, take a breath and make sure you're doing it for the right reasons.

Because You Want to Be a Millionaire

The media often gives that impression that all you have to do is start a business and you'll become rich. Scan the headlines and you'll get the idea that making a million is easy and that having that million makes someone a millionaire, which is definitely not true. Starting a business is costly and the entrepreneur is always the last person to be paid. The average small business owner makes less than they would earning a salary, at least in the beginning.

Many entrepreneurs start their businesses for reasons that have nothing to do with money, but everything to do with their passion. Statistics tell us that one out of two businesses fail in their first year, so your motivation has to be something more important than money. If you fail fast, you're lucky; otherwise, consider how much persistence and courage you need to keep your business going with marginal profit for several years.

Because You're Looking for a Secure Job

Maybe you just got laid off from your job and you figure, why not start a business? Getting fired or laid off is a common precipitator of entrepreneurship. Sometimes it takes that unexpected event to push someone to start the business they have always wanted to start. But keep in mind that failing at your job may be embarrassing, but it's not nearly as awful as having your business fail, especially if you have employees or have taken investor capital. Here's an even more inconvenient fact. On average, small mom and pop type businesses pay their owners, if anything in the first couple years, less than they would have made working for someone else. And you get the privilege of working constantly. What's more, you still won't have job security, because the failure rate of new businesses is 50 percent.

Because You Don't Want to Work for Someone Else

People who dislike working for someone else cite numerous reasons. They want independence — to do what they want, when they want, with no one looking over their shoulder and telling them what to do. They also don't like the idea of spending all their time working for the benefit of someone else, creating wealth for someone else. Nothing is wrong with these reasons, but you may want to ask yourself whether it's the job that's making you feel this way or the idea of working for someone else.

Here's the catch: when you're the CEO of your company, you work for everyone else, including your customers. You have responsibilities to your employees, investors, suppliers, and governmental agencies. Give up the idea that you're independent and free to do what you want. It's simply not the case. You are the face of the company and everyone is looking to you for the answers.

Because You Just Came into Some Money

Having too much money for your venture can have downsides. When you have a lot of money available at the beginning, you may not think as carefully about how you use those resources. The problem with being flush with cash is that if you lose money, you know there's more where that came from. Having a financial safety net means you may take unwarranted risks.

A better plan is to formulate a business concept, test it in the market, and figure out how much money you need to start the business and take it to a positive cash flow on its own. By doing this, you may find that you don't need as much money as you have and you can put the excess away for a rainy day or invest it in something else.

Because You're Not Ready to Retire

You're middle-aged, have years of business experience, are healthy, and have a pension and some savings. Sounds like a great place to be to start a business. It certainly is better than most entrepreneurs have in the beginning. Nevertheless, you must still do the necessary planning and idea testing and use your resources wisely. You also must be comfortable with risk. Your corporate skills may not directly translate into building a new business. Your health is precious, and you must be watchful of staying healthy when stress and anxiety can take a toll. You also must protect your nest egg and be financially prudent.

Before you leap from retiree to entrepreneur, there is a lot to think about. Are there alternatives to starting a business that you may enjoy as much?

Because If the Kid Down the Street Did It, So Can You

Many older adults are walking around shaking their heads, trying to understand all the 20-something (and younger) entrepreneurs and their startups. The Internet and e-commerce seem to have given the advantage to youth and inexperience, while seasoned veterans struggle to comprehend the valuations of no-asset, no-profit enterprises. The kids make it look easy! But I caution you that no startup is easy.

Don't start a business to keep up with the kids. You're in a different place in life. Do something that's meaningful to you. It takes a ton of energy and time to start and run a business. Do you have the energy? Is this how you want to spend your precious time?

Because You Want to Give Everyone in Your Family a Job

Investors often run the other direction when they see a group of relatives running and advising the entrepreneur. To an outsider, this looks like you were going for cheap labor rather than getting the best people for your team. And rather than clean house, a potential investor may just walk away. Likewise, your children may have other ideas about what they want to do with their lives, and your hot idea for a business may not fit with their plans. Don't start a business to give your family jobs they may not want or need. You can take their help if they offer it, but use them as advisors, not employees.

Because You Have a Great Idea

Great ideas are a dime a dozen. You've probably heard the adage, "I'd rather invest in a B idea led by an A team, than invest in an A idea led by a B team." Starting a business is about execution. You may have a great idea, but if you don't have the experience, knowledge, resources, and persistence to make it happen, what's that idea really worth?

Because You Have Passion for a Cause

Let's say you love animals and are concerned about cats and dogs that have no home. You decide you might want to start a pet adoption service, which would require skills that you don't have. There are other ways you can engage with stray dogs and cats without taking the risk of starting a business you know little about. Before you take the leap, visit an owner of an adoption service to find out what each day brings. If you still think you want to start this business, learn as much as you can about how the business works and what it takes to match those cute dogs and cats with the right family.

Instead: Start a Business Because It's What You Most Want to Do

I threw you a curve, ending this list of *don'ts* with a *do*. That's because I want to end on a positive note. If you find yourself always making excuses for why you shouldn't start a business, maybe you shouldn't. You're not feeling the entrepreneurial spirit.

Entrepreneurial types tend to do just the opposite. They rationalize why they *should* start a business and discount any potential negative views. Nothing is wrong with listing all the pros and cons to starting a business. What it boils down to is this: *Do you passionately want to start a business?* Do you think about it day and night? Do you run and rerun scenarios for how it can work (when you should be thinking about other things)? If so, you might have the entrepreneur's virus and the only way to cure it is to start a business.

Chapter 21

Ten Ways to Spark Your Innovative Spirit

Y ou've been thinking about starting a business for a long time now. You know you can do it. All you need is a winning concept. Here are ten suggestions for developing an idea that solves a real problem.

Read about Entrepreneurs

Business magazines featuring entrepreneurs are among the most popular. If you want to inspire yourself with the possibilities, check out some of my favorite titles:

>> *Entrepreneur Magazine,* www.entrepreneur.com/us. One of the longest-running magazines about entrepreneurship. Lots of inspiration here.

>> *Black Enterprise,* www.blackenterprise.com. A good resource for black entrepreneurs since 1970.

>> *The Asian Entrepreneur Magazine,* asianentrepreneur.org. This magazine has become the most authoritative platform on Asian entrepreneurship in 26 countries.

>> *Inc Magazine*, www.inc.com. Known for its annual research on the fastest-growing entrepreneurial companies, it is a great source of stories about entrepreneurs at all stages.

Browse Amazon books for stories and memoirs written by entrepreneurs. Here are a few of the best to get started.

>> *Zero to One,* Peter Thiel (co-founder of PayPal and Palantir and investor in startups)

>> *The Art of the Start 2.0,* Guy Kawasaki

>> *Delivering Happiness: A Path to Profits, Passion, and Purpose,* Tony Hsieh, founder of Zappos

For those who prefer to learn by watching a screen, check out

>> *Super Pumped: The Battle for Uber,* streaming on Netflix.

>> *Print the Legend.* The story of emerging companies MarkerBot and Formlabs working to make 3D printing a consumer product. Streaming on Netflix.

>> *The Dropout.* The story of Elizabeth Holmes and her company Theranos. A lesson on what not to do as an entrepreneur. She was indicted and convicted of fraud. This is the case of a great idea but an entrepreneur with no ethics.

I also recommend the six-season hit HBO series, *Silicon Valley.* It's hilarious and does a good job of making fun of the world of tech startups. But you also get a real sense for how difficult starting is, how much work is involved, and what it's like to deal with investors and partners.

Learn from Innovation Hubs

Nowhere will you find a larger hotbed of entrepreneurial activity, innovation, and new business startups in the earliest stages than at a university. That's because most colleges and universities now have courses in entrepreneurship that prepare students for success as founders. Check out activities in the School of Engineering or the School of Medicine. Much of the innovation on university campuses happens in those schools. The inventors are often looking to partner with businesspeople. You may discover an invention that could spell a wonderful opportunity. You can also inquire about seminars and courses in such things as feasibility analysis, business plan writing, and technology commercialization, to name a few. Schools sometimes offer these opportunities through their extension programs to people from the community who are not registered students. Some schools have developed maker labs to encourage invention and innovation. The innovation environment alone is enough to get you enthusiastic about sharing in the excitement of entrepreneurship.

Find a Difficult Problem and Solve It

The reason I suggest that you find a difficult problem is that you want to come up with something that's not easy for everyone else to solve. You want your innovation and startup concept to be unique. Problems are everywhere. Start by making a list of all the problems you run into in a single day or list all the problems that a university or business might face. Once you get started, you'll find that it gets easier and easier to identify problems. Then pick one that interests you and think about ways to solve it. Of course, make sure you understand the problem completely so you don't miss something important when you're designing a solution.

Spend Time Daydreaming

In a world where we're bombarded 24/7 with distractions, we need to find time to shut everything down and let our minds wander so we can hear ideas when they come to us. And they will. I don't know where your favorite place to daydream is — mine is in nature. The Japanese call it "forest bathing." It can be anywhere. Just make it a place where you can relax and not be disturbed. Keep a notebook nearby so you can record ideas that come to you. Keep one at your bedside as well. Ideas may come to you in dreams.

Save All Your Ideas

Anytime you get an idea about anything related to starting a business, write it down. It may be nothing or at least not something you'll use immediately; but who knows. Down the road, it may become the right idea at the right time. A journal is a great place to store your ideas.

Make an Existing Idea Better

After studying an industry you're interested in, take one of the ideas you've come up with or pick an idea that an entrepreneur had for a new business. Your job is to enhance this idea. See if you can make it even better. It's time to use your creativity and come up with something new. Alternatively, pick an existing product that has been around a long time and find a new use for it.

Spend Time in Airports or Shopping Centers

Find a comfortable place where you have the opportunity to observe passersby. Your goal is to look for problems that people seem to be having. Think of a problem as something that, if you can solve it, might become a business opportunity. Airports are great places to find problems. Alternatively, think of all the things you wish were different. Shopping malls are another great place to observe people and problems.

Use Your Five Senses to Discover a New Industry

We all have five senses to help us understand the world around us: vision, hearing, touch, smell, and taste. Apply your five senses to a product you're interested in and see what you come up with. One or two of the senses may not apply, although don't give up too quickly. Try force associating a sense. I'm betting you'll come up with something. Some of the best ideas come from associating things that don't normally go together. How about chocolate covered potato chips? Or maybe something more practical like Velcro, which was inspired by a walk in the forest that resulted in sticky burrs on the inventor's pant legs.

Talk to Potential Customers

It's very important to start talking to potential customers so you can begin to understand their needs and determine if what you're thinking of doing is something they might be willing to pay for. Potential customers are the best source of information for an aspiring entrepreneur. Spend as much time as possible with customers either talking with them or watching them in their typical environments.

Find a Mentor

Entrepreneurs need someone they can turn to when they're struggling or need inspiration. It's lonely at the top of a business, even a small one. Is there a business owner in your community you admire and would like to model yourself after? Invite this person for coffee and let them know what you admire about how their business runs. Depending on how the business owner reacts, you may ask them to be your mentor. Remember that small business owners are busy people, so assure this person that you are mindful of their time.

A good mentor will be honest and let you know when you're heading in the wrong direction. Although it's helpful if your mentor understands your industry and your business, the ways that mentors are of greatest assistance go well beyond your daily operations. With a great mentor, you can learn how to become an effective leader — a priceless gift.

Index

vertical integration, 307
Vessyl, 58–59
vesting, 165
video catalog exhibitions, 313
VIP clubs, 355
Virgin Atlantic Airways, 17, 60
The Virtual Gurus, 59
virtual tour, 210–212
vision/vision statement, 245–247
VRBO (Vacation Rentals by Owner), 22

W

Wacky Wallwalker, 49
Wall Street Journal, 204
Walmart Stores Inc., 248
Walton, Sam, 248
Ward, Heather, 7
Wasserman, Noam, 161–162
Waste Management, 202
wearables, 81
weather, 113
Webflow, 41
Weissman, Jerry, 273
WeWork, 26–27, 50, 51
Wexner, Lex, 209
Whisolutions.com, 108
wholesalers, 185
Wilson, Andrew, 50
women-owned businesses, 32
Women's Business Enterprise National Council (WBENC), 32
work environment, 35
working capital, 375–379
World Trade Organization, 311
Wrenchead.com, 108

Y

Y Combinator, 58
YouTube, 351

Z

Zapier, 41
Zero to One (Thiel), 406

About the Author

Kathleen R. Allen Ph.D. is an authority in the field of entrepreneurship and the commercialization of new technologies. With over 25 years of experience as an entrepreneur, investor, consultant, author, speaker, and professor, she has counseled startups and rapidly growing companies on feasibility analysis, product adoption, growth strategy, venture capital, and risk management.

Dr. Allen is Professor Emerita of Entrepreneurship at the USC Marshall School of Business, where she founded and led the USC Marshall Center for Technology Commercialization, a collaboration of science, engineering, medicine, and business. She is the author of *Launching New Ventures*, 8th Edition, *Entrepreneurship for Scientists and Engineers* and *Bringing New Technology to Market*, in addition to other books including *Complete MBA for Dummies*, co-authored with Peter Economy. She has also authored many journal articles in her field. For her work, she was awarded Entrepreneurship Educator of the Year in 2014 by the U.S. Association for Small Business and Entrepreneurship. More recently, the University of Southern California awarded her the Faculty Lifetime Achievement Award.

Dr. Allen's personal entrepreneurial endeavors include two successful companies that engage in commercial real estate brokerage, land development, and investment; two technology-based businesses that commercialized patented technologies; and a nonprofit venture that incubated technology and healthcare-related startups in underserved areas in the Midwest. She served for three years as entrepreneur-in-residence at Pratt & Whitney Rocketdyne to determine the feasibility of taking core space shuttle technology into the energy field. From 2014-2017, she was a visiting scholar at the Department of Homeland Security, Science and Technology Directorate, advising on strategies to implement new first responder and cybersecurity technologies.

Dr. Allen holds a PhD in business, an MBA, and an MA in Romance Languages.

Dedication

To all the entrepreneurs I have helped, who have amazed me with their innovations and persistence. It has been a joy to work with you.

Acknowledgments

I would like to give my sincere thanks and appreciation to the talented publishing team at Wiley, particularly Kristie Pyles, Kelsey Baird, Kezia Endsley, and Don Loney. I would also like to thank my family for their unconditional love and support during a time when I was working on two books at once.

Publisher's Acknowledgments

Acquisitions Editor: Kelsey Baird

Managing Editor: Kristie Pyles

Copy Editor: Kezia Endsley

Technical Editor: Don Loney

Production Editor: Tamilmani Varadharaj

Project Coordinator: Kezia Endsley

Cover Image: © G-Stock Studio/Shutterstock

Leverage the power

Dummies is the global leader in the reference category and one of the most trusted and highly regarded brands in the world. No longer just focused on books, customers now have access to the dummies content they need in the format they want. Together we'll craft a solution that engages your customers, stands out from the competition, and helps you meet your goals.

Advertising & Sponsorships

Connect with an engaged audience on a powerful multimedia site, and position your message alongside expert how-to content. Dummies.com is a one-stop shop for free, online information and know-how curated by a team of experts.

- Targeted ads
- Video
- Email Marketing
- Microsites
- Sweepstakes sponsorship

20 MILLION PAGE VIEWS EVERY SINGLE MONTH

15 MILLION UNIQUE VISITORS PER MONTH

43% OF ALL VISITORS ACCESS THE SITE VIA THEIR MOBILE DEVICES

700,000 NEWSLETTER SUBSCRIPTIONS TO THE INBOXES OF *300,000* UNIQUE INDIVIDUALS EVERY WEEK

# of dummies

PERSONAL ENRICHMENT

Staying Sharp

9781119187790
USA $26.00
CAN $31.99
UK £19.99

Facebook

9781119179030
USA $21.99
CAN $25.99
UK £16.99

Guitar

9781119293354
USA $24.99
CAN $29.99
UK £17.99

Investing

9781119293347
USA $22.99
CAN $27.99
UK £16.99

Beekeeping

9781119310068
USA $22.99
CAN $27.99
UK £16.99

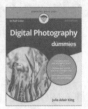

Digital Photography

9781119235606
USA $24.99
CAN $29.99
UK £17.99

Meditation

9781119251163
USA $24.99
CAN $29.99
UK £17.99

Pregnancy

9781119235491
USA $26.99
CAN $31.99
UK £19.99

Samsung Galaxy S7

9781119279952
USA $24.99
CAN $29.99
UK £17.99

iPhone

9781119283133
USA $24.99
CAN $29.99
UK £17.99

Crocheting

9781119287117
USA $24.99
CAN $29.99
UK £16.99

Nutrition

9781119130246
USA $22.99
CAN $27.99
UK £16.99

PROFESSIONAL DEVELOPMENT

Windows 10

9781119311041
USA $24.99
CAN $29.99
UK £17.99

AutoCAD

9781119255796
USA $39.99
CAN $47.99
UK £27.99

Excel 2016

9781119293439
USA $26.99
CAN $31.99
UK £19.99

QuickBooks 2017

9781119281467
USA $26.99
CAN $31.99
UK £19.99

macOS Sierra

9781119280651
USA $29.99
CAN $35.99
UK £21.99

LinkedIn

9781119251132
USA $24.99
CAN $29.99
UK £17.99

Windows 10

9781119310563
USA $34.00
CAN $41.99
UK £24.99

SharePoint 2016

9781119181705
USA $29.99
CAN $35.99
UK £21.99

Fundamental Analysis

9781119263593
USA $26.99
CAN $31.99
UK £19.99

Networking

9781119257769
USA $29.99
CAN $35.99
UK £21.99

Office 2016

9781119293477
USA $26.99
CAN $31.99
UK £19.99

Office 365

9781119265313
USA $24.99
CAN $29.99
UK £17.99

Salesforce.com

9781119239314
USA $29.99
CAN $35.99
UK £21.99

Coding

9781119293323
USA $29.99
CAN $35.99
UK £21.99